TEMPLE UNIVERSITY

Educating for Social Justice

Also available from Lyceum Books

Advisory Editor: Thomas M. Meenaghan, *New York University*

Advocacy Practice for Social Justice
By Richard Hoefer

Diversity, Oppression, and Change
By Flavio Francisco Marsiglia and Stephen Kulis

Career Reflections of Social Work Educators
By Spencer J. Zeiger

Women in Social Work Who Have Changed the World
Edited by Alice Lieberman

Complex Systems and Human Behavior
By Christopher G. Hudson

Social Work Practice with Latinos
Edited by Rich Furman and Nalini Negi

*Essential Skills of Social Work Practice:
Assessment, Intervention, Evaluation*
By Thomas O'Hare

*Caught in the Storm: Navigating Policy and
Practice in the Welfare Reform Era*
By Miguel Ferguson, Heather Neuroth-Gatlin, and Stacey Borasky

The Dynamics of Family Policy: Analysis and Advocacy
By Alice K. Butterfield, Cynthia J. Rocha, and William H. Butterfield

Educating for Social Justice

Transformative Experiential Learning

Edited by

Julie Birkenmaier, PhD
Saint Louis University School of Social Work

Ashley Cruce, MSW, MA
Hunter College School of Social Work of the City University of New York

Ellen Burkemper, PhD
Saint Louis University School of Social Work

Jami Curley, PhD
Saint Louis University School of Social Work

R. Jan Wilson, PhD
Saint Louis University School of Social Work

J. J. Stretch, PhD
Saint Louis University School of Social Work

LYCEUM
BOOKS, INC.

Chicago, Illinois

© 2011 by Lyceum Books, Inc.

Published by
LYCEUM BOOKS, INC.
5758 S. Blackstone Avenue
Chicago, Illinois 60637
773-643-1903 fax
773–643–1902 phone
lyceum@lyceumbooks.com
www.lyceumbooks.com

6   5   4   3   2   1   10   11   12   13   14

ISBN 978-1-933478-41-8

Printed in the United States of America.

Library of Congress Cataloging-in-Publication Data

Educating for social justice : transformative experiential learning / edited by Julie Birkenmaier [. . . et al.].
   p.   cm.
Includes bibliographical references and index.
ISBN 978-1-933478-41-8 (pbk.)
1. Social justice.   2. Experiential learning.   I. Birkenmaier, Julie.
HM671.E37   2010
303.3'72—dc22
                                                      2010001552

Acknowledgments

The authors would like to sincerely thank the Emmet J. and Mary Martha Doerr Center for Social Justice Education and Research for support and guidance. They also thank all of the authors for their contributions.

Contents

Section 3: Social Justice Education Outside the Classroom

Introduction

Teaching Social Justice as an Orienting Value in Social Work Education

Julie Birkenmaier

Ashley Cruce

Ellen Burkemper

Jami Curley

R. Jan Wilson

J. J. Stretch

Social work, as a profession, has struggled over the years with the concept of social justice and has been unable to agree on a universal definition (Galambos, 2008), with implementing social justice in practice (Birkenmaier, 2003), and with teaching and instilling the value as part of the education process (see pp. 75–96). A concrete operationalization of social justice is elusive, and interpretive nuances vary. Yet this concept is touted as the core of the profession of social work, a universal theme within the wide range of social work practice (National Association of Social Workers [NASW], 2008). How can social work education effectively carry out the mandate to teach this important concept and instill a passion for it to the next generation of practitioners who will implement "social justice," when a universally accepted definition is absent?

The historical roots of social justice in social work run deep, and educators are charged with drawing on this rich history in their quest to transfer knowledge and instill passion for social justice. This value of the profession is clearly articulated in the social work *Code of Ethics* with the deliberate ethical principle that "social workers should challenge social injustice" (NASW, 2008, Preamble), and is viewed as a cultural imperative encouraged through the Council on Social Work Education (2008), the National Association of Social Workers (NASW), and other professional organizations. At the root of the challenge is the lack of definition—without a universal definition, how do educators know the content to teach, the goal of social justice (to what shall students and practitioners strive?), and how to evaluate whether the student has learned the concept? Yet social work education has tackled this challenge with gusto, perhaps with the intention of defining and learning about social justice through the "doing."

This volume of work seeks to make important contributions and to add further substance to the conversation about social justice education in social work. Rather than focus solely on defining social justice, the authors share their perspectives on the concept and plunge ahead with the "doing" and "teaching" in the hopes that social work might, as a profession, learn about social justice and be better able to come to an agreement about a definition and its implementation through an inductive process. The authors of this book promote learning and experiencing social justice through utilizing theoretical frameworks within which to engage in action and to reflect. These authors have developed a consensus that transformation in thinking and of behavior is the ultimate goal of social justice education. It is our thesis that, when striving to teach social justice, teachers should aim for an increase in awareness of perspective and an increase in reflection in students, which leads to questions about and a longing for social justice. The awareness of, reflection upon, and the asking of critical questions often result most easily from experience that involves the entire self—mind and body. Disquieting experiences or experiences that result in questioning frames of reference, examining previous opinions, and rethinking previous attitudes can result in such transformations. This volume of work seeks to contribute thoughts, ideas, and concrete examples of student experiences to spur new, innovative andragogy toward instilling students with a passion for social justice work within social work practice. We hope that this volume contributes toward the profession's quest for theory, practice models, and strategies for social justice education.

This work has four sections. The first section focuses on social justice as a concept and provides background on the status of social justice education within social work. In chapter 1, Michael Reisch traces the evolution of the concept of social justice in society in general and in social work in particular. The author implies that the lack of solid consensus about the definition of social justice, practice theories, and interventions has impeded social justice work in social work. By implication, therefore, social work has largely failed to challenge the status quo at the institutional level. The author broadly identifies elements necessary for social workers to work as socially just individuals. Chapter 2 offers the background on the development of the theory of social justice needed to move forward in later chapters. Author Rene Pogue provides a broad overview and the intersections of the development of social justice theory from such pioneer theorists as Rawls, Sen, Merton, Dewey, Habermas, Freire, and Mezirow, and makes important connections between social justice theory and the social work profession. Understanding and appreciating the intersection of theoretical development and the birth of the social work profession is essential to her discussion about the application of theoretical frameworks. She concludes that evidence suggests that social justice learning outcomes may be enhanced when theoretical frameworks are applied in the approach of the curriculum. In chapter 3, David Hodge provides important background on the intersection of spirituality, faith traditions, and social justice work. After pointing out the importance of spirituality to the understanding of social justice for both social workers and clients, Hodge delineates the theoretical link between spirituality and social justice, and discusses sociological data on the relationship between spirituality and efforts to create a more just society at all levels. He provides a number of examples of the ways in which people of faith operationalize understandings of social justice. He concludes with a discussion of the pedagogical implications that flow from the profession's ethical standards and the contributions that spiritually based understandings of social justice contribute to professional discourse. Rounding out the introduction section is chapter 4 by Philip Hong and David Hodge. They provide a snapshot of the status quo in social work education regarding social justice education. From their research of MSW programs around the United States, they find that a lack of clarity of the definition of social justice in classrooms creates a narrow conceptualization of the concept. The authors pose a model for creating consensus-building among students of the concept in the classroom, which will transform student learning and understanding of social justice. In a sense, this model of in-class consensus-building is a form of praxis that emphasizes a deeper hermeneutic of the concept within each class.

The next section of the book, chapters 5 through 10, builds on these foundational chapters to provide real-life, classroom-tested innovations in social justice education within various required and elective courses. In chapter 5, Stephen Pimpare shares his experience of teaching about social justice within a social policy course. He shares two models of the policy change process: a static step-by-step approach and a more flexible and pragmatic view. He describes both the classroom process of preparing students and a social policy assignment designed to instill "hopeful, active realism" in students regarding their ability to affect social policy and promote social justice. Qualitative outcomes indicate a great deal of success toward this goal. The research team of Julie Schroeder and Rene Pogue report in chapter 6 on their efforts to teach about social justice within a research course. The authors utilize transformative theory as a framework for structuring their research methods course. They used an experimental design to gather data over three years from a treatment group that utilized transformative learning activities, while a comparison group experienced a research course without such framework. Qualitative and quantitative results of their research study are shared regarding their use of a "disorienting dilemma" in the classroom to provoke serious, critical self-reflection and rational discourse with the goal of transformative learning. Michael Reisch shares his experience teaching outside of social work to honors students at the University of Michigan in chapter 7, and in doing so, challenges social work education to consider an alternative framework and methods for teaching about social justice. He reports on an undergraduate seminar that examined the multifaceted dimensions of justice through literature, film, art, and music, with a particular emphasis on comparing developments in the United States with those in other parts of the world and on analyzing their implications for social justice–oriented work. He discusses the theoretical and pedagogical foundations of the course, its format and organization, and the impact of the seminar on its participants, including the instructor. Qualitative outcome data suggest students experienced a transformative course and provide food for thought for social work education. The power of art, music, poetry, theater, and film to shape people's thoughts and emotions has long been established, but few attempts have been made in social work programs to use these media in courses about social justice. Chapter 8 shares the creativity of Carla Sofka and Diane Strock-Lynskey, who designed experiences utilizing cemetery work to teach about social justice within elective courses. Students were exposed to social and restorative justice issues through researching the lives of those buried in neglected and abandoned cemeteries, seeking some dignity and recognition for the deceased. Suggestions for replication of the experiences are provided for the curious reader. Cecilia Thomas shares her experience of teaching about social justice within a diversity course in chapter 9. The course was designed to encourage cultural competency with vulnerable populations as well as promote a more multicultural, egalitarian society to determine whether incorporating a transformative learning component in one section of the course enhances social justice education. In an effort to address the overrepresentation of African American children in the state child welfare system, one section of the course utilized a comprehensive community assessment project in a community with a high rate of involvement in the child welfare system. Rounding out this section is chapter 10, wherein Dolly Ford and Linda Ferrise describe their experience of utilizing a "Democracy Lab" within a social welfare course to teach about social justice. The Democracy Lab, an online initiative, involves hundreds of students and faculty members from across the country and was shown to be an important mechanism through which students engage in "dialogue and delibera-tion" about current issues with other students. The participants shared thoughts, experiences, and ideas, and learned about social justice issues from one another—a powerful and, for many, a transformative experience.

The next section, chapters 11 through 15, focuses on transformational experiences in non-classroom-based academic experiences. Julie Birk-enmaier and Ashley Cruce begin this section in chapter 11 with a discus-sion of an innovative program to promote social justice as an explicit goal through the field education experience. Adding to the sparse litera-ture on the potential for field education to offer transformative learning opportunities for social justice education, they describe their program and reflect on the importance of framing practice experience and encouraging students to reflect on their experiences within the value of social justice. In chapter 12, Michael Forster and Tim Rehner describe the transformative power of immersing students in an asset-poor com-munity within a structured "pedagogy of engagement" process. Stu-dents are placed in the community through a university-sponsored agency, and experience transformation as they encounter poverty up close and personal through their clients. Qualitative evidence shows a powerful transformative impact on students. Chapter 13 offers a discus-sion about an international academic experience with Barbara Leh-mann, Nancy Rodenborg, W. Randall Herman, and Sandra Robin. These authors explore the intersection between social justice and trans-formative education within an international context in the process of encouraging further international academic programs. They describe a semester-long program in Mexico, the educational-theory framework utilized, the social justice focus of the program, and student voices that illustrate personal transformation. The authors offer lessons learned, continued challenges, and a sample weekly class schedule to promote the idea that international programs are fertile ground for transforma-tive learning that promote social justice. Chapter 14, by Carol Plummer, Priscilla Allen, and Catherine Lemieux, describes the power of domestic service-learning as transformational learning. The authors relate social justice theory to two service-learning projects: a Teen Court process and the Neighborhood Advocacy project. Described are the conception of the university/community partnerships and the academic course in which each project was nested, along with respective student learning and community change goals. Project evaluation results suggest that domestic service-learning projects hold tremendous power to promote transformative learning. Last in this section is chapter 15 by Donna Har-dina and Ruth Obel-Jorgensen, who describe an opportunity that occurred outside the classroom but within a university, which was uti-lized to teach and engage social work students in direct-action organiz-ing. Academic freedom and its importance for student learning are defined and recent developments related to police surveillance and academic freedom at universities and colleges are described. The authors also discuss the risks involved in direct-action organizing, the application of specific tactical methods, and the outcomes produced. This chapter demonstrates the power of "real-life" events, which add life and substance to classroom teaching and can engage and transform students toward social justice goals. The last section of the book, chapter 16, examines the measurement of learning about social justice. In this chapter, Jan Wilson contributes to the literature with her discussion about approaches to the measurement of transformative learning—how do we know when students "get it"? She traces the history of the measurement of knowledge and proposes ideas for measuring transformative learning.

Together, these chapters describe and analyze the concept of social justice from a secular and spiritual/religious framework, as well as theory and practice of transformational learning. The authors discuss methods and means for students to understand the possibilities and the range of social justice applications to a wide range of practice areas. Some authors deconstruct the concepts, the "doing" or behavior that occurred in interaction with their students and with society, to show possible tools leading toward the reconstruction of a just society. Other authors relate to the cognitive experiences and learning necessary to frame the "doing." Taken as a group, they move the profession further along in the discussion about the concept of social justice and ways in which to structure learning experiences in order to result in transformation in students. Whether in the classroom, field education, service learning, or research settings, transformative learning holds the best promise for long-lasting learning due to the psychological and behavioral change produced through a change in perspective or viewpoint. Through the discussion of theory and the examples of pedagogy, we hope that two conversations can occur simultaneously in the social work profession—the process of coming to a consensus about definition and the operationalization of the definition, as well as defining by "doing"—teaching the concept through experiential learning and promoting transformative learning. Each chapter reflects ways of helping form and transform the student's conscience toward the refining of his or her definition of social justice and the social worker's future implementation of social change and social justice.

References

Birkenmaier, J. M. (2003). On becoming a social justice practitioner. In J. J. Stretch, E. M. Burkemper, W. J. Hutchison, & J. Wilson (Eds.), *Practicing social justice* (pp. 41–54). Binghamton, NY: The Haworth Press, Inc.

Council on Social Work Education. (2008). *Educational policy and accreditation standards.* Retrieved August 25, 2008, from http://www.cswe.org/NR/rdon lyres/2A81732E-1776-4175-AC42-65974E96BE66/0/2008EducationalPolicyand AccreditationStandards.pdf

Galambos, C. (2008). A dialogue on social justice. *Journal of Social Work Education, 44*(2), 1–5.

National Association of Social Workers (NASW). (2008). *Code of ethics.* Washington, DC: Author.

Social Justice and Social Work

CHAPTER ONE

Defining Social Justice in a Socially Unjust World

Michael Reisch

Abstract

A challenge for today's social workers and social work educators is to formulate practice principles that link social justice goals with daily realities and to communicate them effectively to the next generation of practitioners. Through its focus on the inclusion of the "voices" of marginalized groups, its critique of long-standing metanarratives, and its emphasis on the importance of the means by which societies produce or impede the attainment of social justice, postmodernism has added a process-oriented dimension to contemporary thinking (Leonard, 1997). The author provides a broad conceptual framework for social justice education in the twenty-first century.

Educating social work students for social justice practice in the early twenty-first century presents faculty with a particular set of challenges and frustrations. On the one hand, we are compelled by our consciences and professional mandates to emphasize social justice in our teaching. Many of us take seriously the declaration of the revised NASW *Code of Ethics* (2008) that "social workers challenge social injustice . . . [through] social change efforts . . . focused primarily on issues of poverty, unemployment, discrimination, and other forms of social injustice." We try to implement the education policy and accreditation standards of the Council on Social Work Education (CSWE, 2008), which require accredited programs to educate students to promote economic and social justice and combat societal oppression. Our schools' missions often reflect these dictates explicitly, as do our course syllabi.

Yet, despite their thorough immersion in this rhetorical climate, when I ask my students why social workers are not regarded as threats in today's conservative political climate, why they are not harassed by government agencies or attacked by the media (George Will's October 2007 column in the *Washington Post* notwithstanding), as their professional ancestors were repeatedly throughout the twentieth century, they merely shrug. When I tell them that in nations as different as Chile and South Africa social workers have played leadership roles in combating oppressive regimes, students often fail to see the connection to their own work. This reflects both their lack of knowledge about the history of social work in the United States and the inability of social work scholars and educators to bridge the gap between the profession's noble and well-intentioned rhetoric and the realities of practice in our complex and increasingly diverse society.

In fact, despite the increased use of social justice rhetoric, there has been little discussion among social workers or social work educators recently about the frequently contested meaning of this concept or how it can be translated into action on a day-to-day basis. Neither the *Code of Ethics* nor CSWE's Education Policy and Accreditation Standards defines the term or provides clear illustrations of its application. While the goal of social justice implies broad, structural change, most social workers continue to practice with individuals and families and largely fail to make connections between their practice and the profession's underlying philosophy. In addition, the concept of social justice implies a universality that is frequently belied by the profession's emphasis on the specific issues of specific populations. Lacking clear guidance around these critical dilemmas, faculty, students, and practitioners struggle to translate the profession's most compelling ethical imperative into real-world terms. A significant challenge for today's social workers and social work educators, therefore, is to formulate practice principles that link social justice goals with daily realities and to communicate them effectively to the next generation of practitioners.

Evolution of the Concept of Social Justice

For much of human history, the concept of social justice has been applied solely to specific communities. Social justice implied justice for a particular group or population and not for those of different ethnicities or religions. Within these limits, proponents of social justice sought to balance fairness in the distribution of resources with the maintenance of political and social stability (Chatterjee & D'Aprix, 2002). Since the appearance of secular humanism and scientific rationalism in the seventeenth and eighteenth centuries, concurrent to the growth of powerful nation-states and revolutionary movements in the West, debates over social justice have acquired a more universal tone. They have also reflected the tension between the preservation of individual liberty and the attainment of equality of rights and opportunities (Dworkin, 2000). Although there have been periodic attempts in the West to develop a single "universal concept" of social justice (e.g., medieval Christian doctrine; the ideas of eighteenth-century Enlightenment philosophers and political theorists in Europe and North America; the work of German philosophers such as Kant and Hegel; and the numerous documents of revolutionary socialism and anarchism in the nineteenth and twentieth centuries), until the mid-twentieth century there was no systematic attempt to codify social justice in a global way. This first occurred in the United Nations' *Universal Declaration of Human Rights* (1949).

The UN declaration underscored a major theme in the evolution of ideas about social justice: the emergence of a distinction between group-specific and universal concepts and theories. It also reflected the evolving distinction between theories of social justice and theories that explain other forms of justice, such as distributive or retributive justice (Miller, 2001). Although the principles of the UN declaration have rarely been put into practice, by the late twentieth century, major critiques of their underlying, largely Western ideas of social justice appeared. Critics pointed out how the declaration's universal paradigms were either no longer relevant or required extensive modification if they were to serve as effective guides in the contemporary demographic, socioeconomic, and cultural environment (Young, 2001). They also identified two unresolved problems in the attainment of social justice goals. One was the contradiction between social justice ideals and the persistent injustices of the institutional context in which they developed. The other was the tension between justice principles based on individual rights and inequalities rooted in invidious group- or population-based distinctions (Caputo, 2000; Morris, 2002; Nussbaum, 1999).

Historical View of Social Justice in U.S. Social Work

It is widely assumed that contemporary debates over social justice in the United States revolve primarily around liberal and conservative philosophical differences. In this formulation, liberals attempt to balance efforts to distribute societal benefits and burdens more broadly and equitably while protecting individual rights. Conservatives put greater emphasis on individual economic (i.e., property) and political rights and responsibilities and are less supportive of using policy for redistributive purposes (Katz, 2002; Rawls, 1999, 2001). Views of social justice in the United States, however, are far more complex and nuanced. Over the past 200 years, they have been shaped by both secular and religious perspectives ranging from Marxism to postmodernism (Elshtain, 2002; Grogan, 2000).

From Marxism and its various offshoots, social justice proponents derived the values of equality, a positive view of social change, and recognition of the importance of ideas and culture in defining the parameters of a just society (Fraser, 1995). Through its focus on the inclusion of the "voices" of marginalized groups, its critique of long-standing meta-narratives, and its emphasis on the importance of the means by which societies produce or impede the attainment of social justice, postmodernism has added a process-oriented dimension to contemporary thinking (Leonard, 1997). The diverse ideas that inform contemporary views of social justice have led to confusion about its meaning and implications for social work in the twenty-first century (Reisch, 2002).

This ambiguity is not a recent phenomenon; it has been reflected in the profession of social work almost since its inception (Holder, 1922; Wise, 1909). Although social justice has frequently been posited as an alternative to charity within the social welfare field, the social justice mission of social work has been compromised by its drive for professional status in a market-oriented economy (Reisch & Andrews, 2001; Specht & Courtney, 1994; Wenocur & Reisch, 1989). The contradictions between the cause element of social work and its professional function appear in the profession's vocabulary and in the ironic coexistence of practice theories that reflect social justice with professional practices that sustain oppressive conditions (Margolin, 1997). In recent decades, these contradictions have also appeared in the conflicts between universal views of social justice based on hegemonic cultural values and group-specific formulations (e.g., racial or gender justice) articulated by members of oppressed and marginalized populations (Johnson, 2001; Reisch, 2007, 2008; Young, 1990).

Contemporary Views of Social Justice

During the past two decades, in particular, critiques of universal conceptions of social justice have emerged from various perspectives, including neoconservatism, neoliberalism, socialism, feminism, critical race theory, postmodernism, and multiculturalism (Hill Collins, 2000; Morris, 2002; Nussbaum, 1999; Reisch, 2002). For example, there has been a serious schism among philosophers and activists about the contradictions between social justice and human rights agendas in a multicultural but still unequal global environment (Prigoff, 2003). Significant regional and ideological differences have also made it difficult to translate social justice ideals into state-sponsored policies and micro- or mezzolevel practices in public or private institutions.

Most of the recent literature on social justice in the social work field focuses primarily on various manifestations of *injustice*. The strategies proffered to overcome or mitigate these injustices, however, such as culturally competent or nonoppressive practice, rarely move beyond the formulation of abstract principles (Barusch, 2006; Finn & Jacobson, 2007; Gil, 1998; van Wormer, 2004). Perhaps this is because the goal of social justice is largely applied to the macroarena, where only a minority of social workers practice. In addition, the literature presents the injustices experienced by different populations—generally defined by demographic or cultural characteristics—as distinct phenomena with scant references to their common features or systemic roots. In addition, to a considerable extent, these books are atheoretical and make few references to the scholarship on social justice in other disciplines.

By contrast, other works, often written by social work authors outside the United States or by scholars in other fields, emphasize the common effects of recent political/economic and demographic changes such as globalization and neoliberalism on social policy, social work practice, and conceptions of social welfare as a whole (Brodie, 2007; Piven, 2002; Pugh & Gould, 2000; Reisch, 2003). They articulate alternative paradigms, ranging from neoconservatism to Marxism to critical theory, and strive to present alternative approaches to conventional social work. Many of these authors critique welfare capitalism as a social system and argue that traditional social work has been unresponsive to the problems produced by an unrestricted market economy (Isbister, 2001; White, 2000). While these works are conceptually rigorous, their content is difficult to apply to the specifics of daily practice (Appleby, Colon, & Hamilton, 2007; Diller, 2007; Ferguson, Lavalette & Whitmore, 2005; Lum, 2005; Stretch, Burkemper, Hutchison, & Wilson, 2003; Sue, 2006).

Recently, some social work scholars have begun to acknowledge the importance of incorporating social justice concepts and practice principles into both societal goals and daily processes, and into the creation of spaces in which social workers can practice social justice skills effectively and ethically. As Hans Falck (1988) did two decades ago, they assert that this requires social workers to understand the implications of individuals' multiple identities and group memberships. In this analysis, the dialectic between invidious systems of discrimination—based upon race, class, gender, sexuality, ethnicity, nation, religion, ability status, gender expression, and age—and the agency of individuals and groups creates the reality of contemporary institutional structures and shapes people's day-to-day experiences (Hill Collins, 2000). This dynamic is further complicated by the ways in which multiple group identities and social positions—some of which provide unearned advantage and others which produce persistent discrimination—influence one's perspectives on the environment. Complicating the picture further, as societal conditions change, new contradictions emerge, new forms of oppression appear, and new forces for change arise. In addition, multiple conceptions of social justice exist concurrently, even within the same group, organization, or community. Given this complexity, it is hardly surprising that social workers have such difficulty translating values into straightforward practice principles.

Social Justice and Social Work Practice

In her autobiography, Bertha Reynolds (1963) summarized the first attempt by social workers (in the Rank-and-File Movement of the 1930s) to formulate social justice–oriented guidelines for practice. These "five simple principles" implied that the pursuit of social justice within the social work profession occurred *across all methods and fields of practice.* Today's increasingly complex environment requires us to go beyond these broad statements and identify the specific competencies involved. It also requires a thorough critique of the underlying assumptions of our practice frameworks (i.e., their attention to issues of power and the implications of intersecting group memberships) and the importance of decentering our perspectives through reflection and interaction with other participants in the service relationship.

Since the emergence of the profession during the Progressive Era, social workers have assumed that practice with individuals, families, groups, and communities requires an understanding of the relationship between peoples' problems and their environment. It was clear to our professional ancestors that societal structures and institutions produced a wide range of injustices on the personal and community level. Less clear for much of social work's history was the ways in which social injustice was also reflected in the practice theories that underlie social work interventions, in the power differentials between clients and workers, and in the administrative processes employed by service agencies (Margolin, 1997). For many decades, most social workers remained unaware of the ways in which their privileged position as practitioners, their agency's control of critical resources, and the demographic and cultural differences between them and their clients maintained the societal status quo.

During the past several decades, through the influence of a diverse group of scholars, social workers have gradually expanded our understanding of the practice relationship. Social workers now recognize that by assisting clients in reframing aspects of internalized oppression, effective practitioners can help them develop critical consciousness about the nature of social injustice and articulate their own vision of a more socially just society and community. They can also enable people to select and attain goals related to this raised consciousness, which, ideally, are directed at both personal growth and societal change (Saleeby, 2002). Practitioners can sometimes provide assistance through advocacy and social action on behalf of service users, although such work has its own ethical and political challenges (Hoefer, 2006).

In the future, to work effectively toward social justice, social workers will need to possess six major components of social justice skills and knowledge:

- The ability to envision a socially just society and the actions needed to attain it;
- The ability to understand and work with conflict, dialogue, and community;
- The ability to engage in critical thinking about individual and community issues;
- The ability to apply critical self-awareness and use of self in one's practice;
- The ability to develop strategies that integrate the social and political dimensions of the environment with one's personal experience; and
- The ability to engage in praxis—the iterative and ongoing integration of ideas and action through experience, learning, and knowledge generation across domains.

Where Do We Go from Here?
Educating Social Justice Practitioners

A few recent works focus on the educational dimensions of social justice in a global society, in particular those approaches that help people (especially those who possess privilege) learn, think, and grow. They emphasize the prevention, reduction, and overcoming of resistance to change. Despite their application of critical, structural, or postmodern perspectives, and their emphasis on human rights, for the most part they address practice issues with individuals, families, small groups, and communities, rather than problems at an institutional level (Adams, Dominelli, & Payne, 2005; Dominelli, 2004; Goodman, 2001; Lundy, 2004; Pease & Fook, 1999; van Soest & Garcia, 2003). They also do not sufficiently address areas of potential conflicts, unintended consequences, and the effects of underlying biases and assumptions that make social justice work today so complex and problematic. What follows is an attempt to augment these perspectives and outline a framework for social justice education for the field.

THE ROLE OF THEORY IN SOCIAL JUSTICE WORK

Although most students prefer skills-based content to discussions of the theories on which they are based, there are many reasons why theorizing is important for social justice work. First, theorizing is a practical tool, one of the most important for creating effective change. Our explanations of injustice arise from or are articulated through different types of theories, as is our understanding of the change process. Theorizing is also an important means of maintaining one's sanity and equilibrium while working for change, because it balances those forces that sustain injustice and often distort our perceptions; it helps resist the tendency to engage in self-blame, rage, and other defensive or self-destructive reactions to the forces of injustice. Finally, theorizing, especially as a collective endeavor, can help expand our sense of possibility and develop more acute analyses of societal conditions. Each theory can illuminate potential change goals and assist practitioners to develop change strategies that anticipate diverse possible outcomes.

The Roles of Diversity, Oppression, Privilege, and Power

Another fundamental aspect of working for social justice is the need to acquire a basic understanding of the implications of diversity in all of its manifestations. Although differences may arise from diverse sources, including groups' historical experiences, social location, and cultural norms, they are always reflected in their values and goals, conceptions of need and helping, change agendas, and coping styles. Since miscommunication across any of these boundaries can become a social justice issue, we must learn to negotiate them in order to effectively work with people.

Social workers must also become aware of the multiple, often subtle, mechanisms of oppression and privilege that exist in our society and the ways in which the forces that create and sustain them operate through marginalization, domination, cultural hegemony, violence, and the disempowerment of lower status groups. The deviance process, for example, contributes to the maintenance of some forms of privilege and oppression and creates barriers to social justice work if it is not continuously monitored and addressed. Similarly, different ways of conceptualizing power can lead to different approaches to the assessment and analysis of individual and social issues, and the formulation of change strategies. Power can emerge from formal political and economic structures and from the cultural mechanisms that create meaning and worth. Power both creates and rationalizes hegemonic assumptions about acceptable behaviors, attitudes, modes of thinking and personal interaction, and social goals. As Foucault (1994) argues, "disciplinary" processes, which arise from and are sustained by daily organizational and group transactions, also create other forms of power and define acceptable "discourse" about individual and societal problems.

Social justice education, therefore, must emphasize the ways in which various types of structural power both constrain and support our ability to envision possibilities and act in pursuit of our stated goals. Because of our unique location within the institutional fabric of society, social workers must learn ways to manage, challenge, change, and utilize these structural mechanisms *within* the systems in which they occur. This can occur through a variety of strategies, including dialogue, tempered radicalism, the creative use of conflict, coalition building, honoring different standpoints, decentering dominant viewpoints, and negotiating boundaries with those in authority.

Social Justice, Change, and Resistance

Doing social justice work, therefore, requires constant attention to the processes of creating and sustaining change. Even if some social justice goals are attained, new goals will emerge or be recognized. Although conditions must usually be destabilized for desired change to occur, both individuals and institutions often fear and resist alterations to the status quo. This implies that change strategies that do not anticipate, respect, honor, and strive to reduce various types of resistance are likely to create stronger opposition, often called backlash. This is particularly important in social justice work because it involves challenging various types of entrenched power.

Education in this regard must acknowledge the personal dimensions of resistance as well. The same processes that help us survive and find meaning in our lives can also block our ability to recognize injustice. Resistance, therefore, refers to all the mechanisms within a social system that work to maintain stability, even where change may produce a desired result. It includes active, organized opposition, the subversive ways in which people who are oppressed exert dignity and agency in the presence of dehumanizing circumstances, and individuals' difficulty in reflecting upon and understanding the inherent benefits of their position within the social matrix.

Intersectional Humility and Critical Thinking

As mentioned above, in order to work for social justice, practitioners need to be able to envision social justice goals and recognize the sources of injustice, including their manifestations in various forms of privilege and oppression. Two important skills in this regard are intersectional humility and critical structural thinking. Both of these involve "habits of mind," the ability to place oneself in diverse social matrices, and skills in critical analysis—of oneself, one's immediate environment, and the knowledge and tools used in practice. These two set of skills work together and enhance each other.

Intersectional humility allows us to take people's multiple social roles and identities into account while remaining open to alternative ways of understanding and collaborating within and across domains of power. It requires regular self-analysis and monitoring, often in collaboration with others. An important task is to recognize in each context the ways in which our own dimensions of power, privilege, oppression, and difference are associated with these multiple and interacting roles (Hill Collins, 2000). This includes an understanding of our "insider" and "outsider" statuses in working with individuals, families, groups, organizations, communities, and institutions.

Intersectional humility is strengthened if social workers can broaden and "de-center" our own perspectives. One way to do this is to work closely with others who possess different voices and world views in order to learn other ways of "knowing." Intersectional humility also enhances our awareness of the ways in which others perceive us and increases our ability to recognize the importance of context in shaping people's perceptions and behaviors.

Critical structural thinking includes a set of competencies that allows us to identify the sources, manifestations, and mechanisms of injustice and to develop more diverse justice-oriented theories and practices. It involves a critique of the assumptions that underlie knowledge, research methods, theories, and practice interventions. As social justice does not mean the same thing to everyone in the United States and the world, critical structural thinking requires us to decenter the dominant paradigms that guide our practice. It leads to the formulations of such questions as: Who envisions the goals of change and action? Who is responsible for implementing them? Who bears the social costs of such changes or reaps their benefits?

The Personal Dimensions of Social Justice Work

On a more personal level, social workers cannot sustain work for social justice without recognizing and supporting our own strengths and those of others. (I always tell students that social justice work requires them to prepare for a marathon, not a sprint.) This requires finding joy and meaning in work even when failure occurs. In fact, the ability to envision justice is often constrained by a lack of imagination regarding the ways in which justice would affect individuals and their communities.

Working toward a social justice vision in specific practice contexts also requires social workers to assess and build on a wide array of strengths and assets—within ourselves and others. This goes beyond the application of a "strengths perspective" to examine the complexities of incorporating an understanding of our social identities and the role of power in our analysis of doing justice work. It includes the use of accessible language, the acknowledgment of the value of diverse leadership and participation styles, appreciation of indigenous knowledge and experiences, and support for diverse coping and resilience-building strategies.

One important tool linking the personal and theoretical dimensions of social justice work is the concept of praxis. Praxis employs iterative and interactive cycles of theorizing, acting, and reflecting in order to deepen critical consciousness, increase insights about social justice, and identify and reduce barriers to justice. This includes making connections between our theories and experiences; recognizing biased assumptions that underlie presumably universal practice methods; managing the ambiguities and discomfort related to privilege, oppression, and diversity; and employing knowledge and skills for cultural humility. Doing justice through praxis also involves using skills in critical structural thinking and critical consciousness to modify existing theories and generate new knowledge and awareness.

The Organizational Context

Successful social justice–oriented education requires demonstration of ways in which these broad principles can be applied to specific practice settings. A good way to start is to refocus the nature of practice from the traditional dyadic (i.e., worker/client) relationship to one in which the social service agency plays a critical role. Most social services and social change efforts occur through organizations that engage in conscious processes of need definition and assessment; resource development, allocation, and management; issue prioritization; strategic planning; program development and evaluation; and the establishment and maintenance of relationships with clients, constituents, collaborators, and community sponsors. Yet social work education pays little attention to the role of organizations in shaping the nature of social work practice.

This is particularly important because even among organizations with explicit social justice missions and goals, there is frequently a gap between their stated objectives and their day-to-day practice. This failure is reflected in the programs and strategies they create (including the manner by which these programs and strategies are designed, implemented, and evaluated); the nature of worker/client, worker/constituent, and worker/worker interactions; the relationships that exist between the organization and the communities it purports to serve; and the features of the overall organizational culture that shapes patterns of decision making and resource allocation, collegial relationships, and the overall climate of the organization. It undermines their ability to achieve stated goals, diminishes the level of trust within the organization, particularly between workers and clients, and creates barriers between the organization and critical stakeholders.

This contradiction between socially just practice and the socially unjust organizational climate in which it often occurs needs to be directly addressed in the educational process. Students should learn ways in which the attributes of socially just organizations are reflected in their structures and goals; patterns of decision making; means of allocating scarce resources; leadership style; supervision processes; organizational culture; strategies for dealing with intra- and interorganizational conflict; approaches to ethical dilemmas; and use and distribution of technology.

The Community Context

Similarly, since social justice practice occurs in a community context, it is important for students to distinguish between community work directed toward explicitly social justice–related goals and the use of socially just means in community work that lacks such explicit goals. Much of the recent literature on community practice in a multicultural society focuses on the challenges of working across racial and cultural lines, the problems involved in forming and sustaining multicultural

coalitions and alliances, and the need to cultivate increased civic participation, new forms of leadership, and social capital among diverse populations. In addition, it emphasizes the importance of awareness about
the influence of global developments on practice at the local level (Weil,
2005). In combination, these attributes strengthen the ability of practitioners to work toward explicit social justice goals through socially just
means.

A related set of skills involves the use of dialogue and nonviolent
communication in various group settings, whose value in bridging cultural gaps has been recognized by social workers since the 1920s. In
social justice work, the term "dialogue" is often associated with a particular form of intervention—dialogue groups—but, as Freire (1970)
wrote, it can also refer to the use of dialogic education, intragroup and
intergroup communication, and negotiation skills in all forms of
practice.

Linking Policy and Practice

At the same time, in a rapidly changing environment, shaped by economic globalization and major demographic, technological, and socio-
cultural transformation, the relationship between social policies and
social work practice has become both more significant and more complex. Greater attention must now be paid to transnational issues and
the distinctive character of local needs and concerns. In the United
States, the locus of policymaking and implementation has devolved
from the national government to the state and local arenas. Finally, as
a result of globalization, power over policymaking has shifted from the
nation-state to supranational institutions and from the public to the
nonprofit and for-profit sectors. While socially just policies require
greater democratization, many critical policy decisions are increasingly
made through nondemocratic means, often outside of long-standing
political processes.

Despite these changes, it is important for students to learn that
socially just policies can still be promoted from inside even socially
unjust institutions and from the outside, through advocacy and other
forms of community-based social action. This requires students to
understand policymaking processes at multiple levels of government,
as well as within civil society and the corporate sector. They also need
to increase the involvement of low-power groups in the policymaking
process, through the use of participatory action research, community-
based policy advocacy, popular education, and training programs in
public speaking, lobbying, and the use of media.

From a social justice perspective, there are several other aspects of the policy-development process that are frequently overlooked in social work education. One is the need to translate broadly worded legislation into specific socially just programs, which occurs primarily through the budgetary and regulatory processes. Another is the need to safeguard legislative or judicial achievements through ongoing monitoring of policies after they are implemented, often in a decentralized manner. This requires understanding the relationship between federal agencies and state governments; between state agencies and local governments; and between government, in general, and the private sector. Finally, it is increasingly important to evaluate the substantive impact of policy and the process by which it was developed and implemented. In sum, the application of a social justice lens to the policymaking process implies an assessment of the extent to which it expands people's ability to make the critical decisions that affect their lives, increases their share of the tangible and intangible resources they receive, redefines the policy agenda so as to address their needs as they define them, and reduces the level of oppression and unjustified privilege in policymaking spheres.

The Role of Research

Lastly, because of the increased emphasis on the use of evidence-based practice, knowledge generation via research and evaluation, whether through the development of theories or the collection, analysis, and dissemination of empirical data, plays a critical role in social justice work. The growing significance of research enhances the importance of critically examining dominant methodologies, their assumptions about epistemology and the purposes of knowledge development, the criteria for determining valid (i.e., useful) knowledge, the power relationships that exist between researchers and the researched, and the connection between epistemological assumptions and their practice applications. The heightened value given today to quantitative, empirical forms of inquiry runs the risk of producing narrower views of "valid" knowledge that could impede the promotion of social justice.

A social justice perspective, however, acknowledges that power operates regardless of the types of research methods used and that no method innately promotes social justice. Some methods, however, may be more explicit in their social justice orientation or have more potential for promoting social justice processes, for example, by ensuring the inclusion of diverse perspectives and experiences, incorporating attention to the manifestations of power and privilege in the research process, encouraging the development of critical consciousness, and promoting changes at multiple levels (Reisch, Reed, Yoshihama, & Garvin, in press).

Conclusion

In the twenty-first century, social workers' ethical imperative to combat injustice requires them to work toward social justice ends through socially just means. Social workers must acknowledge that the structures, cultural mechanisms, and processes that are necessary to produce progressive social change can also create and maintain forms of injustice. Social workers must recognize, however painful it may be, that social workers have sometimes been complicit in sustaining the very conditions we are obligated to challenge. This implies the need to incorporate ongoing engagement, vigilance, and struggle into social justice practice and educational preparation for that practice.

Recent political, economic, and demographic transformations on a global scale may compel closer attention to the meaning of our historic commitment to social justice in an increasingly diverse environment. Economic globalization has exacerbated prevailing socioeconomic inequalities in the United States and between the global North and South. Within the social welfare field, it has altered sectoral relationships; changed the ideology, vocabulary, and goals of many social service agencies; and contributed to the depoliticization of the profession. Social workers are now compelled to reexamine long-standing assumptions about the role of government in social welfare provision, the role of nonprofits in the social welfare nexus, the nature of worker/client relationships, and the underlying assumptions of our practice theories. Concurrently, demographic changes underscore ways in which contemporary socioeconomic problems can no longer be resolved within existing political boundaries, ways in which social divisions no long occur along a simple majority/minority axis, ways in which the goals of social justice and multiculturalism are not inevitably compatible, and ways in which practice concepts and curricula need to be enhanced to address contemporary realities effectively.

In developing responses to these challenges, it is less important that social workers identify a single "right" social justice approach than it is to remain open to multiple possible explanations and strategies. Perhaps social workers can find common ground in the search for solutions to the social consequences of environmental degradation and climate change or in the articulation of the relationship between the peaceful resolution of local and global conflicts and the pursuit of social justice. Whichever organizing principle is selected, it is critical that efforts are renewed to find new meaning in old concepts, new ways to translate new ideas into concrete actions, and new ways to communicate to the next generation the knowledge and skills required to engage in social justice work.

References

Adams, R., Dominelli, L., & Payne, M. (Eds.). (2005). *Social work futures: Crossing boundaries, transforming practice.* New York: Palgrave MacMillan.

Appleby, G., Colon, E., & Hamilton, J. (2007). *Diversity, oppression and social functioning.* New York: Haworth Press.

Barusch, A. S. (2006). *Foundations of social policy: Social justice in human perspective.* Belmont, CA: Thomson Brooks/Cole.

Brodie, J. M. (2007). Reforming social justice in neoliberal times. *Studies in Social Justice, 1*(2), 93–107.

Caputo, R. (2000). Multiculturalism and social justice: An attempt to reconcile the irreconcilable within a pragmatic liberal framework. *Race, Gender, and Class, 7*(4), 161–182.

Chatterjee, P., & D'Aprix, A. (2002). Two tails of justice. *Families in Society: The Journal of Contemporary Human Services, 83*(4), 374–386.

Council on Social Work Education. (2008). *Curriculum policy statement.* Alexandria, VA: Author.

Diller, J. (2007). *Cultural diversity: A primer for the human services.* Belmont, CA: Thomson.

Dominelli, L. (2004). *Social work: Theory and practice for a changing profession.* Cambridge, UK: Polity Press.

Dworkin, R. (2000). *Sovereign virtue: The theory and practice of equality.* Cambridge, MA: Harvard University Press.

Elshtain, J. B. (2002). *Jane Addams and the dream of American democracy: A life.* New York: Basic Books.

Falck, H. S. (1988). *Social work: The membership perspective.* New York: Springer.

Ferguson, I., Lavalette, M., & Whitmore, E. (2005). *Globalisation, global justice and social work.* London: Routledge.

Finn, J. L., & Jacobson, M. (2007). *Just practice: A social justice approach to social work.* Peosta, IA: Eddie Bowers.

Foucault, M. (1994). The subject and power. In J. B. Faubion (Ed.), *Power: Essential works of Foucault, 1954–1984* (pp. 326–348). New York: Free Press. (Original work published 1982)

Fraser, N. (1995). From redistribution to recognition? Dilemmas of justice in a post-socialist age. *New Left Review, 212*, 68–93.

Freire, P. (1970). *Pedagogy of the oppressed.* New York: Seabury.

Gil, D. (1998). *Confronting injustice and oppression: Concepts and strategies for social work.* New York: Columbia University Press.

Goodman, D. J. (2001). *Promoting diversity and social justice: Educating people from privileged groups.* Thousand Oaks, CA: Sage Publications.

Grogan. C. (2000). Principles of social justice. *Social Service Review, 74*(4), 668–671.

Hill Collins, P. (2000). *Black feminist thought: Knowledge, consciousness, and the politics of empowerment.* New York: Routledge.

Hoefer, R. (2006). *Advocacy practice for social justice.* Chicago: Lyceum Books.

Holder, A. C. (1922). *The settlement idea: A vision of social justice.* New York: MacMillan.

Isbister, J. (2001). *Capitalism and justice: Envisioning social and economic fairness.* Bloomfield, CT: Kumarian Press.

Johnson, A. (2001). *Privilege, power, and difference.* Mountain View, CA: Mayfield.

Katz, M. B. (2002). *The price of citizenship: Redefining the American welfare state.* New York: Holt.

Leonard, P. (1997). *Postmodern welfare: Reconstructing an emancipatory project.* Thousand Oaks, CA: Pine Forge Press.

Lum, D. (2005). *Cultural competence, practice stages, and client systems: A case study approach.* Belmont, CA: Thomson.

Lundy, C. (2004). *Social work and social justice: A structural approach to practice.* Peterborough, ON: Broadview Press.

Margolin, L. (1997). *Under the cover of kindness: The invention of social work.* Charlottesville: University Press of Virginia.

Miller, D. (2001). *Boundaries and justice: Diverse ethical perspectives.* Princeton, NJ: Princeton University Press.

Morris, P. M. (2002). The capabilities perspective: A framework for social justice. *Families in Society: The Journal of Contemporary Human Services, 83*(4), 365–373.

National Association of Social Workers. (2008). *Code of ethics* (Rev. ed.). Washington, DC: Author.

Nussbaum, M. S. (1999). *Sex and social justice.* New York: Oxford University Press.

Pease, B., & Fook, J. (Eds.). (1999). *Transforming social work practice: Postmodern critical perspectives.* London: Routledge.

Piven, F. F. (2002). Welfare policy and American politics. In F. F. Piven, J. Acker, M. Hallock, & S. Morgen (Eds.), *Work, welfare and politics: Confronting poverty in the wake of welfare reform* (pp. 19–33). Eugene: University of Oregon Press.

Prigoff, A. W. (2003). Social justice framework. In J. Anderson & R. W. Carter (Eds.), *Diversity perspectives for social work practice* (pp. 113–120). Boston: Allyn and Bacon.

Pugh, R., & Gould, N. (2000). Globalization, social work, and social welfare. *European Journal of Social Work, 3*(2), 123–138.

Rawls, J. (1999). *A theory of justice* (Rev. ed.). Cambridge, MA: Harvard University Press.

Rawls, J. (2001). *Justice as fairness: A restatement.* Cambridge, MA: Belknap Press of Harvard University Press.

Reisch, M. (2002). Defining social justice in a socially unjust world. *Families in Society: The Journal of Contemporary Human Services, 83*(4), 343–354.

Reisch, M. (2003). Welfare reform, globalization, and the transformation of the welfare state. In M. Ruiz Gonzalez (Ed.), *Community organization and social policy: A compendium.* San Juan, PR: Editorial Edil (in Spanish).

Reisch, M. (2007). Social justice and multiculturalism: Persistent tensions in the history of U.S. social welfare and social work. *Studies in Social Justice, 1*(1), 67–92.

Reisch, M. (2008). From melting pot to multiculturalism: The impact of racial and ethnic diversity on social work and social justice in the United States. *British Journal of Social Work, 38*(4), 788–804.

Reisch, M., & Andrews, J. (2001). *The road not taken: A history of radical social work in the United States.* Philadelphia: Brunner-Routledge.

Reisch, M., Reed, B. G., Yoshihama, M., & Garvin, C. (in press). *Doing justice: Working for change in a changing world.* New York: Oxford University Press.

Reynolds, B. C. (1963). *An uncharted journey: Fifty years growth in social work.* New York: Citadel Press.

Saleeby, D. (2002). *The strengths perspective in social work practice.* Boston: Allyn and Bacon.

Specht, H., & Courtney, M. (1994). *Unfaithful angels: How social work abandoned its mission.* New York: Free Press.

Stretch, J. J., Burkemper, E. M., Hutchison, W. J., & Wilson, J. (2003). *Practicing social justice.* New York: Haworth.

Sue, D. W. (2006). *Multicultural social work practice.* Hoboken, NJ: John Wiley & Sons.

United Nations. (1949). *Universal declaration of human rights.* New York: Author.

Van Soest, D., & Garcia, B. (2003). *Diversity education for social justice: Mastering teaching skills.* Alexandria, VA: Council on Social Work Education.

Van Wormer, K. (2004). *Confronting oppression, restoring justice: From policy analysis to social action.* Alexandria, VA: Council on Social Work Education.

Weil, M. (2005). Introduction. In M. Weil, M. Reisch, D. N. Gamble, L. Gutierrez, E. A. Mulroy, & R. A. Cnaan (Eds.), *The handbook of community practice* (pp. xi–xvi). Thousand Oaks, CA: Sage.

Wenocur, S., & Reisch, R. (1989). *From charity to enterprise: The development of American social work in a market economy.* Urbana: University of Illinois Press.

White, J. E. (2000). *Democracy, justice, and the welfare state: Reconstructing public care.* University Park: Pennsylvania State University Press.

Will, G. (2007, October 14). Code of coercion. *Washington Post,* p. B-07.

Wise, S. S. (1909). The conference sermon: Charity versus justice. In A. Johnson (Ed.), *Proceedings of the national conference of charities and corrections* (pp. 20–29). Fort Wayne, IN: Fort Wayne Publishing Company.

Young, I. M. (1990). *Justice and the politics of difference.* Princeton, NJ: Princeton University Press.

Young, I. M. (2001). Equality for whom? Social groups and judgments of injustice. *Journal of Political Philosophy, 9*(1), 1–18.

CHAPTER TWO

Theoretical Frameworks for Effective Social Justice Education

Rene Pogue

Abstract

Social justice education may be improved when theoretical frameworks are used in its design, planning, and evaluation. Theory provides not only the language students need in order to understand the breadth, depth, and nuance of social justice but the means to inspire students and move them to seek social justice. This chapter summarizes the contributions of pioneer social justice theorists and makes important connections between social justice theory and learning outcomes.

> *The good we secure for ourselves is precarious and uncertain until it is secured for all of us and incorporated into our common life.*
>
> —Jane Addams

When traced to its liberal arts roots, the fundamental purpose of American higher education is to achieve a humanistic vision of *civitas.* A shift in that perspective occurred in the United States with the advent of the land-grant movement and its emphasis on practical education and dedication to building a workforce inclined toward agriculture and mechanical fields (Lucas, 1994). Although distinctly different, both approaches seek to fulfill a purpose to produce citizens able to improve society. In spite of this commonality, the differences in the liberal and practical arts perspectives of higher education are still vigorously argued today (Kyle, 2005) and are particularly relevant to the place social justice education holds in the academy.

Middle ground in the dispute is a view that asserts that the best purposes of a college education are fulfilled when students have the useful knowledge and technical skill that their selected occupations require, and the awareness that they are actors in society, where their actions may have moral, civic, and social effects for good or ill (Hansen, 1995; Rehm, 1990). This balanced perspective assumes that the best university education prepares students to make a wage and to make a life that adds to civil society; to assume an occupation and to answer a "calling." While many scholars believe a dual mission of this sort is essential to higher education and to society (Armstrong & Miller, 2006; Harkavy, 2000; Lemann, 2004), others take an even more liberal view that social justice education is a vital ingredient in fulfilling the best purposes of higher education (Karger & Hernandez, 2004; Kyle, 2005).

While social justice education adds to a college education in general, it is particularly important to professional programs such as nursing, education, and counseling. In social work programs, social justice education is an essential standard (Council on Social Work Education [CSWE], 2008) and vital to making social work practice a just activity (Burkemper & Stretch, 2003; Finn & Jacobson, 2003). In fact, social work's professional commitment to social justice is embedded in the values, principles, ethics, and traditions that identify the profession (Birkenmaier, 1999; Morris, 2002; National Association of Social Workers [NASW], 2008; Swenson, 1998; Wakefield, 1998). To add to the dialogue about social justice education, this review of literature provides an outline of philosophical and educational perspectives of social justice education, examines the intersection between social work and social justice education, and considers scholarship and research in the field.

Social Justice Theory

Social justice education is often grounded in formal social justice theories about what constitutes a fair share of a society's assets and who should be entitled to those assets. Other dimensions of social justice are revealed when issues of fair treatment (procedural justice), just deserts (retributive justice), and restorative justice are considered (Van Soest, 1995). The standard for social justice education in social work is economic justice (CSWE, 2008) and a theoretical framework most cited is Rawls (University of Washington, 2007).

RAWLSIAN THEORY

A Harvard professor until his retirement in 1991, John Rawls is renowned as one of the most important political philosophers of the twentieth century and a foremost social justice theorist (Korsgaard, Sen, Thompson, & Scanlon, 2005). In his most acknowledged work, *A Theory of Justice*, Rawls (1971) set forth a set of principles, or requisite conditions, that form the basis of his theory of social justice. The first of these is "the circumstances of justice," which make human cooperation both possible and necessary. Second is "the formal constraints of the concept of right," which are determined when principles of right (or justice) are applied to adjusting the individual claims one makes on others and their social institutions. Third, "the veil of ignorance" involves screening out self-awareness of self-interests that interfere with the objectivity required for realizing just purposes. Finally, "the rationality of the contracting parties" seeks to claim from society primarily those benefits that society is capable of conveying, otherwise referred to as "primary goods."

The cornerstones of the theory are two core principles. First is the greatest equal liberty principle, which asserts that the "just" distribution of liberty is contingent on each person having an equal claim to the fullest extent of basic liberty that is compatible with a system of like liberty for all others. The second principle is stated in two parts, which assert that social justice is contingent on arranged social and economic inequalities that are "(a) reasonably expected to be advantageous to all" (Rawls, 1971, p. 60) (this is the difference principle) and "(b) attached to positions that are open to all" (the fair equality of opportunity principle) (Rawls, 1971, p. 60). In Rawls's theory, the redress that the disadvantaged have is based on the Difference Principle and is reserved only for those judged to make some effort on their own behalf or that of others (Millgram, 2000, p. 535; see also North, 2006; Reisch, 2002). In this last respect, Rawls's theory of justice makes a distinction between those worthy and unworthy of his notion of distributive justice.

In essence, Rawls theorized that social justice is accomplished through a social contract that seeks to distribute to each worthy person the fullest extent of all rights and benefits that it is possible for all to enjoy; arrangement of compensatory social and economic inequities that benefit all, especially the least advantaged worthy members of society; and individual willingness to enter into the social contract that requires setting aside self-interest or believing that one's self-interests are best served by the contract (Rawls, 1971; see also Bentley, 1973).

When introduced, Rawls's theory was accepted as a new paradigm for understanding social justice and marked a turning point in theory development. However, his perspective of distributive justice was criticized for its limited applicability to the real world, where "people are not necessarily free, rational or just, where disobedience exists and punishment may be necessary" (Bentley, 1973, p. 1073). Rawls (1993) responded to these criticisms by broadening his definition of *primary goods* to include rightful claims to intangibles such as self-respect, and he offered up his partial compliance theory to explain the practical limitations of his ideas (Morris, 2002; see also Brock, 1973). Today, Rawls's theory serves as foundation for the Western paradigm of social justice, which is based on fair distribution of tangible and intangible societal goods (Kymlicka, 1988). Although Rawls's theory covers a great deal of ground, examining other theories is necessary to add greater dimension to our conceptual understanding of social justice.

THE CAPABILITIES APPROACH

Pioneered by Nobel Prize–winning economist Amartya Sen, the capabilities perspective looks for social justice beyond the traditionally drawn borders of distributive justice theory. In theory, Sen (1985) agrees with Rawls that fair distribution of primary goods is essential to human well-being and social justice. However, Sen views the equitable distribution of primary goods as a means to an end, not an end unto itself. Sen agrees that going the way of fair commodities distribution to ensure human welfare and social justice is all well and good, but he argues that is not the best place to stop a search for social justice (1985, p. 15; see also Morris, 2002). Generally speaking, the capabilities perspective sees distributive justice as only one part of an equation that adds up to states of social justice. Those who accept the capabilities perspective take a point of view that begins with questions about "what makes a good life for a person" (Morris, 2002, p. 368). From a capabilities perspective, answers to that question focus not on primary goods, as Rawls suggested, but on "substantial freedoms." Substantial or positive freedoms are those that lead to all sorts of resources that can help an individual become functionally capable of achieving a good life as he or she sees it (Sen, 1999; see also Garrett, 2005).

A law and ethics professor and noted philosopher, Martha Nussbaum's (1999) ideas contribute richly to the capabilities approach to social justice. Nussbaum asserts that human worth and dignity entitles every person to a rightful political claim to those central capabilities that are essential for well-being (see also Morris, 2002). In Nussbaum's view, just societies must have a safety net constructed of the "central capabilities," which are those that allow citizens to live as human beings. Sen and Nussbaum agree that self-determination is a pivotal principle in a theory of social justice that expects societies to make capabilities available but leaves it to individuals to decide to use them (Nussbaum, 1999; Sen, 1999).

SOCIAL CONSTRUCTION OF SOCIAL JUSTICE

While some theorists wrestle with the elements that constitute social justice and ways to achieve it, Robert K. Merton (1957) theorized about the human understandings of social justice that are socially constructed. Unlike his philosopher counterparts who theorized about social justice, Merton was a sociologist whose theories are based on extensive original research that he conducted to test ideas about reference groups and reference individuals. Merton's findings revealed two processes by which individuals formulate personal frames of reference about social justice. The first involves comparisons individuals make between just and unjust situations in their experience; the second is an evaluation of whether the implications of the comparison can be generalized to "virtually every area of the behavioral and social life" (Jasso, 2002, p. 332).

Based on his research, Merton derived a complicated formula for justice evaluation that can be useful to researchers, but the overlap he found between reference group and justice theory is more universally relevant to those who are interested in social justice education. Specifically, Merton's reference group theory teaches us that individuals use many reference groups when making comparisons to determine the justness of a situation, while justice theory explains that individuals may sort through many comparisons that produce a different justice evaluation each time (Jasso, 2002). The implication for social justice education is that the weight and momentum of interpersonal, social interaction is critical to learning about social justice. For educators, Merton's theory clarifies how shared social constructions of social justice are formed and shift over time. In the process, the lessons Merton's theory teaches are pivotal to understanding not only social justice, but how to teach it.

As basic tools for social justice education, Rawls's theory, and those that follow from it, accomplishes the expectation of theories: the means to describe and explain what social justice means and, in part, ways it can be achieved. Likewise, social justice theories provide the grounds on which to make predictions about the just states of human affairs in a variety of particular circumstance. Merton's theory informs us about the ways individuals collectively conceive social justice, which, in turn, informs teaching about social justice. Taken together, a range of social justice theories are both background and instruction for planning and executing social justice education.

Education Theory and Social Justice Education

Social justice theories supply the conceptual detail and language required to develop content for social justice education and, likewise, some direction about effective ways to teach it. Education theories supply us with direction and assurance that teaching can accomplish the complex knowledge, skill, and conative learning outcomes sought in social justice education; aims that include adding knowledge but, also, social consciousness, desire, volition, and striving for social justice. As theoretical notions about social justice are evolving, so too are notions about social justice education. Some education traditions are long-standing, while others more contemporary.

From the Settlement House Movement of the early 1900s and the Action-University Movement of the 1960s, contemporary social justice education often takes form as an educational *experience* involving charitable services in needy communities or as social advocacy (Robinson, 2000). In many incidences, these planned educational experiences take shape in service-learning activities that are intended to help students develop a social consciousness and patterns of engaged citizenship (Lemieux & Allen, 2007; Reich, 2005; Saltmarsh, 2005). In other cases, dialogue (Dessel, Rogge, & Garlington, 2006), classroom instruction (Viggiani, Charlesworth, Hutchison, & Faria, 2005), or integrative (Birkenmaier, 2003) approaches are taken to teach social justice and professional principles. Most of these activities can be traced to classic or modern education theories, but very few who report their efforts draw a clear connection between social justice education and reliable education theory. This chapter supposes that strengthening knowledge about education theory is a reasonable course of action to achieving the best outcomes in social justice education and one that could revive desirable practice patterns and standards set at the time the profession was born.

DEWEY'S THEORY OF EXPERIENCE

Regardless of either liberal or practical arts persuasion, John Dewey's (1938) theory of experience is accepted as a bedrock education theory throughout the academy. As philosopher and theorist, Dewey acknowledged—but avoided—the debate about whether education should prepare students for practical trades or a higher purpose. Instead, he tried to debunk unfounded notions that an education is vocational when it is useful and liberal when it is practically useless. Demonstrating the false nature of the dichotomy to defuse the conflict, Dewey traced the problem back from the division between theory and practice to our received mind/body dualism. To illustrate, Dewey argued that the contrast between culture and utility reflects the breach between leisure and labor and how both of these distinctions originate in classism, which, in turn, leads to the antidemocratic social arrangements that serve as a source for philosophical dichotomies in every direction (Dewey, 1916,

p. 258; Higgins, 2005, p. 443). Dworkin (1959) noted that Dewey perceived education as an unconscious process of self-discovery in the present, whose ultimate objective is to create a greater sense of authenticity. In these respects, Dewey distinguishes education that teaches citizenship skills from that which stimulates and activates learner's humanitarian impulses. Both have benefits, but the latter not only raises consciousness; it moves the learner to action.

To balance the argument in theory and practice, Dewey proposed an alternate view of vocational education; one that embraces a fuller sense of vocation that includes any well-defined social role. From its broadest vantage point, Dewey's view of vocational education recognized the aesthetic and existential dimensions embedded in educational experience (Dewey, 1897, 1938; Higgins, 2005) and understood that without insight into the psychological structure and activities of students, the process of education is bound to be arbitrary and haphazard (Dewey, 1897, 1938; Higgins, 2005). Dewey's theory "is that experience arises from the interaction of two principles—continuity and interaction" (Neill, 2005). Continuity is that every person's future is influenced by each experience he or she has. Interaction refers to the phenomena that present experience is a consequence of the interaction between an individual's past experiences and present situation. According to Dewey, the effect of an experience is not predetermined and must be evaluated on the impact it has on one's present and future and his or her individual ability to contribute to society. Throughout his theory, Dewey emphasized that, in order for education to accomplish its aims, educators must be aware of the subjective nature of experience and understand students' past experiences. According to Dewey, a theory of experience gives educators a solid foundation on which to organize subject matter in ways that capitalize on students' past experiences and provide experiences that may open them up to future growth, which will increase their likely contributions to society (Dewey, 1938; Neill, 2005). During Dewey's time, his theory of experience was considered somewhat radical. The degree to which his advice now seems like common sense is an indication of the degree to which his theory has become deeply embedded.

In essence, Dewey's theory directs us not only to know our students, but to understand the differences in their past experiences and in our own. Where social justice education is concerned, Dewey would likely advise us to be aware of the contemporary world and its effects on our students as more remote historic events may have influenced our own. Because the long-term stakes can be high, it seems reasonable for social justice educators to follow Dewey's useful advice.

FROM PEDAGOGY TO ANDRAGOGY

Based on distinctions in Latin roots of the terms, "andragogy" has been used to refer to adult learning, while "pedagogy" refers to children's learning. Malcolm Knowles (1970) is regarded as the central figure in U.S. education in the second half of the twentieth century (Smith, 2002) for his adult education theory and for popularizing the conceptual difference between pedagogy and andragogy. At the core of Knowles's theory are four andragogical assumptions that adults (a) move from dependency to self-directedness, (b) draw upon their reservoir of experience for learning, (c) are ready to learn when they assume new roles, and (d) want to solve problems and apply new knowledge immediately (Knowles, 1970).

Based on core assumptions drawn from theories of adult development, Knowles's andragogy emphasizes that adults are self-directed and expect to take responsibility for decisions. Knowles makes certain recommendations for tailoring instruction to adult learners. Based on developmental theory, he recommends that instruction for adults should be more process than content oriented. Knowles advises educators to draw adult students' experience into the learning process. His theory also recommends that educators focus on the immediate relevance of subject content to students' jobs and personal lives, and emphasize a problem-centered approach (Knowles, 1980).

Knowles's education theory also relies on principles of democracy. The seven-step process that composes the technology of andragogy calls on educators to (a) set a cooperative learning climate; (b) create mechanisms for mutual planning; (c) arrange for a diagnosis of learner needs and interests; (d) enable the formulation of learning objectives based on diagnosed needs and interests; (e) design sequential activities for achieving the objectives; (f) execute the design by selecting methods, materials, and resources; and (g) evaluate the quality of the learning experience while rediagnosing needs for further learning (Knowles, 1970). Knowles's andragogical theory provides a good set of basic guidelines for adult learning and essential background for planning social justice education. Like Dewey, Knowles reminds us of the essential value of individual experience—past and present—to education.

TRANSFORMATIONAL LEARNING THEORY

Transformational learning theory builds on the theoretical background previously discussed and is a particularly satisfying fit for social justice education that reconciles practical and liberal educational intentions. When translated to education practice, transformative education is a highly experiential, introspective, and dialogical process. In these respects, it is easy to see Dewey and Knowles's footprints in contemporary, formal transformative learning theory, which is built on ground covered in the philosophies of Jürgen Habermas and Paulo Freire.

A German philosopher, critical theorist, and contemporary of Rawls (Hart, 1990), Jürgen Habermas's education theory identified three learning domains based on different aspects of social existence. Together, the domains form a learning taxonomy that locates a resonant place for social justice education. The work knowledge domain represents instrumental knowledge and refers to the way one controls and manipulates one's environment. Learning in the knowledge domain best fits with empirical/analytic sciences that rely on hypothetical/deductive theories. The practical knowledge domain is that which is concerned with human interaction, or *communicative action.* According to Habermas, historical/hermeneutic disciplines that emphasize descriptive social science, history, aesthetics, and so forth, belong to the practical knowledge domain (Brookfield, 2005; Kreber & Cranton, 2000). The emancipatory knowledge domain involves critical self-awareness. The emancipatory learning domain refers to *self-knowledge* or self-reflection. Emancipatory learning involves the insight that occurs when one takes interest in the way his or her history and biography determine self-perception, roles, and social expectation and the ways in which those have manifested in the way one sees oneself, one's roles, and social expectations. Emancipatory-domain learning is the transformed consciousness, or *perspective transformation,* that one achieves through reflection. Habermas believed that our desire to grow, develop, and obtain self-knowledge and freedom is our emancipatory interest. Habermas's theory concludes that emancipatory learning involves critical reflection about the world and critical self-reflection (Cranton, 2006; Mezirow, 1981).

What Habermas adds to transformational learning theory in logic, Paulo Freire's "pedagogy of possibility" adds in soul. Freire was a Brazilian native who moved between the political and social arenas as a Brazilian government official, a U.S. academic, and South American social and political activist. Through his experiences as a political prisoner and work with the oppressed underclass, Freire came to reject what he referred to as the "banking model" of education, wherein teachers act as "depositors" of knowledge into students, who act as passive recipients. Instead, he embraced the possibilities that education can create when it is, by it very nature, empowering. Freire proposed a "pedagogy of the oppressed," which relies on "problem-posing" education and self-reflection as a basis for critical awareness, or conscientization. Freire defines conscientization as a kind of learning that focuses on exposing social and political contradictions, and acting against oppressive elements in one's life. Freire believed dialogue was praxis that empowers and leads to social action for social justice. Because of its nature, Freire's contributions to transformational learning theory come closest to political activism that is at the heart of social justice (Freire, 1998, 2000; Glass, 2001).

Together, Habermas and Freire certainly laid conceptual groundwork, but when it comes to discussions of contemporary transformational learning theory, all roads lead to Jack Mezirow. Mezirow's transformative learning theory is based on an assumption that all learning is change, but not all learning is transformative. According to Mezirow and Associates (1990), transformational learning occurs only when there is change in a learner's *"frame of reference* which encompasses cognitive, conative, and emotional components and is composed of two dimensions: *habits of the mind* and *a point of view"* (emphasis added) (p. 17). Further, Mezirow's (1997) theory supposes that transformational learning requires a "disorienting dilemma," which is defined as an experience that is sufficient to cause students to "lose their bearings set by an existing frame of reference" (p. 5). In practice, Mezirow believes that the disorienting dilemma acts as a catalyst for critical self-reflection and rational discourse necessary for transforming existing frames of reference. When the process occurs, so too does transformational learning (Mezirow, 1997; Mezirow & Associates, 2000). Habermas, Freire, and Mezirow's views broadly outline the essential cognitive rational dimensions of present thought about transformative learning. Their developmental view of transformative learning theory takes a narrative approach that uses students' own stories to demonstrate that personal change occurs as a result of negotiating developmental transitions (Baumgartner, 2001; Daloz, 1999).

A fourth perspective takes an integrative, rather than developmental, approach that adds an extrarational dimension to understandings of transformational learning. The integrative approach accepts and attends students' existential and intrapsychic aspects where emotions, imagination, intuition, and spirituality may be located; in other words, the place where human capacity and motivation for change and transformation reside (Dirkx, 1998; Kovan & Dirkx, 2003; Taylor, 2000). The integrative approach recognizes that transformative learning is a process by which students make meaning of the world and of their place in it and, at the same time, develop personal wholeness or individuation (Dirkx, 1998).

Dirkx's integrative four-lens approach draws from Freire's emancipatory education; Mezirow's cognitive/rational perspective; the developmental approach taken by Daloz; and Dirkx's own exploration of the role of spiritual, extrarational, and emotional elements (Mori, 2005). Dirkx's (1998) approach draws a link between learning and spirituality, and concludes that transformative learning can lead students to greater self-understanding, a deeper commitment to humanity, and a true vocational calling.

Beyond theoretical suppositions, certain methods of instruction are derived from transformational education theory. For instance, Mezirow (1997) tells us that it is necessary to identify or devise a disorienting dilemma that upsets students' existing frames of reference as a catalyst for transformative experience that leads to cognitive and conative change or learning. For example, instructors who use study abroad or service-learning programs, particularly in extreme conditions such as prison or inner city slums, may do so with the intention of creating an experience that vigorously challenges students' frames of reference, thereby igniting social justice learning.

Those who take a developmental approach to transformative learning assert that less-combustible experiences can be successfully carried out when they are carefully guided to create a situation through which learners become liberated from the constraints of existing habits of mind and points of view and, in turn, become capable liberators of social injustice (Baumgartner, 2001; Daloz, 1999). Applying the integrative approach begins with the belief that deepest transformations are born from processing experiences that are emotionally or psychically charged enough to reach students' interior lives where intuition and spirituality reside (Dirkx, 1998; Kovan & Dirkx, 2003; Taylor, 2000). Instructors who take an integrative approach rely on process dialogue and conversations about students' experience, self-examination, critique, and personal growth. Because of its humanistic and humanitarian orientation, transformational learning theory can be useful as a framework for social justice education design and evaluation.

Social justice theories supply content for social justice education. Education theories provide a conceptual framework and derived instructional methods that can be useful for planning and evaluating social justice education with greater confidence. Where social justice education is critical, so too is the utility of formal theories that guide it. In social work, theoretical foundations for social justice education can be considered particularly important.

Social Justice and Social Work Education

The connection between social work and social justice education occurred near the birth of the profession in the United States when Jane Addams, a noted social reformer and founder of social work, first met John Dewey, a noted psychologist, philosopher, education reformer, and theorist. Although their known association preceded the founding of the Settlement House Movement, once the doors were open to Hull

House in 1889, Dewey was a noted visitor there. Nearly a year later, Dewey founded the Chicago School of Pragmatism, which came to have a profound and lasting effect on American scholars and activists (Martin, 2002). In 1892, Addams fell into association with the Chicago School as an associate and writer, and when the settlement became incorporated, Dewey became a member of the Hull House board of directors (Hamington, 2006). These associations served to strengthen their shared commitments to "the value of a robust democracy as well as the importance of education that engaged the student's experience" (p. 5). Described as great public philosophers and "intellectual soul mates," over their long association, Addams and Dewey maintained a fertile exchange of ideas. In the process, Dewey helped to shape Addams's ideas about scientific method in social service, and she undoubtedly influenced Dewey's education "theory of experience" (Engle, 2002; Hamington, 2006; Robinson, 2000; Westbrook, 1993). So important was their influence on one another, that Dewey named one of his daughters for Addams, and she later wrote the eulogy for Dewey's son. After her death, Dewey paid a final tribute to Addams when he dedicated to her *Liberalism and Social Action*, one of his most important books (Hamington, 2006).

When the history is known, the importance of Dewey's philosophy to social work cannot be disputed. The pragmatist philosophers of the Chicago School—Dewey in particular—are credited with formally shaping the American view of social justice (Deegan, 1990; Feffer, 1993). Dewey saw a conflict between old morals and the industrializing country, which he believed posed a threat to the democracy on which social justice depends. Dewey's theory of democracy predicted the new world would win out, and if democracy were left to stand, it would only be by democratic methods. In Dewey's view, democracy is a way of life, not merely a form of politics. Dewey's theory of democracy and his social justice ideals followed his instrumental philosophy and the value he placed on experience (Martin, 2002; Metz, 1969). Certainly, these ideas added fuel to the Progressive Movement and steam to the motivations of reformers such as Addams.

In fact, some suggest that as a profession, social work made its greatest contribution to social justice in America during its birth and infancy in the age of pragmatist theory and the Progressive Era (Karger & Hernandez, 2004). With the origination of the Settlement House Movement, Addams established, at once, a laboratory for both social work practice and education that was grounded in social justice principles. Consequently, Addams's legacy is imprinted on the profession at large and inspires contemporary social work education. Like Dewey, Addams believed the best guarantor of social justice was a robust democracy in which all were welcome to participate. With this commitment in mind,

Addams took up the standard of the Progressive Movement sweeping through American politics. From that position, Addams—and many noteworthy others such as Ellen Gates Starr and Florence Kelly—became social activists and social workers (Sklar, 1985). Directed by their progressive sensibilities, Addams (and those who became attached to the settlement movement) developed an array of social and human services and trained a workforce able to help the disadvantaged develop the human capital required to be active citizen-participants. In practice, settlement houses were both service centers and educational laboratories, where professional methods were conceived, tried, and evaluated. The range of Hull House activities has been described in some detail.

> Among other things, it operated a day nursery, a free employment bureau, the city's first public playground, a cooperative living club for single working women, a public kitchen serving cheap meals, a cooperative coal association, and a wide variety of courses dealing with nutrition, house-keeping, child care, and prenatal education. Hull House sponsored ethnic folk fests at which immigrants displayed and sold their Old World arts and crafts. It also played host to labor unions, with the residents even walking the picket lines and organizing boycotts of uncooperative employers. Its residents were deeply involved in political campaigns and lobbied vigorously for legislation on all levels of government. (Buenker, 1999, p. 16)

It is easy to identify the precepts of Dewey's theory of experience in action for both worker and client in the range of activities that occurred in the social settlements and to think, because of the relationship between Addams and Dewey, that what went on there had as much to do with testing education theories as developing an activist profession.

Addams's history is a testament to how deeply social justice runs in the veins of professional social work. During her career, she and her colleagues participated in organizing the National Child Labor Committee, the National Women's Trade Union League, and the National Association for the Advancement of Colored People (Davis, 1964a, b). Addams's understanding that circumstances in America echoed threatening international conditions added fuel to her compassion and passion for social justice. With respect to social justice education, her accomplishments stand in bold relief in the history of professional social work and are relied on in social work education to inspire, motivate, and socialize.

Addams and Dewey's influence on one another, the development of social work practice and education, and contemporary theories about social justice education seem evident on the face of their individual accomplishments and confirmed by the nature of their associations over their lifetimes. It is acknowledged that both Addams and Dewey embraced the scientific method; and settlement house practices shared much in common with Dewey's educational "theory of experience" (Casil, 2006, Martin, 2002, Metz, 1969), which is the bedrock of contemporary notions about education (Knowles, 1970).

Tracing the connection between Addams and Dewey shows the long and strong association between professional social work and education theories that offer a source of assurance about the validity and reliability of social justice education and practice. While new education theories have prospects for helping to improve methods and insure results, social justice education, research, and scholarship can be another source of support and assurance about the practices we select to accomplish social justice education objectives.

Scholarly and Research Evidence

As scholarly ideas about teaching social justice emerged in the literature, so have some systematic investigations that rely on trustworthy research methods. Both have much to contribute to our knowledge and understanding about the elements that constitute effective social justice education. Scholars acknowledge the importance of research evidence to social justice education (Allen, 1997; Atweh, Kemmis, & Weeks, 1998; Birkenmaier, 2003; Longres & Scanlon, 2001) and just social work practice (Gambrill, 2001; Tyuse, 2003). Others criticize research paradigms of the past and encourage us to look for new theoretical models (Voode & Gallant, 2002) that can guide social justice education with greater assurance.

A review of literature revealed a steady stream of comment, discussion, and theory-developing dialogue about transformational learning theory and social justice. There is also a body of anecdotal evidence that encourages us to believe sweeping efforts such as systematically integrated social justice curriculum supported by enthusiastic faculty (Birkenmaier, 2003) and more modest methods in service-learning projects (Lemieux & Allen, 2007) can help teach and socialize students to care about and act for social justice.

In addition, there is a slight and slow-growing body of research-based evidence into social justice education. Reported studies that investigate the outcomes of planning and evaluating social justice education based on accepted educational theories are few and far between, but the results are interesting (Brown, 2006, 2005; Schroeder & Pogue, 2010). As a starting place, the available research encourages the idea that effective methods for accomplishing social justice education objectives can be systematically identified and replicated with confidence.

An outstanding example is Nagda, Gurin, and Lopez's (2003) investigation of an educational model constructed from several schools of thought and practice including multicultural education and critical pedagogy; Freirean dialogic education; and Kolb's model of active, experiential learning. A resulting model for planning social justice education was drawn from these perspectives and formed in two parts: active learning and engaged learning. A range of educational activities were planned to investigate dimensions of the model. Results showed that different aspects of social justice learning gains associated with each element of the model and demonstrated a possible qualitative difference consistent with transformational principles. Specifically,

> Active learning may facilitate progress from concrete experiences to theoretical and conceptual abstraction (such as structural thinking). Engaged learning, and its effects, seem to suggest an application of classroom reflections to everyday phenomena and immediate social environments (such as in active thinking and socio-historical understanding that have to do with understanding people's behavior—own and others—and their causes. (p. 187)

These findings demonstrate that active learning has an effect on one's own agency, whereas engaged learning has an effect on one's capabilities to act at a mezzolevel to effect change. Although these findings are interesting enough on their own, they confirm the potential value of theory-based planning and evaluation of social justice education.

Another relevant study investigated learning outcomes from a social justice course designed on an andragological framework that included adult learning theory, critical social theory, and transformative learning theory (Brown, 2006). Subjects were graduate students in an educational administration program who were enrolled in a course that focused on social justice in educational leadership. The course emphasized social justice issues in the context of a course focused on the social contexts of educational leadership. Students participated in a variety of transformative learning assignments, including reflective analysis journals and an integrative, reflective seminar dedicated to critical self-reflection and discourse about students' internship experiences. Findings showed significant growth in participants' (a) self-awareness through critical self-reflection, (b) acknowledgment of others through rational discourse, and (c) action through policy praxis.

A 2004 study (Williams & Reeves, 2004) stands out for specifically applying the principles of Dewey's theory of experience and aspects of Mezirow's model for transformative learning to planning and evaluating social justice learning in social work education. Subjects in this study were students engaged in experiential learning via a service-learning project working with burn victims. The course design included critical reflection and discourse components not unlike those outlined in Mezirow's transformative learning model. Researchers concluded that these planned educational strategies help students integrate social work core values such as social justice into developing perceptions of their personal and professional selves. Because results point to specific dimensions in a teaching and learning situation, they suggest that further research into planning and evaluating social justice education against theoretical frameworks may be worthwhile.

More generally, when a social work curriculum as a whole was investigated, Van Voorhis and Hostetter (2006) found that students who completed an MSW degree achieved learning gains associated with conative social justice education objectives. Results showed that students completing an MSW degree did, in fact, have a significantly greater commitment to client empowerment and social justice advocacy. More often, studies seek to identify intended social justice learning outcomes from a specific teaching activity or method of instruction. These studies are important because the resulting evidence helps to build confidence in social justice education beyond what is known anecdotally.

For instance, one study applied qualitative methods to explore the results of using contemporary literature in social justice education (Viggiani et al., 2005). Reading selections were chosen for content most likely to challenge students' frames of reference in regard to social issues such as poverty and inequality. Researchers concluded that literature provides a better catalyst than case studies, because students become more intimately engaged with the characters. According to researchers, the result was that students gained deeper and more meaningful understanding of the human condition as a predicate for motivating social justice–seeking practice.

Multicultural issues such as diversity and oppression are required content in all social work programs. In one such course, instructors based a number of course activities on transformative learning principles (Schmitz, Stakeman, & Sisneros, 2001). Students were required to conduct ethnographic interviews of others to discover their own hidden perspectives. The experience served the purpose of a disorienting dilemma and was followed with critical self-reflective activities. Findings from the study conducted over six semesters were "overwhelmingly positive," showing that students accomplished shifts in perspective and personal growth consistent with transformative learning.

Conclusion

A number of scholars have called for a revival in the civic and moral mission in higher education. There have been vigorous debates in social work that raise concerns over the social and professional consequences of loosening a strong connection with its social justice roots. The literature demonstrates continued commitments to social justice education in social work curricula. Some research is available to support that such efforts are effective, and when theoretical frameworks are applied, evidence suggests learning outcomes may be enhanced.

In social work education, certain professional commitments to empowerment and advocacy are considered strong associates with social justice education. Consequently, social work curricula are laced with general social justice education. While most of the body of research in this arena takes an indirect approach into investigating the impact of social work education on social justice learning outcomes, the evidence does encourage us to believe that the considerable efforts instructors make do, in fact, have desirable effects for our students and the profession.

The central premise of this chapter is that social justice education may be improved when theoretical frameworks are used in its design, planning, and evaluation. The logic is that theory provides not only the language students need to understand the breadth, depth, and nuance of social justice, but the means to inspire students and move them to seek social justice. While identifying social injustice helps to stimulate humanitarian impulses toward social action, theoretical concepts are the substance that fuels and directs social action. Given the importance to the profession, and to society at large, greater knowledge about the effect of social justice education on students, professional practice, and society at large is worth further pursuit.

References

Allen, J. A. (1997). Social justice, social change and baccalaureate degree generalist social work practice. *Journal of Baccalaureate Social Work, 3*(1), 14–16.

Armstrong, P., & Miller, N. (2006). Whatever happened to social purpose? Adult educators' stories of political commitment and change. *International Journal of Lifelong Education, 25*(3), 291–305.

Atweh, B., Kemmis, S., & Weeks, P. (1998). *Action research in practice: Partnership for social justice education.* New York: Routledge.

Baumgartner, L. M. (2001). An update on transformative learning. *New Directions for Adult and Continuing Education, 89,* 15–24.

Bentley, D. J. (1973). John Rawls: A theory of justice. *University of Pennsylvania Law Review, 121*(5), 1070–1078.

Birkenmaier, J. M. (1999). Promoting social justice within the practicum. *New Social Worker, 6*(2), 13–15.

Birkenmaier, J. M. (2003). On becoming a social justice practitioner. *Social Thought, 22*(2/3), 41–54.

Brock, D. W. (1973). Symposium: John Rawls's *A Theory of Justice. University of Chicago Law Review, 40*(3), 486–499.

Brookfield, S. (2005). Learning democratic reason: The adult education project of Jurgen Habermas. *Teacher College Record, 107*(6), 1127–1168.

Brown, K. M. (2005). Social justice education for preservice leaders: Evaluating transformative learning strategies. *Equity & Excellence in Education, 38*(2), 155–167.

Brown, K. M. (2006). Leadership for social justice and equity: Evaluating a transformative framework and andragogy. *Educational Administration Quarterly, 42*(5), 700–745.

Buenker, J. D. (1999). The progressive era in Illinois: "Launching Pad" for "New Women." In K. A. Sculle (Ed.), *Illinois history teacher* (pp. 1–29). Retrieved September 22, 2007, from http://www.lib.niu.edu/ipo/1999/iht719915.html

Burkemper, E. M., & Stretch, J. J. (2003). The right of justice: Contributions of social work practice-research. *Social Thought, 22*(2/3), 1–6.

Casil, A. S. (2006). *John Dewey: The founder of American liberalism.* New York: Rosen Group.

Council on Social Work Education. (2008). *Educational policy and accreditation standards.* Retrieved September 1, 2007, from http://www.cswe.org/CSWE/accreditation

Cranton, P. (2006). Rethinking evaluation of student learning. *Higher Education Perspectives, 2*(1). Retrieved March 24, 2007, from http://www.oise.utoronto.ca/highered/viewarticle.php?id=76&layout=html

Daloz, L. A. (1999). *Guiding the journey of adult learners.* San Francisco: Jossey-Bass.

Davis, A. F. (1964a). Settlement workers in politics, 1890–1914. *Review of Politics, 26*(4), 505–517.

Davis, A. F. (1964b). The social workers and the Progressive Party, 1912–1916. *American Historical Review, 69*(3), 671–688.

Deegan, M. J. (1990). *Jane Addams and the men of the Chicago School: 1892–1918.* Edison, NJ: Transaction.

Dessel, A., Rogge, M. E., & Garlington, S. B. (2006). Using intergroup dialogue to promote social justice and change. *Social Work, 51*(4), 303–315.

Dewey, J. (1897, January). My pedagogic creed. *School Journal, 54,* 77–80. Retrieved March 19, 2007, from http://www.infed.org/archives/e-texts/e-dew-pc.htm

Dewey, J. (1916). *Democracy and education: An introduction to the philosophy of education.* London: Macmillan, 1951.

Dewey, J. (1938). *Experience and education.* New York: Macmillan, 1997.

Dirkx, J. M. (1998). Transformative learning theory in the practice of adult education: An overview. *PAACE Journal of Lifelong Learning, 7,* 1–14.

Dworkin, M. S. (1959). *Dewey on education: Selections.* New York: Teachers College Press.

Engel, L. J. (2002). Saul Alinsky and the Chicago School. *Journal of Speculative Philosophy, 16*(1), 50–66.

Feffer, A. (1993). *The Chicago pragmatists and American progressivism.* Ithaca, NY: Cornell University Press.

Finn, J. L., & Jacobson, M. (2003). Just practice: Steps toward a new social work paradigm. *Journal of Social Work Education, 39*(1), 57–78.

Freire, P. (1998). *Pedagogy of freedom: Ethics, democracy, and civic courage.* Lanham, MD: Rowman & Littlefield.

Freire, P. (2000). *Pedagogy of the oppressed.* (M. B. Ramos, Trans., 30th anniversary ed.). London: Continuum International.

Gambrill, E. (2001). Evaluating the quality of social work education: Options galore. *Journal of Social Work Education, 37,* 418–429.

Garrett, J. (2005). *Amartya Sen's ethics of substantial freedom.* Retrieved March 19, 2007, from http://www.wku.edu/~jan.garrett/ethics/senethic.htm

Glass, R. D. (2001). On Paulo Freire's philosophy of praxis and the foundations of liberation education. *Educational Researcher, 30*(2), 15–25.

Hamington, M. (2006). Jane Addams. *Stanford encyclopedia of philosophy.* Retrieved March 20, 2007, from http://plato.stanford.edu/entries/addams-jane/

Hansen, D. T. (1995). *The call to teach.* New York: Teachers College Press.

Harkavy, I. (2000). The role of universities in advancing citizenship and social justice in the 20th century. *Education, Citizenship and Social Justice, 1*(1), 5–37.

Hart, M. (1990). Critical theory and beyond: Further perspectives on emancipatory education. *Adult Education Quarterly, 40*(3), 125–138.

Higgins, C. (2005). Dewey's conception of vocation: Existential, aesthetic, and educational implications for teachers. *Journal of Curriculum Studies, 37*(4), 441–464.

Jasso, G. (2002). Some of Robert K. Merton's contributions to justice theory. *Sociological Theory, 18*(2), 331–339.

Karger, J., & Hernandez, M. T. (2004). The decline of the public intellectual in social work. *Journal of Sociology and Social Welfare, 31*(3), 51–68.

Knowles, M. (1970). *The modern practice of adult education: Andragogy vs pedagogy.* New York: Associated Press.

Knowles, M. S. (1980). *The modern practice of adult education: From pedagogy to andragogy.* Englewood Cliffs, NJ: Cambridge Adult Education.

Korsgaard, C., Sen, A., Thompson, D., & Scanlon, T. (2005, May 19). John Rawls: Faculty of Arts and Sciences–Memorial Minute. *Harvard University Gazette.* Retrieved September 4, 2007, from http://www.hno.harvard.edu/gazette/2005/05.19/24-mm.html

Kovan, J. T., & Dirkx, J. M. (2003). "Being called awake": The role of transformative learning in the lives of environmental activists. *Adult Education Quarterly, 53*(2), 99–118.

Kreber, C., & Cranton, P. A. (2000). Exploring the scholarship of teaching. *Journal of Higher Education, 71*(4), 476–495.

Kyle, K. (2005). To see or not to see the crisis in the academy: A call for action. *Social Justice, 32*(3), 128–147.

Kymlicka, W. (1988). Rawls on teleology and deontology. *Philosophy and Public Affairs, 17*(3), 173–190.

Lemann, N. (2004). Liberal education and professionals. *Liberal Education, 90*(2), 12–17.

Lemieux, C. M., & Allen, P. D. (2007). Service learning in social work education: The state of knowledge, pedagogical practicalities, and practice conundrums. *Journal of Social Work Education, 43*(2), 309–320.

Longres, J. F., & Scanlon, E. (2001). Social justice and the research curriculum. *Journal of Social Work Education, 37*(3), 447–463.

Lucas, C. J. (1994). *American higher education: A history.* New York: St. Martin's Press.

Martin, J. (2002). *The education of John Dewey.* New York: Columbia University Press.

Merton, R. K. (1957). *Social theory and social structure.* New York: Free Press.

Metz, J. G. (1969). Democracy and the scientific method in the philosophy of John Dewey. *Review of Politics, 31*(2), 242–262.

Mezirow, J. (1981). A critical theory of adult learning and education. *Adult Education Quarterly, 32*(1), 3–24.

Mezirow, J. (1997, Summer). Transformative learning: Theory to practice. *New Directions for Adult and Continuing Education, 74,* 5–12.

Mezirow, J., & Associates (1990). Fostering critical reflection in adulthood: A guide to transformative and emancipatory learning. San Francisco: Jossey-Bass.

Mezirow, J., & Associates. (2000). *Learning as transformation: Critical perspectives on a theory.* San Francisco: Jossey-Bass.

Millgram, E. (2000). Mill's proof of the principle of utility. *Ethics, 110*(2), 282–310.

Mori, I. (2005, May). *Distance education technology symposium.* Presentation at the Distance Education Technology Symposium, Athabasca University, Alberta, Canada.

Morris, P. M. (2002). The capabilities perspective: A framework for social justice. *Families in Society: The Journal of Contemporary Human Services, 83*(4), 366–373.

Nagda, B. A., Gurin, P., & Lopez, G. E. (2003). Transformative pedagogy for democracy and social justice. *Race, Ethnicity and Education, 6*(2), 165–191.

Neill, James. (2005). *500 word summary of Dewey's "Experience & Education."* Retrieved September 4, 2007, from http://wilderdom.com/experiential/SummaryJohnDeweyExperienceEducation.html

National Association of Social Workers. (2008). *Code of ethics.* Washington, DC: Author.

North, C. E. (2006). More than words? Delving into the substantive meaning(s) of "social justice" in education. *Review of Educational Research, 76*(4), 507–535.

Nussbaum, M. C. (1999). *Sex and social justice.* New York: Oxford University Press.

Rawls, J. (1971). *A theory of justice.* Cambridge, MA: Harvard University Press.

Rawls, J. (1993). *Political liberalism.* New York: Columbia University Press.

Rehm, M. (1990). Vocation as personal calling: A question for education. *Journal of Educational Thought, 24*(2), 114–125.

Reich, R. (2005). Service leaning and multiple models of engaged citizenship. *Journal of Education, 186*(1), 23–27.

Reisch, M. (2002). Defining social justice in a socially unjust world. *Families in Society: The Journal of Contemporary Human Services, 83*(4), 343–354.

Robinson, T. (2000). Service learning as justice advocacy: Can political scientists do politics? *Political Science & Politics, 33*(3), 605–612.

Saltmarsh, J. (2005). The civic promise of service learning. *Liberal Education, 91*(2), 50–55.

Schmitz, C. L., Stakeman, C., & Sisneros, J. (2001). Educating professionals for practice in a multicultural society: Understanding diversity and oppression. *Families in Society: The Journal of Contemporary Human Services, 82*(6), 612–622.

Schroeder, J. A., & Pogue, R. (2010). An investigation of transformative education theory as a basis for social justice education in a research methods course. In J. M. Birkenmaier, A. Cruce, E. Burkemper, R. J. Wilson, J. Curley, & J. Stretch (Eds.), *Educating for social justice: Transformative experiential learning* (pp. 103–118). Chicago: Lyceum Books.

Sen, A. (1985). *Commodities and capabilities.* Amsterdam: Elsevier Science.

Sen, A. (1999). *Development as freedom.* New York: Random House.

Sklar, K. K. (1985). Hull House in the 1890s: A community of women reformers. *Signs, 10*(40), 658–677.

Smith, M. K. (2002). Malcolm Knowles, informal adult education, self-direction and andragogy. *The Encyclopedia of Informal Education.* Retrieved September 19, 2007, from http://www.infed.org/thinkers/et-knowl.htm

Swenson, C. R. (1998). Clinical social work's contribution to a social justice perspective. *Social Work, 43*(6), 527–537.

Taylor, E. W. (2000). Analyzing research on transformative theory. In. J. Mezirow & Associates (Eds.), *Learning as transformation: Critical perspectives on a theory in Progress* (pp. 151–180). San Francisco: Jossey-Bass.

Tyuse, S. W. (2003). Social justice and welfare reform: A shift in policy. *Social Thought, 22*(2/3), 81–95.

University of Washington. (2007). *Most cited law books.* M. G. Gallegher Law Library. Retrieved September 19, 2007, from http://lib.law.washington.edu/ref/mostcited.html

Van Soest, D. (1995). Peace and social justice. In. R. J. Edwards et al. (Eds.), *Encyclopedia of social work* (19th ed., Vol. 3, pp. 1810–1817) Washington, DC: NASW Press.

Van Voorhis, R. M., & Hostetter, C. (2006). The impact of MSW education on social worker empowerment and commitment to client empowerment through social justice advocacy. *Journal of Social Work Education, 42*(1), 105–119.

Viggiani, P. A., Charlesworth, L., Hutchison, E. D., & Faria, D. F. (2005). Utilization of contemporary literature in human behavior and social justice coursework. *Social Work Education, 26*(1), 57–96.

Voode, R., & Gallant, J. P. (2002). Bridging the gap between micro and macro practice: Large scale change and a unified model of narrative-deconstructive practice. *Journal of Social Work Education, 38*(3), 439–458.

Wakefield, J. C. (1988). Psychotherapy, distributive justice, and social work: Part I. Distributive justice as a conceptual framework for social work. *Social Service Review, 62*, 187–210.

Wakefield, J. C. (1998). Psychotherapy, distributive justice, and social work: Part 2: Psychotherapy and the pursuit of justice. *Social Services Review, 62,* 353–382.

Westbrook, R. B. (1993). *John Dewey and American democracy.* New York: Cornell University Press.

Williams, N. R., & Reeves, P. M. (2004). MSW students go to burn camp: Exploring social work values through service-learning. *Social Work Education, 25*(4), 383–398.

CHAPTER THREE

Spirituality and Social Justice: Theoretical Frameworks, Exemplars, and Pedagogical Implications

David R. Hodge

Abstract

This chapter focuses on the relationship between spirituality and social justice, concepts that are intrinsically linked in the lives of many clients. After noting the growing interest in spirituality among the general public, the theoretical link between spirituality and social justice is discussed along with sociological data on the relationship between spirituality and efforts to create a more just society at the micro-, mezzo-, and macrolevels. To illustrate how people of faith commonly operationalize understandings of social justice, a number of exemplars drawn from the Christian tradition are delineated, some of which may be considered radical. The chapter concludes with a discussion of the pedagogical implications that flow from the profession's ethical standards and notes the contributions that spiritually based understandings of social justice can contribute to professional discourse.

Interest in spirituality is growing among the general population in the United States (Gallup & Jones, 2000; Gallup & Lindsay, 1999; Wuthnow, 2007). Although variously understood, spirituality is commonly defined as an individual's relationship with God or the transcendent (Gallup & Jones, 2000; Gilbert, 2000; Hodge, 2005b; Wuthnow, 2007).

As an interior, existential construct, spirituality includes a dynamic, motivational dimension (Hodge, 2003).

Although the reasons for the growing interest in spirituality are complex, the trend can be explained in part by the broader philosophical shift toward postmodernism. While modernity affirmed a strictly materialistic universe, this worldview is increasingly seen as fundamentally flawed (Gray, 2008; Lyotard, 1979/1984). As the limits of modernity have come into sharper focus, interest in more holistic understandings of reality, which include a spiritual dimension, has increased. Given that postmodernism appears poised to gain intellectual currency for the foreseeable future, spirituality is likely to be a salient component of the cultural landscape for quite some time.

The growing interest in spirituality has important ramifications for a profession that claims social justice as a primary value. Spirituality and social justice are often intrinsically linked (Moss, 2005; Smith, 1996; Wood, 1999). For individuals for whom spirituality is central to their personal ontology, it is difficult if not impossible to understand social justice apart from spirituality.

Yet despite the link between spirituality and social justice, most social work educators, practitioners, and students report receiving little, if any, content on spirituality during their graduate educations (Canda & Furman, 1999; Heyman, Buchanan, Musgrave, & Menz, 2006; Murdock, 2005; Sheridan, 2004; Sheridan & Amato-von Hemert, 1999). Similarly, content analysis reveals that material on spirituality is essentially absent from a wide array of professional literatures (Cnaan, Wineburg, & Boddie, 1999; Hodge, 2002a; Hodge, Baughman, & Cummings, 2006; Tompkins, Larkin, & Rosen, 2006). In short, the profession appears to have largely overlooked the relationship between spirituality and social justice.

This chapter is designed to address this gap in the literature by delineating the theoretical and empirical links between spirituality and social justice, exemplars that illustrate these concepts, and the resulting pedagogical implications. First, however, the theoretical relationship between spirituality and social justice is discussed. In other words, the following section explains why spirituality is often intrinsically related to the concept of social justice, particularly among people who are spiritually committed.

Spirituality and Social Justice

In order to identify injustice, it is necessary to have a moral framework through which to evaluate the world (Smith, 1996). Without the ability to, in a sense, rise above the status quo, it is impossible to recognize unjust situations. If the norms of the present environment are used to assess that environment, then it is not logically possible to posit that something is unjust. To evaluate entities as unjust requires an independent standard, an ability to assess the present environment in relationship to this standard (Stark, 2003).

Spiritual traditions—the context in which spirituality is typically expressed, developed, and learned—provide such a standard. Spiritual traditions can be understood as a shared set of beliefs and practices, developed in community over time with others who share similar understandings of transcendence, which are designed to mediate an individual's connection to the transcendent (Hodge, 2000). It is important to note that spiritual traditions exist in both structured, organized forms, such as the Catholic Church, and also in more unstructured, fluid forms, such as the new age or syncretistic movement.

In addition to providing a worldview to explain events as they are (Maslow, 1968), spiritual traditions also typically offer a framework for envisioning the world as it should be (Smith, 1996). By positing moral standards—formal or informal notions about what is right, just, and fair—spiritual traditions provide an external framework for assessing the world. To the extent that the status quo does not conform to the standard, action is implicitly called for to right the wrong.

Essentially all spiritual traditions affirm the notion of social justice (Marshall & Koeugh, 2004; Moss, 2005). How justice is understood or operationalized may, at times, vary between spiritual traditions (Wilson, 2008). Since spiritual traditions reflect different worldviews, they can articulate different understandings of exactly what constitutes a just society (Richards & Bergin, 2000; Van Hook, Hugen, & Aguilar, 2001). As an abstract principle, however, the concept of social justice is widely affirmed.

For spiritually motivated individuals, this concept provides the impetus for action. It is important to emphasize that a symbiotic relationship exists between individually oriented spirituality and communally oriented spiritual traditions (Smith, 1996; Wilson, 2008). As noted above, spirituality typically includes a motivational dimension. In contrast, the moral standards affirmed by various spiritual traditions typically do not engender action in and of themselves. The motivation to address injustice flows from a person's connection with the transcendent. Although the social reinforcement of like-minded individuals plays a role in the process, at a certain base level, the motivational energy that animates investment in the pursuit of a more socially just society emanates from one's spirituality.

By way of qualification, it should be noted that action is not necessarily required to address a situation that is deemed to be wrong or unjust. Other factors enter into the decision-making matrix (Hodge &

Wolfer, 2008). If a particular issue is highlighted as unjust by a particular tradition, action to address the situation may or may not be appropriate depending upon a variety of the other variables that influence how individuals should best respond in a given environmental context.

Spiritual leaders in congregational settings often reinforce the call to social justice (Cnaan & Boddie, 2001). A content analysis of sermons (N = 95) from the Jewish and diverse Christian traditions revealed a "regular diet" of social justice messages focused upon improving the lot of human beings in the United States and the rest of the world (Brewer, Kersh, & Petersen, 2003). In fact, content devoted to social justice exceeded that devoted to personal morality. Across all the traditions examined, social justice messages were the most common type of content delivered.

As Moss (2005) notes, beliefs and behaviors are affected by how people view the world. Individuals who derive their worldviews from their spiritual traditions are provided with a framework to assess justice and a rationale to pursue its realization. In turn, their spirituality provides the motivation to work toward a more socially just society. In the following section, some of the ways in which this motivation is manifested are discussed.

Working Toward a More Socially Just Society

Social justice can be promoted through many different avenues. One way to think about these various options is to consider actions at the micro-, mezzo-, and macrolevels. For example, a more just society can be promoted by personal actions on an individual level, organizing and implementing programs to address specific needs, and structural change that seeks to alter governmental policies.

INDIVIDUAL ACTIONS

In keeping with the tenets of their traditions, spiritually engaged people are actively involved in bettering society (Brooks, 2006; Wuthnow, 1994). Consider, for example, those who give money to organizations that help people who are poor and needy. Individuals who are members of spiritual traditions give more to help those in need compared with those who are unaffiliated (Regnerus, Smith, & Sikkink, 1998). Among those who are affiliated with a spiritual tradition, the more one attends services, and the more salient one's spiritual beliefs are, the more one gives to assist those who are poor and needy. In other words, those who exhibit the most generosity to the disadvantaged are consistent

attendees whose spirituality is very important to them. Although variations exist, this general pattern is found across spiritual traditions (Regnerus et al., 1998).

It is important to note that the commitment to improving human
welfare extends to a broad range of concerns. For instance, compared
with secularists, those who attend services in their spiritual tradition
approximately once a week or more give more to charity and volunteer
more often (Brooks, 2006). These spiritually engaged individuals are
also more likely to give to secular causes (e.g., United Way), and are
more likely to volunteer for secular causes. For example, they are more
likely to give to friends and family, donate blood, give food or money to
a homeless person, return change to cashiers when given more than
was due, and express empathy for those less fortunate than themselves.

In fact, Brooks (2006) states that those who are spiritually engaged
are more charitable in essentially every measurable way. Regardless of
how charity is measured, individuals who are spiritually engaged tend
to be more giving of their personal time and resources than those who
are secular. In keeping with the above research, this personal commitment to a better society generally holds true across spiritual traditions.

PROGRAMMATIC EFFORTS

In addition to personal actions to create a more just society, people of
faith are engaged in programmatic efforts to build a better society
through various faith-based organizations, such as congregations
(Cnaan, Boddie, & Kang, 2005; Cosgrove, 2008; Ebaugh & Pipes, 2001;
Wilson, 2008). Compared with other types of community organizations
(e.g., schools, libraries, tenants' associations), congregations are the
most prevalent and long-standing actors in most neighborhoods
(Cnaan, Sinha, & McGrew, 2004). This is particularly the case in poverty-
stricken communities.

A number of studies suggest that approximately 90 percent of congregations, regardless of size or ethnic composition, offer at least one
social service program to help those in need (Cnaan et al., 2004). Collectively, the array of social programs mimics that provided by professional secular social service agencies (Cnaan & Boddie, 2001). The most
commonly served groups include children, youths, the elderly, people
who are homeless, and those who are poor (Cnaan et al., 2004).

The city in which perhaps the most research has been conducted is
Philadelphia. The average congregation in this city designates more
than two-fifths of its budget to help people in need and improve quality
of life (Cnaan & Boddie, 2001). In comparison, the average corporation
in the United States reportedly allocates about 1 percent of its pretax

net income to charitable contributions (Cnaan & Boddie, 2001). A conservative estimate of the collective value of the social services provided by these Philadelphia-based congregations is approximately a quarter of a billion dollars annually.

To provide another point of comparison, the total social services budget of the city of Philadelphia is roughly half a billion dollars (Cnaan et al., 2004). In other words, local congregations voluntarily provide about one-third of the annual cost devoted to social services in Philadelphia. According to Cnaan and Boddie (2001), the programs provided by city congregations often function as the social safety net for people in need.

STRUCTURAL CHANGE

While some observers argue that the best measure of commitment to disadvantaged groups is individual actions, others contend that support for structural change is the most appropriate barometer (Regnerus et al., 1998). Because of the magnitude of certain problems, government action is needed. Poverty is often cited as a signal example of such a problem. It is argued that poverty can be eliminated, or at least mitigated, through structural change in society.

Contrary to the perceptions that exist in some circles, traditional believers are supportive of structural change (Clydesdale, 1999; Hart, 1992). Relative to modernists, orthodox religious believers are more likely to hold a communitarian outlook in which society is collectively responsible for providing for those in need, reducing inequality, and intervening in the economy to meet the needs of the larger community (Davis & Robinson, 2006). These findings have been replicated in diverse societies in Africa, Asia, Europe, and the United States (Davis & Robinson, 1997, 1999, 2006).

For example, in the United States, orthodox believers are more likely to support structural change to reduce economic inequality (Davis & Robinson, 1997). Specifically, they are more likely to support government-provided jobs for those in need, spending on Social Security, giving profits to workers rather than shareholders, and holding organized labor in high regard. This general pattern of results has been confirmed by other research conducted with American samples (Clydesdale, 1999; Hart, 1992).

To better understand the relationship between spirituality and social justice, it may be helpful to transition from the broad theory and sociological data profiled above to specific examples. Due to the prevalence of Christianity among clients in the United States, the following content focuses upon various expressions of social justice drawn from this tradition (Richards & Bergin, 2005). Building upon the theory discussed above, the following section describes some of the conceptual rationales that provide the foundation for social change efforts within the Christian tradition. It may be helpful to view the following discussion as a type of proxy for other spiritual traditions while also bearing in mind that specific rationales and exemplars will vary from tradition to tradition.

A Christian Framework for Social Justice

As is the case with other spiritual traditions, Christianity provides adherents with a worldview that establishes a moral framework for evaluating society (Moss, 2005). This evaluative lens is grounded in the biblical narrative (Wolterstorff, 2007). Although no single, universally agreed-upon biblical narrative exists, a number of widely held theological beliefs serve to inform understandings of social justice (Hanawalt & Lindberg, 1994; Kliksberg, 2003; Linthicum, 2001; Wolterstorff, 2007). Among the most important are the concepts of the *imago dei* and community (Formicola, 2005).

THE *IMAGO DEI*

The *imago dei*, or the image of God, refers to the belief that humans are created in God's image (Formicola, 2005). In some mystical manner, each human being reflects the likeness of God. Although this notion has been interpreted in various ways, it is widely taken to imply the adoption of a certain stance toward human beings (Hoekema, 1986).

At a foundational level, it implies that all human beings have inherent worth and dignity (Evangelium vitae, 1995). This ethic is radically inclusive (Stetson & Conti, 2005). Every human being reflects God's image. Every human being has innate value, regardless of age, beliefs, gender, physical impairment, mental disability, race, religion, sexual orientation, or social class (Bowpitt, 2000).

Since this worth and dignity is based upon humans' status as created beings, it is not dependent upon the extant social norms that exist in a given culture (Ruston, 2004). Thus, in some sense, this construct is a universal, transcultural entity. Regardless of whether or not cultures, societies, or governments recognize the intrinsic worth of persons, it still exists from a Christian perspective (Stark, 2003).

In addition to describing the world as it is, the *imago dei* provides a standard for measuring the world as it should be (Evangelium vitae, 1995). If human beings have innate worth and dignity as God's image bearers on Earth, then it follows that people should be treated in a manner that reflects this status (Bowpitt, 2000). Entities characterized by value and worth implicitly call for treatment in keeping with these innate characteristics.

While what constitutes appropriate treatment has been a source of ongoing debate within Christian circles, a number of precepts are widely held (Formicola, 2005). For example, at a more abstract level, the *imago dei* implies that human interactions are important and should be characterized by respectful interchanges that convey the mutual worth of the participants, that a certain standard of living is necessary to preserve the dignity of people, and the notion that human beings are endowed with certain rights that are universal in nature.

To the extent that people are not treated in keeping with their status as image bearers, then the situation is unjust and, in principle, calls for remedial efforts (Smith, 1996). To follow up on the above three examples, discriminatory human interactions, poverty, and human rights violations are typically viewed as problems that call for action. Depending upon the context, the action may be personal, programmatic, or structural. The central point is that action is required, at least in principle, to ensure that people are treated as they should be, in a just manner reflective of their ontological status as image bearers.

COMMUNITY

The *imago dei* should not be understood in a strictly individualistic manner (Evangelium vitae, 1995). Human beings are called to be in relationship with one another. The image of God is, in a certain sense, truly manifested only within the context of the human community (Hoekema, 1986). For instance, people are only able to communicate the value and dignity of human beings when they are in relationship with other human beings.

Consequently, Christians are called to have a communitarian outlook in which human beings are envisioned to be in relationship with one another (Davis & Robinson, 2006). People should not live for just their own gain, but should also consider the needs of others (Evangelium vitae, 1995). In other words, people are responsible for assisting other members of the human family.

In addition to affirming just relationships among the larger human family, Christians also manifest uniquely transformative communities (Marsh, 2005). In other words, Christians are called to form communities of believers that seek to model an alternative way of living. In turn, these communities function to transform the world around them.

Martin Luther King Jr. reportedly referred to these social networks as the "beloved community" (Marsh, 2005). In the face of a society that often devalues humanity, Christians form communities that model an alternative way of living. A new social space is formed within the flow of human history. These beloved communities reveal to people that God stands on the side of truth, love, and justice.

ADDITIONAL CONSIDERATIONS

It is important to reiterate that many other theological beliefs inform understandings of social justice in addition to concepts like the *imago dei* and communitarianism. For instance, the notion of stewardship is a key tenet in the biblical narrative (McCammack, 2007). As stewards entrusted by God with the care of his creation, Christians are called to care for the environment. Environmental degradation violates this standard and calls for action to ensure that the creation is passed on to future generations in an equitable manner (Girotti, 2008).

As implied above, Christian tradition is also multivocal. Various subtraditions and movements within the larger tradition typically highlight different strands of the biblical narrative. Consequently, not all self-identified Christians would necessarily agree upon what constitutes a socially unjust situation as different theological tenets are often brought to bear on a given issue.

For instance, some regulations that help protect the environment may negatively affect economic growth that helps alleviate poverty. While some Christians may prioritize assistance to the poor, others may favor environmental protection (McCammack, 2007). As a result, Christians from different denominations, and even within denominations, can find themselves on opposite sides of a given issue (Hunter, 1991; Nesbitt, 2001).

Christians operationalize the relatively abstract principles discussed above in multiple forms. Space constraints preclude an overview of all the expressions of social justice that exist within the Christian tradition. However, to provide a sense of how these principles are operationalized, some current examples are delineated in the following section.

Advocating for Social Justice

In addition to caring for the environment, Christians are engaged in many other activities to promote social justice. Many of these activities flow, either directly or indirectly, from the concepts discussed above. Although other theological tenets may also be used to support the social justice efforts profiled below, in a sense, they can all be seen as stemming from the notion of the *imago dei*. In other words, these efforts seek to operationalize the belief that all human beings have worth and value and should be treated with dignity and respect in a communitarian context.

Some representative examples of social change efforts that reflect these values might include mainline Protestants supporting living-wage ordinances (Parker, 2000); Hispanic Pentecostals advocating for humane treatment of immigrants (Espinosa, 2007); Evangelical Christians creating support programs for prisoners (Johnson, 2004); or Catholics working for a "culture of life" in which economic and social resources are used to support people who are poor, sick, disabled, and old, and the unborn (Evangelium vitae, 1995; Martin, 2005).

A variety of methods, both conventional and nonconventional, have been employed to achieve the desired goal of supporting the dignity and worth of each person. Since the social justice efforts of spiritual groups are informed by distinct worldviews, these groups often employ alternative, nonmainstream methods to achieve their goals (Tyndale, 2003). For instance, building upon King's notion of the "beloved community," Christians have formed what some have called "radical communities" (Marsh, 2005). The following subsection discusses one organization emanating from the black church that is dedicated to creating an alternative approach to challenging social injustice in urban settings.

CHRISTIAN COMMUNITY DEVELOPMENT ASSOCIATION

John Perkins founded the Christian Community Development Association (CCDA) in 1989. The CCDA works in "under-resourced communities" (Gordon, 2008). Its vision is the holistic restoration or transformation of such communities.

The CCDA grew out of the unfinished work of the civil rights movement (Marsh, 2005). Although other actors contributed, the civil rights movement emanated from the black church of which Perkins was a part (Day, 2001). Based upon his belief that blacks were intrinsically equal to whites, Perkins organized a series of peaceful marches and business boycotts in late 1960s in Mississippi designed to end segregation and secure equitable access to resources (Marsh, 2005). For his efforts, Perkins was beaten and tortured by local police officers, almost to the point of death.

Growing out of his work in poor black communities, Perkins developed the "three Rs": relocation, reconciliation, and redistribution. These three principles function as the CCDA's philosophical backbone (Stafford, 2007). Together, these principles help create radical communities that take the social agenda initiated by the civil rights movement to the next level (Berk, 1989; Marsh, 2005).

RELOCATION

Relocation entails moving into communities in which the poor live. Perkins believes that people who are poor are created with gifts, talents, and abilities, and consequently are best situated to solve their own problems. Those outside the community who attempt to help are intrinsically patronizing, regardless of their intentions. Due to their social location, it is impossible for outsiders to avoid a top-down perspective. Such an outside, top-down approach is implicitly condescending to community members who understand the problems from the inside out. While it is impossible to completely alter one's social location, it is possible to mitigate its effects by changing one's physical location and becoming a member of the community itself.

By relocating into the community and seeking to compassionately serve its members, it is possible to adopt a relatively inside, bottom-up approach. Living engagement helps turn people who are poor from statistics into friends. A relational bond is created that honors the dignity and worth of each person. A sense of connectedness is developed among individuals. As the CCDA puts it, relocation transforms *you*, *them*, and *theirs* into *we*, *us*, and *ours* (Gordon, 2008). In short, relocation results in a fundamental ontological shift in perspectives that lays the foundation for all subsequent interactions.

RECONCILIATION

The second principle is reconciliation, which involves both vertical (with God) and horizontal (with people) dimensions. In keeping with Perkins's holistic anthropological understanding, spiritual needs are addressed through reconciliation with God. Spiritual reconciliation with God results in a life dedicated to loving God and others in a multi-dimensional manner that addresses people's felt needs.

Reconciliation also entails breaking down barriers that segregate people. This typically difficult process requires the open and honest sharing of differing viewpoints (Marsh, 2005). The physical, psychological, and spiritual wounds incurred as a result of societal oppression are often difficult for others from more privileged backgrounds to hear. Repentance, restitution, and forgiveness are also hard but necessary steps on the path to an authentic reconciliation that results in restored relationships between people.

REDISTRIBUTION

The third principle is redistribution or the just distribution of goods and resources. Communities of color and lower economic status are often characterized by unjust structures that inhibit residents' ability to better their environments. Members of wealthy communities expect equitable distribution of resources in their communities as a manner of course. However, law enforcement, court systems, businesses, banks, and other institutional actors often exhibit bias in their interactions with those who do not have the economic, political, or social power to ensure the just treatment and allocation of resources (Gordon, 2008).

To empower people requires the redistribution of resources so that people who are poor are able to help themselves (Rukshan, 2006). Just distribution includes not only the redistribution of economic assets, but perhaps more importantly, redistribution of knowledge, skills, and relationships. As residents gain access to these new resources, communities can be transformed.

It is important to emphasize that these three principles are intertwined and together form a holistic approach to community development (Berk, 1989; Stafford, 2007). When people with resources commit to living among the poor (relocation), and seek to love and serve their neighbors as themselves (reconciliation), then redistribution naturally occurs as people share their assets to improve the welfare of the community. As newcomers adopt the vision of the existing community residents and share their skills and goods with their neighbors to collectively address community problems, a more just allocation of resources occurs (Gordon, 2008).

Perkins's three Rs provided the basis for an integrated community in West Jackson, the Mississippi city's first modern interracial community (Marsh, 2005). By the summer of 1976, a comprehensive slate of social ministries had been created, which included a children's ministry, study center, medical clinic, thrift shop, family health center, housing cooperative, mortgage company for the poor, clothing distribution center, Bible school, communication and printing office, and the first rural health program in the South targeted toward improving the lives of African Americans (Marsh, 2005).

Since the creation of the CCDA in 1989, this basic three-dimensional model has been replicated in urban areas around the United States and internationally (Gordon, 2008; Rukshan, 2006). Currently, the CCDA consists of over 600 organizations operating in more than 200 cities (Gordon, 2008; Rukshan, 2006). Further, the CCDA is itself part of a larger Christian movement dedicated to community development (Marsh, 2005).

In addition to efforts designed to promote social justice domestically, Christians are also actively involved in more internationally oriented concerns. These efforts are manifested in American and foreign contexts. Indeed, in many nations, people of faith provide over half the educational and health services (Marshall, 2004). In a manner analogous to urban areas in the United States (Cnaan et al., 2004), spiritually based organizations are often the only service providers that remain in poor communities among what some call "failed nation states" (Marshall, 2004). Some Christian contributions to this larger effort to promote a more equitable international social order are reviewed below.

PROMOTING SOCIAL JUSTICE INTERNATIONALLY

To help eliminate poverty, Mennonite believers played an instrumental role in creating what became known as the fair-trade movement (Wolfer & Del Pilar, 2008). Fair-trade organizations, such as Ten Thousand Villages, provide a marketing outlet in the United States and Canada for artisans in developing countries. As an alternative to conventional international trading practices, fair-trade organizations seek to establish trading partnerships that promote sustainable development for excluded and disadvantaged artisans by providing an equitable return on their products.

Drawing upon the biblical concept of the jubilee, Christians developed the Jubilee debt relief campaign (Marshall & Koeugh, 2004). This movement advocates canceling the debt of the world's poorest nations. Through the forgiveness of debt that keeps poor nations in a state of economic bondage to rich nations, poor countries are able to pursue development strategies.

Numerous organizations seek to empower the poorest of the poor in developing nations. For instance, World Vision, perhaps the largest Christian relief and development agency in the world, has helped equip India's "untouchables" or, as they would tend to self-identify, Dalits (Linthicum, 2002). Through its Organizing People for Progress program, World Vision imparts the skills local Dalit communities need to solve their own problems.

For instance, in one city, approximately six thousand Dalits living on the streets were rounded up, placed in the back of army trucks, driven to an inaccessible floodplain with no housing, services, or even vegetation, and dumped off without supplies (Linthicum, 2002). After providing emergency food, health care, and shelter, World Vision personnel worked with the Dalits to develop a strategy to address the situation. Through collective action, the Dalits were able to convince governmental leaders to provide services and housing for all their community members.

Similarly, Catholics have created International Movement ATD Fourth World, or simply ATD Fourth World, an organization dedicated to ending extreme poverty (Marshall & Koeugh, 2004). Toward this end, it seeks to work with the very poor, enabling them to conduct research on poverty and develop solutions. Working in partnership with the extreme poor, ATD Fourth World focuses on supporting families and changing policies that perpetuate poverty.

In addition to poverty alleviation, Christians have been involved in human rights advocacy and the promotion of democratic civil society. Human trafficking, or what some call the modern-day slave trade, has reached "epidemic proportions" (United Nations Office on Drugs and

Crime, 2005), providing organized crime syndicates with their largest source of revenue after the sale of narcotics and arms (U.S. Department of State, 2004). Evangelical Christians, echoing their historical role in ending slavery in the west (Stark, 2003), played an instrumental role in passing the *Victims of Trafficking and Violence Protection Act of 2000* (P.L. 106–386) (Hertzke, 2004; Skinner, 2008). This legislation seeks to penalize traffickers and provide services to victims while encouraging nations around the world to address the issue of human trafficking (Hodge, 2008).

Working across spiritual traditions, evangelical Christians also played a pivotal role in the passage of the *International Religious Freedom Act* (P.L. 105–292) in 1998, as well as related legislation such as the *Sudan Peace Act* (P.L. 107–245) in 2002 (Hertzke, 2004). Article 18 of the United Nations' (1948/1998) *Universal Declaration of Human Rights*—the right to religious freedom—is one of the most ignored and widespread human rights violations in the world (Marshall, 2000). These legislative initiatives seek to, respectively, protect these basic human rights around the world and end the religiously animated war in Sudan through peaceful means.

In addition to challenging the excesses of individualistic capitalism in the United States, Catholic leaders have often been strong advocates for human rights and democratization throughout the developing world (Wood, 1999). Advocating for a "third way," Catholic leaders have confronted various authoritarian regimes on both the left and the right (Formicola, 2005). The church played a key role establishing democracy in Eastern Europe, Latin America, and the Philippines (Burleigh, 2007; Hertzke, 2004; Osa, 1996). Further, the shift from dictatorships and Marxism to democratic societies was accomplished through peaceful means.

Many other examples of domestic and internationally oriented efforts to create a more just world exist (Borer, 1996; Lindsay, 2007; Marshall & Koeugh, 2004; Parker, 2000). Hopefully the above content provides some understanding of how spirituality can inform and motivate the pursuit of social justice. It should be noted that the pursuit of a just society is often a collaborative process; other groups often played a role in the examples cited above. For instance, while evangelical Christians were central actors in the passage of human trafficking legislation, feminists also played an important role (Hertzke, 2004).

It should also be mentioned that spiritual traditions do not always inspire socially just actions. For instance, the Catholic Church has, on occasion, supported, rather than confronted, authoritarian regimes. Spiritual traditions can function as a source of oppression in much the same way that secular worldviews can oppress people (e.g., secular environmentalists who commit acts of violence against people in the name of the environment) (Taylor, 1998).

To reiterate, social justice is a concept that spans spiritual traditions (Marshall & Koeugh, 2004; Moss, 2005). Poverty and suffering, for instance, typically represent deviations from what should be. Consequently, most spiritual traditions express concern for the poor and excluded (Marshall, 2004). Examples include the annual donation of a percentage of one's total wealth to help the poor in Islam, programs to feed the hungry in Sikhism, and efforts to assist the disenfranchised in the syncretistic tradition. Consequently, as noted above, it may be helpful to view the expressions delineated herein as a type of proxy for related expressions within other traditions—particularly when considering the pedagogical implications.

Pedagogical Implications

The intrinsic link between spirituality and social justice suggests a number of pedagogical implications. Perhaps the most important stems from the profession's ethical standards. In the following section, the pedagogical implications and challenges that flow from these ethical standards is discussed. The section concludes by noting the contributions that spiritually based understandings of social justice can contribute to professional discourse.

ETHICAL CONSIDERATIONS

According to the NASW *Code of Ethics* (2008), "social workers promote social justice and social change with and on behalf of clients" (Preamble). Service to others is elevated above self-interest. Although many understandings of social justice exist (see Reisch, Chapter 1, this volume), social workers are ethically called to advocate for clients' understanding of social justice rather than personal understandings that reflect their own self-interests. The approach to social justice articulated in the code is not *top down*, but *bottom up* in the sense that social workers "seek to enhance the capacity of people to address their own needs" (NASW, 2008, Preamble).

In order to promote social change with and on behalf of clients, it is necessary to have some understanding of how various client populations view social justice (Sue & Sue, 2008). For example, effective, ethical advocacy on behalf of various immigrant populations is predicated upon developing one's knowledge and appreciation of the groups' experiences, needs, and desires. Without some knowledge of clients' worldviews, it is difficult, if not impossible, to pursue social change on their behalf (Hodge, 2005a). In order to challenge social injustice on behalf of clients, one must know how clients operationalize the concept.

This line of reasoning implies that social work instructors have an ethical duty to equip students with the necessary skills, attitudes, and knowledge so that they can advocate for their clients, including those clients whose understandings of social justice are informed by their spirituality (Sue & Sue, 2008). The stance articulated by the *Code of Ethics* is inclusive. The code does not state that social workers should only promote social justice on behalf of secular clients. Indeed, discrimination based upon religion is explicitly proscribed by the code (NASW, 2008). Generally speaking, instructors are called to train students so that they can promote justice on behalf of all clients.

Other ethical standards also speak to the issue of classroom content. Specifically, while social workers are called to promote social justice on behalf of all client groups, they are ethically enjoined to pay particular attention to the perspective of those who are vulnerable, oppressed, and living in poverty (NASW, 2008). In keeping with global demographics, devout, mainstream spiritual believers are disproportionately drawn from disenfranchised populations in the United States (Jenkins, 2002). Traditional or orthodox believers are disproportionately likely to be African American, Latino, Native American, female, and members of the working class or the poor (Davis & Robinson, 1997; Hodge, 2002b; McAdams, 1987; Smith & Faris, 2005; Taylor, Chatters, & Jackson, 2007).

In short, social work educators are ethically called to equip future social workers so that they can advocate on behalf of spiritually motivated clients. This is particularly the case with traditional spiritual understandings widely held by the groups mentioned in the preceding paragraph. In the same way that students are currently prepared to advocate for more secular understandings of social justice, students should be trained to provide services that acknowledge, accept, and are responsive to clients' spirituality, including services that involve advocacy that reflects the concerns of people of faith (Van Soest, 1996).

As implied above, many different spiritual traditions exist (Richards & Bergin, 2000; Van Hook et al., 2001). A unique worldview and a corresponding understanding of what constitutes a just society characterize each tradition. Due to the number of extant spiritual traditions in the United States, it is not realistic to cover all the spiritually based understandings of social justice that exist in a single graduate social work program (Eck, 2001; Melton, 2003).

One way to address this issue is to cover those understandings that future social workers are likely to encounter in their practice. In a manner analogous to common practice in many diversity courses, the demographics of the larger catchment area that a given social work program serves would inform social justice content. A program located in a geographic area disproportionately populated by, for example, adherents to syncretistic spirituality, would include social justice content from this perspective.

To facilitate learning of locally prominent traditions, educators might include activities in their courses designed to promote this end. For instance, students might be offered the opportunity to participate in service programs sponsored by various spiritual traditions. Another option is to allow students to select a tradition and then give a presentation on its understanding of social justice.

CHALLENGES TO INCORPORATING SPIRITUAL UNDERSTANDINGS

It is important to acknowledge that presenting alternative understanding of social justice in an unbiased manner may be a challenge for some instructors. People of faith may hold understandings of social justice that differ from those affirmed in the dominant secular culture (Tyndale, 2003). Even when shared goals exist, the means used to achieve those goals often differ.

For instance, while most social workers would likely agree with the Christian Community Development Association's goal of transforming underresourced urban communities, some may have difficulties with the three-dimensional development model based upon relocation, reconciliation, and redistribution. Some social workers, for example, may be uncomfortable with the notion of relocating to poverty-stricken urban areas. Others may disagree with the holistic anthropology that seeks to address spiritual, as well as material, felt needs. Yet others may believe that the notion of extensively redistributing their personal resources is too radical to be seriously considered.

When faced with alternative models of reality, it can be difficult for instructors to present content in an empathetic manner that engenders the abilities to work within the context of clients' worldviews (Sue & Sue, 2008; Wambach & Van Soest, 1997). Students may be particularly sensitive to instructors' cues regarding spiritual content (Eckstein & Turman, 2002). Consequently, it is important for instructors to engage in self-reflection and monitor their classroom behaviors to ensure that content is relayed in an ethical manner.

Some students may also experience difficulty developing empathetic understandings of perspectives that differ from their own. One way to help overcome such resistance is to emphasize points of congruence with existing secular frameworks. For example, some of the methods employed by CCDA are similar to those used by grassroots organizers during the Progressive Era and the Depression. Highlighting areas of congruence between dominant secular perspectives and spiritual perspectives may help engender a fuller understanding of the latter.

CONTRIBUTIONS OF SPIRITUALITY TO SOCIAL JUSTICE DISCOURSE

Although presenting diverse constructions of reality can be a challenging experience, it is also important to note the potentially beneficial outcomes. These benefits include an enhanced ability to provide services to clients, increased congruence with the *Code of Ethics*, personal and professional growth as one develops the ability to see the world through alternative worldviews, and the potential to develop new, innovative ways to address problems. This latter outcome may warrant some additional commentary.

More specifically, diversity may be an intrinsic good, helping to spur advancement and innovation (Hodge, Wolfer, Limb, & Nadir, 2009; Putnam, 2007). Worldviews serve to refract reality, highlighting certain data while simultaneously obscuring other information (Kuhn, 1970). Accordingly, spiritual worldviews may underscore options that secular worldviews may overlook. Advancement occurs more rapidly as different perspectives examine problems, such as poverty. Innovation is furthered as various perspectives cross-pollinate and new solutions are created.

The fair-trade movement serves as an example of an innovative, spiritually based antipoverty strategy that has achieved some degree of mainstream acceptance (Wolfer & Del Pilar, 2008). As noted above, fair-trade organizations seek to empower excluded and disadvantaged artisans in developing countries by providing them with an equitable return on their products. Even though this approach does not rely upon conventional, lowest-cost pricing, it is now widely accepted as an important strategy for addressing poverty. Yet when Edna Ruth Byler, the founder of Ten Thousand Villages, started selling handcrafted products out of the trunk of her car more than sixty years ago, it was widely seen as a radical, even foolish idea.

In the same way, it is likely that many current understandings of social justice, whether secular or spiritual, will be accepted as mainstream at some point in the future. Methods that are considered ineffective or even radical now will eventually become accepted as mainstream in the future. By incorporating social justice strategies into educational programs that reflect the worldviews of diverse client populations, the profession is ultimately better positioned to solve societal problems.

Conclusion

For many clients, social justice and spirituality are intimately and necessarily connected. In order to provide ethically grounded services to such clients, it is critical that social workers be familiar with common understandings of social justice among the various spiritual traditions they commonly encounter in practice settings. To help readers along this road, this chapter has introduced the theoretical and empirical links between spirituality and social justice and illustrated these concepts with examples drawn from the Christian tradition. Readers are encouraged, however, to continue the journey on their own by building upon the presented content. By enhancing our understandings of social justice, we add new tools to our professional toolbox, enabling us to better serve the needs of those who are poor and disadvantaged.

References

Berk, S. E. (1989). From proclamation to community: The work of John Perkins. *Transformation, 6*(4), 1–6.

Borer, T. A. (1996). Church leadership, state repression, and the "spiral of involvement" in the South African anti-apartheid movement, 1983–1990. In C. Smith (Ed.), *Disruptive religion* (pp. 125–143). New York: Routledge.

Bowpitt, G. (2000). Working with creative creatures: Towards a Christian paradigm for social work theory, with some practical implications. *British Journal of Social Work, 30*(3), 349–364.

Brewer, M. D., Kersh, R., & Petersen, R. E. (2003). Assessing the conventional wisdom about religion and politics: A preliminary view from the pews. *Journal for the Scientific Study of Religion, 42*(1), 125–136.

Brooks, A. C. (2006). *Who really cares: The surprising truth about compassionate conservatism.* New York: Basic Books.

Burleigh, M. (2007). *Sacred causes: The clash of religion and politics, from the great war to the war on terror.* New York: HarperCollins.

Canda, E. R., & Furman, L. D. (1999). *Spiritual diversity in social work practice.* New York: Free Press.

Clydesdale, T. T. (1999). Toward understanding the role of Bible beliefs and higher education in American attitudes toward eradicating poverty, 1964–1996. *Journal for the Scientific Study of Religion, 38*(1), 103–118.

Cnaan, R. A., & Boddie, S. C. (2001). Philadelphia census of congregations and their involvement in social service delivery. *Social Service Review, 75*(4), 559–580.

Cnaan, R. A., Boddie, S. C., & Kang, J. J. (2005). Religious congregations as social service providers for older adults. *Journal of Gerontological Social Work, 45*(Suppl. 1/2), 105–130.

Cnaan, R. A., Sinha, J. W., & McGrew, C. C. (2004). Congregations as social service providers: Services, capacity, culture, and organizational behavior. *Administration in Social Work, 28*(Suppl. 3/4), 47–68.

Cnaan, R. A., Wineburg, R. J., & Boddie, S. C. (1999). *The newer deal: Social work and religion in partnership.* New York: Columbia University Press.

Cosgrove, J. (2008). Congregations globalizing social justice. *Social Work and Christianity, 35*(4), 374–390.

Davis, N. J., & Robinson, R. V. (1997). A war for America's soul? The American religious landscape. In R. H. Williams (Ed.), *Cultural wars in American politics* (pp. 39–61). New York: Aldine De Gruyter.

Davis, N. J., & Robinson, R. V. (1999). Their brothers' keepers? Orthodox religionists, modernists, and economic justice in Europe. *American Journal of Sociology, 104*(6), 1631–1665.

Davis, N. J., & Robinson, R. V. (2006). The egalitarian face of Islamic orthodoxy: Support for Islamic law and economic justice in seven Muslim-majority nations. *American Sociological Review, 71*(2), 167–190.

Day, K. (2001). Putting it together in the African American churches: Faith, economic development, and civil rights. In P. D. Nesbitt (Ed.), *Religion and social policy* (pp. 181–195). Walnut Creek, CA: AltaMira Press.

Ebaugh, H. R., & Pipes, P. (2001). Immigrant congregations as social service providers: Are they safety nets for welfare reform? In P. D. Nesbitt (Ed.), *Religion and social policy* (pp. 95–110). Walnut Creek, CA: AltaMira Press.

Eck, D. L. (2001). *A new religious America.* New York: HarperCollins.

Eckstein, N. J., & Turman, P. D. (2002). "Children are to be seen and not heard": Silencing students' religious voices in the university classroom. *Journal of Communication and Religion, 25*(2), 166–192.

Espinosa, G. (2007). "Today we act, tomorrow we vote": Latino religions, politics, and activism in contemporary U.S. civil society. *Annals of the American Academy, 612,* 152–171.

Evangelium vitae. (1995). Retrieved December 27, 2005, from http://www.vatican.va/holy_father/john_paul_ii/encyclicals/documents/hf_p-ii_enc_25031995_evangelium-vitae_en.html

Formicola, J. R. (2005). The political legacy of Pope John Paul II. *Journal of Church and State, 47*(2), 235–242.

Gallup, G. J., & Jones, T. (2000). *The next American spirituality: Finding God in the twenty-first century.* Colorado Springs, CO: Victor.

Gallup, G. J., & Lindsay, D. M. (1999). *Surveying the religious landscape.* Harrisburg, PA: Morehouse.

Gilbert, M. (2000). Spirituality in social work groups: Practitioners speak out. *Social Work with Groups, 22*(4), 67–84.

Girotti, G. (2008). *Vatican bishop points to modern social sins.* Retrieved May 4, 2008, from http://www.catholicnewsagency.com/utiles/myprint/print.php

Gordon, W. L. (2008). *The eight components of Christian community development.* Retrieved May 4, 2008, from http://www.ccda.org/philosophy

Gray, M. (2008). Viewing spirituality in social work through the lens of contemporary social theory. *British Journal of Social Work, 38,* 175–196.

Hanawalt, E. A., & Lindberg, C. (Eds.). (1994). *Through the eye of a needle: Judeo-Christian roots of social welfare.* Lanham, MD: Thomas Jefferson University Press.

Hart, S. (1992). *What does the Lord require? How American Christians think about economic justice.* New York: Oxford University Press.

Hertzke, A. D. (2004). *Freeing God's children: The unlikely alliance for global human rights.* Lanham, MD: Rowman & Littlefield.

Heyman, J., Buchanan, R., Musgrave, B., & Menz, V. (2006). Social workers attention to clients' spirituality: Use of spiritual interventions in practice. *Aretê, 30*(1), 78–89.

Hodge, D. R. (2000). Spirituality: Towards a theoretical framework. *Social Thought, 19*(4), 1–20.

Hodge, D. R. (2002a). Does social work oppress evangelical Christians? A new class analysis of society and social work. *Social Work, 47*(4), 401–414.

Hodge, D. R. (2002b). Equally devout, but do they speak the same language? Comparing the religious beliefs and practices of social workers and the general public. *Families in Society, 83*(5/6), 573–584.

Hodge, D. R. (2003). The intrinsic spirituality scale: A new six-item instrument for assessing the salience of spirituality as a motivational construct. *Journal of Social Service Research, 30*(1), 41–61.

Hodge, D. R. (2005a). Social work and the house of Islam: Orienting practitioners to the beliefs and values of Muslims in the United States. *Social Work, 50*(2), 162–173.

Hodge, D. R. (2005b). Spiritual life maps: A client-centered pictorial instrument for spiritual assessment, planning, and intervention. *Social Work, 50*(1), 77–87.

Hodge, D. R. (2008). Sexual trafficking in the United States: A domestic problem with transnational dimensions. *Social Work, 53*(2), 143–152.

Hodge, D. R., Baughman, L. M., & Cummings, J. A. (2006). Moving toward spiritual competency: Deconstructing religious stereotypes and spiritual prejudices in social work literature. *Journal of Social Service Research, 32*(4), 211–232.

Hodge, D. R., & Wolfer, T. A. (2008). Promoting tolerance: The imago dei as an imperative for Christian social workers. *Journal of Religion and Spirituality in Social Work: Social Thought, 27*(3), 297–313.

Hodge, D. R., Wolfer, T. A., Limb, G. E., & Nadir, A. (2009). Expanding diversity in social work discourse: Exploring the possibility of a theistic perspective. *Journal of Religion and Spirituality in Social Work: Social Thought, 28*(1), 202–214.

Hoekema, A. A. (1986). *Created in God's image.* Grand Rapids, MI: Eerdmans.

Hunter, J. D. (1991). *Culture wars.* New York: Basic Books.

Jenkins, P. (2002). *The next Christendom.* New York: Oxford University Press.

Johnson, B. R. (2004). Religious programs and recidivism among former inmates in prison fellowship programs: A long-term follow-up study. *Justice Quarterly, 21*(2), 329–354.

Kliksberg, B. (2003). Facing the inequalities of development: Some lessons from Judaism and Christianity. *Development, 46*(4), 57–63.

Kuhn, T. S. (1970). *The structure of scientific revolutions* (2nd ed.). Chicago: University of Chicago.

Lindsay, D. M. (2007). *Faith in the halls of power.* New York: Oxford University Press.

Linthicum, R. (2001). Building heaven and creating hell: The Bible on economic, political and religious systems and their people. *Social Policy, 31*(4), 34–47.

Linthicum, R. (2002). Doing community organizing in the urban slums of India. *Social Policy, 32*(2), 34–38.

Lyotard, J.-F. (1979/1984). *The postmodern condition: A report on knowledge* (G. Bennington & B. Massumi, Trans.). Minneapolis: University of Minnesota Press.

Marsh, J. C. (2005). Social justice: Social work's organizing value. *Social Work, 50*(4), 293–294.

Marshall, K. (2004). Faith perspectives for development institutions: New faces of compassion and social justice. *International Journal, 59*(4), 893–901.

Marshall, K., & Koeugh, L. (2004). *Mind, heart, and soul in the fight against poverty.* Washington, DC: World Bank.

Marshall, P. (2000). *Religious freedom in the world.* Nashville, TN: Broadman and Holman.

Martin, E. J. (2005). The U.S. Catholic bishops and welfare policy: Guidelines for reform and reauthorization. *International Journal of Public Administration, 28*(13/14), 1187–1209.

Maslow, A. H. (1968). *Toward a psychology of being.* Princeton, NJ: D. Van Nostrand.

McAdams, J. (1987). Testing the theory of the new class. *Sociological Quarterly, 28*(1), 23–49.

McCammack, B. (2007). Hot damned America: Evangelicalism and the climate change policy debate. *American Quarterly, 59*(3), 645–668.

Melton, J. G. (2003). *The encyclopedia of American religions* (7th ed.). Detroit: Gale Research.

Moss, B. (2005). *Religion and spirituality.* Lyme Regis, UK: Russell House.

Murdock, V. (2005). Guided by ethics: Religion and spirituality in gerontological social work practice. *Journal of Gerontological Social Work, 45*(1/2), 131–154.

National Association of Social Workers. (2008). *Code of ethics.* Retrieved September 15, 2009, from http://www.socialworkers.org/pubs/code/code.asp

Nesbitt, P. D. (2001). *Religion and social policy.* Walnut Creek, CA: AltaMira Press.

Osa, M. (1996). Pastoral mobilization and contention: The religious foundations of the solidarity movement in Poland. In C. Smith (Ed.), *Disruptive religion* (pp. 67–85). New York: Routledge.

Parker, R. (2000). Progressive politics and, uh, God. *American Prospect, 11*(5), 32–37.

Putnam, R. D. (2007). E pluribus unum: Diversity and community in the twenty-first century. *Scandinavian Political Studies, 30*(2), 137–174.

Regnerus, M. D., Smith, C., & Sikkink, D. (1998). Who gives to the poor? The influence of religious tradition and political location on the personal generosity of Americans toward the poor. *Journal for the Scientific Study of Religion, 37*(3), 481–493.

Richards, P. S., & Bergin, A. E. (Eds.). (2000). *Handbook of psychotherapy and religious diversity.* Washington, DC: American Psychological Association.

Richards, P. S., & Bergin, A. E. (2005). *A spiritual strategy for counseling and psychotherapy* (2nd ed.). Washington, DC: American Psychological Association.

Rukshan, F. (2006). The core values of Christian community development as reflected in the writings of the apostle Paul. *Social Work and Christianity, 33*(4), 355–373.

Ruston, R. (2004). *Human rights and the image of God.* London: SCM Press.

Sheridan, M. J. (2004). Predicting the use of spiritually-derived interventions in social work practice: A survey of practitioners. *Journal of Religion and Spirituality in Social Work, 23*(4), 5–25.

Sheridan, M. J., & Amato-von Hemert, K. (1999). The role of religion and spirituality in social work education and practice: A survey of student views and experiences. *Journal of Social Work Education, 35*(1), 125–141.

Skinner, E. B. (2008). *A crime so monstrous: Face-to-face with modern-day slavery.* New York: Free Press.

Smith, C. (Ed.). (1996). *Disruptive religion: The force of faith in social-movement activism.* New York: Routledge.

Smith, C., & Faris, R. (2005). Socioeconomic inequality in the American religious system: An update and assessment. *Journal for the Scientific Study of Religion, 44*(1), 95–104.

Stafford, T. (2007). Grandpa John: A new generation of urban activists is shaped by John Perkins. *Christianity Today, 51*(3), 48–51.

Stark, R. (2003). *For the glory of God: How monotheism led to reformations, science, witch-hunts, and the end of slavery.* Princeton, NJ: Princeton University Press.

Stetson, B., & Conti, J. G. (2005). *The truth about tolerance.* Downers Grove, IL: InterVarsity Press.

Sue, D., & Sue, D. (2008). *Counseling the culturally diverse: Theory and practice* (5th ed.). Hoboken, NJ: John Wiley & Sons.

Taylor, B. (1998). Religion, violence, and radical environmentalism: From Earth First! to the Unabomber to the Earth Liberation Front. *Terrorism and Political Violence, 10*(4), 1–42.

Taylor, R. J., Chatters, L. M., & Jackson, J. S. (2007). Religious and spiritual involvement among older African Americans, Caribbean Blacks, and non-Hispanic whites: Findings from the National Survey of American Life. *Journal of Gerontology, 62B*(4), S238–S250.

Tompkins, C. J., Larkin, H., & Rosen, A. L. (2006). An analysis of social work textbooks for aging content: How well do social work foundation texts prepare students for our aging society? *Journal of Social Work Education, 42*(1), 3–23.

Tyndale, W. (2003). Idealism and practicality: The role of religion in development. *Development, 46*(4), 22–28.

U.S. Department of State. (2004). *Trafficking in persons report.* Retrieved May 13, 2005, from http://www.state.gov/g/tip/rls/tiprpt/2004/34021.htm

United Nations Office on Drugs and Crime. (2005). *Fact sheet on human trafficking.* Retrieved May 12, 2005, from http://www.unodc.org/unodc/en/trafficking_victim_consents.html

United Nations. (1948/1998). *Universal declaration of human rights.* Retrieved February 27, 2006, from http://www.un.org/Overview/rights.html

Van Hook, M., Hugen, B., & Aguilar, M. A. (Eds.). (2001). *Spirituality within religious traditions in social work practice.* Pacific Grove, CA: Brooks/Cole.

Van Soest, D. (1996). The influence of competing ideologies about homosexuality on nondiscrimination policy: Implications for social work education. *Journal of Social Work Education, 32*(1), 53–64.

Wambach, K. G., & Van Soest, D. (1997). Oppression. In R. L. Edwards (Ed.), *Encyclopedia of social work* (19th ed., pp. 243–252). Washington, DC: NASW Press.

Wilson, C. E. (2008). *The politics of Latino faith: Religion, identity, and urban community.* New York: New York University Press.

Wolfer, T. A., & Del Pilar, K. (2008). Ten Thousand Villages: Partnering with artisans to overcome poverty. *Social Work and Christianity*, *35*(4), 449–472.

Wolterstorff, N. (2007). *Justice: Rights and wrongs*. Princeton, NJ: Princeton University Press.

Wood, R. L. (1999). Religious culture and political action. *Sociological Theory*, *17*(3), 307–332.

Wuthnow, R. (1994). *God and mammon in America*. New York: The Free Press.

Wuthnow, R. (2007). *After the baby boomers: How twenty- and thirty-somethings are shaping the future of American religion*. Princeton, NJ: Princeton University Press.

CHAPTER FOUR

A Review of Social Justice Courses: Toward Transformative and Cooperative Learning

Philip Young P. Hong, PhD

David R. Hodge, PhD

Abstract

This chapter analyzes the content of thirty-one social justice syllabi from twenty-seven MSW programs. The results indicate that the level of foci for these courses was diversity-integrated and they had group justice orientation. The coverage of social justice content areas was narrow in perspectives and specific in conceptualizations. While many courses mixed top-down and bottom-up approaches in teaching methods, there were only three cases with strong bottom-up models. Syllabi were issue-based rather than philosophically or theoretically based. Social justice–related terminologies promoted by NASW and CSWE were only partially reflected. Implications for empowering and transformative pedagogy are discussed.

The authors would like to thank the Emmett J. and Mary Martha Doerr Center for Social Justice Education and Research at Saint Louis University, School of Social Work, for supporting this project. We also extend our appreciation to Bryan Burda at Loyola University Chicago and Greg Shufeldt at Saint Louis University, who provided research assistantship on this project.

Introduction

Although the underlying assumption in the social work profession is that "social justice is definable, desirable, and possible" (Longres & Scanlon, 2001, p. 448), no common definition of social justice exists to inform social work practice. "Social justice" is a term that is loosely defined, and this concept can be understood in many different ways (Boucher & Kelly, 1998; Reisch, 2002; West, 1998). According to Reisch (2002), this concept can be used as "a rationale for maintaining the status quo, promoting far-reaching social reforms, and justifying revolutionary action" by as many groups as one can name, such as liberals, conservatives, religious fundamentalists, and radical secularists (p. 343). In this regard, social justice is often socially constructed and can be manipulated to support the biased definitions of many different interests of individuals and groups (Caputo, 2002). Therefore, defining social justice may be like describing the proverbial elephant as understood by blind observers (Lebacqz, 1986).

A central challenge to teaching about the application of social justice in all levels of social work practice is confusion over the referent definition of social justice (Longres & Scanlon, 2001). Social justice in the eyes of one group can be social injustice to another. Hence, the key question that drives this exploratory study is whether there exists a certain pattern in the current practices of teaching social justice in accredited MSW programs in the United States. In this chapter, we explore the ways in which social justice content is introduced in social justice courses toward the aim of strengthening the social justice content and, in doing so, advancing the profession's mission and it social impact.

We begin by overviewing a debate on individual and group-based conceptualizations of social justice. Then we review pedagogical approaches to social justice in social work. Guided by previous literature, we conduct a systematic content analysis of social justice syllabi from selected graduate social work programs (N = 31). The findings obtained from the content analysis include results of univariate analyses by each of the key themes and bivariate correlation analyses. We then highlight points of congruence and dissonance that exist between social justice conceptualizations reflected in the syllabi and traditional NASW and CSWE keywords associated with the concept. We conclude by drawing some implications about how the level of dissonance may limit the ability to implement various social justice strategies in practice.

Social Justice in Social Work Education

GROUP VERSUS INDIVIDUAL JUSTICE

According to Pelton (2001), social justice can be constructed as (1) an individual rights issue, often categorized by basic human needs, diversity, nondiscrimination, equality, and universal social policies, and (2) a group/community issue categorized by historical discrimination, oppression, marginalization, and selective social policies. The former view, favored by Pelton (2001), rejects any discriminatory government policies that violate individual rights by providing selective benefits on the basis of group identity. He maintains that an approach not based on individual rights will induce contentious identity politics among various groups, whether they are dominant or subordinate. In response to this argument, Scanlon and Longres (2001), without disagreeing with Pelton's position, suggest that group-based remedies need to be added to the securing of universal human needs when significant disparities exist across group boundaries. However, Holody's (2002) critical response to Scanlon and Longres (2001) emphasized the importance of the latter view, as he argued that the "fight for social justice must be fought on the terms of the dominant class" (p. 199).

Promoting social justice has been one of the major aspects of the social work profession (Morris, 2002; Reeser & Leighninger, 1990; Saleebey, 1990). Is social work's commitment to social justice about "all" people and at the same time those who are "historically oppressed and marginalized"? The National Association of Social Workers (NASW) *Code of Ethics* recognizes social justice as one of the core values of the profession. Its ethical principle reads, "Social workers challenge social injustice." The Preamble of the *Code of Ethics* states that the primary mission of social work profession is "to enhance human well-being and help meet the basic human needs of 'all' people, with particular attention to the needs and empowerment of people who are vulnerable, oppressed, and living in poverty" (NASW, 2008, p. 1). Balancing the needs of all people and those of various marginalized groups is what the NASW officially promotes. Yet there seems to be greater emphasis put on challenging social injustices through social change, "particularly with and on behalf of vulnerable and oppressed individuals and groups of people" (NASW, 2008, p. 5).

Building upon the code, the Counsel on Social Work Education's (CSWE, 2008) Educational Policy and Accreditation Standards (EPAS) also require accredited social work programs to be grounded in the profession's core values, including social justice. For instance, EP 1.1 requires social work educational programs to be grounded in

> service, social justice, the dignity and worth of the person, the importance of human relationships, integrity, competence, human rights, and scientific inquiry. . . . These values underpin the explicit and implicit curriculum and frame the profession's commitment to respect for all people and the quest for social and economic justice. (p. 2)

Although the standards provide more specific applications to the process and outcomes of social work education, and include an emphasis on at-risk populations, there is relatively less mention of how to involve all people. The CSWE standards do not define or operationalize social justice, but allow for a diversity of understandings based on either individuals or groups.

PEDAGOGY OF SOCIAL JUSTICE

In keeping with the diversity of social justice definitions, a number of viewpoints have appeared in the literature regarding how to integrate social justice into social work education (Reisch, 2002). Reeser and Leighninger (1990) proposed a specialization in social justice with courses designed to "develop students' critical consciousness as to learn social change strategies" (p. 73). As they state, the goals of this specialization are to

1. Develop tools for the analysis of the political, economic, and social structures of society and an understanding of how these structures lead to oppression;
2. Acquire a vision of the necessary elements of a just society that will foster the provision of the basic needs of all members of that society and promote the realization of the full potential of that society's people. Emphasis is on the student developing and articulating his or her own vision; and
3. Develop an understanding of the power of the people to change unjust structures and develop the skills necessary for leadership in the empowerment of people to move toward a just society.

These goals highlight the importance of understanding the systemic nature of personal consequences, exploring various theoretical and philosophical underpinnings of social justice models, and learning skills for bottom-up empowerment strategies to promote social change.

Recent literature follows these proposed goals from more than a decade ago and discusses the importance of using critical theory as a form of learning through reflection and empowerment to become stronger agents of change for the clients at multiple levels of practice and research. In the area of research, O'Connor and O'Neill (2004) have discussed how qualitative research methods are particularly well suited for the integration of social justice. Patterson (2004) examined how social justice can be interfaced into aging content. A number of educators have suggested that facilitated dialogue between different groups represents an ideal way to promote social justice (Dessel, Rogge, & Garlington, 2006; Nagda et al., 1999). Drawing heavily from postmodern thought, Finn and Jacobson (2003) have argued that current theoretical models are inadequate to meet the challenges of the twenty-first century and argue for a new, social justice–based practice model entitled the "just practice" framework.

Longres and Scanlon (2001) found that social work faculty members tend to "promote a broad and inclusive definition of justice," free-associating the concept with fairness, equity, parity, and equalizing rather than providing a formal definition (p. 460). While there was a lack of familiarity with social justice–related literature, the range these free associations covered were consistent with the diversity of social justice definitions. In this context, social work education then becomes a good testing ground for how best the social justice content can be introduced to students as a way of empowering them to become effective practitioners at all levels—micro, mezzo, macro, and global—working with multiple interests in a highly complex and divisive world.

RESEARCH QUESTIONS

There is little evidence from previous investigations of the full scope of how social justice content is delivered within social work. Few empirical studies exist in social work literature that examines the content and method of teaching among social justice courses from a wide range of MSW programs. Although narrower in scope, a survey of sixty graduate social work programs conducted in 1986 suggested that 50% offer at least one social justice–related course (Reeser & Leighninger, 1990). Another study analyzed the social justice content reflected in research courses taught in one state institution of higher learning (Longres & Scanlon, 2001). Bronstein, Berman-Rossi, and Winfield (2002) examined the gap between the perceptions of faculty and students and found that faculty assess themselves as teaching more content on broad-based oppression than what students feel they are learning. More recently, Hong and Hodge (2009) examined the definition of social justice implicitly reflected in MSW social justice course syllabi and summarized the bottom-up overarching definition as follows: "Based on the professional values of social work, social justice is a process of taking action to 'do justice' and an outcome of achieving justice-related goals and overcoming injustices, particularly for vulnerable groups in society" (p. 215).

In this regard, the purpose of this study is to systematically review the content of social justice courses covering a broader set of questions. Research questions we ask are:

1. To what extent do social justice courses reflect individual versus group-based approaches to understanding the concept?

2. What are the major content areas of social justice definitions covered in these courses?
3. What are some methods of transactions used in teaching social justice?
4. How congruent are the conceptualizations of social justice reflected in the syllabi with NASW and CSWE keywords associated with social justice?

Methods

SAMPLING

In October 2006, a letter was sent by e-mail to 190 CSWE accredited MSW programs describing the purpose of the study. The letter included a six-point survey regarding social justice courses:

1. Whether the social justice is infused in multiple courses or the program offers an explicit social justice course or courses;
2. If infused, which course(s) it is concentrated in;
3. What the title of the courses are if social justice is covered in a single course;
4. Whether these courses are foundation- or concentration-level courses;
5. How recently the social justice courses were taught; and
6. What the current enrollment is in the social justice courses and whether the enrollment is trending up or down.

Initially, forty-three schools responded to the survey. A follow-up e-mail was sent a month later to programs that had yet to respond by November 2006, and sixteen additional programs responded to the second e-mail. A total of fifty-nine programs responded, which provided a response rate of 30.9%.

Copies of current social justice course syllabi, along with the names of professors teaching these courses, were requested in the letter. Eight individual professors who have taught explicit social justice courses were contacted, of which three personally responded with course syllabi, and two returned the surveys through departmental staff. Fifteen syllabi were obtained from the surveys and through direct contact with instructors. Additional syllabi searches were made through Internet course listings of all 190 programs, from which fifty-four total social justice–related courses were identified. This list included all fifteen received from the surveys and by instructors. The Web search accessed sixteen additional syllabi, yielding a total of thirty-one syllabi from twenty-six social work programs. This represented 57% of the total number of identified social justice–related courses.

Syllabi qualified for analysis if the course titles either specifically included the word "justice" or if the course description particularly emphasized social justice. These courses were differentiated from syllabi that focused primarily on human and cultural diversity. All CSWE regions (1–10) but regions 1 (CT, ME, MA, NH, RI, and VT) and 3 (DE, DC, MD, PA, VA, and WV) were represented among the programs whose social justice syllabi were included in this study. Twenty-one out of thirty-one syllabi were explicit social justice courses, and the remaining ten were social justice–related courses that strongly reflected social justice themes and content.

ANALYSIS

First, a descriptive analysis by each survey question was conducted from the data obtained from fifty-nine MSW programs. Programs were coded as "infused" if they indicated that the social justice content appeared in multiple courses throughout the curriculum; as "explicit" if they had representative social justice courses; and as "both" if the content was both infused and explicit. Infused programs were categorized by which areas in the curriculum the social justice content appeared most. The characteristics of programs with specific social justice courses were tallied by the course levels (foundation or concentration), frequency of course offering, and enrollment trend.

Second, a content analysis was conducted on thirty-one MSW-level social justice syllabi. A coding scheme was developed based on the first three research questions, which provided the categories for collecting information from each syllabus in the sample—level of foci, coverage of social justice content, and method of teaching. The first two sets of variables were used for manifest content analysis, which involved examining the obvious and clearly evident data (Grinnell, 1993). The course content areas that we focused on were course descriptions, objectives, outlines, readings, and assignments. The level of foci included whether the main focus was on diversity ($=1$) or primarily social justice ($=0$) and whether the course's main emphases were on group ($=1$) or individual justice ($=0$). The coverage of social justice content represented the extent to which the range of multiple definitions was introduced in these courses and was categorized into general ($=1$) or specific coverage ($=0$).

Furthermore, a latent content analysis, examining the present but not-so-evident data (Grinnell, 1993) involved drawing out the method of teaching social justice from either the didactic or experiential teaching approaches. Strozier (1997) defined didactic as "traditional teaching methods such as lectures, classroom discussion, papers, and tests" and experiential method as using in-class tasks and process groups (p. 68). It is also important to note that experiential learning occurs through direct encounter (mock role-play and situational activities in class) and direct participation in events of life (learning through reflection) (Brookfield, 1984). Courses with any experiential-learning exercise component were coded as a bottom-up teaching method (=1) and those with primarily didactic teaching as a top-down approach (=0). As reflection is a large component of experiential learning (Kolb, 1984), it was coded separately to represent a reflective praxis method (=1) (Brookfield, 1990). Additional analysis was conducted to decipher whether the teaching methods were philosophically based (=1) or issue based (=0). Syllabi were considered philosophically based when course orientation focused on philosophical or theoretical literature (e.g., Rawls's distributive justice) when introducing the concept of social justice. On the other hand, issue-based syllabi laid out selected issues (e.g., racial discrimination) or events (e.g., Civil Rights Movement) that would be considered as social justice issues by the instructor.

Third, in order to address the fourth research question—whether there are any gaps between the general content of these courses and what is promoted by NASW and CSWE—examined through a manifest content analysis by highlighting some keywords for congruence and dissonance. Major keywords used were: "poverty," "unemployment," "discrimination," "oppression," "cultural and ethnic diversity," "access to needed information," "services," and "resources," "equality of opportunity," "advocacy," "social change," and "meaningful participation in decision making for all people." Based on these groupings, we investigated whether there were any differences in the way that the social justice definition was introduced or promoted.

Lastly, a correlation matrix of all variables from the content analysis was examined in order to explore the relational tendencies between key characteristics present in the syllabi. To examine potential co-occurrence of these characteristics, a Pearson product-moment correlation was used with a two-tailed test of significance.

Findings

SURVEY RESULTS

Of fifty-nine MSW programs responding to the survey, 81.4% (n = 48) identified as following an infusion model. The authors' curriculum review of the sampling frame (N = 190) over the Internet indicated that this was nearly consistent with 82.6% (N = 157) having an infusion model. No program was found to have an explicit model; rather, the remaining 18.6% (n = 11) followed "both" an infusion model with specific social justice courses. Among forty-eight programs that used the infusion model, 29.2% (n = 14) reported having social justice content in all courses. Policy courses (83.3%, n = 40) was the most frequent answer, followed by practice (66.7%, n = 32), HBSE (60.4%, n = 29), and human diversity courses (52.1%, n = 25). Research, values/ethics, and introduction to social work had only a few responses.

Seven out of eleven programs that offered both infused and explicit models reported introducing the social justice courses at both foundation and concentration levels. The remaining four offered them as foundation-level courses. All but one program that had not offered the course recently taught these social justice courses at least once a year. Enrollment in these courses for the most part has either remained steady (n = 5) or gone down (n = 4) over the years.

SYLLABI CONTENT DISTRIBUTION

The three key areas of content were the level of foci, the covered content areas of social justice, and the teaching method. As for level of foci, a slight majority of social justice courses (n = 17; 54.8%) examined in this study integrated diversity as the major content of social justice (see Table 4.1). The remaining fourteen (45.2%) focused primarily on the principles and models of social justice. Also, twenty-one syllabi (67.7%) had a group justice focus, while the rest integrated both individual and group-based approaches to understanding social justice. A great majority of the syllabi (n = 22; 71%) were evaluated as having specific coverage of social justice definitions.

Slightly less than half of the syllabi (n = 14; 45.2%) primarily used a top-down method of teaching. The other portion (n = 17; 54.8%) mixed both the top-down and bottom-up method of learning by incorporating experiential learning projects and assignments. Only three syllabi promoted student generated bottom-up definitions to be discussed to enhance critical thinking skills and dialogue. Encouraging some form of reflection as part of student learning was found only in fourteen syllabi (45.2%). Content delivery was for the most part issue-based (n = 21; 67.7%) and only eight had a philosophical approach, with two mixing both approaches.

The social justice conceptualizations represented in the syllabi were narrow and group-based in that they particularly highlighted discrimination, oppression, diversity, advocacy, and social change as key elements. This became more evident when examining syllabi for

TABLE 4.1   Description of social justice syllabi (n = 31)

Variables	Frequency	Percentage
Level of foci		
Diversity content		
Diversity oriented (= 1)	17	54.8
Primarily social justice (= 0)	14	45.2
Group vs. individual justice		
Group justice (= 1)	21	67.7
Individual and group justice (= 0)	10	32.3
Covered content areas of social justice		
Coverage of definitions		
General (= 1)	9	29.0
Specific (= 0)	22	71.0
Teaching methods		
Top-down vs. bottom-up		
Mix of top-down and bottom-up (= 1)	17	54.8
Top-down (= 0)	14	45.2
Use of reflective method (= 1)	14	45.2
Delivery of content		
Philosophical (= 1)	10	32.3
Issue based (= 0)	21	67.7

congruence and dissonance to the key NASW and CSWE terminologies that are used in connection with the value and principle of social justice. As shown in Table 4.2, highly congruent were discrimination (n = 25; 80.6%), oppression (n = 29; 93.5%), cultural and ethnic diversity (n = 25; 80.6%), advocacy (n = 23; 74.2%), and social change (n = 23; 74.2%). Only about half (n = 17; 54.8%) specifically discussed the issue of poverty. A rather low level of congruence was found for unemployment (n = 3; 9.7%), access to needed information, services, and resources (n = 7; 22.6%), equality of opportunity (n = 10; 32.3%), and meaningful participation in decision making (n = 5; 16.1%).

BIVARIATE CORRELATIONS

As can be observed in Table 4.3, diversity-oriented syllabi were more likely to focus only on group justice (r = .48, p < .01), less likely to include general coverage of definitions (r = −.42, p<.05), and less

TABLE 4.2 Reflection of NASW and CSWE social justice content

Content areas	Frequency	(%)
Poverty	17	54.8
Unemployment	3	9.7
Discrimination	25	80.6
Oppression	29	93.5
Cultural and ethnic diversity	25	80.6
Access to needed information, services, and resources	7	22.6
Equality of opportunity	10	32.3
Advocacy	23	74.2
Social change	23	74.2
Meaningful participation in decision making	5	16.1

likely to incorporate philosophical or theoretical approaches to teaching ($r = .49$, $p < .01$). Examining the association with NASW key concepts of social justice, these syllabi were correlated negatively with unemployment ($r = -.36$, $p < .05$), social change ($r = .54$, $p < .01$), and meaningful participation in decision making ($r = -.49$, $p < .01$), and positively with discrimination ($r = .38$, $p < .05$) and cultural and ethnic diversity ($r = .54$, $p < .01$).

Group justice–focused syllabi, as mentioned above, tended to be diversity oriented. These courses were less likely to present general coverage of definitions ($r = -.47$, $p < .01$). These syllabi were associated less with philosophical orientation to content delivery ($r = -.58$, $p < .01$). Interestingly, group justice–focused syllabi had negative correlations with advocacy ($r = -.41$, $p < .05$) and social change ($r = -.41$, $p < .05$). Courses that introduced a wide spectrum of definitions as indicated above had negative correlations with integrating diversity content and focusing primarily on group justice. These courses were more likely to have philosophical and theoretical approaches to teaching ($r = .78$, $p < .01$) and had greater tendencies to include content material on social change ($r = .38$, $p < .05$).

As for teaching methods, syllabi that were coded as having some aspects of bottom-up approaches were correlated with courses using reflective methods in thinking of social justice ($r = .56$, $p < .01$). Surprisingly, bottom-up courses had a negative correlation with the presence of social change in the syllabi content ($r = -.39$, $p < .05$). This may have been due to including all courses that had *any* bottom-up component, which were the courses that were primarily top-down. Courses that use reflective teaching methods had positive correlations with unemployment ($r = .36$, $p < .05$) and access to needed information, services, and resources ($r = .44$, $p < .05$). Philosophical and theoretical teaching methods, as stated earlier, contained less diversity

TABLE 4.3 Correlation matrix of variables used in content analysis (n = 31)

	(1)	(2)	(3)	(4)	(5)	(6)	(7)	(8)	(9)	(10)	(11)	(12)	(13)	(14)	(15)	(16)
Diversity integrated	(1) 1.00															
Group justice	(2) **.48**	1.00														
General coverage of definitions	(3) **−.42**	**−.47**	1.00													
Teaching method 1 (bottom-up)	(4) −.04	.21	.15	1.00												
Teaching method 2 (reflection)	(5) −.09	−.07	.13	**.56**	1.00											
Teaching method 3 (philosophical)	(6) **−.49**	**−.58**	**.78**	.07	.07	1.00										
Poverty	(7) −.30	−.35	.01	.09	.17	.07	1.00									
Unemployment	(8) **−.36**	−.24	.27	.30	**.36**	.01	.30	1.00								
Discrimination	(9) **.38**	.01	.13	.05	−.05	−.01	−.12	.16	1.00							
Oppression	(10) .03	.10	.17	.03	−.29	−.10	.03	.09	.20	1.00						
Cultural and ethnic diversity	(11) **.54**	−.16	.13	.05	.28	−.01	.05	.16	**.59**	−.13	1.00					
Access to needed information, services, and resources	(12) .03	.04	−.18	.18	**.44**	−.21	.03	.35	−.13	**−.49**	.27	1.00				
Equality of opportunity	(13) .21	−.11	.02	−.07	.21	−.18	−.07	.24	.16	−.10	.34	**.45**	1.00			
Advocacy	(14) −.24	**−.41**	.22	−.24	.24	.09	.06	.19	.08	−.16	.08	−.03	.09	1.00		
Social change	(15) **−.54**	**−.41**	**.38**	**−.39**	−.06	**.41**	.06	.19	−.10	.15	−.2 9	−.21	−.07	**.50**	1.00	
Meaningful participation in decision making	(16) **−.49**	−.26	.11	−.13	−.05	−.12	**.40**	**.45**	−.23	.12	−.23	.18	.26	.26	.26	1.00

Note: **Bold** indicates significant correlation at p < .05, and **<u>bold underlined</u>** indicates p < .01.

content, less group justice focus, and general coverage of definitions. This approach yielded a positive correlation with social change ($r = .41$, $p < .05$).

Notably, there was significant copresence of cultural and ethnic diversity and discrimination ($r = .59$, $p < .01$); equality of opportunity and access to needed information, services, and resources ($r = .45$, $p < .05$); advocacy and social change ($r = .50$, $p < .01$); and meaningful participation in decision making with poverty ($r = .40$, $p < .05$) and unemployment ($r = .45$, $p < .05$).

Discussion

Courses examined in this study, in general, were diversity oriented and provided a group justice orientation. They represented specific rather than general perspectives on social justice. There were only three cases with clearly strong bottom-up approaches, while many combined a mixed approach. The courses were issue based rather than philosophically or theoretically based. Some gaps were found between the conceptualizations of social justice reflected in the syllabi and the social justice–related terminologies promoted by NASW and CSWE. Poverty; unemployment; access to needed information, services, and resources; equality of opportunity; and meaningful participation in decision making had relatively less representation compared with discrimination, oppression, cultural and ethnic diversity, advocacy, and social change. These findings suggest that the content of social justice courses seems as diverse as the orientations of the instructors teaching these courses and fragmented rather than fully reflecting what the profession promotes.

Both NASW and EPAS in principle seem to suggest a human rights approach that balances social justice for all people and those who are socially excluded. However, as found in this study, social work education in practice may be leaning toward preferential treatment for more pressing issues or populations. This emphasis does not necessarily mean that the courses neglect the need to include all people, but it could invite critics to question its legitimacy. This pedagogical practice may help explain some recent professional controversies. In at least two instances, state-funded social work programs appeared to use the concept of social justice to rationalize what were claimed to be discriminatory practices (Office of University Communications, 2006; Ressler, 1998). The experience of some minority students in these programs is consistent with qualitative research exploring the perceptions of traditional Christians in social work (Ressler & Hodge, 2003, 2005). More specifically, respondents reported that social justice was operationalized in what was perceived to be an oppressive manner that was inconsistent with the profession's ethics.

In 2006, the National Association of Scholars (NAS), an academic organization devoted to the defense of academic freedom, petitioned the federal government regarding CSWE's social justice standards (Balch, 2006). The NAS cited a number of examples in which social justice was operationalized in a capacious manner that arguably led to discrimination against student voices. Given the lack of conceptual clarity and the potential for abuse, the NAS contended that the CSWE should either drop its social justice requirements or lose its federally granted accreditation monopoly. A renewed call was issued in 2007, in which the NAS was joined by the Foundation for Individual Rights in Education and the American Council for Trustees and Alumni (Lukianoff, Balch, & Neal, 2007).

To some degree, these controversies involve how Christian perspectives are viewed within social work. Accordingly, it may be useful to compare the various Christian models of social justice with NASW and CSWE keywords that we examined in this study. Drawn from McCormick's (2003) work, Table 4.4 presents one summary of various models of social justice. This overview is particularly pertinent because it includes a broad range of social justice theories. Included in those theories are Christian models of social justice.

While opinions may differ, the four Christian models of social justice—Christian realism, Catholic social thought, liberation theology, and biblical justice—are relatively consistent with the professional definition as reflected in the NASW and CSWE. For instance, the Christian models of social justice include concepts such increasing the power of victims; balancing power relations between groups; promoting civil, political, and economic rights; transforming oppressive economic, cultural, and political social structures; standing in solidarity with those who are poor; and upholding a preferential option for those who are poor and marginalized. These concepts would seem to be largely congruent with the professional definition as a significant overlap appears to exist.

This implies that the controversies may not be rooted in the concept of social justice itself. Rather, the central issue may be the way in which social justice is taught. If this is the case, then NAS and other actors concerned about academic freedom may be addressing the wrong issue by calling for CSWE to drop social justice content from its accrediting standards. The question may simply be that the profession's pedagogical practice in teaching social justice needs improvement in terms of how individual biases are organized and discussed in an academic setting.

TABLE 4.4   Nine Models of Justice

Utilitarianism	The just choice is that which produces the greatest good. Actions that promote the overall happiness and security of society at large are typically just.
Libertarianism	Each person should have as much autonomy or liberty as possible without violating others' freedoms. Rights to life and property should be largely free from constraints, including those imposed by government.
Social contract (John Rawls's formulation)	Justice as fairness, operationalized as a social order in which (1) each person has equal access to basic liberties and (2) social and economic inequalities are allowed to exist only when they improve the situation for those who are poor and marginalized.
Complex equality	An egalitarian and pluralist vision of justice that seeks to prevent domination and tyranny by those with power. Justice is preserved by promoting a decentralized mosaic of actors, goods, and standards.
Feminist ethic of care	Emphasizes the relational, social, and interdependent character of persons. Posits an ethic of care while calling for the expression of compassion and concern for those in need.
Christian realism	Premised upon the presence of personal and systemic sin. To counter self-interest, justice requires increasing the power of victims and working to balance power in both political and economic realms between various groups.
Catholic social thought	Promotes a broad range of civil, political, and economic rights while uncovering, confronting, and transforming oppressive and sinful social, political, and economic structures. Justice also entails standing in solidarity with, and upholding, a preferential option for the poor and marginalized
Liberation theology	Calls for the liberation of the poor from economic, cultural, and political oppression. Stresses the need for confrontational struggle against sinful social structures that foster inequality.
Biblical justice	Largely drawn from biblical precepts. Protects the poor and the victimized while working to eliminate economic, political, and religious structures that oppress and alienate them.

Source: Adapted from McCormick (2003).

Our bivariate correlation analyses indicated that syllabi that emphasize group justice tend to be diversity oriented and have narrow coverage of social justice definitions. Both diversity- and group-justice–oriented courses were likely to be issue based rather than philosophically based. Philosophically based syllabi covered a diversity of social justice definitions. Surprisingly, social change was less prevalent in diversity-oriented and group-justice syllabi and appeared more commonly in syllabi with general coverage of social justice perspectives and those that are philosophically based. Meaningful participation in decision making had lower tendency to appear in diversity-oriented syllabi. There seems to be a pattern of diversity-oriented and group-based syllabi being less diverse when it comes to introducing a wide array of perspectives on social justice from which critical thinking skills can emerge.

These findings are tentative, however, and no firm conclusions are to be drawn from this exploratory study without being confirmed by additional research. The results can only be interpreted with the limitations in mind. First, one could question the fact that course syllabi are good indicators of all the course material and what students learn from these courses (Harris, 1995). It is possible that instructors make their own interpretations of the syllabi and the delivery of the content could be conditioned by their personal teaching style. Students may interpret the same course material differently depending on their personal situations. Second, content analysis of syllabi is a common method in social work (Lacasse & Gomory, 2003; Longres & Scanlon, 2001; Strozier, 1997), but it may not be a clearly objective method because researchers' own subjective interpretations may be interjected into coding various categories (Tsang, 2001). Therefore, replication of this study with a larger sample of syllabi would be encouraged. Also, qualitative content analyses of objectives, descriptions, and assignments of the courses could help further strengthen the results.

Authors' Reflections on Transformative Social Justice Education

Social work programs incorporate social justice content into their curricula in a variety of ways. Some operationally define social justice and incorporate these definitions into their course content. Others do not define the term, yet assume that some form of "right" definitions exist as different cases of oppression and injustice are discussed in class. The former could either be too narrow in scope or too broad to the extent that it no longer is a definition. As reported in the Findings section, the latter type of approach dominates in social work education. Students in this environment would be left to wonder individually if there is a "right" way they ought to think. Oftentimes, instructors are not able to intervene as empowering educators in classroom controversies. It is common that they lean toward a particular definition that dismisses many students' interests, including some conservative ideas.

The authors find both of these cases to be approaches that exclude many helping initiatives and rather limit the transformative process for some who are at different stages of agreement with what are already established or assumed definitions of social justice. Transformative education centers on the hope that change is possible toward a vision for a more just society (Hope & Timmel, 1995, p.16). The transformative process is defined by what Paulo Freire (1972) calls praxis or reflection and action. It is a model of popular education that respects and empowers each member of the community to take ownership of the learning process and to realize the shared vision of the new society. Feminist pedagogy is rooted in these principles and encourages students to engage in "honest confrontation, dialogue, and reciprocal interaction" and "border crossings" (Crabtree & Sapp, 2003, p.132). Transformation takes place in a cooperative learning environment as students "open [their] minds and hearts so that [they] can know beyond the boundaries of what is acceptable, so that [they] can think and rethink" (hooks, 1994, p.12).

Practices of offering specific views of social justice are not considered transformative in nature and fail to empower social work students and engage them in reflective processes. While this study had limitations in terms of making any conclusive remarks on bottom-up teaching methods due to only three truly bottom-up syllabi being present in the sample, it was evident that syllabi with group-justice orientation tended to be limited in scope and leaned toward being issue based. Social work education in a highly contentious era needs to educate its students to become leaders in bridging various definitions of social justice by being able to lead transformative processes for others. Exclusion of alternative definitions can only trigger dismissal of nontraditional ideas to social work. This in turn would lead to exclusion of creative ideas and debates that could emerge through transactions among students, and this would limit transformations from taking place by not being able to share different ideas and reflecting upon them. Therefore, a mixture of introducing a wide spectrum of theoretical and philosophical ideas of social justice and a bottom-up reflective process of learning to define social justice as a way of empowering students to become active critical thinkers is suggested.

Suggestions for Teaching Social Justice

As Scanlon and Longres (2001) suggest, "only social justice movements with goals that will benefit large numbers of citizens and which recognize the shared human rights of all individuals are likely to foster widespread political engagement" (p. 442). We argue that this practice can be incorporated into transformative and cooperative learning experiences in the classroom when discussing social justice issues. As suggested by our findings, social change appears in courses that entertained a wide coverage of social justice definitions and those that incorporated theoretical and philosophical discussions on social justice. Overcoming the unease of having different ideas to permeate social work classrooms would assist the students in becoming better agents of change by not overreacting to contentious issues. Only then can actions be matched with passion that will be longer lasting for coalition building and social/community change at large.

To this end, we suggest consideration of a combined approach of an intergroup dialogue approach (Dessel, Rogge & Garlington, 2006; Nagda et al., 1999) and the "just practice" paradigm (Finn & Jacobson, 2003) in promoting a reflective transformative social justice education. After introducing the philosophical and theoretical perspectives on social justice from a wide range of disciplines (i.e., nine models of justice in Table 4), students could complete an individual paper in which they provide their own definitions of social justice. Students could conceptualize individually within the academic literature what constitutes social justice from their own perspectives. This assignment could challenge students to present the importance of social justice, define what is meant by a just society, list itemized criteria for distinguishing something that is unjust from just, assign appropriate weight to each criterion by importance, identify alternative or competing definitions, provide the target population with which one would associate the definition, and give examples of relevant issues to which one can apply this definition of social justice.

We also suggest a "transcend" method of conflict resolution (Galtung, 2000), to be applied to the process of building common student-driven social justice definitions. Students could be asked to merge all individual papers into one common class paper by the end of the semester. This process can get contentious depending on how unyielding a student is to other individual conceptualizations of social justice. Students would not only be building critical-thinking skills to generate one's own definition, but also develop negotiation and coalition-building skills to work through disagreement and contention during the process of merging the definitions with their peers. Formulating an overarching definition is a way of bringing diverse interests together to agree on how to conceptualize social justice and apply it in practice. This consensus-building process can provide a forum by which creative individual and social rights–based definitions of social justice can emerge, which in turn could suggest ideas for universal programs, comprehensive measures, and institutional approaches to combating injustices.

Transformative social justice education can bridge conflicting views on social justice by nurturing innovative ideas through reflection and critical-thinking exercises. Use of debates and structured controversy has been found to significantly enhance cooperative learning (Keller, Whittaker, & Burke, 2001; Steiner, Brzuzy, Gerdes, & Hurdle, 2003). We suggest a Designated Devil's Advocate (DDA) as an instructional tool whereby the instructor would secretly assign a student who could work in collaboration with the instructor to create an open and safe environment for discussions on controversial issues. The DDA would come to class prepared to radically oppose major presenting views offered by other students. Everyone in the classroom would be informed that there is a DDA for each week, whose role is to widen the level of foci and the coverage of social justice perspectives by presenting arguments on the other end of the spectrum for particular issues.

Conclusion

A transformative and cooperative learning process can prepare students in the classroom to meet these challenges in the real world. The DDA approach to promoting critical-thinking skills, the top-down instructors' theoretical and philosophical guidance to learning a wide array of social justice definitions from the literature, and the bottom-up process of formulating an overarching definition of social justice are suggested as ways to empower students. Only as empowered agents can they bring diverse interests together to reflect various aspects of social justice once thrown into the contentious world. In fact, the process of merging various definitions does not necessarily entail agreeing on a specific definition applicable to providing a solution to every problem. Instead, this merging is a process of transforming oneself and others to move from being captured in the narrow confines of conflict to building broad definitions of social justice by building coalitions through cooperatively creating common social justice goals. Social justice is an outcome and process for all empowered individuals as they continue to engage in this transformative and cooperative process.

References

Balch, S. H. (2006). *Political tests for aspiring social workers are unconstitutional.* Retrieved June 16, 2007, from http://www.nas.org/nas-initiatives/CSWE-initiative/cswe_agwunob i.pdf

Boucher, D., & Kelly, P. (1998). *Social justice: From Hume to Walzer.* New York: Routledge.

Bronstein, L., Berman-Rossi, T., & Winfield, B. (2002). Beyond cultural specificity: Teaching the impact of oppression on all clients' lives. *Journal of Progressive Human Services, 13*(2), 43–59.

Brookfield, S. D. (1984). *Adult learners, adult education, and the community.* New York: Teachers College Press.

Brookfield, S. D. (1990). *The skillful teacher: On technique, trust, and responsiveness in the classroom.* Oxford: Jossey-Bass Publishers.

Caputo, R. K. (2002). Social justice: Whither social work and social welfare? *Families in Society: The Journal of Contemporary Human Services, 83*(4), 341–342.

Council on Social Work Education. (2008). *Educational policy and accreditation standards.* Washington, DC: Council on Social Work Education.

Crabtree, R. D., & Sapp, D. A. (2003). Theoretical, political, and pedagogical challenges in the feminist classroom: Our struggles to walk the walk. *College Teaching, 51*(4), 131–140.

Dessel, A., Rogge, M. E., & Garlington, S. B. (2006). Using intergroup dialogue to promote social justice and change. *Social Work, 51*(4), 303–315.

Finn, J. L., & Jacobson, M. (2003). Just practice: Steps toward a new social work paradigm. *Journal of Social Work Education, 39*(1), 57–78.

Freire, P. (1972). *Pedagogy of the oppressed.* New York: Continuum.

Galtung, J. (2000). *Conflict transformation by peaceful means: The transcend method.* Geneva: United Nations Publications.

Grinnell, R. M. (1993). *Social work research and evaluation* (4th ed.). Itasca, IL: F.E. Peacock Publishers.

Harris, S. M. (1995). Ethics, legalities, professionalism, and the professor: A document analysis. *The American Journal of Family Therapy, 23*(1), 38–47.

Holody, R. (2002). Social justice and social work. *Journal of Social Work Education, 38*(1), 198–199.

Hong, P. Y. P., & Hodge, D. R. (2009). Understanding social justice in social work: A content analysis of course syllabi. *Families in Society, 90*(2), 212–219.

hooks, b. (1994). *Teaching to transgress: Education and the practice of freedom.* New York: Routledge.

Hope, A., & Timmel, S. (1995). *Training for transformation: A handbook for community workers* (Book 1). London: ITDG Publishing.

Keller, T. E., Whittaker, J. K., & Burke, T. K. (2001). Student debates in policy courses: Promoting policy practice skills and knowledge through active learning. *Journal of Social Work Education, 37*(2), 343–355.

Kolb, D. A. (1984). *Experiential learning: Experience as the source of learning and development.* Englewood Cliffs, NJ: Prentice Hall.

Lacasse, J. R., & Gomory, T. (2003). Is graduate social work education promoting a critical approach to mental health practice? *Journal of Social Work Education, 39*(3), 383–408.

Lebacqz, K. (1986). *Six theories of justice: Perspectives from philosophical and theo-logical ethics*. Minneapolis, MN: Augsburg Publishing House.

Longres, J., & Scanlon, E. (2001). Social justice and the research curriculum. *Journal of Social Work Education, 37*(3), 447–463.

Lukianoff, G., Balch, S. H., & Neal, A. D. (2007, March 14). *NAS, FIRE, ACTA challenge CSWE accrediting status*. Retrieved June 16, 2007, from http://www.nas.org/nas-initiatives/CSWE-initiative/cswe-jointly_eround2/FIRE-ACTA-NAS_re_CSWE.pdf

McCormick, P. T. (2003). Whose justice? An examination of nine models of justice. *Social Thought, 22*(2/3), 7–25.

Morris, P. M. (2002). The capabilities perspective: A framework for social justice. *Families in Society: The Journal of Contemporary Human Services, 83*(4), 365–373.

Nagda, B. A., Spearmon, M. L., Holley, L. C., Harding, S., Balassone, M. L., Moise-Swanson, D. et al. (1999). Intergroup dialogues: An innovative approach to teaching about diversity and justice in social work programs. *Journal of Social Work Education, 35*(3), 433–448.

National Association of Social Workers. (2008). *Code of ethics* (Rev. ed.). Washington, DC: Author.

O'Connor, D. L., & O'Neill, B. J. (2004). Toward social justice: Teaching qualitative research. *Journal of Teaching in Social Work, 24*(3/4), 19–33.

Office of University Communications. (2006). *Missouri state settles lawsuit with Emily Brooker*. Retrieved February 19, 2007, from http://www.news.missouristate.edu/releases/27833.htm

Patterson, F. (2004). Motivating students to work with elders: A strengths, social construction, and human rights and social justice approach. *Journal of Teaching in Social Work, 24*(3/4), 165–181.

Pelton, L. (2001). Social justice and social work. *Journal of Social Work Education, 37*(3), 433–439.

Reeser, L. C., & Leighninger, L. (1990). Back to our roots: Towards a specialization in social justice. *Journal of Sociology and Social Welfare, 17*(2), 69–87.

Reisch, M. (2002). Defining social justice in a socially unjust world. *Families in Society: The Journal of Contemporary Human Services, 83*(4), 343–354.

Ressler, L. E. (1998). When social work and Christianity conflict. In B. Hugen (Ed.), *Christianity and social work* (pp. 165–186). Botsford, CT: North American Association of Christians in Social Work.

Ressler, L. E., & Hodge, D. R. (2003). Silenced voices: Social Work and the oppression of conservative narratives. *Social Thought, 22*(1), 125–142.

Ressler, L. E., & Hodge, D. R. (2005). Religious discrimination in social work: Preliminary evidence. *Journal of Religion and Spirituality in Social Work, 24*(4), 55–74.

Saleebey, D. (1990). Philosophical disputes in social work. Social justice denied. *Journal of Sociology and Social Welfare, 27*(2), 29–39.

Scanlon, E., & Longres, J. F. (2001). Social justice and social work. A reply to Leroy Pelton. *Journal of Social Work Education, 37*(3), 441–444.

Steiner, S., Brzuzy, S., Gerdes, K., & Hurdle, D. (2003). Using structured controversy to teach diversity content and cultural competence. *Journal of Teaching in Social Work, 23*(1/2), 55–71.

Strozier, A. (1997). Group work in social work education: What is being taught? *Social Work with Groups, 20*(1), 65–77

Tsang, A. K. T. (2001). Representation of ethnic identity in North American social work literature: A dossier of the Chinese people. *Social Work, 46*(3), 229–243.

West, D. (1998). Beyond social justice and social democracy: Positive freedom and cultural rights. In D. Boucher & P. Kelly (Eds.), *Social justice: From Hume to Walzer* (pp. 232–252). New York: Routledge.

Classroom-Based Social Justice Education

CHAPTER FIVE

Hopeful, Active Realism: A Pedagogy of Critical Social Policy

Stephen Pimpare

Abstract

Simplistic views of the policymaking process can foster unrealistic expectations in future social workers about the possibility for social progress. This chapter describes one effort to confront this challenge in a core social welfare policy course for second-year MSW students. After reviewing theories of the policy process, the chapter reviews a social policy assignment designed to instill "hopeful, active realism" in students regarding their ability to affect social policy and promote social justice. Qualitative outcomes are provided.

A commitment to social justice is among the core values of the social work profession (Healy, 2001; NASW, 2008). The thorny question of "what *is* justice?" has been an issue at least since Plato's *Republic*, and it remains hotly contested territory. For the purposes of this chapter, NASW's concise definition can suffice: "Social justice is the view that everyone deserves equal economic, political and social rights and opportunities" (NASW, 2007, n.p.).

This definition is an explicitly *redistributive* conception of justice, one that is rooted in a belief that there are universal or human rights that transcend the legal obligations of government. It is a bold statement, which may be one reason that it has been contested and recently challenged as being inherently partisan (National Association of Scholars, 2007). This is no mere abstract affirmation of principle, moreover, in that the NASW *Code of Ethics* compels action in the pursuit of justice:

> Social workers should engage in social and political action that seeks to ensure that all people have equal access to the resources, employment, services, and opportunities they require to meet their basic human needs and to develop fully. Social workers should be aware of the impact of the political arena on practice and should advocate for changes in policy and legislation to improve social conditions in order to meet basic human needs and promote social justice. (NASW, 2008)

Perhaps because of the long-standing commitment of social workers to being agents of change, some have argued that social work and social workers have had a naïve understanding of policymaking (Ehrenreich, 1985; Polsky, 1991; Reisch & Andrews, 2001; Specht & Courtney, 1994; Wagner, 2000). These critics claim social work has adopted an idealized version of the Progressive Era's emphasis on the value of expertise, believing that by educating policymakers and the public to sound and just policies, genuine forward-thinking change would result. There is little in American history to suggest that this is the case. There is too much emphasis on the power of ideas alone and in the belief that what is right and just will prevail if only people *knew*. This belief is especially pernicious in social work education. Simplistic views of the policymaking process can foster unrealistic expectations in future social workers about the possibility for social progress. Social workers enter the profession and are confronted with a daunting array of formidable obstacles, including entrenched bureaucracies peopled with petty bureaucrats and a Byzantine political system. The naïveté of some social workers under these circumstances can cause feelings of discouragement and a sense of being overwhelmed, and can lead them to believe that they have failed. Too little knowledge about the complexity and irrationality of public policymaking can, in this way, contribute to burnout (Figley, 2002).

On the other hand, it is well documented that social work students already tend to prefer micropractice or casework over macrolevel analysis and advocacy (Adams, 2004; Weiss & Kaufman, 2006), and that, as Weiss, Gal, Cnaan, and Majlaglic (2002) write, "In practice most social workers do not take part in activities aimed at bringing about [social] change." (p. 60) One risks exacerbating these conditions by belaboring the obstacles they face to achieving policy progress. Moreover, while change is seldom easy, ideas *do* matter, change *is* possible, and the accumulated power of small acts of activism and resistance can achieve results. As an educator who was a student of John Dewey wrote: "Most children can face and welcome the fact that they can change their environment, that their own actions can be those of social reconstruction. On the other hand, many adults find it almost impossible to accept the potential for change that lives within them" (Rodgers, 2006, p. 1276).

Can faculty alert students to the reality that meaningful change is difficult under the best of circumstances (and it is almost never the best of circumstances) while fostering a commitment to try, nonetheless? This chapter describes one effort to confront this challenge in a core social welfare policy course for second-year MSW students, and argues that one need neither abandon a critical view of American politics and policymaking nor present a dewy-eyed view of how change happens. The intent was to help students acquire that critical view of American politics and policymaking while, at the same time, helping them to identify places in the political opportunity structure where they could exert leverage and have real chances for achieving modest successes, which they might then draw upon as inspiration over the course of their careers. That goal is here identified as a "hopeful, active realism," which draws its inspiration from research that shows that service- and experiential-learning approaches can improve students' substantive knowledge of public policy (Anderson & Harris, 2005), bolster their confidence in their ability to affect policy and their willingness to try to do so (Hamilton & Fauri, 2001; Rocha, 2000), and further enrich their commitment to the pursuit of social justice, however they might come to define it (Weiss, Gal, & Cnaan, 2005).

Theories of the Policy Process:
Normalizing Irrationality and Uncertainty

The course began by introducing students to two competing theoretical frameworks for understanding policymaking: first, what Paul Sabatier (2007) calls "the stages heuristic" and then, John Kingdon's (1995) "multiple streams" model (see also Cohen, March, & Olsen 1972).

The stages model will be generally familiar, in part because it mimics the clinical process. It is also a framework often used in public policy texts (see, e.g., Anderson, 2003; Peters, 2004; Theodoulou & Kofinis, 2004; for an overview of a broad range of other policy theories, see Sabatier, 2007; Theodoulou & Cahn, 1995). The stages model typically asserts that there is a normal and predictable process by which public policies are created and offers a linear and logical framework for tracking the policymaking process.

- The process begins with *problem definition* or *identification*, in which one of the many social conditions that are always present is singled out as requiring action. Newspaper articles, university or government studies, or dramatic public events are often the source.
- The next stage is *agenda-setting*, in which those who have the power to affect change (often lawmakers) decide to act upon the problem.
- Agenda-setting is followed by *formulation*, the actual drafting of a law, a new regulation, or an executive order.
- *Adoption* or *legitimation* comes next, which marks the formal ratification or codification of the solution settled on during the previous stage. This is often the passage and signing of a new law.
- The process is nearly complete with *implementation*, in which the executive agencies set out to enforce the new law or put the new policy practices into effect.
- Finally comes *evaluation*, in which the success or failure of the policy intervention is judged. In an ideal world, the process would then begin again, as we learn from our efforts and seek to refine our solutions to reduce the problem even further. Thus, this model is also referred to as the "policy cycle."

Note that such a policymaking world is rational, orderly, and progressive—one stage leads to another. One might find fault with this model. The stages model has the virtue of simplicity, which it achieves by sacrificing accurate descriptions of the usual functioning of the political and policymaking world. This model is useful, to be sure, especially as an initial means of explaining to students, who may be many years past their last American government or civics course, why and how new laws or rules are made. Nonetheless, as Sabatier's (2007) name for it reveals, it is best understood as a heuristic device, or as an overgeneralized way to simplify a complex process.

By contrast, Kingdon's (1995) multiple streams model describes a contingent world in which the accident of timing and the allocation of power and influence at just that moment become essential factors in describing the realistic opportunities for change. Kingdon's model is a rather postmodern and constructed framework for making sense of change (or the lack of change). Kingdon argues that policymaking forces travel in three separate "streams." The *politics* stream carries the context: which party controls which branches of government, which executive agencies are jockeying for control, which potential leaders have influence and how much influence with which actors inside and outside of government. The *solution* stream carries the policies themselves: as Kingdon observes, in virtually every office in Washington, DC, there is a shelf of reports and white papers advocating particular policy changes and indicating political actors' preferred policy solutions. Some want to reduce carbon emissions or increase welfare benefits or toughen prison sentences or privatize social security. These proposals are always available, waiting for their time to surface. In the final stream reside the policy *problems* themselves, the social conditions—income inequality, lack of health care, gun violence, and so on—that travel constantly through the stream. It is only when, argues Kingdon (1995), a "policy entrepreneur" is able to successfully join these streams in pursuit of a particular goal that change is likely to occur, and that is often only when events cause a "policy window" to open. This policy window, or window of opportunity, is created by, for example, a news report from the Congressional Budget Office, or a death attributable to negligent health care or a school shooting. Policy entrepreneurs have their favorite policies that they are constantly trying to enact, and these entrepreneurs devote their efforts to finding just the right time in the politics stream and a way to attach their solution to a problem, any problem.

An example Kingdon (1995) offers is transportation policy. Since the 1960s there have been ardent advocates for increased investment in public transportation. During the height of the environmental movement, these advocates argued that this solution could help reduce pollution. During the energy crisis of the 1970s, they offered that same solution as a remedy for scarce fuel. In the 1980s they argued that mass transit would help ease a new concern, congestion in large cities. The solution never changed, only the problem to which advocates sought to attach it. A more recent policy window was the destruction of the World Trade Center. The events of September 11 created an urgency to act in Congress, and the Capitol was soon flooded with lobbyists offering the same solutions they always offered, now arguing that they knew how to best help prevent terrorism. So, as Massachusetts Congressman Edward J. Markey told the *New York Times* (Rosenbaum, 2001):

> No self-respecting lobbyist [has not] repackaged his position as a patriotic response to the tragedy: The challenge is terrorism. The answer is re-establish telecommunications monopolies. The challenge is terrorism. The answer is to drill for oil in the Arctic Wildlife Refuge. The challenge is terrorism. The answer is a $15 billion retroactive tax break to scores of corporations.

The intent of the instructor was to juxtapose the "rational" and the "irrational" models and to encourage students to be comfortable with the latter as a legitimate expectation in policymaking. They did not need to approve of it, but they did need to make peace with the fact that irrationality must be considered when trying to explain the timing and manner in which policies change and further, to be strategic about ways in which to advocate for change.

Students' initial frustration with Kingdon's model was not insignificant and was, perhaps, partly due to the abstraction of the model, but also to the manner in which the model can pull the floor out from under one, making happenstance just as, if not more, important than sound policy, democratic support, electoral power, or other more traditional factors. Further, Kingdon's model upends the usual belief about the ways those more familiar policy stages progress, since in Kingdon's world, solutions often exist before problems are identified. It is nonetheless important to normalize chaos and uncertainty in pursuit of a sophisticated, contingent understanding of policymaking, and to moderate expectations about the reasons and ways in which change comes to pass.

Theory into Action: An Exercise in Policy Analysis and Change

With Kingdon's model as a foundation, the exercise in policy analysis and change began with a review of the basic institutions and actors in the American political system, in which students were asked to focus on a policy problem that was of particular interest to them, whether at the agency, municipal, state, or national level. Their choices mirrored their diversity, and included Medicare Part D; domestic violence among immigrant women and the Violence Against Women Act; public funding for private schools; the genocide in Darfur; changes in welfare law after the 1996 reform; the food stamp shelter deduction; laws regarding the informal job market for day laborers; policies affecting young men and women aging out of foster care; administrative supports for overburdened caseworkers; the affordability of higher education in poor communities of color; and other policy problems. Because students chose the policy area themselves, the instructor hoped that it would be easier to sustain their interest and passion throughout the course, a hope that seems to have been borne out by the experience.

Focusing solely on their policy, students were then asked to move through a series of increasingly more applied and engaged assignments. Their first task was to craft a five-page position-neutral policy brief, as if they were legislative assistants for an elected representative. This presented them with the challenge of separating themselves from their own biases and policy preferences, since they were asked to assume that (a) the instructor was their boss (e.g., a city council person, congressperson, state legislator, mayor, agency head); (b) their supervisor possessed no knowledge of the issue; (c) there was an impending vote that would require them to stake out a position; and (d) they needed to decide both the best policy approach and the wisest political position. Students were reminded that *they* were not elected, and therefore it was not their role to advocate for one position over another, but rather to gather as much information as they could and present it so that the elected official might make a fully informed decision. This was difficult for many students, and more than a few went through several rounds of revision before the instructor was satisfied that they had laid out the issue clearly, comprehensively, and in a neutral manner.

Students were then asked to interview any person directly affected by their policy or anyone actively engaged in advocacy or service delivery around the issue. After overcoming their initial trepidation about approaching a stranger for an interview, they emerged with an even more sophisticated understanding of the policy issue. This exercise also provided opportunities for the class to discuss effective interviewing techniques, from the virtues of asking general or specific questions to ways in which to follow up in a manner that elicits the desired information. While the instructor's experience with ethnographic research facilitated this discussion, any good qualitative research methods text could help other instructors guide students (see, e.g., Holstein & Gubrium, 1995; Patton, 2001; more generally, for many of these exercises, Kush, 2004, proved a valuable resource. Some useful worksheets from the book entitled *Your Personal Advocacy Inventory,* "Critical Pieces of Information About Your Elected Officials," "Personal Legislative Agenda," "Bill Analysis Worksheet," and "Preparing for the Opposition," are available online at http://www.josseybass.com/go/one houractivist).

Using the research they had amassed and the knowledge they had acquired, students were then asked to write a letter to one of their own representatives and to advocate a particular action: they were finally allowed to stake out a position. As one might expect, that position was more thoughtful and more nuanced than it had been when they began and, in at least two cases, was a very different opinion than the one with which they began.

Students were given one week to follow their letter with a telephone call, and instructed to request a meeting with the official or one of his or her staff members. Almost none of the students initially believed that anything would come of the telephone call, especially those contacting

U.S. House members or senators. This presented an opportunity to talk about constituent service and its importance for reelection. These activities also created space to discuss the value that they now had as experts in the area and to explain that their expertise was something truly useful that elected officials need and welcome. All but one were successful in their efforts, although most of the meetings were with staff members, not with the officials themselves, with the exception of one student meeting with a city council person and one with an agency director. These meetings with staff persons provided the opportunity to examine the crucial role of staff, and illustrated the manner in which staff interacted with their elected officials. The tactic used throughout this course was to introduce the policy literature not for its own sake, but as a means toward gaining insight into students' firsthand experiences.

Students were surprised that they were able to arrange in-person meetings; most were doubly surprised that they were taken seriously. All of the students, to one degree or another, reported that they felt a new sense of their power to reach out to policymakers and a faith in their ability to have their voices heard. Most students indicated that they would make a habit of calling their officials' offices and trying to arrange meetings with their staff when there is an issue they wanted to address. Informal and unsystematic follow-up by the instructor with students from this class has revealed that a few have, in fact, done just that.

The class also discussed the role of media and mass public opinion in policymaking, and the ways in which to best present ideas and arguments so that they would be attractive to an editor. They next were asked to craft an op-ed article or a letter to the editor, and to try to publish it in any appropriate print or online source. The class discussed the importance of targeting the right outlet for publication and reviewed ways of framing ideas for maximum reach and effect. Here students were less successful (as was to be expected), but one student published an op-ed in a small, local newspaper; two placed articles in their agencies' newsletters; and a fourth was able to post an entry on a blog sympathetic to his issue.

The students' final task was to communicate their key learning either about the substance of their issue or about the process of advocating for change to any of their communities, whether neighborhood, workplace, or school. The student focusing on Darfur and Sudan became a leader in a universitywide organization that sponsored teach-ins on the issue, organized protests in New York's Central Park, and ultimately helped to bring busloads of students to a national protest in Washington, DC. Other students engaged in more modest education campaigns. One distributed flyers helping students understand the particulars of the new Medicare drug benefit and providing resources that could be used to find information that would help students offer knowledgeable advice to clients. Another student spoke with the school's student government leaders to educate them about her issue, and another produced a professional-looking brochure that included the contact information for the relevant staff person at the U.S. congressperson's office, urging recipients of the brochure to call and make their voices heard.

Outcomes and Conclusion

Throughout this process, the class focused attention on case studies about the timing of, reasons behind, and ways in which policy change occurs, as well as accomplishments that individuals and small groups historically can and cannot effectively achieve. Over the course of the semester, students were continually asked to evaluate their own experiences against Sabatier's (2007) and Kingdon's (1995) academic theories. Students emerged with the hoped-for acceptance of the fact that influencing policy was difficult, frustrating, and almost inevitably slow, but that with perseverance and a thoughtful, hard-nosed evaluation of the places in which they could find spaces to communicate and to cajole, they could, in fact, create change.

For many students, their accomplishments were significant and even unexpected. One student was offered, and accepted, a full-time job by the executive director of the not-for-profit organization he interviewed because the executive director was so impressed with his knowledge and commitment. Another testified before a public hearing of his town council, and is now involved in the community's efforts to solve the problem on which he focused. One student has been systematically updating the Wikipedia entry on his policy area while simultaneously working to change the rules of his local food co-op so that it better serves food stamp recipients. Yet another convinced her agency to have monthly town hall–style policy meetings during staff lunch breaks, while another organized on-site training workshops at her agency.

During the oral presentations to the class, in which students were asked to discuss the substance of their policy area or the process of becoming an advocate, almost all chose to discuss some aspect of their activism. Yet perhaps because their policy knowledge was acquired in pursuit of another goal, they emerged with a more sophisticated, substantive knowledge than, it seemed to the instructor, had students in previous semesters without this active learning component. While this is merely impressionistic, it does seem to bear out previous findings that such classroom techniques, as noted previously, can improve students' policy knowledge, bolster their confidence, and further enrich their commitment to the pursuit of social justice, however they might come to define it (Anderson & Harris, 2005; Hamilton & Fauri, 2001; Rocha, 2000; Weiss, Gal, & Cnaan, 2005).

Student evaluations of the course included comments, with some frequency, on the difficulty of the material, but also recognized a new kind of understanding as a result. Qualitative comments included:

> Challenging and demanding . . . The need to advocate for policy change was made clear, along with realities of making such changes.

> I will always remember one of the lecture notes that said "too often social workers presume that policy change merely requires sound policy analysis . . . it's merely a matter of showing people the evidence." That was my thinking until this course.

Some responded favorably to the format of the course:

> I liked the structure of the assignments, which required us to submit small assignments throughout the semester as opposed to writing one long paper at the end.

But more importantly, many students reported a new feeling of personal and even shared empowerment, as this sample reveals:

> I also really liked the hands-on nature of the course. I found the experience quite empowering. I also enjoyed the last two classes. The other students really shined in their presentations. I would have liked to have heard more about their projects throughout the semester.

These are, one hopes, lessons that they have internalized and ones that they will carry with them for the rest of their lives as social workers and as citizens. It is worth noting that while students' narrative course evaluations were longer, more detailed, and more attuned to the *process* of their learning than in the previous semester, the quantitative evaluations showed no significant difference. The results of this limited experience suggest that further efforts, and more systematic evaluation of results, are warranted.

This model of teaching policy advocacy may not be adaptable on the whole. It can, however, help others think about ways in which to incorporate pedagogies of active learning in social policy courses in order to give MSW students the following: (a) a realistic, critical *understanding* of the actual operations of the political world; (b) the *tools* with which they can make their voices heard; and (c) the practical, personal *experience* that can help instill confidence that they can affect change, with the acceptance that it will rarely be quick and seldom easy.

References

Adams, P. (2004). Classroom assessment and social welfare policy: Addressing challenges to teaching and learning. *Journal of Social Work Education, 40*(1), 121–142.

Anderson, D. K., & Harris, B. M. (2005). Teaching social welfare policy: A comparison of two pedagogical approaches. *Journal of Social Work Education, 41*(3), 511–526.

Anderson, J. E. (2003). *Public policymaking.* Boston: Houghton Mifflin.

Cohen, M., March, J., & Olsen, J. (1972). A garbage can model of organizational choice. *Administrative Science Quarterly, 17*(1), 1–25.

Ehrenreich, J. H. (1985). *The altruistic imagination: A history of social work and social policy in the United States.* Ithaca, NY: Cornell University Press.

Figley, C. (2002). *Treating compassion fatigue.* New York: Routledge.

Hamilton, D., & Fauri, D. (2001). Social workers' political participation: Strengthening the political confidence of social work students. *Journal of Social Work Education, 37*(2), 321–332.

Healy, L. M. (2001). *International social work: Professional action in an interdependent world.* New York: Oxford University Press.

Holstein, J. A., & Gubrium, J. F. (1995). *The active interview.* New York: Sage.

Kingdon, J. W. (1995). *Agendas, alternatives, and public policies.* New York: Harper Collins.

Kush, C. (2004). *The one-hour activist: The 15 most powerful actions you can take to fight for the issues and candidates you care about.* San Francisco: Jossey-Bass.

National Association of Scholars. (2007). *The scandal of social work education.* Retrieved September 14, 2007, from http://www.nas.org/nas-initiatives/CSWE-initiative/soswe_scandal/scandal_soc-work-ed_11sep07.pdf

National Association of Social Workers. (2007). *Issue fact sheets: Social justice.* Retrieved September 13, 2007, from http://www.socialworkers.org/pressroom/features/issue/peace.asp

National Association of Social Workers. (2008). *Code of ethics* (Rev. ed.). Washington, DC: Author.

Patton, M. Q. (2001). *Qualitative research and evaluation methods.* New York: Sage.

Peters, B. G. (2004). *American public policy: Promise and performance.* Washington, DC: CQ Press.

Polsky, A. J. (1991). *The rise of the therapeutic state.* Princeton, NJ: Princeton University Press.

Reisch, M., & Andrews, J. (2001). *The road not taken: A history of radical social work in the United States.* Ann Arbor, MI: Sheridan Books.

Rocha, C. J. (2000). Evaluating experiential teaching methods in a policy practice course: The case for service learning to increase political participation. *Journal of Social Work Education, 36*(1), 53–63.

Rodgers, C.R. (2006). " 'The turning of one's soul'—Learning to teach for social justice: The Putney Graduate School of teacher education (1950–1964)." *Teachers College Record, 108*(7), 1266–1295.

Rosenbaum, D. E. (2001, December 3). Since Sept 11, lobbyists use new pitches for old pleas. *New York Times.*

Sabatier, P. A. (Ed.). (2007). *Theories of the policy process.* Boulder, CO: Westview.

Specht, H., & Courtney, M. E. (1994). *Unfaithful angels: How social work has abandoned its mission.* New York: Free Press.

Theodoulou, S. Z., & Cahn, M. A. (1995). *Public policy: The essential readings.* Boulder, CO: Westview.

Theodoulou, S. Z., & Kofinis, C. (2004). *The art of the game: Understanding American public policy making.* Belmont, CA: Thomson-Wadsworth.

Wagner, D. (2000). *What's love got to do with it? A critical look at American charity.* New York: New Press.

Weiss, I., & Kaufman, R. (2006). Educating for social action: An evaluation of the impact of a fieldwork training program. *Journal of Policy Practice, 51*(1), 5–30.

Weiss, I., Gal, J., & Cnaan, R. A. (2005). Does social work education have an impact on social policy preferences? A three-cohort study. *Journal of Social Work Education, 41*(1), 29–47

Weiss, I., Gal, J., Cnaan, R., & Majlaglic, R. (2002). What kind of social policy do social work students prefer? A comparison of students in three countries. *International Social Work, 45*(1), 59–81.

CHAPTER SIX

An Investigation of Transformative Education Theory as a Basis for Social Justice Education in a Research Methods Course

Julie Schroeder
Rene Pogue

Abstract

This chapter reports a study that investigates the merits of transformative education theory as a framework for both planning social justice education activities and evaluating student learning outcomes in a graduate research-methods course. The chapter provides an overview of transformative education perspectives and theoretical principles that are applied in the design of a comparative study of educational activities intended to accomplish social justice education objectives. Results of the study show significant differences when learning experiences are planned with transformative learning principles in mind. Implications for using transformative learning theory as a basis for planning and evaluating activities for social justice education are considered.

Commitments to social justice and to social change are hallmarks that distinguish social work from other helping professions. These commitments are formally acknowledged in the profession's ethical code (NASW, 2008) and in standard requirements for accredited social work education (CSWE, 2008). Consequently, understanding methods for inducing commitments to these ideals is essential to teaching, training, and socializing professional social workers.

In this chapter, we provide an overview of transformative education perspectives and theoretical principles as applied in the design of a comparative study of educational activities intended to accomplish aims of social justice education. Further, we describe the design and outcomes of an investigation into the merits of applying transformative education theory as a framework for both planning social justice education activities and evaluating student learning outcomes within a research course.

Review of Literature

In social work literature, the trend in planning and evaluating social justice education is generally limited to designing an activity that resonates with general concepts of social justice or an element in formal social justice theory. This approach appears to stimulate creativity in teaching social justice concepts and provides one basis for determining positive outcomes of those efforts. However, as foundation for designing, planning, and evaluating educational activities with social justice aims in mind, general definitions of social justice or discrete elements in social justice theory provide an insufficient framework within which to investigate the degree that teaching may reach students' interior lives in ways that generate the intrinsic motivations desirable in professional social work. Transformative education theory holds more promise for adding dimension to our knowledge and ability to exact desired learning outcomes that encourage intrinsic motivations that lead social work professionals to actively seek social justice and to engage in just social work practice.

TRANSFORMATIVE FRAMEWORK FOR SOCIAL JUSTICE EDUCATION

A primary expectation in transformational learning theory is that educational experiences can change students' perspectives of themselves and their world in ways that lead to commitment to social justice and action for just social change. Given these ideals, transformative learning theory is identified as a particularly fitting framework for planning and evaluating educational experiences designed to promote the aims of social justice education (Brown, 2004, 2005, 2006; Hughes & Sherry, 1997; Nagda, Gurin, & Lopez, 2003; Pearson, 1999).

In the literature on transformational learning, all roads appear to lead to Jack Mezirow (1981), whose early conceptualization of *perspective transformation* corresponds to Habermas's (1970) *emancipatory action* learning domain, and Freire's (1970) *conscientization* concept. Building on these ideas and the premise that all learning is change but not all learning is transformative, Mezirow and Associates (1990, 2000) developed a richly textured education theory which posits that the transformed in transformational learning is a *"frame of reference* which encompasses cognitive, conative, and emotional components and is composed of two dimensions: *habits of the mind* and *a point of view"* (Mezirow, 1997, p. 5, emphasis added). According to Mezirow (1997; Mezirow & Associates 2000), when theory is translated to transforming educational practice, the required ingredients are experience, critical reflection, and rational discourse (see also Brown, 2005; Boyd, 1991; Cranton, 1994, 2000; Kegan, 1994).

To create transformative learning experiences, certain suppositions and methods have been drawn from theory. For instance, Mezirow (1997) believes that an emotionally charged "disorienting dilemma" that causes learners to lose their bearings set by an existing frame of reference is essential as a catalyst for transformative learning (see also McGregor, 2004). There are others who view transformative learning as a developmental process rather than a combustible experience. Those who hold to a developmental perspective theorize that the key ingredient in transformative education is critical self-reflection that takes place in an environment where all students are free to examine the constraining habits of mind and points of view that limit their freedom as actors against social injustice in the world (Baumgartner, 2001; Daloz, 1999). Those who take an integrative approach believe that the critical element in transformational learning is guided rational discourse, by which students process educational experiences that are sufficiently charged—emotionally or psychically—to reach students' interior lives, the places where intuition, spirituality, and yearnings for social justice reside (Dirkx, 1998; Kovan & Dirkx, 2003; Taylor, 2000). Regardless of which element is emphasized, most theorists agree that transformational learning requires a safe and accepting circumstance wherein all learners are fully free to learn at a transforming level.

Because of its humanistic and humanitarian orientation, transformational learning theory is well suited as a framework for social justice education design and evaluation (Mertens, 1999). When distinct theoretical perspectives are holistically considered, the essential elements of transformative learning clearly emerge to include experience, critical self-reflection, and rational discourse. While preference or circumstances may lead to emphasizing one element over others, consideration of all is advised in design and planning curricula and educational activities. In addition to serving as a valuable tool for planning social justice education, the essential elements in transformational learning theory provide a framework against which to test the depth, breadth, and nature of social justice education.

THEORETICAL FRAMEWORKS OF SOCIAL JUSTICE

Social and economic justice are touted as cornerstones of professional social work (CSWE, 2008; NASW, 2008). In theory, the two are treated not as interchangeable, but as kin. In fact, the relationship is a dependent one because social justice depends on economic justice, but economic justice alone does not ensure the fullest measure of social justice.

Rawls's (1971) theory of justice is frequently favored in social work literature for its emphasis on distributive justice as it explains reasons for and ways in which social and economic injustice help to marginalize some while other prosper (Morris, 2002; Reisch, 2002; Van Wormer, 2003). Merton's (1957) justice theory takes another road, emphasizing ways in which individuals form ideas about what is and is not just by a comparison of one's own lot in life with others, and seeks to evaluate perceived justice or injustice (Jasso, 2000). By its nature, Merton's theory gives clues to the means by which human beings' habits of mind and points of view about social justice are formed and open to revision. When ideas about the core elements of social and economic justice are teased apart, a typology of justice emerges for a fuller expression of social justice that includes protective, corrective, restorative, distributive, and representational justice (Chatterjee & D'Aprix, 2002). In simple terms, all explanations of social justice begin with *suum cuique*, "giving everyone his own or his due," or "to each his own" (Tsanoff, 1956, p. 12). At a purely sentient, intuitive level, an acceptable understanding of social justice is that it is about fairness.

For this study, we view our teaching, research, and service through the lens of these and other ideas about social justice. Social justice ideals provide the stimulus for not only this study, but our whole approach to satisfying expectations of the academy and of the social work profession. Our social justice orientation adds passion to our work and makes us advocates in our roles as scholars, teachers, helpers, and learners.

VALUE ADDED TO SOCIAL JUSTICE EDUCATION

Whether it is integrated or strategically placed, social justice instruction can be easily located in curricula design and pedagogical methods in many masters-level social work courses. However, integrating social justice into research courses is made more difficult by CSWE requirements that allow only one methods course. This allowance leaves little room for layering social justice issues into research courses as a place where students are free to explore their "habits of mind" or "points of view" about anything other than ways to best deal with a course that most would rather not take. For many students, learning research methods tends to be a disorienting dilemma in and of itself. Because we are committed to creating opportunities for students' transformational learning and growth, we experimented with layering social justice issues—content nearer to the locus of most students' native humanitarian motivations—into the design, planning, and evaluation of a research course. Beyond enriching the course, we speculated that students would become less resistant and more engaged in learning research if the connection between the subject of the course and the object of the profession were successfully combined. In other words, we developed a way in which to teach research methods using a disorienting dilemma of a different sort, one that could result in serious critical self-reflection and rational discourse with the goal of transformative learning.

DESIGN ISSUES

The social work research-methods course that served as the "treatment condition" for this study was designed, planned, and executed by the first author of this chapter. Theoretical foundations were selected by the coauthor. Analysis of outcomes was a conjoint process. A primary intention in course design was to create conditions in a research-methods class in which transformational learning was possible. To accomplish this primary aim, the design required planning for a sustainable, emotionally engaging situation—if not a completely disorienting dilemma—wherein students would have a textured cognitive, behavioral, and conative learning experience that integrated a set of research course objectives with exposure to social justice issues and constructs. To accomplish this aim, the death penalty was selected as a social justice issue and problem against which to simulate and learn research methods.

Using the death penalty in this context created opportunity for a disorienting dilemma. It further supplied a background against which educational experience and outcomes might stand in bolder relief against the magnificent life-and-death stakes and multilayered social justice issues attendant to the problem. By design, the research-methods course provided enriched opportunities for students to accomplish a variety of course objectives, including learning about (a) the importance of theory and ways in which theoretical content is used to develop measurement instruments; (b) research design; (c) ethics and informed consent; (d) development of a pretest/posttest educational intervention; (e) becoming research participants; (f) data collection, analysis, and interpretation; and (g) rational discourse about the research process and the social justice issues at hand, as well as critical reflection about students' own frames of reference and points of view about capital punishment.

A TRANSFORMATIVE PLAN

An overview. For three consecutive years, the course plan was applied and data collected in a foundation-level social work research-methods course at a large research-extensive university in the southern United States. By design, the planned activities that were implemented in the course required students to assume roles of both researcher and research participant/subject. Assuming both roles created a desirable educational condition, or experience, in which students' personal frames of reference about capital punishment might be challenged. Further, focusing research practice simulations and follow-up activities on capital punishment added a potentially disorienting dimension to class activities for many students and provided all a mechanism for understanding and integrating research and policy. Designing activities to occur both independently and in groups was intended to capitalize on Merton's (1957) ideas about the power of reference groups in social constructions.

The educational plan began with an introduction to solid theoretical foundations provided to us by legal scholars. Theoretical constructs added to an understanding of why people support or oppose the death penalty and also added to critical self-reflection and guided rational discourse necessary for transformative learning. Further, exposing students to theoretical constructs helped them understand the importance of survey questions that integrated content representing domain in legal justice theory and practice: deterrence, retribution, cost, innocence, and adversarial and appellate system issues. Exploring these issues laid the foundation for the educational intervention that students received while acting as research subjects.

Disorienting conditions. When students assumed the role of research subject, each went through the process of informed consent, completed a twenty-item Likert-scale pretest survey of attitudes toward capital punishment and took part in a one-hour lecture aided by PowerPoint slides that covered the history of capital punishment, the theoretical issues, and a variety of social justice issues, including ways that race, poverty, inadequate legal representation, prosecutorial misconduct, geography, cost, age, gender, and the race of the victim all played vital roles in identifying those who are charged with and tried for a capital offense. The educational lecture was considered the first educational intervention in the treatment condition. Following the one-hour (treatment) condition, each student assumed the role of research subject and completed the posttest and a thirteen-item Likert-type survey with short-answer questions about the value of the teaching method, the capital punishment content, and questions about the origin of each student's thoughts and beliefs about capital punishment. The instructor developed all instruments.

In the following class period, students assumed the researcher role and discussed a method to develop the data set used for data analysis and coded each instrument. The instructor entered and analyzed the survey data and developed a PowerPoint presentation of the results. Students were presented with the findings of their study and were guided through periods of critical self-reflection and rational discourse about the research findings and their frames of reference regarding the death penalty.

From the first class meeting, the instructor controlled conditions and modeled behavior in ways to create an open and expressive environment where students could be free to learn not only about research and social justice, but about themselves and their relationship to others and the world at large. Investigation of results of our educational plan to teach about social justice in the context of a social work research-methods course followed two paths. The first avenue was a quantitative investigation that involved implementing research methods as content and practice experience as well as data useful to the analysis of the results of our instructional plan. The second avenue was a qualitative inquiry that relied on instructor documentation. A detailed design plan can be found in the Appendix.

Quantitative Inquiry

METHODS

Participants. Participants were 177 masters-level social work students enrolled at a large public university in the southern United States. Informed consent was obtained from all participants. The consent form indicated that the study's purpose was to educate students on pretest/posttest research design and on the issue of capital punishment. Students were informed that they could choose not to participate in the study or withdraw at any time without penalty. Ninety-eight (55%) participants were in their foundation (first) year of the social work program, while seventy-one (40%) were in their advanced (second) year. This information was not available for eight (5%) of participants.

One hundred ten participants composed the experimental group, and sixty-seven were in the comparison group. The mean ages for these groups were 29.48 years and 28.79 years, respectively. Other demographic information was collected from participants in the areas of gender, religion, marital status, and political preference. Complete demographic information was not available for all participants because some failed to complete all or part of the demographic sheet.

Procedures. Participants' knowledge, attitudes, and beliefs about capital punishment were measured using a survey designed specifically for use in this study. The same survey was used for the pretest and posttest. This survey consisted of twenty statements assessing five domains: deterrence, retribution, cost, innocence, and system issues. Participants were asked to rate each statement on a scale from one (strongly disagree) to five (strongly agree).

Reliability of this survey as both a pretest measure and posttest measure was calculated using an alpha coefficient. Results indicated that this survey is reliable for use in research (α = .7872 and .8391, respectively). As a result of the reliability analysis, the researchers determined that the survey could be used as a cumulative measure; therefore, a total-score variable was calculated for each participant.

The pretest/posttest educational intervention was undertaken using foundation and advanced MSW students in sections of research and policy classes. Comparison data (posttest only) was taken from students in research, policy, differential diagnosis, and practice classes. Thus, participants in the experimental group completed the same survey both before and after the intervention, while participants in the comparison group completed the survey only once and did not receive any part of the intervention.

Members of the experimental group completed a thirteen-item exit survey that questioned students on the value of the intervention in assisting them in better understanding pretest/posttest research design and whether they (a) thought they would be able to implement this type of design in a practice setting, (2) enjoyed this type of teaching method, (3) enjoyed the capital punishment content, and (4) learned enough to educate others on the issues surrounding the death penalty. Students were also queried about ways in which their views had been developed, including friends and family, the media, other classes, and religious beliefs. Lastly, students were asked about theoretical arguments that most influenced any change in their attitudes about the death penalty.

RESULTS

Pretest/posttest results. In order to assess whether or not the experimental and comparison groups were alike in their knowledge, attitudes, and beliefs about capital punishment prior to the implementation of the intervention, an independent samples t-test was calculated using total scores for the pretests of both groups. No significant difference was found between the means of the two groups (t = 3.831, df = 173, p = .000).

A paired samples t-test was used to test the effect of the intervention on the experimental group. The mean total scores for this group dropped from 55.6 on the pretest to 49.0 on the posttest, a difference that was found to be statistically significant ($t = 10.834$, $df = 102$, $p = 0.000$). Further analysis was used to compare the comparison group pretest scores ($M = 54.9$) and the experimental group posttest scores ($M = 49.1$). Once again, this change in scores was found to be significant ($t = 3.831$, $df = 173$, $p = 0.000$). These results suggest that strategies for teaching about social justice in the context of a research course led to positive transformational learning gains with respect to students' points of reference (Mezirow & Associates, 1990) about the death penalty.

Exit survey. Exit survey responses were gathered from seventy-nine students. Of those students, 84.4% ($n = 65$) agreed or strongly agreed that this learning experience assisted them in better understanding pretest/posttest research design. Some 74% ($n = 57$) of students agreed or strongly agreed that they learned enough from this exercise to be able to implement this type of design in a practice setting. As many as 86% ($n = 68$) of students agreed or strongly agreed when asked if they enjoyed this type of learning activity. In all, 89% ($n = 70$) of students either agreed or strongly agreed that they learned a great deal about the issue of capital punishment. Finally, nearly two-thirds of students (60.6%, $n = 48$) agreed or strongly agreed that as a result of this learning experience, they could educate others on the issues surrounding the death penalty.

Just over one-third (34.2%, $n = 26$) reported that prior to this learning experience they had held their views about capital punishment for from less than one year to ten years. Only 16% ($n = 12$) stated that they had held their views throughout their entire lives. Just over 10% of students (12%, $n = 9$) reported not knowing how long they had held their current views. Just 4% of students ($n = 3$) had developed their views since their undergraduate programs. Finally, 16% ($n = 12$) stated that they had been previously undecided prior to this learning experience.

When questioned about the influences that were responsible for their views on the death penalty, 31% ($n = 23$) were influenced by friends and family, 49% ($n = 37$) were influenced by the media, 11% ($n = 8$) cited religious beliefs, 23% ($n = 17$) cited other college coursework, and 12% ($n = 9$) reported developing their ideas about the issues based on their own belief systems.

When questioned about the issues surrounding the death penalty that surprised them the most, 62% ($n = 48$) reported being most surprised about the costs involved from arrest through execution of offenders. This was followed by the problem of innocence (21%, $n = 16$)

and the misconduct within the adversarial system (18%, n = 14). Finally, when we asked students if they thought this was a worthwhile teaching method, 89% (n = 69) of students responded with agree or strongly agree. Some 91% of students (n = 72) either agreed or strongly agreed that other social work students should have access to this information.

Against education theories (Daloz, 1999; Dirkx, 1998) that advise about the importance of relying on students' experience, these results suggest positive learning gains that were both satisfying and meaningful to them. Further, the results raise questions about the power of reference groups (Merton, 1957) in the process of students' formulating and changing their opinions regarding the death penalty. Results of the empirical investigation are insufficient to draw conclusions. However, these results do raise interesting questions.

Qualitative Inquiry

The qualitative aspects in this study were applied as the course unfolded over three years. To the degree to which coinvestigators were able, accepted qualitative research methods (Cresswell, 1998; Marshall & Rossman, 1999) were applied in design, data collection, and analysis. Because the qualitative aspects of the study developed over time, we acknowledge limitations in method of this aspect of the study. However, we believe the findings have an added measure of trustworthiness beyond an anecdotal level.

Qualitative data were collected over the three-year course of the investigation. These data were in the form of the instructor's record of (a) students' participation in class research practice simulations, (b) content of dialogue with students during lecture periods, (c) response content contained in periods of guided critical self-reflection and rational discourse, (d) instructors' behavioral observations, and (e) follow-up work with and observations of select students. These data were processed and discussed with the study coauthor to add to the trustworthiness of the data analysis and interpretation (Cresswell, 1998; Marshall & Rossman, 1999). In each of the three years of the plan, the observable results of each educational activity supplied confirming evidence of transformative learning outcomes.

For all three years, the qualitative findings appeared to support the significant change identified in quantitative measures. Students reflected on their initial opinion, or lack thereof, about the death penalty and ways that the intervention had helped them to crystallize their points of view about the issue. Interestingly, one of the students had served on a capital jury that had sentenced an offender to death. She stated that she had come into this classroom exercise as a devout proponent of capital punishment, but as a result of the intervention, began to seriously question her own beliefs and her own role in that death vote. She later became graduate assistant to this first author and coauthored an article on death penalty mitigation that was published in the journal *Social Work* and presented at the National Organization of Forensic Social Workers' annual conference on the same topic. (Schroeder & Bordelon, 2002; Schroeder, Guin, Pogue, & Bordelon, 2006). The trajectory of this student's learning seems to confirm theoretical assumptions (Daloz, 1999; Dirkx, 1998) and notions about the power of capitalizing on students' own experience in transformative processes.

Another student became so interested in the topic that she also became a research assistant and provided the initial analysis of the data for this study. After the final presentation of this course material, yet another student became this first author's graduate assistant. He went on to law school following graduation from the MSW program. He also played a pivotal role in the following outcome to result from this teaching method. Another student requested that the first author supervise her independent study with the goal of writing a grant to garner funding to study the impact of exoneration on former death row inmates. In each of these cases, students confirmed observations that their respective pursuits were sparked by engagement in the planned transformational learning experience. The changes in students' attitudes are consistent with outcomes that theories predict about the ways reference groups may work in learning situations surrounding social justice (Merton, 1957) and in transformative learning that produces conative learning outcomes that move learners to act (Freire, 1998; Mezirow & Associates, 2000).

Evidence of the effectiveness of theory-based educational design and potency of transformational experience continued to follow when, inspired by participation in the research methods class, a group of students petitioned the dean of the school of social work to request a corrections course be developed by the instructor. In response, a course titled Social Work and Corrections was developed and taught. While the course included a variety of content relating to corrections, several weeks of reading and discussion were dedicated to capital punishment. Serendipitously, the theater department at the university was sponsoring *The Exonerated*, a Broadway play about death row inmates exonerated with DNA evidence. The corrections class took an active role in planning a variety of activities that promoted university and community discourse on the issues of the death penalty and wrongful conviction. We were greatly honored to have as our guest Kirk Bloodsworth, the first death row inmate freed via DNA. He lectured to both the research-methods class (following the educational intervention) and the corrections class. As a result, the corrections class became so moved by the issues facing persons who are exonerated yet receive no compensation for their lost lives that the graduate assistant mentioned in the previous paragraph took the lead and, with the assistance of the entire corrections class, worked with the Innocence Project New Orleans in advocating for and witnessing the passage of a compensation statute in the state legislature. These incidences are a representative sample of the observable outcomes of transformative process through which students were liberated from constraining frames of reference and, in turn, became capable liberators and agents for social change and justice.

Discussion

The data suggest that prior to the learning experience, there was no significant difference in attitudes toward capital punishment between social work students in the intervention group and their peer counterparts. However, following the learning experience, support for the death penalty dropped significantly in the intervention group compared with their peer counterparts. This suggests that creating a disorienting dilemma assisted students in losing their bearings set by an existing frame of reference. In turn, a significant change in attitudes followed students' freely participating in repeated opportunities for critical self-reflection and guided rational discourse.

Qualitative and anecdotal evidence discussed earlier describes that students gravitated toward opportunities to pursue social justice through social change efforts, which confirmed for us that some students' learning experience had, indeed, been transformative. We believe using transformational learning theory in the course design, planning, and evaluation served several critical purposes. First, applying theory to course design and planning led us to creatively integrate social justice education with research methods; in turn, emphasizing the link between social justice and social work research helped to buffer the common fears and resistance that social work students typically have toward research courses. Second, casting every student in roles as both researcher and research participant created an encouraging condition for examining their most deeply held views about a variety of social justice issues. Third, repeated opportunities to participate freely in critical self-reflection and rational discourse helped create conditions that, in one respect, minimized students fear and resistance to research course content and, in another respect, opened doors to transformative outcomes. In some cases, our taking a transformative approach to teaching and learning moved many students to push them-selves farther than they had ever expected about an issue that they never expected to address in a social work research-methods class. Many were motivated to advocate for policy change in the state legisla-ture and, through their work, made it possible for persons who had suffered wrongful arrest, conviction, and imprisonment for a murder they did not commit to gain the right to compensation from the state that sentenced them to die.

Conclusion

The apparent success of our effort leads us to conclude that further investigation into the benefits of using transformative educational the-ory as a basis for designing, planning, and evaluating social justice edu-cation is warranted. Given the highest aspirations for higher education to benefit all of mankind, it seems particularly worthwhile to employ teaching methods that, by nature, help students fulfill the highest call-ings of their chosen vocations. The role that social justice education can play in accomplishing these aims is certain enough to stimulate continued exploration of ways to best achieve those noblest aims.

References

Baumgartner, L. M. (2001). An update on transformative learning. In S. B. Merriam (Ed.), *New directions for adult and continuing education* (Vol. 89, pp. 15–24). San Francisco: Jossey-Bass.

Boyd, R. D. (1991). *Personal transformations in small groups: A Jungian perspective.* New York: Routledge.

Brown, K. M. (2004). Leadership for social justice and equity: Weaving a transform-ative framework and pedagogy. *Educational Administration Quarterly, 40*(1), 77–108.

Brown, K. M. (2005). Social justice education for preservice leaders: Evaluating transformative learning strategies. *Equity & Excellence in Education, 38*(2), 155–167.

Brown, K. M. (2006). Leadership for social justice and equity: Evaluating a trans-formative framework and andragogy. *Educational Administration Quarterly, 42*(5), 700–745.

Chatterjee, P., & D'Aprix, A. (2002). Two tails of justice. *Families in Society: The Journal of Contemporary Human Services, 83*(4), 374–386.

Council on Social Work Education. (2008). *Educational policy and accreditation standards.* Washington, DC: Author.

Cranton, P. (1994). *Understanding and promoting transformational learning: A guide for educators of adults.* San Francisco: Jossey-Bass.

Cranton, P. (2000). Individual differences and transformative learning. In J. Mezirow (Ed.), *Learning as Transformation* (pp. 184–204). San Francisco: Jossey-Bass.

Cresswell, J. W. (1998). *Qualitative inquiry and research design: Choosing among five traditions.* Thousand Oaks, CA: Sage.

Daloz, L. A. (1999). *Mentor: Guiding the journey of adult learners.* San Francisco: Jossey-Bass.

Dirkx, J. M. (1998). Transformative learning theory in the practice of adult education: An overview. *PAACE Journal of Lifelong Learning, 7,* 1–14.

Freire, P. (1970). *Pedagogy of the oppressed.* New York: Herter and Herter.

Freire, P. (1998). Cultural action for freedom. *Harvard Educational Review, 68*(4), 471–521.

Habermas, J. (1970). *Toward a rational society.* Boston: Beacon Press.

Hughes, K., & Sherry, T. (1997). Doing it together: Only transformative education is compatible social justice. *Adults Learning, 9*(3), 9–14.

Jasso, G. (2000). Some of Robert K. Merton's contributions to justice theory. *Sociological Theory, 18*(2), 331–339.

Kegan, (1994). *In over our heads: The mental demands of modern life.* Cambridge, MA: Harvard University Press.

Kovan, J. T., & Dirkx, J. M. (2003). "Being called awake": The role of transformative learning in the lives of environmental activists. *Adult Education Quarterly, 53*(2), 99–118.

Marshall, C., & Rossman, G. B. (1999). *Designing qualitative research.* Thousand Oaks, CA: Sage.

McGregor, S. L. T. (2004). Transformative learning: We teach who we are. *Kappa Omicron Nu Forum, 14*(2). Retrieved August 22, 2008, from http://www.kon.org/archives/forum/14-2/forum14-2_article4.html

Mertens, D. M. (1999). Inclusive evaluation: Implications of transformative theory for evaluation. *American Journal of Evaluation, 20*(1), 1–14.

Merton, R. K. (1957). *Social theory and social structure.* New York: Free Press.

Mezirow, J. (1981). A critical theory of adult learning and education. *Adult Education, 52*(1), 3–24.

Mezirow, J. (1997, Summer). Transformative learning: Theory to practice. *New Directions for Adult and Continuing Education, 74,* 5–12.

Mezirow, J., & Associates. (1990). *Fostering critical reflection in adulthood: A guide to transformative and emancipatory learning.* San Francisco: Jossey-Bass.

Mezirow, J., & Associates. (2000). *Learning as transformation: Critical perspectives on a theory.* San Francisco: Jossey-Bass.

Morris, P. M. (2002). The capabilities perspective: A framework for social justice. *Families in Society: The Journal of Contemporary Human Services, 83*(4), 366–373.

Nagda, B. A., Gurin, P., & Lopez, G. E. (2003). Transformative pedagogy for democracy and social justice. *Race, Ethnicity and Education, 6*(2), 165–191.

National Association of Social Workers. (2008). *Code of ethics* (Rev. ed.). Washington, DC: Author.

Pearson, N. K. (1999). Social action as collaborative transformation. *Women's Studies Quarterly, 3*(4), 99–113.

Rawls, J. (1971). *A theory of justice.* Cambridge, MA: Harvard University Press.

Reisch, M. (2002). Defining social justice in a socially unjust world. *Families in Society, 83*(4), 343–354.

Schroeder, J., & Bordelon, D. (2002, April). *Mitigating circumstances and death penalty decisions.* Presented to the 19th annual National Organization of Forensic Social Work conference, St. Louis, Missouri.

Schroeder, J., Guin, C., Pogue, R., & Bordelon, D. (2006). The impact of mitigating circumstances on death decisions: Using evidence-based research to inform social work practice in capital trials. *Social Work, 51*(4), 355–364.

Taylor, E. W. (2000). Analyzing research on transformative theory. In. J. Mezirow & Associates (Eds.), *Learning as transformation: Critical perspectives on a theory in progress* (pp. 151–180). San Francisco: Jossey-Bass.

Tsanoff, R. A. (1956). Social morality and the principle of justice. *Ethics, 67,* 12–16.

Van Wormer, K. (2003). Restorative justice: A model for social work practice with families. *Families in Society, 84*(3), 441–448.

Appendix: A Plan for Social Justice Education in a Social Work Research-Methods Course

Step One: Instrument Construction
- Included a lecture on the relationship between conceptual development of a research area and questions, and the operationalization of related concepts
- Discussion of levels of measurement and instrument construction

Step Two: Research Design
- Assists students in determining the best way to assess changes in attitudes
- Lecture on educational interventions in social work (e.g., in-service presentations to agency peers).
- Lecture of pretest/posttest design
- Lecture on institutional review boards and voluntary consent

Step Three: A Disorienting Dilemma—Who Lives, Who Dies, Who Cares?
- Distribute and discuss consent form
- Students sign consent forms agreeing to participate
- Students complete pretest
- Students are presented with a one-hour educational intervention that provides them with not only an example of a research method but also a disorienting dilemma
- Students complete posttest
- Answer any questions about the process
- Assign writing assignment about the content

Step Four
- Students examine the pretest/posttest
- Students identify questions that address the five constructs discussed during step one
- Students develop a code sheet using the instrument
- Hands-on data set development

Step Five
- Instructor analyzes data
- Presents results to students

Step Six
- Students meet in small groups to discuss the findings and ways that they related to their own attitudes pre- and postintervention
- In-class discussion about issues and ideas developed in the small-group setting

Step Seven
- Review and clear up any issues regarding the analysis of items and internal consistency
- Focus on content and meaning found in the results

Step Eight
- Allow ample time for active and sometimes intense rational discourse on the death penalty
- Invite students to discuss their previous frames of reference and ways in which those frames may or may not have changed
- Charge students with devising ways in which they might use this type of educational intervention to reach other students
- Reinforce the value of research and inferential statistics in measuring change over time

CHAPTER SEVEN

Teaching About Social Justice Through a Multimedia Format

Michael Reisch

Abstract

Sweeping global social and political changes have transformed how people think about freedom, equality, justice, and human rights and dramatically restructured societal institutions and social relationships. These changes have serious implications for the field of social work and its commitment to social justice. This chapter reports on a seminar that examined the multifaceted dimensions of justice through literature, film, art, and music. It analyzes how effective it was to teach material on social justice in this manner as compared with more traditional methods of pedagogy, which the course instructor and his colleagues have used for many years.

The sweeping social and political changes of the past century have transformed the way people think about such fundamental concepts as freedom, equality, justice, and human rights (Pelton, 2005; Prigoff, 2003). They have dramatically reshaped global perspectives about gender, race, class, religion, and sexuality; restructured societal institutions and social relationships; fundamentally altered the nature of war and peace; and questioned the purpose of human existence itself (Fraser, 2005). These changes have serious implications for the field of social work and its historic commitment to social justice (Dominelli, 2004; Finn & Jacobson, 2003; Gil, 1998; Lundy, 2004; Reisch, 2007). This chapter reports on an undergraduate seminar that examined the multifaceted dimensions of justice through literature, film, art, and music, with a particular emphasis on comparing developments in the United States with those in other parts of the world and on analyzing their implications for social justice–oriented work. The chapter will discuss the theoretical and pedagogical foundations of the course, its format and organization, and the impact of the seminar on its participants, including the instructor. It will also assess the effectiveness of teaching material on social justice in this manner as compared with more traditional pedagogical methods used by the course instructor and his colleagues.

Seminar Description

CONCEPTUAL FRAMEWORK

Social justice has been a central normative component of social work in the United States since the early twentieth century. Although the revised NASW *Code of Ethics* (2008) makes the pursuit of social justice an ethical imperative of the profession, there is still considerable ambiguity about the meaning of this concept and how it can be applied to practice, policy, and research. This ambiguity stems from largely unacknowledged tensions between universal views of social justice and those with more selective implications for different demographic groups (Reisch, 2007). Current social work discourse presumes a complementary relationship between these diverse perspectives when they may often be in conflict (Yee & Dumbrill, 2003). To respond effectively to twenty-first century demographic and political/economic realities, social work educators must attempt to resolve this conflict through their teaching and research.

In developing the seminar, the instructor used a definition of social justice that incorporated both its substantive goals and the processes by which these goals are developed, implemented, and evaluated (Gil, 1998). Substantive goals include the more equitable distribution of resources, power, rights, opportunities, and status through policies, programs, and services that hold vulnerable groups harmless (Rawls, 1990), emphasize collective and mutual responsibility (Reynolds, 1951), focus on people's common humanity (Towle, 1945), and stress multiple forms of helping that reflect diverse conceptions of need (Green, 1998). Process dimensions of social justice include the promotion of meaningful, democratic participation in all phases of decision making so that people are empowered and their voices are genuinely heard (Hill Collins, 2000).

For many years, the seminar instructor—a professor in the School of Social Work and the Undergraduate Honors Program at the University of Michigan, who teaches the history and philosophy of social welfare, contemporary social policy, theories and methods of social action and social change, and community organizing—has been influenced by the work of Paulo Freire (1970, 1990) and attempted to incorporate dialogical methods into his courses. Although often difficult to implement because of deeply entrenched habits of learning and teaching, Freire's concepts of praxis, dialogical education, and conscientization can be far more effective in stimulating students' understanding of complex and often painful issues than traditional pedagogy. They can also enable students to undergo a transformative process that allows them to find the deeper meaning of abstractions like justice, power, and privilege; connect them more clearly to their personal and work experiences; and apply them to their practice.

In contrast to what Freire termed "the banking concept" of education (1970), which he argued perpetuates the forces of domination, exploitation, exclusion, and objectification, a focus on dialogue enables students to relate their learning experience to the conditions of their lives. By "naming the world," they are transformed from objects who passively accept what social and cultural institutions impose on them to actors who possess the tools to question, challenge, think critically, and act (Reisch, Wenocur, & Sherman, 1981). This occurs through the development of critical consciousness, a process Freire called conscientization. It is distinguished from naïve or romantic consciousness in two fundamental ways: it analyzes the contradictions in societal institutions and dominant ideologies; and it promotes praxis—the ongoing reflection on the interrelationship between thought and action (Van Soest & Garcia, 2003).

Postmodern ideas and social constructionism, particularly regarding matters of personal and group identity, positionality, privilege, and oppression also contributed to the design of the seminar (Giroux, 2000; Laird, 1993; Van Soest, 2003; Van Soest & Garcia, 2003; Young, 2000). These approaches, often derived from Foucault (1977, 1979) or Derrida (1976), enable students to grasp the multiple and often hidden levels of meaning in language, the power inherent in all social relationships and the ways in which seemingly mundane objects, representations, and daily transactions reflect mutually accepted and institutionalized forces of privilege and oppression (Chambon, Irving, & Epstein, 1999). Foucault's work, in particular, emphasizes the importance of critical thinking in unmasking the motives behind the normative practices of professions. Several authors have observed how social work and social work education embody similar patterns (Dominelli, 2004; Howe, 1994; Margolin, 1997; Pease & Fook, 1999).

Although the power of art, music, poetry, theater, and film to shape people's thoughts and emotions has long been established (Gitlin, 2003; McLuhan, 2001; Shikes, 1969), few attempts have been made in social work programs to use these media in courses about social justice (Adams, Bell, & Griffin, 1997; Dudziak, 2005; Garcia & Van Soest, 2006; Sowers & Rowe, 2007; Van Soest & Garcia, 2003; Van Wormer, 2004). Explicit efforts to link consciousness-raising, justice-focused education and various cultural forms, however, have been widespread in other fields like drama (Boal, 1982).

Despite the absence of such models, long-standing frustrations with traditional, often prescriptive curricular requirements in schools of social work created a personal motivation for the instructor to teach social justice in this format. Although there is considerable emphasis today on the attainment of educational outcomes (CSWE, 2008), these outcomes are largely cast in measurable—quantitative—empirical terms. They are more closely correlated with students' acquisition of specific, demonstrable knowledge and practice skills than with the transformation of their attitudes, underlying assumptions, worldviews, fundamental values, or relationship skills. This is ironic since the goal of empowerment assumes that such transformation is essential for clients and communities to integrate the political/economic and psychosocial dimensions of their lives, recognize their strengths or assets, and assert greater control over the decisions that affect them (Gutierrez & Lewis, 1999). In order to assist people in this empowerment process, social workers must undergo a similar transformation (Reisch et al., 1981). Part of this transformation is the acquisition of new insights into patterns of communication and relationships that are rarely subject to such scrutiny (Bourdieu, 1977; Coates & McKay, 1995).

The honors seminar provided a limited opportunity to address this gap in students' education. It enabled the instructor to engage in more innovative and experimental approaches to teaching with fewer preconceived or prescribed outcomes. The use of multimedia content allowed students to be more creative in interpreting what they read, observed, heard, or experienced. By eliminating the usual professionally oriented "filters" through which most learning about social justice is transmitted, it also gave them a wider choice of means to express their thoughts and feelings in more candid and less guarded ways. Lastly, by giving students some control over the syllabus, the seminar empowered them to introduce songs, poems, and images of their choosing every week and through their final projects. In other words, it modeled the Freirean concept of "naming the world" and widely held ideas about empowerment in a very practical sense.

SEMINAR DESCRIPTION

The eighteen students who enrolled in the seminar in the 2006 winter term were sophomores in the university's Honors Program; all were nineteen or twenty years old. The eleven women and seven men had a wide range of majors: five in biology (mostly premed), three in business, three in English, art history, and political science; and one each in music, anthropology, and organization studies. Although the seminar was fairly diverse in terms of race and ethnicity—more than one-third of the class consisted of students of color—nearly all the students came from privileged backgrounds. Only five of the students were Michigan residents; nearly half came from the Chicago, New York, or Washington, DC, areas. Only four of the students initially indicated they had a career goal that was justice oriented; one expressed an interest in doing missionary work. All of the students indicated from the outset a preference for open-ended discussions, visual experiences, and participatory forms of learning. Many expressed an interest in music, literature, art, history, and politics. Most of them were sophisticated in terms of their exposure to different parts of the country and the world through travel. All were conversant with the latest trends in popular culture, including current slang, information technology, and modes of verbal communication.

The seminar met for three hours weekly over the course of a semester. The instructor facilitated the seminar, but the students' weekly journals on the assigned readings, films, music, and art identified the themes and questions that served as the core of each week's discussion. These journals were posted on a course Web site several days before the seminar met in order for all participants to access them. Prior to each seminar session, the instructor extracted and synthesized the journals' major themes and questions to guide the seminar. He returned the journals ungraded, but with extensive comments.

As in the selection of readings, images, music, and films, discussion questions were deliberately framed to be provocative in order to stimulate dialogue among the seminar participants. While some of the questions were abstract and philosophical, others were personal or political in nature. For example, in the session "Justice and Freedom," discussion questions included the *personal* (What limits on freedom currently exist [or should exist] in our society? Which of these limitations are justified and why?); the *political* (Whose responsibility is it to preserve freedom and enable those who are not free to become free?"); and the *philosophical* (Is freedom a "zero sum game" in a multicultural society?). Often, discussion questions explicitly linked concepts derived from the assigned readings or films—especially from poems, song lyrics, or letters—to current issues. For example, a poem by Lawrence

Dunbar (1986), "We Wear the Mask," was used to illustrate contemporary barriers to racial justice. The song, "Bread and Roses" (Oppenheim, 1992), introduced a discussion of the meaning of gender justice in the twenty-first century. The blacklisted film *Salt of the Earth* underscored the multiple dimensions of justice and human identity in today's globalized world.

Course readings included social scientific research from multiple disciplines, philosophical essays, poems, short stories, plays, and song lyrics. Students were required to watch both documentary and dramatic films inside and outside class; observe artistic images ranging from painting to cartoons; visit and write about an exhibit of art and poetry by prison inmates; and attend several concerts and lectures on campus. Students also had to attend and reflect upon several activities of their own choosing from among the university's many scheduled events on the Martin Luther King Jr. holiday. Classes often included a discussion of music ranging from traditional folk songs to contemporary hip-hop and world music. Students were encouraged to bring in music or images they felt related to social justice (or injustice) or its applications to domestic or foreign issues. Many did so.

The first assignment was an analytic essay (five to eight pages) that required students to discuss some aspect of justice within one of the following frameworks:

- How the *same issue* has been presented during the *same period* in two or more *different forms* (e.g., literature and art);
- How the *same issue* has been presented during the *same period* in two or more *different parts of the world* or in two or more *different groups* within the *same part of the world*;
- How the *same issue* has been presented in the *same medium* in the *same part of the world* during two or more *different eras.*

Additional assignments included a joint seminar presentation on a topic of the students' choosing and a final project that could take the form of a paper, film, video, or DVD; a piece of creative fiction (short story, poetry, one-act play, screenplay, song); a piece of music, art or sculpture; a photo exhibit; or some combination of the above. The presentation and project had to connect the theme of justice selected with either an issue of policy or practice/action. Students were encouraged to be as imaginative and provocative in their presentations as possible. Many of the seminar participants responded well to this challenge.

After an introductory class in which general concepts were presented through three very different formats—a poem entitled "Injustice," by Pablo Neruda (1981); a short essay by philosopher Judith Shklar titled (1990) "Justice and Injustice"; and a short documentary film, *What Is*

Justice?—each seminar session addressed a different dimension of justice. Due to the breadth of each issue, the material was organized around specific subtopics or contemporary manifestations of a particular aspect of justice or injustice.

For example, the second class, which coincided with the Martin Luther King Jr. holiday, was titled "Racial Justice: The African American Experience." It was followed by required participation in and written reflection on several events during the university's Martin Luther King Jr. celebration. The class "Gender Justice" coincided with events on International Women's Day. This session was not limited to traditional issues such as abortion, but examined women's political and economic rights from multiple contemporary cultural perspectives, including Islam and Hinduism.

Many of the seminar sessions were organized around a provocative question or theme. For example, the class "Justice and Sexuality" posed the question, Is gay liberation sufficient? by showing a film, *All God's Children: Tongues Untied,* about gay African American men. The class "Justice and Religion" focused on the question, What is divine justice? by showing excerpts from several films about religious intolerance. This led to a particularly interesting discussion since two of the students had worked as missionaries.

The session "Justice and Freedom" asked the question, Which takes precedence, individual freedom or group justice? in light of the ongoing controversy in the state over a ballot proposition to ban the use of affirmative action. The class "Justice and Equality" examined whether these principles applied to individuals or groups. The session "Justice and Human Rights" placed the issue in the context of globalization and the vast dichotomies between the global North and South.

Several sessions addressed controversial aspects of justice that emerged specifically from students' journals. The session on "Retributive Justice" examined whether certain forms of punishment, such as the death penalty or the identification of child molesters, were just. The session "Justice and Peace" asked if these two goals were compatible in an unjust world. With the Iraq War and 9/11 as context, the penultimate class session asked how we can address conflicts of justice when different interpretations of its meaning exist.

The assigned readings attempted to balance the presentation of each subject in several ways. First, by using different types of media to present the material, the readings illustrated how different uses of language, image, and atmosphere conveyed different aspects of a particular subject. For example, reading Ida Wells-Barnett's (1984) essay on lynching in the South stirred different thoughts and feelings than hearing Billie Holiday sing "Strange Fruit" or seeing photos of crowds entertaining themselves at a lynching.

Second, in order to break down stereotypes, avoid the appearance of using the seminar for advocacy purposes (Fish, 2007), and stimulate reflection and dialogue, the readings tried to integrate diverse views on the topic from writers or artists with diverse backgrounds and ideologies. The instructor, who left it to the students to draw their own conclusions, presented these viewpoints without comment. A primary role of the instructor was to place the different perspectives in their historical context.

Third, using multimedia sources increased the points of access to the material for the students. Some students learn more effectively by reading; some by watching film or viewing visual images; and others learn best through media that have more explicitly emotional overtones, such as music or poetry. Most students found that a combination of sources evoked the most powerful and lasting impressions of the material, enabling them to understand it at multiple levels and, as a result, be transformed by the experience.

The students selected challenging and often provocative topics for their in-class presentations, many of which linked historical and contemporary events, although this was not an explicit requirement. Topics included a comparison of events in Rwanda and Darfur with the Nazi Holocaust; the viability and feasibility of the idea of inherited guilt (the "sins of the fathers"); the role of mass media in shaping popular perceptions of racial minorities and women; and post-9/11 views of justice. While the majority of the eight presentations used traditional print materials to collect most of their information, others used a variety of multimedia sources. All of the students employed at least two different types of media in their presentation formats.

For example, one presentation, "Political Justice," used newspaper cartoons and photographs to discuss how political biases shaped people's images of certain individuals and parties. The presentation on gender justice relied heavily on song lyrics, especially from hip-hop and rap music, and clips of TV and radio advertising to illustrate sexist stereotyping. The discussion "Racial Justice and the Media" analyzed local news broadcasts and showed video clips from the Internet to demonstrate racial biases in reporting about crime, welfare, education, and terrorism. Finally, the presentation "Art and Justice" showed how painters, from Kathe Kollwitz to Fernando Botero, used art to convey evolving yet universal ideas about what constitutes justice and injustice.

To an even greater extent, students' final projects demonstrated the creative uses of media in expressing different aspects of justice. Two students mounted photo exhibits, one about homelessness, the other about the ways in which consumerism reflects the disparities between rich and poor. One student put together a multimedia montage of songs, stories, and drawings about the impact of the 1960s on our society's conception of justice. Another student wrote a short story that consisted of a correspondence between a father and a daughter about their different views of justice in today's world. Finally, one student took an enormous risk by writing the lyrics of a song about race and justice, "Keep Breathing," and performing it for the first time in class.

TRANSFORMATIVE ASPECTS

Freire (1970) emphasized the ways in which the development of critical consciousness through dialogue enabled people to transform their relationship to the environment from one of object (i.e., being acted upon) to one of subject. One aspect of what he termed "conscientization" was the acquisition of the ability and confidence to "name the world" (Freire, 1970), and to acknowledge the right and capacity of others to do likewise. Similarly, Hill Collins (1990) and Young (1990, 2000), among others, focus on the ways in which the educational process can make students aware of their personal and social relationship to power, oppression, and privilege, and thereby transform their approaches to dealing with others. This has applications to both interpersonal and community practice (Dominelli, 2004; Lundy, 2004; Reed, Newman, Suarez, & Lewis, 1997; Rose, 2000).

Over the course of the semester, students underwent a modest transformation in this direction. This is consistent with the view of empowerment "as beginning with the smallest of individual actions" (Van Soest & Garcia, 2003, p. 98). In the seminar, they became increasingly comfortable expressing their views on controversial subjects in their journals and, above all, in class discussions. They focused less on a frequently heard concern of students regarding the need for safety and took risks with themselves and with each other. Through ongoing dialogue, they learned how to question or challenge classmates' opinions without provoking personal confrontations.

In addition, students began to understand, at both an emotional and a cognitive level, the ways in which injustice, oppression, and privilege affected them personally. The men in the seminar became more aware of the ways in which their gender-based privilege influenced their interactions with peers, even in the relatively benign confines of the classroom. The white students in the class recognized the ways in which their race granted them certain unspoken and largely unacknowledged advantages in their day-to-day existence. The perspectives of all the students on the concept of justice broadened considerably through these discussions as much as through assigned readings, films, art, and music. The various means used in the seminar to expose students to different ideas and experiences opened them up to alternative ways of seeing the world to a far greater extent than would have been accomplished by didactic presentations or nonfictional reading assignments alone.

In their final journal entries and class evaluations, nearly all the students commented on these aspects of the course. One student wrote:

> This course had the most thought-provoking, provocative and sincere discussions about the world around us. [The] . . . diverse methods of learning and interacting with the material . . . taught us . . . that we should never take anything as given; we should always question why things are and how they got this way.

Another student connected the educational approach used explicitly with issues of power and justice by stating:

> Seeing and hearing injustice hold a different power than simply reading about injustice . . . The open-endedness of this class makes it a good forum for discussion about issues sensitive to people from diverse backgrounds. . . . Learning not only about what I want to hear, but also what I should hear, makes me feel like a more responsible member of society. . . . This course force[d us] . . . to confront preconceived, stereotypical ideas.

A third remarked:

> One cannot truly grasp some of the injustices that we discussed without viewing some of the films that documented them. . . . I [also] enjoyed . . . listening to how people constructed their own views on a particular subject. These discussions allowed me to reflect on how I came to my own conclusions and gave me a chance to rethink some of the issues and my own ideas.

The diverse portrayals of justice and injustice enabled students to overcome the different forms of denial in which they all engaged. This is another critical component of the transformation process. Many students cited specific readings, films, or assignments as being particularly powerful or influential. A premed student wrote, "The photography project I did forced me to think a lot about the topic [of homelessness] and how to approach it from a different angle." A classmate commented:

> The journal assignments that required us to visit the Martin Luther King, Jr. Day events and the Prison Art Show . . . were

crucial in helping me to shed my ignorance and challenge stereotypes that I have may have held. . . . I feel that I . . . am better equipped to help justice be realized in my own life.

A student who acknowledged his initial resistance to the material confessed:

Having spent the semester as the resident "bad guy" of the class, it was an eye-opening experience. It got tiring being part of every oppressive majority, but it also afforded me a unique outlook. I felt that the class was a very intriguing exploration of the overwhelming idea of justice. It was through discussions of its applicability that . . . [I have continually thought about] the "desirability" of a just society and what a just society is. This is the most valuable nugget I take from this class.

A student interested in social activism and the law described that she became aware of her transformation through her reaction to the final reading of the semester, the poem "Always There Are the Children," by Nikki Giovanni (1974):

I think I viewed this poem differently than I would have a few months ago. . . . I dismissed past problems as history that should be studied and observed, but not necessarily as problems that currently require action. [The poem] made me realize that I am in the process of transitioning from one of the children in the poem to the next generation that is responsible for providing the children with wisdom and nourishment.

A student majoring in music brought his particular insight to the course:

I liked your choice of videos, especially *Amandla* [a film about the use of song in the South African freedom movement]. It was great [to see] . . . how the songs spread the ideas of the movement more than literature and political activism. . . . Music's ability to convey messages . . . makes it one of the most powerful tools in teaching about any subject.

A business major was particularly moved by contact with previously unknown issues:

> Certain readings, like the article about the school in East St. Louis, and certain exhibits, like the Prison Arts exhibit, struck me because they educated me about things that I was legitimately ignorant about. I think the moral I got out of this class is that . . . finding a solution to a problem isn't just about recognizing it, it's about understanding why that problem exists and what can be done to fix it.

For some students, the seminar process itself was transformative, because it allowed them to express their anger, ignorance, or pain about the subject matter in a nonjudgmental environment. This also reflected their acquisition of an understanding of justice that incorporates an assessment of both its ends and means. A student of art history wrote:

> This class . . . allowed me to understand and connect different issues, such as the civil rights and feminist movements, to understand how they are related and why they are important. It was so interesting for me to see and learn about conflicts that extend beyond my own Eurocentric sphere. . . . I appreciated being able to connect my art history background with contemporary social issues. However, the most interesting part of this class has been being able to listen and learn from my classmates' opinions.

An English major from a self-acknowledged privileged background had the following reflection, which had clear implications for the social work values of developing equal and empathetic relationships with those with whom we work:

> [Although] I've known about poverty and injustice . . . throughout my whole life, they were always distant concepts. . . . This seminar truly made me think and question my own values and way of life . . . [by] allow[ing] us to be both the creator and the recipient. . . . This . . . made me think more critically about my own values and priorities [and] see other points of view from a less biased perspective. [It also] made me more aware and empathetic towards everyone.

According to Freire (1990), another critical element in the transformation process is the ability to translate critical consciousness into action. Perhaps the most important transformative aspects of the course were the effects the course had on students' ideas about justice and on the roles they could play in its attainment. In their self-assessments, several students referred to the specific knowledge and skills they developed and demonstrated an awareness of the active role they played in their own transformation.

A student who was, by her own description, disinterested in politics at the beginning of the semester commented:

> I looked forward to our discussions every week because it was the one time when I could voice my opinions about important issues and hear the opinions of others. . . . I became more interested in current events as a result. . . . More than anything, this class has taught me how to argue effectively and listen fairly.

This reflected an unspoken theme of the course: to teach students how to argue effectively and listen fairly.

Another student reflected:

> Some of my favorite essays and films are the ones that have challenged my beliefs the most. . . . I think that my personal definition of justice is now comprised of specific examples, images, and complex relationships between individuals and groups of people. . . . Because I am much more aware now of some of the issues that exist in today's society, I believe that the recognition of a problem is the first step towards an effective solution.

Another theme that emerged was the way the course content challenged students' beliefs and helped them develop a personal definition of justice. Two students specifically remarked on how the use of different media shaped their views of justice. One wrote, "What I really appreciated about this course is that it showed me that all the various forms of justice are connected. . . . This is why it is important for people with specific issues to band together so that they are not simply looked over in the mainstream movements." Another commented:

> A factor that helped keep class fun and interesting was the variety of mediums through which the concepts were introduced. . . . If I had to pick one thing I garnered from this class experience, it would be the notion that an individual can effect social change, although a group working together as a team is a more effective way to make an impact. . . . I realized how much this class made me think about how I

wanted to live in more of a concrete way than any other class
I have ever taken.

A final element of the transformation process was the ability of students to begin to understand that their individual situations related to
the global dimensions of justice (Van Soest & Garcia, 2003). Many of
them were able to link this understanding with newfound recognition
of the importance of collective action, and the role that individual efficacy and agency played in effecting social change. Nearly all the students indicated that the seminar led them to think about, as one put it,
"issues both in greater depth and in different perspectives," rethink
career choices, and broaden their awareness of the world and its problems. Despite the frequent illustrations of injustice presented in the
seminar, most of the students concluded the semester with a combination of anger about people's lack of awareness and guarded optimism
about the future.

A student interested in social activism reflected:

> Somewhere along the line, we seem to have lost our concep-
> tion of a worldwide community; perhaps we were never truly
> a global community and the modern fracturing is merely an
> exaggeration of past divisions. It is that fracturing that I think
> a course like this seeks to remedy. . . . I cannot say that I have
> developed greater problem-solving techniques over the past
> semester and that I now have answers to the many questions
> I included in my journals. However, I can say that I have a
> better grasp of the world around me, and of the struggles that
> others endure on a daily basis.

A classmate agreed:

> I think we will make little progress unless we have the cour-
> age and vision to hope for positive change in the future. . . .
> The most important common denominator connecting all
> our readings together across the semester seems to be this
> hope in the future. . . . I want to be one of those people
> brave enough to recognize the mistakes of our past and
> work to end the consequent injustices that plague our
> present. . . . I have begun to realize that defining justice is
> not a simple matter of listing words like fairness, equality,
> and freedom. . . . I think that, in part, justice means creating
> a world in which we are all able to do so without unfair bur-
> dens placed on us or identities forced upon us by society to
> pull us down. . . . I do not believe that only one true path
> exists to achieving justice; I think that justice means holding

individuals responsible for their actions. . . . While justice may take many different forms, if we recognize the common bond of humanity between all of us, we can truly work toward achieving justice.

In the final session, the students completed a brief self-evaluation of their class participation, which the instructor used as the primary basis of determining this portion of their grade (10% in all). Nearly all of the students gave themselves ten points out of ten. Several commented that "as the semester progressed, [they] felt more comfortable and ready to engage in the class discussion." Others wrote that they appreciated "the opportunity to talk and discuss things without worrying about grades or whether the professor would agree with [them]."

The students were also asked to write one question and one comment on any subject related to the course on a piece of paper and toss it anonymously into a hat. We then passed around the hat and, in turn, students read aloud what their classmates had written. Several of these comments stimulated lively discussions and were good ways for the seminar to wrap up.

- We probably will never attain justice, but it's worth a try.
- I think we all need to make sure we continue to address these issues and urge others to do the same.
- Sensitivity and awareness are the only ways to end injustice.
- Does anyone in their actions consistently advocate for justice?
- Judging by our discussion this semester, are our actions in Iraq considered just?
- Is America justified in imposing itself and democracy on the rest of the world?
- What can we, as individuals, do to make the world more just?
- Maybe the world will never be fair; maybe justice can't exist without injustice.

LESSONS LEARNED (A PERSONAL REFLECTION)

Although I had taught many graduate-level courses in which undergraduates and non-social-work students had enrolled, this seminar was the first undergraduate course and the first course outside of a school of social work that I had taught for about twenty years. For the most part, the experience was very enjoyable and stimulating, and the students were refreshing in their openness and honesty. I always felt more energy after the seminar than I did before it started—a good indication of the positive nature of the experience. I particularly enjoyed the opportunity to discuss materials from a wide range of sources and see how students reacted to them.

Another, more unexpected result of the course was how much I learned from the students about their perceptions of current issues; their understanding of politics, culture, and society; and their perspectives on mass media, literature, and art. The comfort and trust that we built together in the seminar enabled us to cross both cultural and generational boundaries. Unexpectedly, I overcame some of my dislike for hip-hop music, and the students tolerated the exposure I gave them to folk music and the blues.

The seminar experience made me realize the limitations and constraints of social work education, particularly in regard to teaching about justice. Despite its rhetorical commitment (CSWE, 2008; NASW, 2008), much of the content on this topic in schools of social work is presented in a noncritical and fairly narrow fashion (Garcia & Van Soest, 2006; Sowers & Rowe, 2007; Van Soest, 1992; Van Wormer, 2004). In the face of ongoing and recent challenges to the ideology of the profession (National Association of Scholars, 2007), social work educators should not become defensive about our underlying values. Instead, through rigorous inquiry and open-ended dialogue, we should explore the complex, nuanced, and dynamic meaning of social justice in an increasingly diverse environment.

It seems, however, that at present, social work educators do not have sufficient confidence in the righteousness of our values to be open to diverse opinions on the subject. Consequently, course syllabi and classroom discussions rarely delve deeply into the meaning or implications of difficult and controversial topics such as the relationship between social justice and multiculturalism (Fraser, 2003, 2005; Reisch, 2002, 2007). Both students and faculty are so concerned that their views may not conform to some unstated standards of propriety that they often fail to take intellectual or personal risks. Without such risk-taking, transformative growth cannot occur, particularly in an educational environment. We appear to have forgotten that dialogue is an opportunity to stimulate healthy differences among us, not to suppress them. The use of multiple media formats proved to be a catalyst to stimulating this type of dialogue.

Finally, I learned some specific lessons that I hope to apply to future editions of the course, which may be useful for other instructors teaching similar material. One is to find a way to convey my own ideas without dominating the conversation and suppressing the views of the students. An effective means of doing this was to give everyone in the seminar the authority to select the music used to introduce and close each session. Another was to have the students, through their journals, determine the questions and issues that would guide the discussion. It was also useful to allow open-ended interpretations of images, music, poetry, and films rather than look for predetermined correct answers.

In addition, it was important to respect the silences in the classroom, especially when students were confronted with emotionally powerful words or wrenching images, such as those of lynching or the Holocaust. This helped make the class a more egalitarian experience in which I facilitated rather than led the seminar.

Another lesson was that certain types of music and film seem to be more conducive to creating a response in students than others. Perhaps because music is such a personal medium, students connected more powerfully with music that was familiar, such as hip-hop or reggae. While they appreciated the lyrics of folk songs, their emotional responses to such music were more muted. Similarly, students preferred dramatic films to documentaries and contemporary documentaries to those made even a decade ago. The instructor was struck by the fact that documentaries that still seemed fresh to him were already dated in the students' eyes. It was also apparent that viewing films as a group evoked more powerful responses than having students watch them alone outside class. Experiential assignments also proved to be very valuable, especially the required visit to the Prison Arts Project.

Finally, I learned that it is important to be patient yet persistent when discussing sensitive subjects, such as homosexuality, racial tensions, gender differences, and religion. Even controversial material can be presented in a nonthreatening way if a classroom atmosphere of trust and mutual respect exists. Students must be made to feel comfortable and safe expressing their discomfort and insecurities. This required me to model active listening and resist making judgments, however subtle, about students' ideas with which I differed. Often, combining images, words, and music or beginning the seminar with songs, slides, a short video, or a political cartoon helped set the right mood.

Over the course of the semester students became increasingly comfortable discussing controversial topics in depth, critiquing each other's ideas, and challenging each other in a nonthreatening but risk-taking manner. They felt freer to admit their ignorance, convey their feelings, articulate their fears, show their discomfort, and relate their dreams. Visual media, music, and occasionally poetry were more likely to evoke such responses than nonfiction essays. Sometimes, to make the latter more effective, it was useful to put them in historical context by assigning them in conjunction with a film or song and to underscore the innovative or cultural aspects of these works by connecting the ideas they were expressing to contemporary discourse on today's issues.

Although the seminar required a great deal of preparatory work, it was work of a different nature. Instead of polishing a lecture or PowerPoint slides, the instructor spent more time thinking about ways in which to convey the meaning of different aspects of justice and ways in which different media could be used together to express different elements of a related theme. One anonymous comment in a student's evaluation, however, made all the hard work worthwhile: "This class changed my outlook on life."

References

Adams, M., Bell, L., & Griffin, P. (Eds.). (1997). *Teaching for diversity and social justice.* New York: Routledge.

Boal, A. (1982). *Theatre of the oppressed.* New York: Routledge.

Bourdieu, P. (1977). *Outline of a theory of practice* (R. Nice, Trans.). Cambridge, MA: Cambridge University Press.

Chambon, A., Irving, A., & Epstein, L. (1999). *Reading Foucault for social work.* New York: Columbia University Press.

Coates, J., & McKay, M. (1995). Toward a new pedagogy for social transformation. *Journal of Progressive Human Services, 6*(1), 27–43.

Council on Social Work Education. (2008). *Educational policy and accreditation standards.* Alexandria, VA: Author.

Derrida, J. (1976). *Of grammatology* (G. Spivak, Trans.). Baltimore: Johns Hopkins University Press.

Dominelli, L. (2004). *Social work: Theory and practice for a changing profession.* Malden, MA: Polity Press.

Dudziak, S. (2005). Educating for justice: Challenges and openings in the context of globalization. In I. Ferguson, M. Lavalette, & E. Whitmore (Eds.), *Globalisation, global justice and social work* (pp. 141–153). London: Routledge.

Dunbar, L. (1986). We wear the mask. In R. Abcarian & M. Klotz (Eds.), *Literature: The human experience* (p. 528). New York: St. Martin's Press.

Finn, J. L., & Jacobson, M. (2003). *Just practice: A social justice approach to social work.* Peosta, IA: Eddie Bowers.

Fish, S. (2007, March 24). Advocacy and teaching. *New York Times,* p. A-13. Retrieved March 24, 2007, from: www.nytimes.com

Foucault, M. (1977). *Discipline and punish.* London: Allen Lane.

Foucault, M. (1979). Truth and power. In M. Morris & P. Patton (Eds.), *Michel Foucault: Power, truth, and strategy* (pp. 29–48). Sydney, Australia: Feral Publications.

Fraser, N. (2003). Social justice in the age of identity politics. In N. Fraser & A. Honneth (Eds.), *Redistribution or recognition? A political-philosophical exchange* (pp. 7–109). London: Verso.

Fraser, N. (2005, November–December). Reframing justice in a globalizing world. *New Left Review, 36,* 69–88.

Freire, P. (1970). *Pedagogy of the oppressed* (M. B. Ramos, Trans.). New York: Seabury.

Freire, P. (1990). A critical understanding of social work (M. Moch, Trans.). *Journal of Progressive Human Services, 1*(1), 3–9.

Garcia, B., & Van Soest, D. (2006). *Social work practice for social justice: Cultural competence in action, a guide for students.* Alexandria, VA: Council on Social Work Education.

Gil, D. (1998). *Confronting injustice and oppression: Concepts and strategies for social workers.* New York: Columbia University Press.

Giovanni, N. (1974). Always there are the children. In *The women and the men: Poems* (p. 56). New York: William Morrow and Co.

Giroux, H. A. (2000). Racial politics, pedagogy, and the crisis of representation in academic multiculturalism. *Social Identities, 6*(4), 493–510.

Gitlin, T. (2003). *The whole world is watching: Mass media and the making and unmaking of the new left.* Berkeley: University of California Press.

Green, J. (1998). *Cultural awareness in the human services.* Boston: Allyn & Bacon.

Gutierrez, L., & Lewis, E. (1999). *Empowering women of color.* New York: Columbia University Press.

Hill Collins, P. (1990). *Black feminist thought: Knowledge, consciousness, and the politics of empowerment.* New York: Unwin Hyman.

Hill Collins, P. (2000). *Black feminist thought: Knowledge, consciousness, and the politics of empowerment.* New York: Routledge.

Howe, D. (1994). Modernity, postmodernity, and social work. *British Journal of Social Work, 24*(5), 513–532.

Laird, J. (1993). *Revisioning social work education: A social constructivist approach.* New York: Haworth Press.

Lundy, C. (2004). *Social work and social justice: A structural approach to practice.* Peterborough, ON: Broadview Press.

Margolin, L. (1997). *Under the cover of kindness: The invention of social work.* Charlottesville: University of Virginia Press.

McLuhan, M. (2001). *Understanding media: The extensions of man.* London: Routledge.

National Association of Scholars. (2007). *Report on social work education.* Washington, DC: Author.

National Association of Social Workers. (2008). *Code of ethics.* Washington, DC: Author.

Neruda, P. (1981). Injustice (A. Reid, Trans.). In K. Vanden Heuvel (Ed.), *The nation, 1865–1990: Selections from the Independent Magazine of Politics and Culture* (pp. 509–510). New York: Thunder Mouth Press.

Oppenheim, J. (1992). Bread and roses. In M. Schneir (Ed.), *Feminism: The essential historical writings* (pp. 305–306). New York: Vintage Press.

Pease, B., & Fook, J. (Eds.). (1999). *Transforming social work practice: Postmodern critical perspectives.* New York: Routledge.

Pelton, L. H. (2005). *Frames of justice: Implications for social policy.* Somerset, NJ: Transactions Publishers.

Prigoff, A. W. (2003). Social justice framework. In J. Anderson & R. W. Carter (Eds.), *Diversity perspectives for social work practice* (pp. 113–129). Boston: Allyn & Bacon.

Rawls, J. (1990). *A theory of justice.* Cambridge, MA: Harvard University Press.

Reed, B. G., Newman, P., Suarez, Z., & Lewis, E. (1997). Interpersonal practice beyond diversity and toward social justice: The importance of critical consciousness. In C. Garvin & B. Seabury (Eds.), *Interpersonal practice in social work: Promoting competence and social justice* (pp. 44–78). Boston: Allyn & Bacon.

Reisch, M. (2002). Defining social justice in a socially unjust world. *Families in Society, 83*(4), 343–354.

Reisch, M. (2007). Social justice and multiculturalism: Persistent tensions in the history of U.S. social welfare and social work. *Studies in Social Justice, 1*(1), 67–92.

Reisch, M., Wenocur, S., & Sherman, W. (1981). Empowerment, conscientization, and animation as core social work skills. *Social Development Issues, 5*(2/3), 108–120.

Reynolds, B. C. (1951). *Social work and social living.* New York: Citadel Press.

Rose, S. (2000). Reflections on empowerment-based practice. *Social Work, 45*(5), 403–412.

Shikes, R. (1969). *The indignant eye: The artist as social critic from the fifteenth century to Picasso.* Boston: Beacon Press.

Shklar, J. N. (1990). Justice and injustice. In *The faces of injustice* (pp. 15–19). New Haven, CT: Yale University Press.

Sowers, K. M., & Rowe, W. S. (2007). *Social work practice and social justice: From local to global perspectives.* Belmont, CA: Thomson/Brooks Cole.

Towle, C. (1945). *Common human needs.* Washington, DC: Social Security Administration (reprinted by NASW).

Van Soest, D. (1992). *Incorporating peace and social justice into the social work curriculum.* Washington, DC: National Association of Social Workers.

Van Soest, D. (2003). Advancing social and economic justice. In D. Lum (Ed.), *Culturally competent practice: A framework for understanding diverse groups and justice issues* (pp. 350–351). Pacific Grove, CA: Brooks/Cole.

Van Soest, D., & Garcia, B. (2003). *Diversity education for social justice: Mastering teaching skills.* Alexandria, VA: Council on Social Work Education.

Van Wormer, K. (2004). *Confronting oppression, restoring justice: From policy analysis to social action.* Alexandria, VA: Council on Social Work Education.

Wells-Barnett, I. (1984). Southern horrors: Lynch law in all its phases. In J. Anderson (Ed.), *Outspoken women: Speeches by American women reformers, 1635–1935* (pp. 206–220). Dubuque, IA: Kendall/Hunt.

Yee, J. Y., & Dumbrill, G. C. (2003). Whiteout: Looking for race in Canadian social work practice. In A. Al-Krenaw & J. R. Graham (Eds.), *Multicultural social work in Canada: Working with diverse ethno-racial communities* (pp. 98–121). Don Mills, ON: Oxford University Press.

Young, I. M. (1990). *Justice and the politics of difference.* Princeton, NJ: Princeton University Press.

Young, I. M. (2000). Five faces of oppression. In M. Adams, W. J. Blumenfeld, R. Castanada, H. W. Hackman, M. L. Peters, & X. Zuniga (Eds.), *Readings for diversity and social justice* (pp. 35–49). New York: Routledge.

Appendix: How to Design a Course
Utilizing Multimedia Format

PREPARING THE SYLLABUS

1. Consult faculty in other disciplines, such as English, ethnic studies, theater, film, and art history for suggested readings, films, and images.
2. Think of each subtopic or class session in terms of its relationship to a contemporary issue or event to enable students to connect to the theme more easily.
3. Design assignments to build on each other and provide for maximum opportunities for discussions to enhance students' ability to dialogue about controversial subjects.
4. Whenever possible, connect topics and assignments to activities occurring in the university, surrounding community, holidays, and current events.
5. Build in sufficient space in the syllabus to allow students to suggest readings, films, music, etc., and to respond to unexpected developments.
6. Create various means for students to complete assignments such as in-class presentations and final projects. This reflects a strengths or asset-based approach to education, analogous to popular practice frameworks in the social work field.
7. Emphasize critiques/comments rather than grades in giving students feedback, particularly important when returning students' journals and their first assignment.

CONDUCTING CLASS SESSIONS

1. Emphasize your role as facilitator, not leader or sole expert. This requires expressing your views in a way that neither prejudges nor dominates conversation.
2. Create class ground rules for discussions during the first class session.
3. Use students' journals (or Web site discussion postings) to structure the discussion questions that form the basis of the outline of each class session.
4. Use a Socratic rather than a didactic style of teaching to stimulate dialogue; open up diverse lines of inquiry and allow controversial perspectives to be introduced.
5. Respect classroom silences, especially when discussing emotionally powerful or controversial topics. Be patient, yet persistent, in drawing out students' voices.
6. Whenever possible, watch films, videos, etc. in a group setting, rather than assigning them to students to watch outside of class.

7. Be sure to mix contemporary music, films, and literature, ideally chosen by the students' themselves, with your own selections. Try to promote comparisons not only about the subject matter, but also about the manner in which it is presented.

8. Balance the presentation of each topic with illustrations from various media.

9. Set the mood of each class session with music or an image at the outset. Encourage students to bring in their own music or images for this purpose. This helps students make the transition from more traditional classroom settings and subtly underscores the emotional and psychological aspects of the transformation process.

CHAPTER EIGHT

Utilizing Cemetery Work as a Mechanism for Teaching Social Justice and Engaging Students in Restorative Justice Efforts

Carla J. Sofka

Diana Strock-Lynskey

Abstract

This chapter will provide an overview of two undergraduate social work courses that utilized cemetery work projects to teach about social justice. Each course explored academic and practice-based constructs, such as disenfranchised grief, social justice, restorative justice, and transformative learning. Students applied these constructs to the initiation of a process for reestablishing "sacred spaces" for the deceased within each of their communities of origin. The projects were undertaken with deceased Albany Almshouse residents and with deceased Jewish community members residing in a Jewish cemetery in the village of Yselyub, Belarus.

Cemeteries represent sacred ground—places to honor and respect the memory of those who have died and for the living to maintain a connection to those who were significant to them during life. Harvey (2006) noted that "cemeteries have historically been seen . . . as sacred spaces, and that aspect should not be forgotten" (p. 295). According to Zelinsky (1994), "deciding how to bestow our earthly remains is a response to one of the central challenges in defining what it means to be human" (p. 29). Sadly, there are circumstances where this has not been the case. For example, during periods of rapid growth in some American cities, unmarked and forgotten graves and even entire cemeteries of the poor were relocated and even destroyed to make way for expansion. During and after wars and catastrophic occurrences such as the Jewish Holocaust and other mass acts of genocide, oppressors have used the desecration and even total destruction of cemeteries as the ultimate tactic to dehumanize and annihilate an entire culture (Strock-Lynskey, 2007).

This chapter will provide an overview of two undergraduate social work courses offered at Siena College, a four-year college founded by the Franciscans and grounded in the Catholic and liberal arts traditions, located in Loudonville, New York. Through the use of student-based service-learning cemetery work projects, each course explores academic and practice-based constructs, such as disenfranchised grief, social justice, restorative justice, and transformative learning. Students then apply these constructs to the initiation of a process for reestablishing sacred spaces for the deceased within each of their communities of origin. The service-learning cemetery work projects undertaken related to two very distinct communities: (1) deceased Albany Almshouse residents buried within Albany Rural Cemetery, located just outside of Albany, New York, and (2) deceased Jewish community members residing in a Jewish cemetery that had been desecrated during World War II located in the village of Yselyub, Belarus.

Framework for Courses

SERVICE-LEARNING

Service-learning is defined and described as a pedagogical approach that combines a credit-bearing educational experience with an organized service activity (Nnakwe, 1999). The service activity not only meets community needs but is an empowering approach that provides students with opportunities to develop and apply skills within an experiential learning opportunity that embodies specific social work values, such as a respect for diversity and social justice (Bringle & Hatcher, 1996; King, 2003; Lemieux & Allen, 2007). Ngai (2006) notes that service-learning is "ideally suited to achieving both the personal and academic goals of students and the broader goals of civic responsibility and social justice" (p. 165). This definition of service-learning is similar to Maxwell's (2002) definition of transformative learning, which "involves experiencing a deep, structural shift in the basic premises of thought, feelings and actions" along with a "shift of consciousness that dramatically and irreversibly alters our way of being in the world" (p. 18). Maxwell (2002) also notes that this shift of consciousness involves one's understanding of ourselves, relationships with other humans, one's understanding of relations of power in interlocking structures of class and race, and can involve one's sense of possibilities for social justice.

SOCIAL JUSTICE

The National Association of Social Workers (NASW) defines social justice, a core value of the social work profession, as "the view that everyone deserves equal economic, political and social rights and opportunities" (NASW, 2007, p. 1). The Council on Social Work Education's (2004) curriculum standards stresses the importance of integrating content into social work courses on social justice, grounded in an understanding of human rights. Typically, such content focuses on the role of social workers in addressing the needs of marginalized, disenfranchised, and oppressed populations.

GRIEF

When placed within the context of the cemetery restoration work undertaken for each of these projects, the concept of disenfranchisement is interrelated with another very complex concept, that of grief. According to Doka (1989), grief is disenfranchised due to a loss being defined as socially insignificant or when the loss itself is not socially validated. This disenfranchisement of the deceased or the bereaved can be due to the fact that either or both are viewed as a member of a socially devalued or marginalized population. Residents of almshouses throughout the United States were not recognized as legitimate members of their own communities or were shunned by members of the community at the time of their deaths due to their poverty status. During the Jewish Holocaust, survivors could not outwardly engage in mourning or grief out of fear that acknowledgment of relationships with the decreased could jeopardize one's safety or bring about one's own death. In addition, entire communities were eliminated, leaving no trace of their existence, with no one to acknowledge and mourn their loss.

RESTORATIVE JUSTICE

Under these circumstances, the cemetery work extended beyond the realm of social justice and into what has been referred to as "restorative justice" (Zehr, 2002). Within the restorative justice practice community, there has been a good deal of debate about the definition of restorative justice. One of the founders of the restorative justice movement, Zehr (2002) offers the following working definition: "restorative justice is a process that seeks to involve, to the extent possible, those who have a stake in a specific offense and to collectively identify and address harms, needs and obligations, in order to heal and to put things as right as possible" (p. 37). Pavlich (2005) further clarifies that "healing in this sense involves meaningfully addressing contextually defined needs following a crime" (p. 32). Marshall (1996) emphasizes that this process also involves finding constructive ways "to resolve collectively how to deal with the aftermath of the offense and its implications for the future" (p. 37). Historically, restorative justice efforts have been directed toward providing alternative remedies for addressing serious harm or death that has occurred as the result of violating the rights of others. In keeping with this, restorative justice models have focused on offenders being given the opportunity to demonstrate redress toward the individuals, family members, and related communities that they have harmed (McLaughlin, Fergusson, Hughes, & Westmarland, 2003; Strickland, 2004). In the 1990s, the restorative justice movement began to focus more broadly on citizens and communities as entities suffering harm and also requiring healing and repair (Bazemore & Schiff, 2001). Restorative justice practice efforts have also been undertaken in schools and workplaces and been utilized for addressing larger community issues and processes (Zehr, 2002). Mulligan (2001) discusses the connection between cemetery restoration and healing among mental health care consumers. More recently, some efforts have also focused on the concept of "community responsibility," which Pavlich (2005) defines as

> The need for a community to deal with the aftermath of a crime, and to ensure that the community becomes (or remains) a safe, secure and collectively meaningful space for all members. The main objective is to restore a community's fabric . . . and building community strength by requiring communities to deal with the criminal event through restorative processes (p. 33).

Daly (2003) maintains that "given the extraordinarily diverse meanings of the term [restorative justice] and the contexts in which it has been applied, it is important . . . to bound the term to a particular context and set of practices" (p. 196). Inherent in whatever set of restorative justice practices that may be utilized are some common values and principles.

The Prison Fellowship International Project (PFIP) (2007) serves as one example of a program that draws from principles that are consistent with other restorative justice models and frameworks, and exemplifies the broader purposes of this student-based service-learning cemetery project work. Among the major principles of the PFIP (2007) are that (1) justice requires that we work to restore those who have been injured (the first priority being the individual victims and the second priority being the community, to the degree possible); (2) those most directly involved and affected (by crime) should have the opportunity to participate fully in the response if they wish; and (3) government's role is to preserve a just public order, and the community's is to build and maintain a just peace.

The PFIP also emphasizes the following practices that are consistent with other restorative justice models: (1) *Encounter:* Creating opportunities for victims, offenders, and community members who want to do so to meet to discuss the crime and its aftermath; (2) *Amends:* Expecting offenders to take steps to repair the harm they have caused; (3) *Reintegration:* Seeking to restore victims and offenders to whole, contributing members of society; and (4) *Inclusion:* Providing opportunities for parties with a stake in a specific crime to participate in its resolution and to share responsibilities for restorative justice through partnerships for action (Pavlich, 2005; PFIP, 2007; Zehr, 2002).

Typically, restorative justice efforts are initiated within a "present context," that is, in relation to a recent victim and community. Pavlich (2005) states that "the notion of healing is meant to be a future-orientated gesture insofar as it tries to rectify, to the greatest possible extent, the harm of a past criminal event" (p. 32). With regard to the cemetery projects highlighted in this chapter, restorative justice efforts were initiated posthumously to attempt to remedy past harm caused to collectives of individuals (peoples) or communities who had been systematically victimized through the use of oppression, discrimination, and even genocide. In addition to this, a unique aspect of both projects was their emphasis on finding meaningful, engaging mechanisms that might be used to either establish or reestablish a rightful resting place for the deceased (of a prior generation) within their communities of origin (among community members who do not have a recognized relationship with the deceased). In the case of the Yselyub, Belarus, project, it was also hoped that these activities would begin to reestablish not only a rightful resting place, but also a rightful place, within the history of this village, for its Jewish community members and for the past history of Belarus's involvement in and response to World War II. To do so required the need to establish (many years after the fact) that harm had occurred and that the extent of this harm was such that a current intervention was necessary to restore the rightful status of these members within the present community. For each project, community-based commemorative and memorial activities were then employed as strategies for beginning to restore a sense of justice. Such strategies have been found to be particularly beneficial to engage in within a community when people who have been subjected to the gross violation of human rights want public recognition of the harm they have suffered (Cunneen, 2006) or to prevent disenfranchisement of grief when victimization results in the loss of life of an individual or groups of people (Danieli, 2006). A more in-depth overview of the specific methodologies utilized in the development and implementation of each of these projects follows.

Project #1: Albany Almshouse Cemetery Project (Albany, New York)

In January of 2002, while erecting a protective tent around a construction site, workers unearthed graves that were determined to be part of the long-forgotten Albany Almshouse cemetery. As additional information was released about the history of the cemetery and the paupers who were laid to rest there, so grew the controversy regarding whether or not to further delay the construction that was interrupted by this discovery. There had been two prior incidents during which this cemetery and its residents became newsworthy. In 1989, a construction crew uncovered five coffins behind a New York State Health Department laboratory near this location. In 1992, the Division of Hazardous Waste Remediation reported that this laboratory had dumped between one hundred and two hundred gallons of solvents on this abandoned cemetery, described in the newspaper as a "burial ground for paupers and poisons" (Wehrwein, 1992).

A headline that appeared in the *Albany Times Union* several years after this reflected the sad reality that these individuals had previously been treated this way: "Forgotten in life, interrupted in death" (Benjamin, 2000). Shortly after this, the Charitable Leadership Foundation in Clifton Park, New York, donated funds for the archaeological excavation of the cemetery and to rebury the residents at Albany Rural Cemetery. However, several months later, these funds and tolerance for construction delays were exhausted and a decision was made to halt the excavation efforts. A local citizen's response to this decision follows: "The decision to terminate the ongoing archaeological excavation of the Albany Almshouse cemetery is reprehensible from both a moral and scientific standpoint" (Willis, 2002).

After discussions and research, a decision was made to create a new unit in a social work elective course on death, dying, and grief. Students enrolled in this course cut across all majors and all academic years, and included male and female students from various religious and socioeconomic backgrounds. This new unit merged content on memorialization with a community-based service project that provided students with the opportunity to engage in activities that are consistent with restorative justice practices. Students were first introduced to concepts that served to set the stage for their service project and the development of task groups that would focus on the design and implementation of a memorial service for the almshouse residents. The concept of disenfranchised grief and circumstances contributing to disenfranchisement were introduced through an assigned reading from Doka (1989) and classroom discussion. Inclusion of content on the cost of dying and the role of poverty provided an opportunity to talk about the history of the Albany Almshouse and practices related to burial of the indigent in the community.

Students were then asked to read articles from the newspaper archives about the previously described events, and a subsequent class activity focused on the creation of a timeline of events from the discovery of the remains to their reburial at Albany Rural Cemetery. Conversations during this activity revealed that the students were incensed by what had occurred and the language that was used in the articles, and were motivated to explore what could be done to correct these injustices in some way. These conversations and questions provided the perfect opportunity to discuss the concept of restorative justice, and to pose the question about whether this type of justice could be accomplished posthumously. Since students had been introduced to content about strategies for memorialization in an earlier unit of the course, students began to discuss the idea of a memorial service as a strategy to accomplish this goal.

We reviewed a list of potential components of memorial services and rituals. Students were encouraged to keep this list in mind as they began to research an individual resident of the Almshouse. This research was conducted at the Albany Town Hall of Records, with the assistance of staff. Albany County is fortunate to have extensive original records from the Almshouse in its collection, including the admissions book, the discharge book, and monthly reports from the Almshouse physician.

To ensure that students selected an individual who had died while residing at the Almshouse, each student began by choosing an individual from the discharge book whose reason for discharge was listed as "death." Next, by using both admissions and discharge records, students could obtain a mixture of demographic and situational information about each resident (concept of *encounter*). In addition to age and religious affiliation, records described each person's racial and ethnic background and indicated if the person was an immigrant from another country. Last known residence was also listed as well as whether or not the person had living relatives. Information about the individual's occupation and his or her physical health was available. When reading the language that was used to describe the Almshouse residents in the original records and the newspaper coverage of recent events, the students were appalled. A rich discussion ensued about the presence of stigma and discrimination toward the poor in our society. Students made a commitment to discontinue the use of derogatory language and would educate others about the lives of the disenfranchised; thus, their aim to decrease the use of such language in relation to the poor reflected the concepts of *amends* by proxy and guarantee against repetition.

Students constructed a biographical sketch of their chosen resident. When these sketches were read in class, it became clear that common characteristics of the almshouse residents included the lack of financial resources, poor health or physical disabilities, transient lifestyles, and the absence of living family. Information was also presented on the religious backgrounds and nationalities represented among the group. This information was then used by the students to determine the types of prayers (Protestant, Catholic, and Jewish) that would be selected for the memorial service to ensure that it reflected the beliefs of those being memorialized. Information that students had gathered about resident's countries of origin was later used to obtain small flags that were placed along with two American flags around the Almshouse burial site marker during the memorial service.

A team of students was responsible for creating the program for the memorial service. In order to commemorate each individual's life during the service, two students created memorial cards with each person's name. Each student honored his or her resident by reading each resident's name while placing a carnation in the resident's honor in a vase by the Almshouse burial site marker, and the list of residents was included in the program. Music selected for the memorial service included a traditional hymn ("Amazing Grace," a song commonly recalled by students as being included in services that they had attended), a contemporary song ("Dust in the Wind" by Kansas), and a song written by one of the students ("In Our Hearts" by Craig Spinelli). Several students compiled the history of the Almshouse and the story of the discovery, removal, and reburial of the almshouse residents in a document that was summarized and distributed during the memorial service. One premed student researched and described information from the physician's reports, which included causes of death, adding another component of storytelling to the service. The instructor was asked by the students to contribute a reading of "Sacred Ground" by John Rainer and the original poem "Potter's Field to Sacred Ground."

In addition to those individuals described above who were present, a social work field educator who works at a local homeless shelter was asked to represent the population of individuals who are currently being challenged by issues of poverty, homelessness, and other types of adversity. His presence (reflecting the concept of *inclusion*) reminded all students that although these injustices continue, each of them has the ability to be involved in working toward the elimination of these injustices. Also invited to attend the service were the historian from the Albany Town Hall of Records who assisted with our quest for information, Charitable Foundation representatives (that had funded the disinterment and reburial), the Albany Rural Cemetery staff, and a popular friar at the college. To create a more permanent addition to the Almshouse burial site, a tree was planted at the burial site, with a plaque identifying it as a gift from the class.

While the students decided against publicizing the service to avoid the potential of changing the quiet and respectful nature of the service, the campus photographer took photos to create a visual record.

Project #2: Restorative Justice for Jewish and Other Community Members (Yselyub, Belarus)

During the summer of 2006, the School of Liberal Arts at Siena College cosponsored the Restoration of Eastern European Jewish Cemeteries Project with Dr. Michael Lozman. The project workgroup consisted of ten Siena students, the dean, a college staff member, Dr. Lozman, and one of the coauthors.

Dr. Michael Lozman, a local orthodontist from Latham, New York, observed firsthand the desecration that invading Nazis in Belarus during World War II had undertaken of the Jewish cemetery in which his ancestors were buried. After learning that other cemeteries throughout Belarus had suffered a similar fate, Dr. Lozman created the project and, partnering first with Dartmouth College and then with the University of New York and State University of Binghamton, completed several prior cemetery restoration projects in various villages within Belarus.

The students involved in this initiative were all enrolled full-time at the college, ranging from first-year freshmen to juniors. Gender was evenly represented with the group consisting of five males and five females. With the exception of one student who was of Latina heritage and one faculty member who was part Native American, all of the other students and chaperones were of Euro-American descent. Dr. Lozman was Jewish and one faculty member was Universalist. The rest of the group was Christian (with one student who also had a parent who is Jewish). The majority had not traveled outside of the United States and none of our members had traveled to Eastern Europe. When asked why they wanted to be involved with this project, some of the students' initial reasons included: an interest in having a travel experience outside of the United States, an opportunity to visit an area of the world previously not accessible, an interest in participating in a more experientially based approach to learning about the Jewish Holocaust, and an interest in social justice.

Due to the need for formal study and preparation for a trip of this sort, the project was reconceptualized to offer the option to participate in the project as a course that included both academic and service components, with the option to enroll as a for-credit course. Six of the ten students selected this option. Course requirements included (1) participation in three two-hour seminars; (2) the viewing and writing of a critique of two media sources that relate to the Jewish Holocaust; (3) a written analysis of *Night* by Elie Wiesel (2006); (4) completion of the educational tours and the service project; (5) completion of a journal; and (6) completion of a final reflection paper. To ensure that the students who completed the project but did not take the course had the opportunity to build rapport with the other students, we decided to conduct an orientation session for the entire group just prior to departure.

The seminars focused on three themes: (1) an overview of the history of Belarus; (2) the personal accounts of a local couple, both of whom have parents who were Jewish Holocaust survivors; and (3) an overview of the interrelationship between historical trauma response and principles of restorative justice.

It was during this last seminar that we earnestly explored the deeper principles and values underlying our rationale for the project. First, we reviewed the traditional definition of disenfranchised grief and then discussed how it might be broadened to apply to the experiences of a community and even an entire culture. As noted by Balakian (1997):

> If the circumstances relating to the disenfranchised grief are especially severe—such as is the case with genocide—the significant others of the deceased may be unable to resolve such grief. . . . When this occurs, the victim('s) culture is held hostage in a wilderness of grief and rage, and is shut out of its moral place in history.

This may lead to the situation that Maria Yellow Horse Brave Heart (2005) refers to as a historical trauma response based on "the cumulative emotional and psychological wounding across generations, including (but not limited to) one's own life span resulting . . . from a cataclysmic history of genocide" (p. 4). Denham (2006) postulates that historical trauma need only include "the conditions, experiences, and events that have the *potential* to contribute to or trigger (such) a response" (p. 31).

The class then discussed that while the specific dynamics of the historical trauma response may differ, it can also be transmitted across generations within families, communities, and cultures by those who had witnessed such acts of injustice but were now allowed to acknowledge them, who indirectly contributed to acts of injustice by acting as bystanders, or who failed to correct such injustices after their occurrence (whether it be in the generation in which the atrocities occurred or in subsequent generations). Next, we focused on the interrelationship between historical trauma and restorative justice. The questions raised by the group assisted us in focusing on the higher purpose of our work and applied directly to the restorative justice principles and values espoused by the Prison Fellowship International Project (2007):

1. To what extent might the principle of working to restore a sense of justice within a community be applied to the village in which we would be completing cemetery restoration work? For example, would the residents be open to our efforts to restore a Jewish cemetery that had existed in their village but had not been respected as such or maintained for more than sixty years? Could we do this in a way that would not come across as judgmental or presumptuous?

2. Given that there had been no Jewish community members in this village since the Nazis had invaded in 1941, would the community members be able to relate to and be willing to participate in our efforts (concept of *inclusion*) to initiate a process to reintegrate the prior Jewish members of their community into the history and fabric of the community through restoring this cemetery to its rightful status of sacred ground?

3. Might this project serve as catalyst for the community to engage, posthumously, in a dialogue about this devastating occurrence in their history (concept of *encounter*)? If so, could this be done in a way that would be empowering rather than retraumatizing?

4. Might the community be willing to claim ownership for the future maintenance of this cemetery (concept of making *amends*) and, in doing so, move toward a just peace through beginning the process of acknowledging feelings of grief and loss?

The ability to place the concepts presented in the course within the specific context of the service-learning experience enabled the group to begin to make the shift of consciousness that Maxwell (2002) stresses is necessary to engage in for transformative learning.

During this discussion, Dr. Lozman also introduced a very important concept: the "mitzvah," explaining:

> Within the Jewish religion, a mitzvah is considered a blessing of the highest order. There are different types of mitzvahs. One type of mitzvah is that of doing a good deed for someone who has died. Since the deceased can never return to offer their thanks, such a deed must be a truly selfless act, engaged in solely for the deceased with no expectations of benefiting the individual who is undertaking it. Cemetery work should be viewed as such an act. From this perspective, we should not expect to receive thanks from the current residents of Yselyub, but rather, focus our energies on the act of restoring the resting places of those who did not have significant others to do so for them. (Strock-Lynskey, 2007, p. 7)

This concept relates very well to those aspects of transformative learning by Maxwell (2002), which have been previously described. Through offering this perspective, Dr. Lozman challenged us to move beyond any self-centered motivations for engaging in this project and toward embracing what Ngai (2006) claims are the broader goals of learning, those of "civic responsibility and social justice" (p. 165).

"Project Restore" (as the trip came to be known) took several months of planning, fund-raising, and preparation. The trip included educational tours of major historical sites within Poland, including the Warsaw Ghetto, the Warsaw Jewish Cemetery, the cities of Warsaw and Krakow, Auschwitz and Birchenau Concentration Camps, as well as within Belarus, the cities of Minsk and Muir, and the Belarus Resistance Movement Museum.

While all these aspects were truly fascinating and very meaningful, the trip to Auschwitz and Birchenau was a life-altering experience that left its mark. As one student stated in his reflective paper:

> The impact of visiting such a place was indescribable. . . . The feel of Auschwitz was like nothing I had ever felt before. This was not a museum or a memorial. . . . This was a place of great hate, sadness, fear and loss. . . . You read about it but seeing it all right in front of you is astounding. . . . This is when it became truly apparent what we were about to do. (Begley, 2006)

As another student also stated, "I think when we left the concentration camps that day we all walked away different people . . . we all learned to understand human suffering on a greater level" (Gaschel, 2006). These examples serve as powerful illustrations of the "shift of consciousness that dramatically and irreversibly alters our way of being in the world," which is characteristic of transformative learning experiences (Maxwell, 2002, p. 18).

Upon arriving in Belarus, our group traveled to the town of Lido (at one time a thriving city with a significant Jewish population), where the group resided while completing cemetery restoration work in the village of Yselyub (a one-hour commute each way daily). While there, the group worked closely with a local school, whose students, faculty, and principal greeted us upon our arrival. After a warm greeting, and following a meal that was prepared by some of the local families and teachers, the group was invited into one of the classrooms for introductions and a presentation by the only two elders in the village still alive to remember the Jewish Holocaust, who shared their memories of the prior Jewish members of their community and their fate. One of our speakers noted:

> One day in 1941, the Nazis arrived in our village and rounded up all our Jewish neighbors (40 families and nearly one-half of the entire village population) and took them away. We heard later that they were all executed. A woman had managed to escape and came back to the village and went to one of our neighbors and asked for help. He was too afraid and turned her away. We don't know what happened to her after this. (Strock-Lynskey, 2007, p. 11)

The group learned that the execution site selected for the village's Jewish families was a corner area in the cemetery that we were there to restore. For the teachers and students, this was the first time that they had heard these stories and learned about this site. In advance of our trip, Dr. Lozman and the school principal had also developed a student essay contest based on examining the relationship between the Holocaust and the Jews of Belarus. This provided an opportunity for the school and community to engage in dialogue about their history and to conduct research on the Holocaust and Belarus's role in the underground resistance movement. These essays were later read at a concluding banquet sponsored by the group. These events illustrate the village's willingness to initiate the process of reintegrating into their collective consciousness, which is associated with restorative justice efforts (PFIP, 2007) through acknowledging the loss of their Jewish community members and the role of Belarus in fighting against genocide. The village also demonstrated its willingness to engage in this process through allowing the young people to actively participate in the cemetery restoration work of the group. The young people worked on the project with the group from beginning to end, enabling the group to accomplish a great deal.

Over the course of six days, the group was able to clear the entire cemetery of major debris, erect a cemetery fence, install a formal entranceway and dedication plaque, and work to locate and restore 160 gravestones. The restoration of the gravestones served as another very significant point of transformation for both the community and the group. The stones became a visible reminder that each site represented a real person that had once existed as a member of the community and assisted to reestablish the sacredness of the cemetery. This process also serves as a powerful example of the major focus of restorative justice according to Pavlich (2005), that of "building community strength by requiring communities to deal with the criminal event through restorative processes" (p. 33).

After a memorial service involving our group, community members, political leaders, and embassy representatives, our students and the village's young people gathered small stones that were placed on each gravestone, a Jewish tradition that we learned signified that someone has visited that grave and honored the deceased. The memorial service and this simple act illustrated very poignantly ways in which commemorative and memorial activities can be used as strategies for making amends and the importance of the inclusion of key stakeholders (PFIP, 2007). The commemorative service offered a way for all participants to value such traditions and to learn how to effectively utilize them to properly acknowledge the deceased Jewish members of this community. The project appeared to have made a long-term impact on the community, as evidenced by an interview conducted after the project's completion with the school's principal, in which she noted:

> To be honest, I feel ashamed we hadn't done this before. It's a great lesson for us in how to respect the dead, no matter what religion they were. I know that the Jewish community of Yselyub consisted mainly of shopkeepers who were respected by the villagers for their charity work. I now feel moved to build an archive and learn more about them. (Vilkos, 2006, pp. 1–4)

Lessons Learned and Suggestions for Replication

When considering possible replication of these projects, certain challenges may be encountered. For example, with regard to the Albany Almshouse Project, while the availability of detailed records and a staff person at the Town Hall of Records to provide access to those records facilitated the success of this project, working backwards from death records to admission records resulted in frustration when the records could not be easily located or when it was discovered that no corresponding data was available. The learning curve required to conduct research without the aid of computerized data was a significant one for several students. In addition to this, due to the rare nature of the Almshouse documents and the absence of financial resources to duplicate them, students were required to go off campus to conduct the research. The location of the Town Hall of Records made the use of public transportation very challenging, and the complicated and varied schedules made it difficult for students without a car to share a ride. Instructors must anticipate the need for sufficient lead time required for students to coordinate schedules and gain access to the records.

With regard to Project Restore, a factor that poses a significant challenge to any group that is considering traveling is that of having a key person (such as Dr. Lozman) or organization who has established important relationships leaders and organizations and who can take the lead on the initial logistics of the project. Utilizing such a person may be imperative, such as in the case of visiting Belarus, which required an "invitation" to be extended from a specific jurisdiction within the country to any individual who wishes to travel to there and required approval of final travel plans by government leadership. In some cases, both passports and visas may be required for travel, and sufficient lead time is needed for these documents. Flexibility is crucial as well, as the group learned only six weeks prior to departure of the exact village in which we would be conducting our work and finalized our travel plans accordingly. Having a specific resource person who resides in the country in which the project takes place may also be essential to a meaningful, educational experience.

Fund-raising for the project also posed a significant challenge. While students paid the equivalent of a three-credit course and faculty travel expenses were offset through the generous support of an international study grant obtained through the college, supplemental funding was still needed to offset costs for items such as the educational trips built into the overall experience, for interpreters, and to purchase materials needed for the completion of the cemetery work (e.g., metal panels that had to be made in Belarus and transported to Yselyub in advance of our arrival; cement that had to be brought in by local contractors; shovels, buckets, picks, and other equipment). While initially it was assumed that it would be relatively easy to secure donations from Jewish-based organizations within the United States, most were unable to do so because of their funding constraints. As a result, aside from donations generously made by a few local synagogues and the college, the additional funding had to be painstakingly raised one donor at a time. Based on this, it is recommended that at least one year be allocated to ensure adequate time has been built in to secure the needed funding.

Gravestone restoration work requires a good deal of knowledge, skills, and access to proper materials (e.g., cleaning solutions, supplies needed to obtain gravestone data, camera equipment). The use of improper materials and methods can result in damaging stones or destroying valuable data that might be needed to locate the deceased. Careful planning is needed to prepare for this aspect of the work. The Association for Gravestone Studies can be utilized as an excellent resource. Of note is that while some colleges and communities may not have the means or access to engage in cemetery restoration work in other countries, many opportunities exist to complete such work within the United States.

Conclusion

The cemetery as sacred ground and cemetery restoration work offer rich opportunities for integrating social and restorative justice and grief resolution efforts into the learning process. Through the unique nature of each project, participants learned that restorative justice work does not have to depend on the original victims having to be a part of this process. Through the use of academic and service-learning activities, students can be engaged in a transformative learning process that enables them to understand another's life experiences through either "alter-casting," the taking on of a particular role to learn the expected behavior associated with that role, and gain perspective and empathy in the process (Pratkanis, 2000) or observing directly the impact of disenfranchisement of a segment of a community on its other members. Through the development of school- and community-based, academic and student partnerships that actively engage community members in social and restorative justice efforts, current generations can learn about past events and work to attain justice on behalf of those previously wronged. In collaboration with community members, students can experience ways in which to put restorative justice principles into practice through identifying effective mechanisms that provide restitution and make amends for past atrocities, and through doing so, assist others in reclaiming a sense of dignity and attain closure.

In the words of Holocaust survivor Elie Wiesel (1985, p. 168), "They have no cemetery; we are their cemetery." Through the development of cemetery project efforts, students can actively participate in service and transformative learning principles, and social and restorative justice models and practices as mechanisms for providing reparation for harm done to disenfranchised groups and communities. As Ngai (2006) states, such service-learning experiences have "the capacity to transform lives, to touch the heart as well as the mind, and to teach many valuable lessons beyond those provided within the confines of the classroom" (p. 174). Through such experiences, students, faculty, and community members can learn that although they may not be able to change the past, all have the power to influence the ways, both locally and globally, that current individuals as well as future generations conceptualize justice, address past injustices, and should they occur, work to not only confront but also to correct any future injustices with the use of social and restorative justice practices.

References

Balakian, P. (1997). *Black dog of fate: An American son uncovers his Armenian past.* Retrieved April 26, 2006, from http://www.facinghistory.org/facing.fha02 .nsf/

Bazemore, G., & Schiff, M. (2001). *Restorative community justice: Repairing harm and transforming communities.* Cincinnati, OH: Anderson.

Begley, C. (2006, Summer/Fall). *Personal reflection paper.* Unpublished manuscript, Siena College, Loudonville, NY.

Benjamin, E. (2000, April 19). Forgotten in life, interrupted in death. *Albany Times Union,* p. A1.

Bringle, R. G., & Hatcher, J. A. (1996). Implementing service learning in higher education. *Journal of Higher Education, 67,* 221–239.

Council on Social Work Education. (2004). *Educational policy and accreditation standards.* Retrieved on September 21, 2007, from http://www.cswe.org/NR/ rdonlyres/111833A0-C4F5-475C-8FEB-EA740FF4D9F1/0/EPAS.pdf

Cunneen, C. (2006). Exploring the relationship between reparations, the gross violation of human rights, and restorative justice. In D. Sullivan & L. Tifft (Eds.), *Handbook of restorative justice* (pp. 355–368). New York: Routledge.

Daly, K. (2003). Restorative justice: The real story. In E. McLaughlin, R. Fergusson, G. Hughes, & L. Westmarland (Eds.), *Restorative justice: Critical issues* (pp. 195–200). Thousand Oaks, CA: Sage Publications.

Danieli, Y. (2006). Elements of healing after massive trauma. In D. Sullivan & L. Tifft (Eds.), *Handbook of restorative justice* (pp. 343–354). New York: Routledge.

Denham, A. R. (2006). *Rethinking historical trauma: Narratives of resilience.* Retrieved April 1, 2007, from http://www.webpages.uidaho.edu/~rfrey/ PDF/Rethinking%20Historical%20Trauma%20Revised.pdf

Doka, K. J. (1989). *Disenfranchised grief: Recognizing hidden sorrow.* Lexington, MA: Lexington Books.

Gaschel, M. (2006, Summer/Fall). *Personal reflection paper.* Unpublished manuscript, Siena College, Loudonville, NY.

Harvey, T. (2006). Sacred spaces, common places: The cemetery in the contemporary American city. *Geographical Review, 96*(2), 295–312.

King, M. E. (2003). Social work education and service learning. *Journal of Baccalaureate Social Work, 8*(2), 37–48.

Lemieux, C. M., & Allen, P. D. (2007). Service learning in social work education: The state of knowledge, pedagogical practicalities, and practice conundrums. *Journal of Social Work Education, 43*(2), 309–325.

Marshall, T. (1996). The evolution of restorative justice in Britain. *European Journal of Criminal Policy and Research, 4*(4), 21–43.

Maxwell, M. (2002). What is curriculum anyway? In E. V. O'Sullivan, A. Morrell, & A. M. A. O'Connor (Eds.), *Expanding the boundaries of transformative learning: Essays on theory and praxis* (pp. 13–22). New York: Palgrave Press.

McLaughlin, E., Fergusson, R., Hughes, G., & Westmarland, L. (2003). Introduction: Justice in the round—Contextualizing restorative justice. In E. McLaughlin, R. Fergusson, G. Hughes, & L. Westmarland (Eds.), *Restorative justice: Critical issues* (pp. 1–18). Thousand Oaks, CA: Sage Publications.

Mulligan, K. (2001, August 3). Caring for patients' graves helps hospitals reconcile with living. *Psychiatric News, 36*(15), 10.

National Association of Social Workers. (2007). *Social justice* (Issue Fact Sheet). Retrieved September 21, 2007, from http://www.socialworkers.org/press room/features/issue/peace.asp

Ngai, S. S. Y. (2006). Service-learning, personal development, and social commitment: A case study of university students in Hong Kong. *Adolescence, 41*(161), 165–176.

Nnakwe, N. (1999). Implementation and impact of college community service and its effect on the social responsibility of undergraduate students. *Journal of Family and Consumer Sciences, 91*, 57–61.

Pavlich, G. (2005). *Governing paradoxes of restorative justice.* London: GlassHouse Press.

Pratkanis, A. R. (2000). Altercasting as an influence tactic. In D. J. Terry & M. A. Hagg (Eds.), *Attitudes, behaviour and social context: The role of norms and group membership* (pp. 201–226). Mahwah, NJ: Lawrence Earlbaum Associates.

Prison Fellowship International Project. (2007). *Restorative justice online.* Retrieved May 20, 2007, online.

Strickland, R. A. (2004). *Restorative justice.* New York: Peter Lang.

Strock-Lynskey, D. (2007, November 16–18). Historical trauma, restorative justice, and Jewish cemetery work, Belarus, Eastern Europe. In C. Brownstein-Evans (Ed.), *The battlefield for human rights: Social workers in the trenches* (pp. 3–19). Proceedings of the 39th annual conference of the New York State Social Work Education Association, White Plains, NY.

Vilkos, Y. (July, 2006). U.S. Catholic students clean up a Jewish cemetery in Belarus. *Global News Service of the Jewish People,* pp. 1–4. Retrieved August 18, 2006, from http://www.jta.org/PAGE-PRINT_STORY.ASP?INTARTICLEID= 16770

Wehrwein, P. (1992, February 4). Burial problem: Paupers field complicates cleanup of chemicals. *Albany Times Union,* p. B6.

Wiesel, E. (1985). Listen to the wind. In I. Abrahamson (Ed.), *Against silence: The voice and vision of Elie Wiesel* (Vol. I, pp. 166–168). New York: Schockens.

Wiesel, E. (2006). *Night.* New York: Hill and Wang.

Willis, P. (2002, August 22). Almshouse graves deserve careful study. *Albany Times Union,* p. A10.

Yellow Horse Brave Heart, M. (2005). From intergenerational trauma to intergenerational healing: A teaching about how it works and how we can heal. *Wellbriety*, 6(6), 1–8. Retrieved April 11, 2006, from http://www.whitebison.org/magazine/2005/volume6/no6.htm

Zehr, H.(2002). *The little book of restorative justice.* Intercourse, PA: Good Books.

Zelinsky, W. (1994). Gathering places for America's dead: How many, where, and why? *Professional Geographer, 46*(1), 29–38.

Appendix: Designing a Cemetery Project

PROJECT #1: RESTORATIVE JUSTICE FOR DISENFRANCHISED
ALMSHOUSE RESIDENTS

1. Locate information about the county almshouse. Possible resources include (a) town records/town clerk/town archives; (b) county courthouse; (c) historical society; (d) public library; (e) local history books; (f) local funeral home records (may have records related to indigent burials); and (g) Web-based information.

2. Search for the following types of information: (a) admissions records for individual residents; (b) medical records/physicians' reports; (c) documents recording discharges; and (d) death records/burial records.

3. Identify location(s) where almshouse residents are buried. This could include (a) Potter's field located near the almshouse property; (b) Potter's field for the town/county in a separate location; (c) disinterrals/reburials that may have occurred in a formerly rural area; and (d) an area where the land was reused and bodies were moved to another burial site.

4. In the classroom, present a lecture and facilitate a discussion about the following: (a) brief history of the local almshouse; (b) describe/define: (i) disenfranchisement experienced due to poverty and dying in poverty, (ii) Potter's field, (iii) disenfranchised grief/absence of memorialization for those dying in an almshouse, and (c) components of ritual/memorial services.

5. Working backwards from the death records, have each student in the class construct a biography of one of the residents, gathering information about (a) length of stay in the almshouse (date of admission/date of death); (b) reason for admission; (c) demographic information (age, gender, race/ethnicity, U.S. citizen or immigrant, religious affiliation or spiritual preference); and (d) cause of death, as well as any other available information.

6. Create a mechanism for students to share information about residents. Options include (a) summary sheet that can be photocopied and shared; (b) brief classroom presentation by each student; and (c) electronic file with a record for each almshouse resident.

7. Group project: Students design a memorial service in honor of the almshouse residents that includes (a) a way to acknowledge each resident; (b) ways to incorporate readings, music, religious/spiritual beliefs of the almshouse residents, heritage (race, ethnicity, homelands of immigrants) and other aspects of residents' lives for which information is available.
8. Conduct a public or private the memorial service. Copies of the materials produced (memorial service program, memorial cards, song lyrics, documentation of the history/summary of additional research) should be archived in the records of all participating organizations.

PROJECT #2: RESTORATIVE JUSTICE FOR DECEASED JEWISH COMMUNITY MEMBERS RESIDING IN CEMETERIES DESECRATED DURING OR AFTER THE HOLOCAUST (YSELYUB, BELARUS)

1. Identify a Jewish cemetery or other cemetery/burial ground in need of restoration that would be suitable to target for a service work project. If you are interested in working with the Restoration of Eastern European Jewish Cemeteries Project on future projects pertaining to Belarus or Poland, contact Dr. Michael Lozman, project director, at mlozman@aol.com or see http://eejhp .netfirms.com/Svir Cemetery.htm. If you are interested in exploring other possible sites for Jewish cemetery restoration work, go to the International Association of Jewish Genealogical Societies/ International Jewish Cemetery Projects Web site at http://www .jewishgen.org/cemetery/. If you are interested in locating other restoration sites, consider (a) contacting the U.S. Department of State for a listing of cemeteries in your area; (b) for information on possible projects pertaining to persons with psychiatric/mental disabilities, contact your state office of mental health, the National Alliance for the Mentally Ill (NAMI), or the Mental Health Association for your state; and (c) for possible projects relating to racially diverse communities, contact the NAACP or other population-specific advocacy groups in your state. The process of narrowing down your site selection should include a fact-gathering phase, which considers factors such as the current political, social, and economic climate; safety, prior project work conducted by other college groups, and the specific nature of such projects; receptivity of the host country/community; and feasibility of gaining fundraising support for the locations you are considering.
2. Establish mechanisms through which a relationship can begin to be established/built with the country/community that will be the focus of your service work efforts. A contact/lead person who can

travel in advance to visit possible project sites, meet with local political leaders and officials (to determine interest in a project, host family visits, the memorial service, and other extracurricular activities), begin to identify the types of and amount of materials that would be needed (as well as anticipated costs), arrange for interpreters, identify suitable lodging sites, and other activities is strongly recommended.

3. Determine the extent of interest within your college/university and broader community.

    a. Identify individuals who are in key positions at your college/ university and within your local community who will assist in promoting and fund-raising for the project. The involvement of at least one or two individuals within the broader community and in key administrative roles that support and are willing to assist in oversight of the administrative and fund-raising aspects of the project is important.

    b. Identify a core group of participants committed to participating in the project. Conduct a general information meeting about the proposed project for the broader campus and community. Prior to the meeting, decisions should be made about type of format (service-learning or credit-bearing course), number of credits, structure of course components, timing of components, etc. Collect contact information of participants, and be prepared to send out several follow-up notices to create a pool of serious participants. Have a mechanism in place for locking individuals into a firm commitment. A strategy that we utilized that worked well was to establish a cutoff date when individuals could elect to withdraw from the project, after which all students who did not withdraw would be billed for the cost of the course (if enrolled) as well as any other identified costs.

4. Create a project workgroup that will address planning, organizing, and fund-raising.

    a. The dean solicited, through e-mail, the names of those who might be interested in the project. We then created a lead team consisting of the project director, dean, a faculty member (myself), and a staff member. Each individual took responsibility for different aspects, such as developing the itinerary, working out travel arrangements, soliciting donations of materials we might bring with us (such as work gloves obtained from a local hardware store), purchasing rubbing paper and other supplies needed for securing gravestone data, making fund-raising contacts, etc. NOTE: If your project involves gravestone restoration work, an excellent resource is the Association of Gravestones Studies.

b. Planning meetings were initially held on a weekly and then on a biweekly basis once our work plan was established. Students participated very heavily in planning meetings and worked on completing tasks such as developing a project brochure and description that were used for student recruitment and fund-raising, conducting presentations to various community groups, and researching possible fund-raising sources online and within their home communities.

5. Ensure in advance that the group is effectively grounded in the broader conceptual frameworks and cultural context that is the central focus of your project work. A copy of the syllabus of the course featured in this chapter can be obtained by contacting Professor Strock-Lynskey at Strock@siena.edu. It is strongly recommended that an additional class/seminar be built into the educational model you utilize, which provides the basics of the language of your host setting and that all participants purchase a travel dictionary to take with them.

CHAPTER NINE

Using Transformative Learning to Enhance Social Justice Learning in Diversity Courses

Cecilia Thomas

Abstract

This chapter presents findings on a study of two diversity courses structured to promote cultural competency with vulnerable populations and to increase student commitment toward a multicultural, egalitarian society by using transformative and experiential learning processes. The disparity of African American children in the child welfare system served as the core issue that framed the students' study, while a second diversity course served as a comparison. Through qualitative data, this study suggests that educators can advance concern for social justice issues through the use of transformative and experiential perspectives that reinforce theoretical concepts taught in the classroom, increase student understanding, and help engage them in community concerns.

Concern for social justice and the elimination of inequity are paramount to the social work profession; however, students can be resistant to learning content on issues related to power differentials, oppression, and discrimination. This reticence may be due to the knowledge or value base required to effectively delve into this subject matter. The study of social justice necessitates much self-refection, critical analysis of one's worldview, and the assessment of emerging social realities.

These same components also make social justice a particularly complicated concept to teach students. Students often have a difficult time understanding the applicability of social justice to real-life issues and are therefore slow to care about these issues on a personal level. In general, helping students understand macrolevel concerns important to social work has been challenging (Anderson & Harris, 2005; Rocha, 2000). Debate continues on the type of educational approaches that may be most appropriate in meeting student learning needs and capturing student interest on this subject matter.

Social justice reflects societal concern for the most vulnerable and oppressed. Social and economic marginalization has severe consequences on such individuals that result in exclusion on a number of levels. Differing outcomes are compounded based on these oppressive and discriminatory processes. According to Van Soest and Garcia (2003),

> Social justice encompasses satisfaction of basic human needs and the equitable sharing of material resources. It aims at universal access to fundamental services in health, education, equal opportunities at the start, protection for disadvantaged persons or groups, and a degree of moderation in the areas of retribution, consumption, and profit. (p. 66)

The National Association of Social Workers' *Code of Ethics* (NASW, 2008) identifies social justice as one of the core values, demonstrating the importance of the pursuit of social change for injustices against vulnerable or oppressed groups. This prime responsibility of professional social workers is further dictated such that "social workers strive to ensure access to needed information, services, resources; equality of opportunity; and meaningful participation in decision making for all people" (NASW, 2008, p. 5). As a basic ideology, social justice encompasses fairness, equity, and equality (Flynn, 1995). Further, as asserted by Barker (2003), social justice refers to "an ideal condition in which all members of a society have the same basic rights, protection, opportunities, obligations, and social benefits" (pp. 404–405).

This chapter presents findings on a study of two diversity courses structured to promote cultural competency with vulnerable populations and to increase student commitment toward a multicultural, egalitarian society by using transformative and experiential learning processes. Content for both courses emphasized understanding sociopolitical processes such as oppression, discrimination, and economic deprivation for populations at risk and the consequences of inequality for individuals and social systems.

Transformative and Experiential Learning Processes

Mezirow (1997) views transformative learning as "the process of effecting change in a frame of reference" (p. 5). The underlying premise of transformative learning provides a conceptual framework that suggests the value of new meaning and understanding through critical self-reflection (Cranton, 1994; Knowles, 1977; Mezirow, 1991) of the assumptions that form the basis of our beliefs (Mezirow, 1997). The transformative process thereby increases one's understanding of the world and the capacity to change toward more inclusive viewpoints (Mezirow, 1990). Some important dimensions of transformative learning involve helping learners become autonomous thinkers, inviting discourse, interactive participation, as well as active cognitive and emotional processes (Mezirow, 1997). Transformative learning also emphasizes "creating an environment in which learners become increasingly adept at learning from each other and at helping each other learn in problem-solving groups" (Mezirow, 1997, p. 11). Grabove (1997) noted this process is one that requires the dual "effort, courage, and authenticity" (p. 90) of student and educator due to potential exposure to risk and vulnerability.

Transformative learning is further enhanced through participatory experiential techniques. According to Kolb (1984), learning is "the process whereby knowledge is created through the transformation of experience" (p. 38). Experiential processes promote discovery learning and employ action projects that are important in transformative approaches (Mezirow, 1997). This emphasizes guiding learners toward "more discriminating, self-reflective and integrative of experience" (Mezirow, 1997, p. 5). Stevens and Richard (1992) suggest that experiential learning involves the immersion of students in an activity and then a reflection of the experience. Theoretically, this process assumes that when the learner understands the value of certain knowledge or skills and is excited about this knowledge, learning can take place (Cantor, 1997).

The literature has suggested that student learning regarding macro-level issues can be effectively enhanced through the use of innovative educational approaches. For example, this body of research has included exploring the utilization of service learning in courses such as research (Anderson, 2002; Rosner-Salazar, 2003) and social welfare policy (Anderson & Harris, 2005). This method has demonstrated benefit by increasing student knowledge, understanding of the topic, life experiences, and sense of civic responsibility (Anderson & Harris, 2005; Myers-Lipton, 1998; Rosner-Salazar, 2003). Existing research on the application of transformative and experiential processes further endorses findings of improved learning for the student (Fineran, Bolen, Urban-Keary, & Zimmerman, 2002; Nagda, Gurin & Lopez, 2003), improved perceived competence (Rocha, 2000), and changes in student attitudes (Quinn, 1999).

The recurrent success of these approaches may be associated with the pragmatic nature of learning employed from a more realistic outlook. Lather (1991) suggested learning can be enhanced and resistance reduced upon acceptance of the realities of issues such as oppression. This suggests learners can then be helped to deal with the emotional aspects of learning such factors as fear or hopelessness, thereby becoming better ready to work toward change. Learning at only the cognitive level can limit the attainment of these crucial feelings (Van Soest & Garcia, 2003) and may inhibit one's motivation to rally for change efforts that alleviate social injustice. Transformative and experiential principles allow the student to directly apply the theoretical components of learning to lifelike circumstances, providing a foundation fundamental to learning and a framework to guide these applied experiences.

In consideration of the difficulty students may experience in embracing and understanding these concepts, different teaching methods for this subject may be warranted. Regrettably, there has been limited study of pedagogical approaches applied to the study of social justice issues. The present study explores the learning and understanding of social justice issues acquired by students from a diversity course, using transformative learning as an underlying approach. The disparity of African American children in the child welfare system served as the core issue that framed the students' study. A second diversity course, taught in a different semester, served as a comparison to the transformative learning students.

The next section identifies social justice as defined in the context of child welfare and highlights the many inequitable patterns evident in this important practice domain.

Transformative Learning Project

RACIAL DISPARITY: AN ISSUE OF CONCERN IN THE CHILD WELFARE SYSTEM

In the child protective service system, the term "disproportionality" has been used to refer to the overrepresentation of African American children and racial disparity. Nationally, the problem is evident from a statistical standpoint. African American children consist of approximately 39% of the children in the foster care system (U.S. Department of Health and Human Services, 2000) while they are only approximately 13% of the total U.S. population (U.S. Census Bureau, 2001).

Differential treatment and subsequently detrimental consequences have plagued African American children in the child welfare system. At the front end, these disparate results include African American children being more likely reported for child abuse (Sedlak & Schultz, 2001) and having higher substantiated reports of abuse (Rodenborg, 2004). Further, African American children have a greater likelihood of removal, (Barth, 1997; Courtney & Wong, 1996; Frame, 2002), remaining in the system longer (Barth, 1997; McMurtry & Lie, 1992), and have a decreased chance for adoption or reunification (Courtney & Wong, 1996; Frame, 2002; Kapp, McDonald, & Diamond, 2001; Smith, 2003; Wells & Guo, 1999).

Disparity is also apparent in terms of service usage in that African American children receive fewer services while in the system (Potter & Klein-Rothschild, 2002). These systemwide discrepancies are found in mental health (Garland, Landsverk, & Lau, 2003), health care utilization as it relates to access, and follow-up health services (Blumberg, Landsverk, Ellis-MacLeod, Ganger, & Culver, 1996; Risley-Curtiss, Combs-Orme, Chernoff, & Heisler, 1996). This is also evident in the child welfare response to families and children. For example, nonwhite families have been found to have fewer contacts or visits from agency caseworkers (Tracy, Green, & Bremseth, 1993). In addition, the proportion of unmet service needs such as housing and employment is disproportionate for African American families, possibly a reflection of the higher need levels for this population (Rodenborg, 2004).

These issues portray some of the equity differentials that exist in the child welfare system and reflect a severe and widespread problem. Regrettably, these system problems have existed for some time but are now causing increased national concern among the practice and research communities (Courtney & Skyles, 2003). This predicament of racial and ethnic disproportionality is viewed as multicausal and embedded in varied conditions such as poverty, cultural insensitivity, policies, practices, and other issues that impact the vulnerability of families. For example, race intersects with poverty in that African American families tend to be poorer, in receipt of welfare, unemployed, and they often reside in large urban areas (Ayón & Lee, 2005; Rodenborg, 2004) and in lower socioeconomic neighborhoods (Saunders, Nelson, & Landsman, 1993). Single parent status of many African American children in the child welfare system (Harris & Courtney, 2003; Rodenborg, 2004) may also be a contributing factor in view of the high rate of poverty for single-headed households. Undoubtedly, any subsequent resolutions for these complex problems must be multicausal and explore understanding societal or community-level issues as well as family and individual needs.

COURSE COMPONENT

The present study focuses on two diversity courses structured to promote cultural competency with vulnerable populations and to increase student commitment toward a multicultural, egalitarian society. Content for both courses emphasized understanding sociopolitical processes such as oppression, discrimination, and economic deprivation for populations at risk and the consequences of inequality for individuals and social systems. Further, students explored action strategies to counter policies, practices, and social institutions that promote inequity. Assignments for these courses consisted of intense readings, large and small discussion groups, journal writings, exploration through film, and student cultural presentations.

An additional transformative learning component was integrated only in the fall 2005 course. This facet consisted of an experiential project conducted in collaboration with the Child Protective Services (CPS) agency. In the summer of 2005, a statewide initiative was launched by CPS to address the overrepresentation of African American children and attest to the agency's commitment to combat these disparaging findings. A subsequent meeting was held with university stakeholders from across the state and a direct appeal was made for assistance in more closely examining this compelling issue.

The local CPS agency targeted a specified community with high CPS involvement and desired to better understand problems that might contribute to CPS intervention. Following discussion with CPS officials, the 2005 diversity class was deemed a resource to help examine intervening factors by means of a community assessment and analysis. An outline of potential research components was submitted to CPS for feedback and to verify interest in specified areas. The overall objectives of the experiential assignment for the students were to enhance student awareness and understanding of social justice ideals with marginalized populations and to relate these features to a realistic community setting.

Preparation for the fall 2005 project included dissemination of information regarding the targeted community to students. Further, a high-level CPS official provided introductory information on the nature of disproportionality, how children were impacted, and challenges facing the agency. This provided a foundation for the students, which helped them gain improved understanding of the community's connection to the specified problem. Further, students had the opportunity for direct interaction with CPS staff to address questions regarding the focus of this project.

The fall 2005 class was divided into six teams to manage the large magnitude of this project, each group focusing on differing components for a comprehensive community assessment (see the Appendix at the end of the chapter). The experiential component required the various groups to research specific resources and needs that affected differing facets of the community, families, and children. This process involved direct observation and description of specified aspects of the targeted community and conducting interviews with the residents/ stakeholders. Finally, students were expected to analyze and synthesize the data and present a final report of the findings to agency representatives. During each class period, time was allocated for the groups to plan their ongoing research, assess progress, and devise strategies to alleviate any identified barriers.

Method

PARTICIPANTS AND SETTING

Participants in this study consisted of a convenience sample of undergraduate students from two social work diversity courses entitled "Diversity in the Helping Professions," taught in the fall 2005 and fall 2006 at a large university in the southwestern United States. The students in the classes represented a number of different disciplines, including social work, rehabilitation studies, liberal arts, and criminal justice. The majority of students from both courses were classified as college juniors and seniors. The content for both courses was basically the same, except the fall 2005 course incorporated transformative learning with an experiential component as a class project ($n = 57$) (The fall 2005 class is hereafter referred to as the "transformative learning students."). A second cohort of students taking the same course the following year (fall 2006), without the experiential component and in a traditional format, served as a means to compare student learning ($n = 62$).

PROCEDURES

Institutional review board approval was obtained from the study-site institution. Students were informed about the voluntary nature of the study at the beginning of the semester, guaranteed anonymity, and were assured that participation or refusal would not impact their grade. Information on participation requirements was provided to the students and they were given the opportunity to ask questions or to have any concerns addressed. Those willing to participate signed consent forms early in the semester.

DATA COLLECTION

Basic, nonidentifying demographic information was collected from both classes, including information on student age, gender, socioeconomic status, and race/ethnicity. Other preliminary information was also collected on the students during the beginning of the semester to assess their knowledge of social justice issues.

Separate instruments were developed for the two classes to collect students' written responses to open-ended questions at the end of the semester. Both classes were asked about their understanding and knowledge of social justice, the necessity of social action, and engaging in social change. Further, qualitative information was obtained from the transformative learning students to assess their learning as a result of participation in the experiential activity. These students' written reports also served as a source of data. Additionally, on the last day of the class, the investigator conducted a one-hour focus group with the transformative learning students. The intent of the focus group was to better grasp the personalized transformative learning that was observed for these students. The focus group was audiotaped and transcribed verbatim.

DATA ANALYSIS

A qualitative approach was utilized to assess the unique aspects of learning that occurred for the transformative learning students, as well as to understand differential or common dimensions of the learning that occurred between the two classes. Qualitative data allows the study of experiences from the participant's perspective (Rubinstein, 1988) and "are a source of well-grounded, rich descriptions and explanation of processes occurring in local context" (Miles & Huberman, 1994, p. 15). Content analysis of all the data sources was examined using the constant comparison method to make comparisons among concepts (Glaser & Strauss, 1967), applying an inductive process of interpretation (Janesick, 1994).

Several techniques were used to enhance data quality through trustworthiness, credibility, and rigor of the data. These included member verifications to determine whether the findings were credible to study participants, peer reviews of the findings, and triangulation of data sources. Data dependability was further evaluated by employing an audit trail (Lincoln & Guba, 1985) to authenticate findings. The investigator coded the data using the line-by-line, iterative reading of transcripts and making notations of emerging patterns or themes (Marshall & Rossman, 1995). Open coding was used to identify emerging categories that adequately fit the data and initially resulted in the generation of sixty-five codes. These codes were reduced to further refine theoretical categories and to identify the major themes prominent to the students' learning.

Findings

PARTICIPANT DEMOGRAPHICS

Demographic data provide a context for understanding the study participants (see Table 9.1). The sample was composed of fifty-seven of the transformative learning students and sixty-two students from the fall 2006 course. For the transformative learning students, the mean age of participants was 33.4 with a range from 21 to 64 years old; the 2006 students had a mean age of 30.7 with ages ranging from 19 to 60. Both classes reflected a more nontraditional student population. The majority of students from both classes had to balance school responsibilities with employment on either a full-time or part-time basis, as well as the ongoing care and responsibilities of families. Over 80% of the population were students of color, which provides some additional dynamics to consider in understanding their experiences with this transformative learning project. The prevalent socioeconomic income range was $20,000–$29,000 for both classes.

STUDENT LEARNING

Distinct differences were evident between the two classes. Learning for the transformative learning students occurred at enhanced levels as a result of participation in the experiential transformative learning project. Four key themes emerged from the data sources that enlighten the learning experiences for the students participating in this added component (see Table 9.2). These were (a) recognizing systematic and complex conditions, (b) interpreting meaning from differing perspectives, (c) connecting through human sensitivity, and (d) advocating for action-oriented change. Exemplars of these themes are provided through the students' voices to more clearly illustrate the impact of their learning.

Recognizing systematic and complex conditions. Students participating in the transformative learning experience recognized the systematic conditions and the realistic impact of social ills in the targeted community. The disparities that faced this area became evident to students along with an understanding of the complexities that intersected social and economic injustices. Students observed that many community resources were nonexistent, and this necessitated residents' reaching outside of their locale for common goods and services that were often inaccessible, such as medical resources and insurance. Other debilitating factors that were observed included the impact of crime, poverty, and limited educational opportunities, all of which, students concluded, resulted in a diminished quality of life for residents. This is in

TABLE 9.1   Demographic Characteristics of Students

Students	Transformative Learning Project $n = 57$ (%)	Traditional Class $n = 62$ (%)
Gender		
Males	13 (22.9)	16 (25.8)
Females	44 (77.2)	46 (74.2)
Race/ethnicity		
African American	36 (63.2)	36 (58.1)
Latino	11 (19.3)	9 (14.5)
Caucasian	6 (10.5)	14 (22.6)
Other	4 (7.1)	2 (3.2)
Age Ranges		
19–25	20 (31.5)	24 (40.7)
26–39	23 (40.5)	25 (42.0)
40–49	7 (12.4)	6 (9.6)
50 +	7 (12.4)	4 (6.0)
Employment		
Full-time/self-employed	41 (71.9)	43 (69.3)
Part-time	9 (15.8)	9 (14.5)
Not employed/other	7 (12.3)	10 (16.1)
Marital Status		
Married	22 (38.6)	22 (35.5)
Divorced	4 (7.0)	8 (12.9)
Single	29 (50.9)	26 (41.9)
Other	2 (3.5)	3 (4.8)
Income		
Less than $10,000	10 (17.5)	6 (9.7)
$10,000–$19,000	7 (12.3)	10 (16.1)
$20,000–$29,000	15 (26.3)	13 (21.0)
$30,000–$39,000	10 (17.5)	9 (14.5)
$40,000–$49,000	2 (3.5)	10 (16.1)
$50,000 +	13 (22.8)	11 (17.8)
Children		
No	19 (33.3)	27 (43.5)
Yes	36 (63.2)	34 (54.8)
Type of Residence		
Renting	27 (47.4)	27 (43.5)
Own home	25 (43.9)	23 (37.1)
Other	5 (8.8)	6 (9.7)

TABLE 9.2 Themes and Sample Indicators

Emerging Themes	Sample Indicators
Recognizing systematic and complex conditions	When each generation has no hope, they will proceed from what they know.
	This area has experienced generations of poverty and many basic needs are absent in the midst of unemployment and neglect prevalent in this community.
	Poverty and race are major factors in how this community lives on a day-to-day basis.
	Economic hardship weakens one's ability to cope with new problems and difficulties; hence they are more likely to succumb to the debilitating effects of negative life events.
Interpreting meaning from differing perspectives	There is very little education or funding for programs to inform these residents or encourage them to become independent and responsible.
	Safe and affordable shelter is difficult for many families with some living in unstable, crowded, or unsafe housing. Many social influences, disadvantages, and other barriers continue to hinder this community. Socioeconomic status is the primary cause of racial, health, and other disparities in this community.
	Employment opportunities, access to health care, poverty, and lack of supported services have affected the life experiences of individuals in this community.
Connecting through human sensitivity	A major prohibitive factor in the receipt of services is insurance. All children deserve to have the best health care. The majority in this community would aspire to something different if given the opportunity.
	It was disappointing to discover the enormous gaps in services for this community.
	People just want to be loved, nurtured, and affirmed, with better alternatives for services.
Advocating for action-oriented change	There are structures in the community that could be changed into one-stop centers, to provide supportive services, immediate identification of needs, and case management.
	There is a need for increased opportunities for celebration and community pride in an effort to reunite this community. Improved community awareness is essential and problems must be confronted. Keeping problems hidden "under the rug" or "patching them up" is not an option.
	Programs need to be developed in which children can get the services they need when families are unable to afford health care.

contrast to the traditional students who were less aware of the social components of marginalization and were less able to demonstrate understanding of the systemic impact of oppression and inequity.

The transformative learning students acknowledged visible signs of deterioration and the systemic nature of these problems, which had previously been minimized or ignored. Students noted that the community was "left behind" and, as summarized by one, "This area is overlooked and people accept and actually expect this community to fail." Another commented, "I have friends that live in this community; it just happens that they do not want to see what I now see." These sentiments were similarly expressed by a student: "It was very sad for me to realize that before this project, I had been visiting the same neighborhood over the year without recognizing these issues." Denial was also evident from both the community residents and community leaders regarding the existing conditions. As remarked by a student, "People want to believe that things have changed, but in many ways they have not." This was viewed as perpetuating the status quo and ultimately generating a cycle of apathy detrimental to the progress of the community at large.

The transformative learning students were more adept at observing the extent of individual-level problems and the subsequent negative effects of disparity. These students could also conceptualize the complexity of the continued impact of social injustice and neglect that was generational. A participant acknowledged learning that

> Societal issues in all areas that were researched affect the outcomes of children's safety, future, and existence. Employment opportunities, access to health care, poverty, and city-supported services have also impacted the life experiences of adults in this community. Children are dependent on parents to provide the financial, emotional, psychological, and physical needs of children entrusted to them. These basic needs are absent in the midst of poverty, unemployment, and neglect prevalent here. Maybe the issue is not the children but in educating, healing, and peeling away the layers of neglect evident among adults.

Students attributed many of the societal conditions to systematic community problems, such as the stress of single parenthood, unemployment, limited educational resources, substandard health care, and housing. Students initially felt that the plight of the community was insurmountable and difficult to solve. The serious nature of these problems and their complexities were summed in a student's statement that

"One person cannot fix these problems . . . it's going to take a community."

Interpreting meaning from differing perspectives. The two diversity classes were also distinguished by their ability to critically analyze the difficulties that may impact societal inequities and social injustice. Learning about the community was evident in many ways for the transformative learning students. They reported learning skills effective in helping them understand and interpret the meaning of phenomenon from new perspectives. For example, they were able to demonstrate a capacity to analyze the interworkings and sociopolitical factors that might affect community outcomes. These students became more knowledgeable about community-level factors that assisted in their capacity to make comparisons of severe disparities across differing communities. Skills in analyzing information were honed through advanced research skills that furthered their understanding of the status of the surrounding area. Students commented on also improving their listening and communication skills as they analyzed the extensive information that was gathered.

Seeing the community differently was a real revelation for some students. One student indicated learning "the status of a community that I know and did not know at all." In the examination of the numerous programs available in the community, these students were able to ascertain the impact of service gaps and limited resources. Students were also able to examine resource utilization and differential access to those benefits and services. Another student who commented on learning further elaborated on "the ability to focus more critically on others and to recognize problems when I see them." This was compounded with a will to know, understand, and further develop these key skills.

Connecting through human sensitivity. Students in the traditional class did not have the added field experience and fell short of personally connecting to and understanding the persuasive nature of social injustice. However, for the transformative learning students, there was evidence of greater sensitivity in embracing new information gained by connecting with the targeted community on a more human level. This served to deepen their understanding of oppression, inequality, and injustice. These students lamented about their findings not only at a cognitive level but an emotional level, particularly given the enormous gaps in services and resources. Moreover, the students acknowledged the added benefit of thinking not just in terms of their "own world." For example, one student reported having previously not thought about injustices, since "[they] didn't happen to me." Another noted that the transformative project put things in perspective. "It's sad to say that I lost where I came from. This project helped us." Others further remarked on the origins of unfair treatment as a result of self-interest and limited societal concern.

Notably, some transformative learning students were beleaguered by the findings and the life experiences of these residents living in the targeted community. There was the expression of grave concern about the circumstances of underserved populations in society. Students used words such as "horrible," "terrible," "disappointing," and "unfair" to describe these discoveries. These social issues remained a concern and were acknowledged by students in other ways as well. As observed by one, "Upon doing this project, I have had an eye-opening experience. It was eye-opening for me because I grew up in this area and I was not aware of many of its problems." Residents from the community who were interviewed related the personal toll of their circumstances and stated, "It appears that no one cares about this area. So therefore, no need to worry about voting, nothing will change." This sense of defeat was difficult for students to accept. One student suggested this viewpoint could lead to even further distressing outcomes in that "people are indeed products of their environment, not always intentionally. It is difficult to get out of 'bad' situations if you do not have access to the necessary tools to help yourself."

Advocating for action-oriented change. Students from the experiential transformative course were open regarding the value of confronting social and economic injustices. One student acknowledged learning "even more so, how much work needs to be done." An open commitment toward broaching the subject of change strategies was most prominent for these students than those in the traditional class. For the transformative learning students, there was a sense that just studying these concepts in didactic, traditional ways was not sufficient, and change strategies needed to be nonstandard. They made the case for change to occur using more creative devices to vitalize and impact learning, demonstrating an interest in developing comprehensive processes toward this endeavor. This was unlike students in the traditional class who were less likely to identify social ills or to indicate concrete change strategies.

The transformative learning students had heartfelt responses for those individuals in the community and were interested in striving for "fairness to all." The targeted community was viewed as needing a lot of assistance and deserving a better life. There was considerable acceptance of strategies to effect change and the necessity of alleviating observed injustices. For example, students were adamant about the need to protect children, and as one reported, "I suggest that we start with the children and focus on their well-being in order to break the cycle that has plagued this community for so many years." A range of community or advocacy strategies were elaborated, including the development of employment and training programs, providing healthier environments for children in the community, teaching cultural awareness, enhancing the availability of medical services, promoting effective parenting, and implementing more educational programs. The importance of maintaining a presence in the community and outreach was another recommendation. One participant observed:

> The organizations and agencies need to have more personal contact with the community and visit the families in their homes to see how they are coping on a day-to-day basis. In other words, instead of these residents seeking out services, organizations need to come to the community.

The transformative learning students reported feeling better prepared and were "encouraged to talk more publicly about social issues," thus speaking out for many who did not have a voice. Another student further elaborated this stance regarding social justice issues: "I learned that we all need to ask questions in efforts to make sure we understand." Students also noted the importance of governmental and religious institutions, and challenged these organizations to play a larger role to affect community change. One report reflected, "We believe collectively, that the government, community, and the church can truly make a difference and do more in funding the debilitating needs of this community."

Discussion and Implications

This exploratory study examined student learning in two different diversity classes. One class incorporated a transformative learning experience in the form of a communitywide social justice project and the other did not. The transformative learning students focused on the disproportionality of African American children in the CPS system and explored a range of contributing elements related to this societal problem, applicable to a targeted community. These students' challenge was to assess and analyze the community in terms of social, economic, and political factors. This involved the completion of a comprehensive community assessment to identify area services, resources, and needs. The inequities that existed in the community included extreme poverty, deterioration, and other societal dilemmas. The transformative learning process provided a unique opportunity for students to examine the effects that limited resources, services, and access may have on communities while reflecting on this knowledge at a cognitive and emotional level. The students conducted this community analysis with consideration of the sustainability of the community and the means to affect more positive outcomes for children.

There has been limited research on the learning that occurs as a result of transformative approaches that emphasize discourse, problem solving, and interactive participation. These components were incorporated in the experiential social justice project described in this study. The project embraced the tenets of transformative learning and translated these into essential skills for students. Further, the transformative learning process supported the application of these processes to enhance student learning.

This study was exploratory and as such does not make claims of cause and effect. There are several evident precautions that must be noted regarding the interpretation of these findings. First, the results may not be transferable to other student populations. A convenience sample was utilized and incorporated only one research site, a university classroom. Additionally, the self-report nature of the data collected and the potential bias of this information must be taken into consideration. Still, these findings provide some beginning understanding of the nature of the learning that can occur for students involved in transformative learning activities.

The child welfare issue highlighted in the present study has broad social implications. In particular, for the transformative learning students, the racial disproportionality problem solidified understanding of systematic inequity with direct and personalized application. Students were better able to engage and process these issues framed in a real societal problem, which is critical to an understanding of social justice. The complex nature of disproportionality and the impact of this issue on the lives of vulnerable children provided a milieu that was well accepted by students.

The main differences that separated the two different diversity classes were the attainment of enhanced skills and the level of insight exhibited by the transformative learning students. Upon reflection of their experiences, the transformative learning students perceived the experiential project as beneficial to their learning as evidenced by four themes. Students were able to recognize systematic conditions and the complexity of these circumstances. They examined the evidence and concluded that injustices had existed for a long time in the community. A better understanding of the community was also expanded throughout the semester, enabling them to comprehend the interplay between the processes of inequity, oppression, and discrimination.

The transformative learning students further gained the capacity to interpret and grasp knowledge from differing perspectives, thereby enhancing essential analytic skills. While the majority of students were of color, many were able to raise their consciousness about their own belief systems and the manner in which these were affected by social and economic concerns. They were able to face the reality of these conditions through new lenses, despite their own social position or biases. They acknowledged that all individuals in society do not have the same opportunities. Thus, the social justice project provided an important foundation for discerning the conditions surrounding them.

Connecting through a sense of humanity was particularly salient for transformative learning students through contact with the community. This project presented students with a social issue that directly impacted the community and the agency and therefore students personalized the reality of the evident disparities that affected vulnerable children. This evoked some strong emotional responses from students and helped them value shared humanity and promoted compassion regarding the status of these residents.

In advocating for action-oriented change, students were able to move beyond the emotional level to see that structural and political change is necessary and possible. Students were able to thoughtfully identify and consider alternatives to alleviate evident community problems. The experience helped to make them better advocates in the alleviation of these social ills.

The illumination of these key themes for the transformative learning students contrasts with the traditional class participants. Specifically, students from the traditional class were more likely to be critical and make statements that disregarded or simplified underlying issues of oppression, inequity, or privilege. These included annotations such as "we are moving in the right direction," "there is room for some improvement but it is stable," and "I think we are in a very strong society." A rich description of learning and understanding was absent, and there was less sensitivity regarding the components of social justice. Further, many of these students conveyed more stereotypical images that did not demonstrate transformation. Therefore, they were also more likely to view themselves as being "mistakenly viewed as discriminatory," "not biased towards anyone," "not racist," and "open to others." There was less evidence of a deeper connection to the substance and the value of social justice concepts.

This study suggests that educators can advance concern for social justice issues through the use of transformative and experiential perspectives that reinforce theoretical concepts taught in the classroom, increase student understanding, and help engage them in community concerns. Such projects can serve to heighten student interest when they have direct applicability as tangible and complex social problems that exist at multiple system levels. These efforts enable students to give back to the community, providing them with a sense of pride and accomplishment. This process may translate to other settings and serve to propel students' investment as stakeholders within their own communities.

Transformative learning approaches can also prove meaningful in other ways. Students can gain essential skills and obtain not only the cognitive components of learning but also the capacity to be emotionally engaged in the human condition, compelling them to extend their energies toward added change efforts. Other side benefits include the opportunity for students to work collaboratively, understand, and listen to one another while also gaining critical research skills. Pedagogy that encourages these aspects of learning is essential and will serve students well as future social work practitioners.

These methods challenge us in other ways. As noted by Van Soest and Garcia (2003), "Teaching and learning about diversity and social justice requires a willingness on the part of both students and educators to work through any unresolved conflicts in relation to their own role and status in an oppressive society" (p. 21). This suggests the important contribution of educators by engaging in a joint learning venture that relies less on didactic approaches and allows a more open exchange between student and educator. Further, this endorses deliberate debate in the educational realm and the integration of fundamental knowledge and skills in diverse forms. Efforts such as these are worth undertaking in our ongoing attempt to promote social justice for those who are vulnerable and oppressed while also passing this passion on to new generations of social workers.

References

Anderson, D., & Harris, B. (2005). Teaching social welfare policy: A comparison of two pedagogical approaches. *Journal of Social Work Education, 41*(3), 511–526.

Anderson, S. (2002). Engaging students in community-based research: A model for teaching social work research. *Journal of Community Practice: Organizing, Planning, Development and Change, 10*(2), 71–88.

Ayón, C., & Lee, C. (2005). A comparative analysis of child welfare services through the eyes of African American, Caucasian, and Latino parents. *Research on Social Work Practice, 15*(4), 257–266.

Barker, R. (2003). *The social work dictionary.* Washington, DC: NASW Press.

Barth, R. (1997). Effects of age and race on the odds of adoption versus remaining in long-term out of home care. *Child Welfare, 76*(2), 285–307.

Blumberg, E., Landsverk, J., Ellis-MacLeod, E., Ganger, W., & Culver, S. (1996). Use of the public mental health system by children in foster care: Client characteristics and service use patterns. *Journal of Mental Health Administration, 23*(4), 389–405.

Cantor, J. (1997). *Experiential learning in higher education: Linking classroom and community*. Columbus, OH: ERIC Clearinghouse on Higher Education.

Courtney, M., & Skyles, A. (2003). Racial disproportionality in the child welfare system. *Children and Youth Services Review, 25*(5/6), 355–358.

Courtney, M., & Wong, Y. (1996). Comparing the timing of exits from substitute care. *Children and Youth Services Review, 18*, 307–334.

Cranton, P. (1994). *Understanding and promoting transformative learning: A guide for educators of adults*. San Francisco: Jossey-Bass.

Fineran, S., Bolen, R., Urban-Keary, M., & Zimmerman, L. (2002). Sharing common ground: Learning about oppression through an experiential game. *Journal of Human Behavior in the Social Environment, 6*(4), 1–19.

Flynn, J. (1995). Social justice in social agencies. In R. L. Edwards (Ed.), *Encyclopedia of social work* (pp. 2173–2179). Washington, DC: NASW Press.

Frame, L. (2002). Maltreatment reports and placement outcomes for infants and toddlers in out-of-home care. *Infant Mental Health Journal, 23*(5), 517–240.

Garland, A., Landsverk, J., & Lau, A. (2003). Racial disparities in mental health service use among children in foster care. *Children and Youth Services Review, 25*(5/6), 491–507.

Glaser, B., & Strauss, A. (1967). *The discovery of grounded theory: Strategies for qualitative research*. Chicago: Aldine.

Grabove, V. (1997). The many facets of transformative learning theory and practice. *New Directions for Adult and Continuing Education, 74*, 89–95.

Harris, M., & Courtney, M. (2003). The interaction of race, ethnicity, and family structure with respect to the timing of family reunification. *Children and Youth Services Review, 25*(5/6), 409–429.

Janesick, V. (1994). The dance of qualitative research design: Metaphor, methodolatry, and meaning. In N. Denzin & Y. Lincoln (Eds.), *Handbook of qualitative research* (pp. 209–219). Thousand Oaks, CA: Sage.

Kapp, S., McDonald, T., & Diamond, K. (2001). The path to adoption for children of color. *Child Abuse and Neglect, 25*, 215–229.

Knowles, M. (1977). The emergence of a theory of adult learning. In M. Knowles (Ed.), *Adult development and learning* (pp. 27–59). San Francisco: Jossey-Bass.

Kolb, D. (1984). *Experiential learning: Experience as the source of learning and development*. Englewood Cliffs, NJ: Prentice-Hall.

Lather, P. (1991). Staying dumb? Student resistance to liberatory curriculum. In P. Lather (Ed.), *Getting Smart: Feminist research and pedagogy with/in the postmodern* (pp. 123–152). New York: Routledge.

Lincoln, Y., & Guba, E. (1985). *Naturalistic inquiry*. Beverly Hills, CA: Sage.

Marshall, C., & Rossman, G. (1995). *Designing qualitative research*. Thousand Oaks, CA: Sage.

McMurtry, S., & Lie, G. (1992). Differential exit rate of minority children in foster care. *Social Research and Abstracts, 28*(1), 42–48.

Miles, M., & Huberman, A. (1994). *Qualitative data analysis*. London: Sage.

Mezirow, J. (1990). *Fostering critical reflection in adulthood*. San Francisco: Jossey-Bass.

Mezirow, J. (1991). *Transformative dimensions of adult learning.* San Francisco: Jossey-Bass.

Mezirow, J. (1997). Transformative learning: Theory to practice. *New Directions for Adult and Continuing Education, 74,* 5–12.

Myers-Lipton, S. (1998). Effect of a comprehensive service-learning program on college students' civic responsibility. *Teaching Sociology, 26,* 243–258.

Nagda, B., Gurin, P., & Lopez, G. (2003). Transformative pedagogy for democracy and social justice. *Race, Ethnicity & Education, 6*(2), 165–191.

National Association of Social Workers. (2008). *Code of ethics of the National Association of Social Workers.* Washington, DC: Author.

Potter, C., & Klein-Rothschild, S. (2002). Getting home on time: Predicting timely permanence for young children. *Child Welfare, 81*(2), 123–150.

Quinn, A. (1999). The use of experiential learning to help social work students assess their attitudes towards practice with older people. *Social Work Education, 18*(2), 171–181.

Risley-Curtiss, C., Combs-Orme, T., Chernoff, R., & Heisler, A. (1996). Health care utilization by children entering foster care. *Research on Social Work Practice, 6*(4), 442–461.

Rocha, C. (2000). Evaluating experiential teaching methods in a policy practice course: The case for service learning to increase political participation. *Journal of Social Work Education, 36*(1), 53–63.

Rodenborg, N. (2004). Services to African American children in poverty: Institutional discrimination in child welfare? *Journal of Poverty, 8*(3), 109–130.

Rosner-Salazar, T. (2003). Multicultural service-learning and community-based research as a model approach to promote social justice. *Social Justice, 30*(4), 64–76.

Rubinstein, R. (1988). Stories told: In-depth interviewing and the structure of its insights. In S. Eeinharz & G. Rowles (Eds.), *Qualitative gerontology* (pp. 128–146). New York: Springer.

Saunders, E., Nelson, K., & Landsman, M. (1993). Racial inequality and child neglect: Findings in a metropolitan area. *Child Welfare, 72*(4), 341–354.

Sedlak, A., & Schultz, D. (2001). Sample selection bias is misleading. *Child Abuse and Neglect, 25*(1), 1–5.

Smith, B. (2003). After parent rights are terminated: Factors associated with exiting foster care. *Children and Youth Services Review, 25*(12), 965–985.

Stevens, P., & Richard, A. (1992). *Changing schools through experiential education.* Columbus, OH: ERIC Clearinghouse on Higher Education.

Tracy, E., Green, R., & Bremseth, M. (1993). Meeting the environmental needs of abused and neglected children: Implications from a statewide survey of supportive services. *Social Work Research and Abstracts, 29*(2), 21–26.

U.S. Census Bureau. (2001). *State and county quick facts.* Washington, DC: Author.

U.S. Department of Health and Human Services. (2000). *Report to the Congress on kinship foster care.* Washington, DC: U.S. Government Printing Office.

Van Soest, D., & Garcia, B. (2003). *Diversity education for social justice: Mastering teaching skills.* Alexandria, VA: Council on Social Work Education.

Wells, K., & Guo, S. (1999). Reunification and reentry of foster children. *Children and Youth Services Review, 21*(4), 273–294.

Appendix: Overview of Transformative Learning Project

The transformative learning students participated in a joint project with the entire class that dealt with a significant community issue involving a vulnerable and oppressed population. The task of the class was to conduct an extensive community assessment considering a number of ecological factors that impact the life circumstances of a targeted community. This incorporated several different aspects of study such as population analysis and identification of community assets, supports, and needs.

The class was divided into six subgroups to address different dimensions of the specified social issue. This process enabled students to better understand the complex issues facing the targeted community, evident problems, and strengths, and enabled them to begin to synthesize these findings and make appropriate recommendations for change strategies. Each group developed a comprehensive document that addressed key areas as described (see Table 9.3).

TABLE 9.3   Select Components of Transformative Project

Dimensions	Description of project components
Societal factors	Describe the broad, societal influences on the community, such as the political structure and processes, economic development, status of employment/unemployment, and power structure. Identify the influence of racism and disparities in health that exist. Address the impact of various policies on injustice. Identify community leaders and their power and influence on the perceptions of community-level problems. Assess the presence of city government and the media in the community.
Community factors	Describe the history, geography, and population of the targeted community. Identify the impact of problems such as incarceration rates, incidence of crime, homelessness, etc. Describe existing housing structures, civic organizations, businesses, shopping/malls, libraries, and museums that are accessible. Address the nature of community participation and involvement. Compare and contrast the factors that affect a strong community. Analyze community strengths and challenges based on the data collected.
Family characteristics	Assess the vulnerabilities and stress impacting families in the community, such as single parenthood, substance abuse, financial resources, domestic violence, health issues, and educational needs. Reflect on the residents' values, interests, and activities. Obtain input from key informant interviews and interviews with service agency representatives in the community.
Child characteristics	Describe child-specific demographics/population of the targeted community. Assess the vulnerabilities and social ills that affect children. Describe the incidence of mental health problems, substance abuse, disabilities, teen pregnancies, etc. that are prevalent in the targeted area. Identify typical caregivers of the children. Obtain input from key informant interviews and organizational entities that serve the community. Assess the overall quality of life for children.
Service delivery system for adults	Describe the service delivery system for adults in the community. Identify the assets and service delivery support for the wide range of needs that exist in the community. Address the eligibility criteria for various service systems, demand, waiting lists, the number of clients served, problems in service utilization, and access to services. Assess the ability of the service system to serve the cultural needs of the community.
Service delivery system for children	Describe the service delivery system for children in the community. Identify the existence and locale of these services. Describe the eligibility criteria for service systems, demand for services, waiting lists, and the number of clients served. Address service utilization issues as they relate to access, barriers, and lack of service delivery supports. Assess the ability of the service system to serve the cultural needs of children in the community.

CHAPTER TEN

Learning About Social Justice Through Dialogue: Democracy Lab

Dolly Ford

Linda Ferrise

Abstract

This chapter examines the ways in which the meaning(s) and values of social justice are explored and articulated through an introduction to the social welfare system course, and ways in which transformative learning occurs when students engage with peers on issues of social justice through dialogue and deliberation. This chapter provides information relevant to educators, administrators, practitioners, and students about an innovative way to engage in learning about social welfare, social justice, multicultural diversity, and civic youth (dis)engagement. This method can be utilized within and outside the boundaries of the traditional classroom.

The authors would like to recognize the hard work and efforts of the faculty at Lock Haven University, Pennsylvania; Regis University's Institute on the Common Good, Denver, Colorado; the faculty of all partnering institutions; and the faculty and associates of the Nova Institute at West Virginia University's Division of Social Work, who have dedicated a great portion of their work to ensuring the success of this project. It is and has been an honor to be a part of a growing network of scholars, practitioners, and students across the globe who are committed to teaching, thinking, and learning with their fellow citizens in mind.

Social work educators strive to emphasize the social worker's advocacy role in the policymaking process in areas of social justice and poverty to promote self-determination, empowerment, and to promote full citizenship for all. The challenge often faced in social work education is bridging the gap between the commitments made to social justice through classroom work and actually practicing social justice (Nagda et al., 1999). This gap offers an opportunity to experiment with innovative ways to explore social justice in the classroom in a way that resonates with each student and promotes a life-long commitment.

The very meaning of "social justice" is unclear, as there is no universal definition of the term. Some would argue the term is used so frequently that the power and value behind its meaning is fading (Dolgoff & Feldstein, 2007). As an underpinning for this chapter, the authors agree that Bell's (1997) definition of social justice aligns with their efforts to promote, teach, and practice social justice:

> Social justice includes a vision of society in which the distribution of resources is equitable and all members are physically and psychologically safe and secure. Social justice involves social actors who have a sense of their own agency as well as a sense of social responsibility toward and with others and the society as a whole. (p. 3)

One way for students to understand and create a commitment to social justice is for the instructor to create space for students to share their perception and personal meaning of social justice. Through the creation of such space, students can weigh the costs and benefits to particular perceptions and arrive at a meaning that holds the power and value that social work educators aim to instill (McDonald, 2005).

This chapter examines the ways in which the meaning(s) and values of social justice are explored and articulated through an introduction to the social welfare system course, and ways in which transformative learning occurs when students engage with peers on issues of social justice through dialogue and deliberation. This chapter provides information relevant to educators, administrators, practitioners, and students about an innovative way to engage in learning about social welfare, social justice, multicultural diversity, and civic youth (dis)engagement. This method can be utilized within and outside the boundaries of the traditional classroom.

There is an emerging civic movement to create space for deliberative discussion that some would argue is loosely defined and others would argue is an emerging field of study and practice known as "dialogue and deliberation." McCoy and Scully (2002) relate this by stating, "The need to expand and deepen civic engagement is a central theme of a

loosely defined and growing civic movement" (p. 117). This civic movement consists of a growing number of citizens and practitioners concerned about the lack of civic engagement and the resulting impacts on
democracy in the United States. A fitting example of an organized network of such citizens/practitioners is the National Coalition for Dialogue and Deliberation (NCDD), an organization with a membership of
over seven hundred individual and organizational members. As stated
on the NCDD Web page,

> The "dialogue and deliberation community" is a loose-knit
> community of practitioners, researchers, activists, artists,
> students and others who are committed to giving people a
> voice and making sure that voice counts. NCDD provides the
> infrastructure needed in this community so we can work
> together to increase both our individual and our collective
> impact. (n.d.)

The authors find this emergence to be a useful and fitting compli-
ment to social work education, theory, and practice. Social workers are
charged to advocate on behalf of those unable to advocate for themselves. Much of this advocacy takes place at local, state, and federal
policy levels. To inform policymakers of the issues one asks them to
address begs those of us as citizens and professionals to become a part
of the political process. "Dialogue can be a powerful tool in helping
social workers meet the needs of people on each level of practice"
(Shatz, Furman, & Jenkins, 2003, p. 482). In micro-, mezzo-, and macrolevels of practice, as a theoretical base, dialogue is useful in psychotherapy and group process and may be used as a tool to reach common
ground and understanding between communities with a history of conflict (Sharma, 1996).

Course Content and Pedagogy

In an undergraduate social work program in the southeastern United
States, the introduction to the social welfare system course is a useful
recruitment tool for students who are undecided in their area of major
study. As a service course open to students of all academic ranks and
majors of the university, this course fulfills a general elective curriculum
requirement. The course draws students from several disciplines,
including psychology, sociology, political science, nursing, and business. The course examines the historical development of organized
social responses to meeting basic human needs, as well as the role of
citizens, the government sector, and the private for-profit and nonprofit

voluntary action sector in shaping those responses. The exploration of the history and current makeup of the welfare state includes highlighting two particular areas throughout class content and discussion: social justice and policy. The discussion of poverty also includes the span of poverty in the United States and around the world, including the disparities of poverty among minority populations and the reasons for such disparities. Textbooks often devote only a chapter or two to racial disparity and poverty, and the implications of such disparity upon the concept of social justice.

Despite the large number of students in the class, the course is presented in a seminar/discussion format. The format of this course involves class lectures on social welfare twice a week for one hour and fifteen minutes. This course has been influenced by the Gurin, Dey, Hurtado, and Gurin (2002) three-part conceptual model of the impact diversity has upon student learning. This model includes (a) structural diversity, or the racial and ethnic makeup of the student body; (b) classroom diversity, including building awareness of diverse groups within the curriculum; and (c) interactional diversity, or fostering opportunities for cross-group experiences and interactions. The course has been developed on an active-learning pedagogical approach through the use of dialogue rather than passive content learning. The intent is to create a learning environment in which the three types of diversity are

> effectively integrated [such that] the three aspects of diversity create both the conditions and opportunities for students that may be discontinuous from their past experiences, create dissonance through the availability of multiple and different perspectives from their own, and provide novel, positive intergroup situations and learning. (Nagda, Kim, & Truelove, 2004, p. 197)

COURSE ENHANCEMENT: FOSTERING TRANSFORMATIVE LEARNING AND CIVIC ENGAGEMENT

Kretzman and McKnight (1993) maintain that communities are functioning at their best when individuals within a community are aware of their knowledge, skills, social preferences, norms, abilities, networks, and other attributes that they can offer to the collective good of the community. Such attributes are collectively known as social capital (Putnam, 2000). A precondition to the realization of social capital within a community is the engagement of community members with one another. "Such opportunities create environments that foster all forms of civic engagement—connecting citizens to each other, to community institutions, to the issues, to policy making, and to the community as a whole" (McCoy & Scully, 2002, p.119). Putnam (2000) identifies the benefits of maximizing social capital as (a) allowing citizens to make collective decisions about community problems; (b) serving as a springboard for momentum building for community advancement; and (c) building awareness of the direct and indirect impacts individuals have upon each other. Putnam (2000) postulates that the realization of social capital may serve as a foundation of being socially just as citizens.

A center of research, teaching, and service within the social work program was funded for two years by the Fund for the Improvement of Post-Secondary Education to participate in a program known as "Democracy Lab" (DL), which is defined as an online learning experience to teach students

> about dialogue and deliberation through an engaging discussion about a current issue. This online course allows students to connect with their peers from across the nation by dividing students from one class into multiple sections. In these sections students interact with each other, share personal experiences and work together to address a current issue of interest. Issues range from topics of race and ethnicity to health care; from the media to government policies. (Democracy Lab, n.d.)

During the 2007–2008 academic year, the DL program involved hundreds of college students and eleven faculty members. Social work students from this program were partnered with students from eight other colleges and universities. Infusing the DL into the course involved dividing the students into online dialogue groups of ten to twelve students from peer institutions. Seventeen separate groups dialogued specifically on the topic "Racial and Ethnic Tensions: What Should We Do?" (National Issues Forum, n.d.), and another six groups dialogued on the topic "Three American Futures: What Direction Do We Take?" (Knauer, 2004). Dialogues on various topics across the eight institutions occurred concurrently over an eight-week period using the National Issues Forum's framework for deliberation provided by the Institute on the Common Good (Regis University, n.d.). The National Issues Forum (NIF) is an organization that aims to bring citizens together to engage in deliberative discussions regarding difficult issues with trained facilitators. These deliberative discussions entail the use of nonpartisan issue guides to facilitate the weighing of possible ways to address a problem. Participants "analyze each approach and the arguments for and against" (National Issues Forums, n.d.). Regis University's Institute on the Common Good provided trained facilitators to facilitate the dialogues.

This national dialogue exposed the students to the lives and experiences of others, enhanced their own understanding of social justice, and placed them in a position to analyze their own contributions toward fostering *or* impeding social justice. The DL experience of civic discourse is a first for many students. Since 2005, a total of 230 students in this program have participated in the DL, and of this total, only six students reported having engaged in a civic dialogue of any kind prior to the DL experience.

The Process

PREENGAGEMENT PREPARATION

Preparation and planning were instrumental to implementation of the DL. Preengagement preparation included the completion of institutional partnerships with faculty and administration of the various disciplines and persuading the students of the value of the activity. As few of the students had engaged in civic dialogue prior to the course, the instructors provided several rationales for participation to the students. For example, the instructors explained that the United States is a nation that seeks to "spread democracy" across the globe, yet very few of us are in dialogue with or engaged with one another within the United States. Students who are advancing their education through higher learning are considered an "elite few" and, as educated people, should seek to be a model for those unable to seek or obtain higher education. Without civic dialogue among the educated, a critical mass of social capital and the opportunities for self-enlightenment remain untapped. The process of assisting students to see the value of civic dialogue also assists them to set a priority of seeking "the good of the whole," the foundation attitude for social justice.

After instructing this course with the DL over three years, two recurring challenges have emerged. First, students often begin the course with a "just world" ideology, which Van Soest (1996) discusses in order to explain that society rewards individuals based upon merit; therefore, if a person behaves meritoriously then society compensates him or her accordingly. Thus, the inverse is also true; therefore, the world must be just. Benabou and Tirole (2006) assert that individuals battle a cognitive dissonance as they aim to maintain a view of a just world, "where effort ultimately pays off and everyone gets their just deserts" (p. 699). When introducing the course content and opening a discussion on students' perceptions of poverty, students often engage in the discussion through the lens of the just world ideology. Students often respond to the discussion by making statements such as, "If people would get and keep their jobs, then they could make it in life," or "I think people who are poor are lazy, I mean, there are jobs everywhere," implying that people get what they deserve.

Van Soest (1996) finds that students' perception of the just world was heightened as a result of the discomfort students felt when exploring issues of oppression. The outcome of this particular course resulted in the opposite effect; that is, once students heard the diverse experiences and perceptions of their peers within the dialogue groups, they began to question the premise of the just world ideology. The just world ideology is a difficult perception to penetrate when encouraging students to think about structural poverty, racism, oppression, and related topics. While difficult for the students to accept initially, the DL experiential learning experience proved to be a powerful way for them to engage in active learning rather than content learning. "Experiential learning builds directly on participant experiences; it acknowledges personal experience as valid knowledge and content for discussion" (Nagda et al., 1999, p. 440).

A second challenge that has emerged each semester is a dualistic mind-set. Students often possess their particular image of reality and, when presented with information contrary to their image, experience difficulty fitting the information into their present perception of reality. Rather than simply hearing and questioning to absorb information presented in a class lecture, the DL experience has served as a useful tool for critical thinking. Students question their own perception of reality when a mismatch with the reality of a peer is shared. Rather than a conversational discussion, engaging in a dialogue about issues of privilege and oppression and reflecting on such issues in a structured way brings a powerful social justice focus to a course (Nagda et al., 1999).

As this course fulfills a general elective for any major, many students expect less-intense course requirements. Over each of the three semesters that DL has been infused into this course, students express confusion and disdain in the first week of class. They are asked to fill out an anonymous index card with a series of information to inform the instructor of the class demographics, as well as to provide their initial impressions of the course after the introduction on the first day. Regarding their initial impression, students have replied as follows:

> I thought this was a class on social welfare and you want me to talk to complete strangers about racial and ethnic tensions, where and how does this fit.

> I have never participated in a project like this, but I am willing to try it out. I am a little nervous about it.

> I have never been in a discussion formatted course in a class this big. I do not like talking in front of people, but the course

sounds like it will be interesting. I think the online dialogues will help me break the ice in sharing my thoughts and opinions, we shall see!

I am a senior in my last semester and needed a class to fill an elective. This is not what I expected at all and I am considering dropping the course. I am not sure how talking to complete strangers about racism is going to a) inform me of the social welfare system and b) make any profound changes in a world that is full of racism it will always exist no matter how much we talk about it. I'm a black female—take it from me, I know.

The above quotes illustrate four different perspectives, each of which would be an asset in the dialogue for the course. It is important to stress to the students that diversity of opinions among the students is essential to the success of the dialogue, and that the instructors will provide guidance and assistance in this new experience of civic dialogue.

In sum, the absolute key to the success of this program is preparing the students for the civic dialogue experience. In the age of the Internet, instructors may assume that students would easily be able to engage in such an online dialogue. However, participating in an online chat room or updating one's social networking account is far different than talking openly about a sensitive issue among strangers when this is often a topic curtailed even among people who are very familiar with one another.

Dialogue Themes and the Fit Between Democracy Lab and the Course Agenda

Democracy Lab offers instructors a variety of topics from which to choose, such as America's role in the world, civic youth disengagement, and news media and society. In this collaboration with the Institute on the Common Good, the instructor chose the topic of racial and ethnic tensions as the most appropriate to integrate into an introduction to social welfare institutions. The dialogue topic was integrated into the general course content by examining, in greater detail, the disparity in poverty and access to public programs between the majority and minority populations in the United States. The dialogues allowed for a rather seamless approach to exploring the inevitable tensions that developed throughout the history of social welfare to the present, when those who needed assistance were and often still are neglected by values and ideologies and thus the categorization between the deserving and undeserving poor.

The initial three weeks of the dialogue were the most challenging, mostly due to the unknown and, for many, the awkwardness of the idea of talking to a group of (mostly) friendly strangers about such a deep-rooted and sensitive issue. Many students felt an initial apprehension about engaging in such a dialogue because many of them had never discussed race and ethnic tension with and among people closest to them (i.e., family, friends, and partners). Yet many students also shared a comfort in sharing their thoughts, feelings, and experiences on this difficult topic because of the protection offered by the anonymity of engaging online and out of the view of their coparticipants.

During the first week, students introduced themselves to each other and began to establish rules of engagement. While some rules are already supplied/suggested by DL administrators, groups tend to be more committed to rules when they have a role in creating them. Some students chose to only identify themselves by name, academic rank, and major. Others shared additional information, such as where they were from, any previous experiences with public discourse, initial apprehensions, and personal goals for the dialogue.

The NIF's framework for deliberating the issues on racial and ethnic tensions provided three plausible approaches to the issues for the discussion. The students used this framework and the issue guide as a springboard for dialogue. In order to deliberate each approach, each week students were provided a set of questions that were developed by the DL administrators, which reflected each of the three approaches. These questions were provided to help students generate answers, thoughts, and questions of their own, which in turn maintained the momentum of the dialogue. Each group had a facilitator, who had been trained in facilitating public deliberation forums and assisted in maintaining the momentum of the dialogue. The facilitator can ask additional questions to clarify a point, highlight a particular comment, or bring the group back to the topic if they go astray. The facilitators also ensure accountability to the rules of engagement the students developed in the first week of the dialogue.

Each instructor participating in DL is free to determine the way in which their students' participation meets course requirements, but DL administrators ask that students be required to post at least four postings (each on different days) per week for the purpose of maintaining dialogue momentum. This posting schedule ensures an even flow of dialogue throughout each week and the semester. The instructor for this course made participation in DL worth 50% of the final grade and attached a point value for each posting. Students were not required to post a particular length per posting, but to post a meaningful, thought-ful response or question to his or her coparticipants. Other instructors have provided students with a rubric to follow in order to receive full credit for the required postings. While not participating directly in the dialogue, the instructor, with assistance of a graduate student, moni-tored the dialogue and counseled students one-on-one when improve-ment in participation was necessary.

It is important to encourage students to maintain an open mind and to be as open about their own background and experiences as they can within their personal comfort levels, reminding them each week that their dialogues would be as meaningful as they hoped them to be by sharing open, thoughtful, and honest reflections of the issues and com-ments raised by others. During these types of conversations, there is a temptation to simply agree with what one's counterparts are relating to avoid potential conflict or disagreement. Groups with the most open introductions tended to develop a momentum and cohesiveness, which kept them engaged at a much higher level than those with more shel-tered introductions. Those groups with a higher level of cohesiveness also tended to hold each other more accountable in two ways: (a) to the rules of engagement they agreed to during the first week and (b) in their commitment to thoughtful, meaningful expression.

The opportunity to collaborate with Regis University's Institute on the Common Good in our participation in DL was a unique way to enhance our curriculum. The exposure of our students, who are mostly from a rural background, to students with more diverse backgrounds within their dialogue groups allowed for themes to surface that may not have otherwise.

Initially, students related their feelings of ignorance regarding issues of racial and ethnic tensions or were fearful of offending another dia-logue member if they shared honest thoughts and experiences. Two themes surfaced throughout the dialogues each semester: (1) many of the students from rural areas were open about their lack of exposure to diversity. Through the dialogue process, they came to recognize that the very lack of exposure either perpetuated racial ideologies through-out their home communities or insulated them from the realities of the racial and ethnic tensions that still exist in the United States; (2) the students from more urban and metro areas shared their experiences of diversity and difference as the norm for them. However, because it was the norm for these students, many shared that initially they felt oblivi-ous to the racial and ethnic tensions within their own communities and at the national level. Those same students related their realization that they had fallen victim to one or more of the "isms" discussed, but never recognized it as such because they lived in such diverse communities.

Finding enough time to cover the traditional course content and preparing students with the tools they need to be successful participants in DL is one of the greatest challenges; however, it is the most important ingredient for a successful DL experience. Two weeks prior to the kickoff of the dialogues, four class sessions are devoted to preparing the students to be active participants. The first two sessions explore definitions of dialogue, deliberation, and debate and the role each model of talk plays in a healthy democracy. The third session of this unit involves a lecture and discussion on the technique of deliberative discourse. Tool kit packets are made containing material about the following topics: (a) ways of handling a participant who is not actively listening; (b) lists of probing questions or statements that might be helpful when the dialogue is "down" or when everyone is in agreement; and (c) ways to maintain group accountability. The fourth and final session of the preparation unit involves an orientation of the DL technology by walking the students through the DL Web page to learn the navigation of the site and ways in which to maximize the tools installed. While time-consuming, these steps are an effective way to gain student buy-in to the activity. Most importantly, completing these steps set the stage for establishing a safe environment in which students may participate.

In addition to regular class exams and quizzes on the social welfare content, completion of one- and two-page pre- and postreflection essays are required to evaluate the impact and perceptions of DL. The following questions are addressed one week prior to the implementation of DL:

1. Prior to officially registering online for the partnership, what were your initial thoughts/reactions to the DL component of the course?
2. Have you ever participated in public discussions (whether online or face-to-face) regarding issues important to you in the past? If not, why not? If so, what was the topic and what was your role in the discussion? Was it effective?
3. What strengths do you believe you offer to your dialogue group (e.g., your life's experiences enrich the dialogue, you are a good communicator, you are a good writer, you have an open mind)?
4. What do you hope to gain/learn from this dialogue?

The following questions are addressed one week following the conclusion of the dialogue:

1. After participating in this program, do you believe you are more comfortable being civically engaged with and among other citizens regarding difficult decisions about difficult issues? Why or why not?

2. Name three things that you discovered about yourself through this process.
3. How do you see yourself using this experience in the future either academically, as a citizen, and/or in your careers (e.g., this could refer to the actual lessons you learned or to any newfound methods of communicating about sensitive issues, any skills you developed regarding group work, or even perhaps applying this method of "talk" with and among your family and friends)?
4. Summarize your final reactions/thoughts—an evaluation of the overall DL experience.

The reflections on these questions serve two purposes: (a) students are given the opportunity to return to the higher-order reflection and thinking outside of the dialogue and classroom, but in their own space and time; and (b) instructors are afforded an opportunity to gain anecdotal insight to the students' experiences and ways to make improvements and to build on elements that are successful. Below are statements taken from the students' reflective essays:

(A female student's predialogue reflection)
I am nervous about DL. I have never participated in a dialogue of any kind. I am particularly nervous because I come from a rural part of the state and have been exposed to little diversity growing up. As a white person, I am not sure I have a whole lot to offer the discussion and I am afraid I might offend someone through my ignorance.

(A male student's postdialogue reflection)
I guess you could say I took being a white male for granted. I did not realize that racism still existed to the extent that it does. I heard stories from other people that sounded like experiences of the 1940s not in 2006. I am kind of embarrassed by my ignorance on this. I feel like my ignorance has only contributed to the problems of racism and oppression. This experience makes me want to know more and be a part of the solution and not the problem.

(A female student's postdialogue reflection)
I really thought this class requirement was going to be a pain in the you know what. I was angry that this was going to entail half my grade. After being a part of this partnership, I have learned more about myself in the last ten weeks than I have in my entire college career and I am one semester away from graduating. I learned some things about myself that I

am not proud of. I realized through this experience that I am in fact a bigot. I never realized my behavior and perceptions were oppressive to people different than me. Like I said, I'm not proud of it, but I'm glad I am aware of it. I no longer want to be a part of the problem. I want to change this about myself and be a part of the solution. I really am grateful for this opportunity.

Each semester, all students are asked to add their reflective essay to the rich collection of qualitative evaluation and insight for the DL. If they wish to make their reflection a part of the evaluative collection, they are asked to submit two copies: one is graded by the instructor and the second is submitted without identifying information (unless they wish to be identified).

The experiences and personal growth revealed in the reflection essays are inspiring and confirm predictions that DL would be a venue for active learning, personal growth, and citizenship. Such an opportunity for transformative learning is at the core of the aim to teach and foster critical thinking and learning.

The Future of Democracy Lab and Lessons Learned

Important lessons have been learned about the use of DL in coursework. Reflecting from the beginning of the DL experience to the present, lessons have been learned in the following key areas: (a) time investment, (b) preparation of students, and (c) evaluative research. While a high degree of time commitment is needed from the instructor engaging in such a program, an assistant such as a graduate student may be helpful in the monitoring and maintenance of the program. However, it is not sufficient to depend upon an assistant to fully capture the details and content of the dialogue in each dialogue group. Careful monitoring of the weekly postings is essential by the instructor to competently debrief with the students in class. The instructor must be fully in tune to the collective experience of the process. Therefore, instructor engagement and regular communication with the assistant are vital.

Laying a foundation by preparing students fully to participate in, for many, a first-time experience in deliberative discourse also cannot be understated. As mentioned earlier, students are often reluctant to participate in such a discussion and making the dialogue a course requirement often generates a heightened reluctance. The overall aim of DL is to address the issue of civic youth *disengagement*. For the purpose of this course, the connection between youth civic disengagement, the intended and unintended consequences of such disengagement on social policy and the welfare state, and social justice is the more specific aim. Yet in order for the students to grasp and *want* to engage, it is important they understand that a disengagement problem exists. Rather than seeing the world as having a number of problems but feeling a lack of power to impact the problems, students can emerge from such an experience with a newfound sense of possibilities. The authors have learned that time spent talking about the issue of civic disengagement and ways in which to be effective participants in civil society can translate into the result of students feeling safer and equipped to fully engage in the DL process, and hopefully beyond.

The final lesson worth noting is the lack of evaluation of this program. While empirical evidence of a transformative learning experience as a result of DL is absent, this is a recognized weakness and one that is being addressed in the current and future semesters. Pre- and post-tests are being developed for program evaluation and will be analyzed. The information gathered from such evaluations will not only enhance the credibility of the program and promote student buy-in for future cohorts but will also aid in securing funding for the future of Democracy Lab.

Conclusion

Democracy Lab can serve as a tool for training in both BSW and MSW programs. Broadly, DL aims to foster civic engagement by offering students an opportunity to engage in civic discourse about difficult issues often requiring difficult decisions—better made by all stakeholders involved, recognizing the essence of the democratic process is that the citizenry actively participate in political processes. Specifically, for social work students, DL offers the opportunity to test students' *knowledge* of important social issues impacting themselves as citizens and the people they serve in the profession; creates a safe venue for students to reflect upon their personal *values* against those of others; and provides students with the opportunity to hone their communication *skills* in group settings. In advanced practice curriculum, DL can be used as a mechanism to study in both direct and indirect practice courses. Some examples include its usefulness in the study and practice of human behavior, both in individual and group settings; the study of ways to empower and organize communities toward collective well-being and within policy courses, DL can be used as a tool to learn ways to weigh the pros and cons of policies proposed or implemented and thus enhance advocacy efforts by raising awareness among policymakers of the often unintended consequences manifested as a result. Democracy

Lab has proved to be a way to bridge the gap between the commitments made to social justice and actually practicing and "living" social justice.

References

Bell, L. (1997). Theoretical foundations for social justice education. In M. Adams, L. Bell, & P. Griffin (Eds.), *Teaching for diversity and social justice* (pp. 3–15). New York: Routledge.

Benabou, R., & Tirole, J. (2006). Belief in a just world and redistributive politics. *The Quarterly Journal of Economics, 121*(2), 699–746.

Democracy Lab: Teaching Democracy Online. (n.d.). *Welcome to Democracy Lab.* Retrieved May 4, 2007, from http://www.teachingdemocracyonline.org

Dolgoff, R., & Feldstein, D. (2007). *Understanding social welfare: A search for social justice.* Boston: Pearson, Allyn & Bacon.

Gurin, P., Dey, E. L., Hurtado, S., & Gurin, G. (2002). Diversity and higher education: Theory and impact on educational outcomes. *Harvard Educational Review, 72*(3), 330–366.

Knauer, J. (2004). *Three American futures: What direction do we take?* Retrieved May 4, 2007, from http://www.teachingdemocracyonline.org/file.php/1/PDFs/issue_three-american-futures.pdf

Kretzmann, J. P., & McKnight, J. L. (1993). *Building communities from the inside out: A path toward finding and mobilizing a community's assets.* Evanston, IL: Center for Urban Affairs and Policy Research, Northwestern University.

McCoy, M., & Scully, P. (2002). Deliberative dialogue to expand civic engagement: What kind of talk does democracy need? *National Civic Review, 91*(2), 117–135.

McDonald, M. (2005). The integration of social justice in teacher education. *Journal of Teacher Education, 56*(5), 418–435.

Nagda, B., Kim, C., & Truelove, Y. (2004). Learning about difference, learning with others, learning to transgress. *Journal of Social Issues, 60*(1), 195–214.

Nagda, B., Spearmon, M. L., Holley, L. C., Harding, S., Balassone, M. L., & Moise-Swanson, D. (1999). Intergroup dialogues: An innovative approach to teaching about diversity and justice in social work programs. *Journal of Social Work Education, 35*(3), 433–449.

National Coalition for Dialogue and Deliberation. (n.d.). *What we're all about.* Retrieved May 4, 2008, from http://www.thataway.org/?page_id=2

National Issues Forum. (n.d.). *Issue Guides.* Retrieved May 4, 2007, from http://www.nifi.org/index.aspx

Putnam, R. (2000). *Bowling alone: The collapse and revival of American community.* New York: Simon and Schuster.

Regis University. (n.d.). *Institute on the Common Good.* Retrieved May 4, 2007, from http://www.regis.edu/regis.asp?sctn=out&p1=icg

Sharma, S. L. (1996). *The therapeutic dialogue: A guide to humane and egalitarian Psychotherapy.* New York: Jason Aronson.

Shatz, M., Furman, R., & Jenkins, L. (2003). Space to grow: Using dialogue techniques for multinational, multicultural learning. *International Social Work, 46*(4), 481–494.

Van Soest, D. (1996). Impact of social work education on student attitudes and
     behavior concerning oppression. *Journal of Social Work Education, 32*(2),
     191–202.

Appendix: A Step-by-Step Process for Participating in a Successful Democracy Lab

The following is a guide for establishing an institutional partnership
with a Democracy Lab, as well as successfully infusing and maintaining
a Democracy Lab to an already existing or new course.

STEP ONE: GETTING CONNECTED TO THE DEMOCRACY LAB NETWORK

- The Democracy Lab Homepage, www.teachingdemocracyonline
  .org, provides helpful orientation information. For information
  about joining the partnership and network, interested faculty can
  contact the associates administrating the program at the Institute
  on the Common Good at Regis University in Denver, Colorado, at
  www.icgregis.org
- Upon entering a partnership, the associates at the Institute on the
  Common Good provide an orientation to the Web site and connection with current faculty and student partners. This network serves
  as a support system to share and learn the lessons learned through
  previous semester experiences.

STEP TWO: COURSE PREPARATION

- Engaging in a Democracy Lab requires a substantial time commitment from the instructor for the initial planning and maintenance.
  However, an assistant can be helpful in many aspects, including (a)
  monitoring the weekly dialogue postings, (b) serving as a point of
  contact for students experiencing any difficulty, (c) providing the
  instructor with feedback on the overall process, and (d) serving as
  a discussion leader in the classroom when debriefing dialogues at
  the conclusion of the week.
- A high level of initial reluctance from students when asked to
  engage in such a controversial topic is to be expected. Tying the
  students' course grade to participation in the Democracy Lab is
  one strategy to provide adequate incentive for student participation. For example, in the social welfare institutions class, participation in Democracy Lab amounted to 40% of the students' grade.
  This percentage translated into the requirement to post four times
  per week on four different days, as well as to write a two-page pre–

and post–Democracy Lab reflection. These requirements ensure student engagement and that students will post on different days. Requiring that students post on different days ensures that students read the postings of their colleagues throughout the week. Students in each semester admitted that had it not been for the posting requirements, they were highly unlikely to remain involved in the dialogue. Students reported in their reflections that once the dialogue gained momentum, they found themselves looking forward to checking the daily postings and going beyond the four-day-a-week posting requirement.

- The written reflections are recommended as a helpful mechanism for students to process their experiences on their own, as well as to prepare them for debriefing with each other in class. These reflections also are helpful to the instructor to gather anecdotal information about the process and reporting such experiences for evaluative purposes for fellow faculty partners and Democracy Lab administrators at the Institute on the Common Good. The institute seeks feedback about the experience of each institution participating in the Democracy Lab program.

- An integral part of the Democracy Lab process is to schedule weekly Democracy Lab Debriefings in class. For example, this class allotted thirty to forty minutes of class time each week to debriefing the process. Not all students are in the same dialogue groups, and this time gave students an opportunity to share their experiences of transformative learning, ideas that were successful, and ways in which to improve participation individually and collectively.

- Instructors may wish to obtain a copy of the National Issues Forum guide on the particular issue of choice in advance. These guides serve as the backbone for deliberating the three approaches to addressing the issue. They are downloadable for students upon registration to the Democracy Lab site. These guides provide a helpful framework for the discussion.

STEP THREE: INTRODUCING DEMOCRACY LAB TO THE CLASS

- Instructors should plan a class time early in the semester for a preengagement preparation unit. This unit might include a discussion surrounding issues such as "Civic Disengagement: Why Is the Body Politic Not Engaged?" A way to begin this discussion might be to create a springboard by raising particular campus and/or community issues about which the students care, but feel powerless, apathetic, or cynical to address as a collective. Generating such a discussion and tying it into the goals and objectives of

Democracy Lab is vital to developing an initial level of student buy-in.

- The distribution of a "How to be a Good Participant" tool kit to the students helps them prepare for their participation and for participation challenges by others. This kit might include readings on the differences between dialogue and debate, a list of probing questions students might use to keep a dialogue active, a list of suggestions in dealing with a nonactive listener or belligerent participant, and other challenges.

STEP FOUR: THE PROCESS—MAINTAINING A DEMOCRACY LAB

- The network of partnering institutions/instructors serves as a tremendous support system and resource. While institutions/instructors vary in many aspects, such as the degree to which they require participation or simply offer extra credit, maintaining ongoing communication with fellow faculty and assistants in order to share experiences, questions, and/or concerns with each other is vitally important. Planning to spend time with fellow faculty, assistants, and Democracy Lab administrators via teleconference calls throughout the semester is a worthwhile investment.
- The Democracy Lab Web site assists in the process of implementing the process as it logs, maintains, and archives all student postings, which in turn, allows for ease in grading.

STEP FIVE: CONCLUDING DEMOCRACY LAB

- The dialogues are typically eight to ten weeks in duration. A final debriefing session during the week after the final week of the actual dialogue serves to provide a forum for evaluation. This allows students the opportunity to share any final thoughts on the entire process, even after a final written evaluation. The final debriefing session provides an opportunity to bring closure to the (hopefully) transformative experience.

Social Justice Education Outside the Classroom

CHAPTER ELEVEN

Reframing Field Education: Promoting Social Justice in Practicum

Julie Birkenmaier
Ashley Cruce

Abstract

This chapter discusses the rationale and possibilities for promoting social justice–oriented professional practice through social work field education. The authors describe an innovative field education model that uses practicum stipends for promoting social justice–oriented practice. The model entails student conceptualization of activities to promote social justice with the aim of improving services and systemic change, a grant-writing experience and a merit-based, competitive award process. The authors discuss the experience in terms of transformative learning, share feedback from students, and provide examples of social justice–focused field experiences in the United States and international agencies. Lastly, tools to replicate the model, as well as targeted supervision questions and seminar assignments, are offered with the overall aim of strengthening the value of social justice in field education.

As a significant part of the social work curriculum, field education provides a powerful and underutilized opportunity to incorporate the core value of social justice into professional practice. In support of the profession's commitment to social justice, scholars have written extensively on social justice content in a wide range of social work courses.

However, the presence of explicit social justice content in field education has received scant coverage in the literature. Consequently, little is known about the concrete ways in which social justice is promoted within field education through student learning activities, supervisory discussions, and field seminar discussions and assignments. Given the limited scholarship and existing approaches, this chapter offers an innovative model to promote social justice within field education, along with targeted supervision questions and seminar assignments. All of these are adaptable within any social work program (with or without scholarship funds for students).

This field-education model uses a formalized proposal process and awards practicum stipends for promoting social justice–oriented professional practice. The model was created by an endowed center dedicated to social justice education and research within a school of social work In this chapter, the authors (1) review the social work literature regarding social justice and field education, (2) discuss transformative learning, (3) present the model and several student case studies in U.S. and international agencies, (4) offer qualitative evaluation data, and (5) share practical strategies for replication and incorporating social justice into field education. The authors discuss the potential of this approach as a method for transformative learning within field education and the potential impact of field education for engendering a life-long commitment to the pursuit of social justice.

Literature Review

Both the definition and overall importance of social justice in social work education have been debated extensively (Abramovitz & Bardill, 1993; Gil, 1998; Longres & Scanlon, 2001; Pelton, 2001; Reisch, 2002; Van Soest, 1992). Various definitions coalesce around the idea that social justice activities are those that seek to influence "the patterns of people's actions, interactions and social relations" (Gil, 1998, p. 39), or work toward "an ideal situation in which all members of a society have the same basic rights, protections, opportunities, obligations and social benefits" (Barker, 2003, p. 354). However, the key difference in definitions centers on the degree to which such efforts seek or advance systemic change, defined as changing the circumstances and the social and institutional systems that lead to discrimination and oppression. Some scholars emphasize social justice work as occurring at the community, society, and policy level, with or on behalf of disadvantaged, vulnerable and at-risk populations (Figueira-McDonough, 1993). Others maintain that clinical, direct-practice social work can also be considered social justice work as clients are empowered toward personal or societal change (Bogo, 2006; Parker, 2003). The authors embrace the full spectrum of social justice–oriented practice and advocate for a broader conception in order to include the widest audience of social workers.

Likewise, scholars continue to debate the extent to which social work education has effectively implemented and maintained its commitment to social justice (Abramovitz & Bardill, 1993; Figueira-McDonough, 1993; Finn & Jacobson, 2003; Gambrill & Patterson, 2001; Pearson, 2003). Numerous articles document the social justice content and emphases in a wide range of social work courses such as diversity (Rabow, Stein, & Conley, 1999; Van Soest, 1992, 1994); research (Holody, 2002; O'Connor & O'Neill, 2004; Scanlon & Longres, 2001); gerontological social work (Patterson, 2004); macropractice (Figueira-McDonough, 1993; Rocca & McCarter, 2003–2004); and clinical social work (Sachs & Newdom, 1999; Swenson, 1998; Wakefield, 1998).

Social Justice in Field Education

As a vital part of social work training, the field-education component provides an untapped opportunity to infuse social justice education. Field education also provides the chance to role-model the importance of a life-long passion for the pursuit of social justice in social work practice. Social work education and accreditation standards fully support the teaching and practice of social justice throughout the curriculum, including field education; however, knowledge about the various ways in which field education can demonstrate and reinforce social justice–oriented practice is limited (Bogo, 2006). The existing literature on social justice and field education primarily falls into two categories: (a) the role of field instructors to infuse social justice content within supervision and (b) as organizing framework for various field-based assignments and projects, both generalist and for specific practice areas.

Several authors focus on the important role of field instructors for infusing social justice in field education. Conrad (1988) found that field instructors are not explicit about their social justice orientation with students for fear that they would be viewed as imposing their personal views on students. Hawkins, Fook, and Ryan (2001) found that, although social workers were aware of the impact of environmental factors, the majority used individualistic terms, and clinical/therapeutic perspectives to discuss their clients, and rarely used social justice terms in practice. Hardina (2006) discusses the unique skills necessary for field supervision in social justice–related practicum and advocates for the creation of a new supervisory model.

The majority of related literature describes the ways in which practicum-based learning assignments can demonstrate and reinforce the core value of social justice. Several authors outline opportunities to address social injustice through a broad range of practicum activities, including micro- and macrolevel activities across diverse practice areas (Sachs & Newdom, 1999). Others describe field activities and projects for particular areas, such as international social development (Ladbrook, 1987), environmental justice (Rogge, 1993), macropractice (Gamble, Shaffer, & Weil, 1994), and community organizing (Hardina, 2006). For instance, Rogge (1993) calls for the inclusion of environmental justice and equity in social work curriculum and for the creation of field placements with agencies addressing environmental hazards (e.g., lead poisoning; toxic waste; and air, water, and ground contamination) in disenfranchised communities. Hardina (2006) provides a conceptual model for "social justice internships" focused on community organizing and social-action skills. Finally, Gutierrez (2006) stresses the importance of engaging and preparing social work students for greater political and civic engagement in the twenty-first century within her call for a reconceptualization of field placements as sites of community engagement, political advocacy, and civic participation. In sum, the related literature describes some of the potential for field education to provide learning opportunities about work toward social justice goals.

The educational purpose, rather than an apprenticeship approach, of field education is explicated in the Educational Policy and Accreditation Standards (CSWE, 2003). A key feature of field education is the use of an educational model, whereby students learn by both doing and integrating their learning into their values, knowledge, and skills (Bogo, 2006). Thus, in order to teach about social justice in field education, students must explicitly engage in activities that address social justice, be prepared to articulate the concept of social justice, and integrate social justice into their personal and professional values, knowledge, and skill base. A structured, field-based educational process focused on social justice and social work practice is essential to achieve these ends. As a structured learning experience, field education not only holds great potential for learning, but also for engaging the student in an experience that can lead to perspectives that are "more inclusive, discriminating and integrative of experience" (Cranton, 2006, p. 19) or offering transformative learning.

Over twenty-five years ago Mezirow used the term "perspective transformation" to describe the developmental process observed in women who participated in college reentry programs. In referring to this process, now known as transformative learning, Mezirow coined a term to describe the ways in which education facilitated an increase in their self-confidence. Since then, transformative learning has been the subject of hundreds of journal articles, dissertations, books, at least one international conference, and a new scholarly journal. In addition, there are graduate courses and seminars, as well as doctoral and master's-degree programs specifically featuring transformative learning and transformative education (Cranton, 2006).

Altering a student's frame of reference involves several aspects of the learning experience. An important element for the shifting of a frame of reference is the need for students to be open to considering alternative perspectives and a different frame of reference (Cranton, 1997). Mezirow (1997) later wrote that a frame of reference is composed of cognitive, conative, and emotional components, the dimension of "habits of the mind" and a point of view. Although there is no one right way to achieve transformative learning, altering a frame of reference can occur through a carefully structured reflection on a disorienting dilemma or an emotionally charged experience that spurs students to question their previous assumptions and perspectives. The dilemma also serves as catalyst for critical self-reflection and discussion necessary for questioning existing perspectives, assumptions, and frames of reference (Mezirow, 1997, 2000). Such reflection and processing must be guided to assist students to objectively examine their assumptions, perspectives, and points of view to carefully inspect their previous frame of reference, which has emerged from their experiences, emotion, intuition, values, spirituality, and other core elements (Cranton, 2006). Transformative learning is personal, imaginative, intuitive, and emotional—it involves the head and the soul. A critical reflection on the assumptions on which our interpretations, beliefs, and points of view is key to transformative learning (Mezirow, 1997). A single event can prove instrumental in transformative learning, or such learning can take place gradually over time (Cranton, 2006).

Field education holds the potential to facilitate transformative learning, as many of the key elements are components of the guided educational experience. For example, students must determine their learning needs within the structure of the learning agreement; have access to reflection resources; have access to outside influences that impact their learning; have a feedback mechanism through their coworkers and field instructor; learn time management; and be involved with group work that can also be a mechanism for self-reflection (Pilling-Cormick, 1997). In short, field education may be an untapped educational opportunity to purposively enable students to utilize their field experiences to examine their assumptions and habits of mind toward the goal of transformative learning.

A Model to Promote Transformative Learning

Since 1997, one field-education model that has been utilized at a midwestern social work program involves a merit-based competition for social justice practicum stipends. Within the program, an endowed center promotes social justice within social work education and practice through a variety of education, advocacy, and research opportunities. The practicum stipends assist the center to carry out their mission to promote social justice with students in practicum. In this model, a practicum site is selected by students, and they develop a proposal for the stipend in the semester prior to the field placement. This process ensures a critical examination of social work practice in the framework of social justice and prompts students to consider both short-term benefits and long-term systemic change as a part of social work practice.

In the proposal, students must clearly define practicum activities that will address at least two of the center's three goals: (a) alleviation of poverty and suffering and the improvement of services for vulnerable populations; (b) development of educational programs and social policies that lessen discrimination or oppression; and (c) social action for social change. The following are activities that students have completed to address the respective center goals:

> For Goal (a): case management, needs assessments, group work, resource referrals, and program evaluation;
> For Goal (b): training modules, peer-mentoring programs, youth leadership programs, legislative policy changes/proposals, advocacy, letter writing, and meeting with lawmakers; and
> For Goal (c): lobby days, demonstrations, rallies, petition drives, voter registration drives, get-out-the-vote efforts, and accountability meetings.

Upon completion of the practicum, students must accomplish two to three outcomes or products that raise public awareness and serve as resources for their clients, the agency, the school, and the center. Legislative fact sheets, letters to editors, op-ed pieces, newsletter articles, posters, videos, and formal presentations are examples of past student products. Stipends are awarded for field placements that have a strong micropractice/macropractice connection (or are able to connect the structural issues involved in individual or family client issues), include efforts to address systemic causes of discrimination and oppression, and work toward systemic change.

Proposals are solicited and accepted every semester and reviewed by a committee that consists of faculty, practicum faculty liaisons, and community practitioners. The committee makes funding decisions based on a number of factors, including the degree to which the center's goals will be met (explicated above), the quality and depth of the learning activities proposed, and the degree to which the student has been realistic about potential accomplishments within a semester time frame. Workshops and a proposal worksheet are offered in order to assist students, and in some cases, the proposal has been included as a required course assignment. If awarded, the student and practicum faculty liaison jointly prepare a stipend contract that outlines the student's specific activities, products, and an agreement to complete a midterm and final report; however, the contract does not replace the traditional practicum learning agreement. The stipend activities to be completed must also be incorporated into the traditional learning agreement. The student is then given a tuition award or monetary stipend, which varies in amount depending on practicum location (e.g., local, out-of-state, international). The stipend covers tuition for three credit hours, with additional funds for travel and housing expenses for the out-of-state and international sites. Throughout the student's practicum, the center works closely with the field education office and faculty practicum liaisons to monitor the practicum stipend and facilitate the overall learning process. Field instructors of these students agree in writing to the tasks and activities that are proposed in the application, and cosign the contract, attesting to the possibility that the proposed learning activities are possible and supported by the agency.

Case Studies

Since 1997, seventy-four social justice practicum stipends have been awarded for U.S.-based (63) and international field sites (11). The type of agency settings and areas of social work practice involved in the funded practica have been diverse. Student recipients have worked in many areas, including faith-based community organizing, labor organizing, legal services, child welfare, youth development, community health, veteran health care, mental health, civil rights, voter rights, prisoner advocacy, state-level Latino affairs division, refugee resettlement, immigrant rights, school social work, housing and homelessness, economic development, gerontological social work, and international social development. MSW students in all concentrations are eligible (community, family, and health/mental health) and have been recipients; however, the community concentration students have applied in greater numbers and have been awarded at the highest rate (53%). Students in this concentration focus on community and organizational practice, and tend to be students with the strongest interest in the social justice aspect.

Several case studies of student recipients illustrate and exemplify the social justice–oriented practice that has occurred: three at locally based agencies, one at an out-of-state agency, and one with an international organization.

Student A (MSW) provided case management and facilitated a support group for formerly incarcerated women at a locally based organization. Working in conjunction with a statewide nonprofit advocacy organization and its criminal justice taskforce, she organized three advocacy days in the state capitol for women and children. The advocacy focused on educating legislators and asking for their support on specific bills focused on more long-term drug and alcohol treatment options for nonviolent offenders. She created fact sheets, talking points, and other materials to lobby. She also organized a Mother's Day rally to educate the community about the harm done to children of incarcerated parents. She was successful in getting her letter to the editor published in the major local newspaper about funding such treatment programs; her other stipend products included a grant proposal for the agency, a newsletter article for the center, and a binder with information on lobbying and advocating for treatment options for nonviolent offenders.

Student B (BSW) worked at a locally based organization with refugee youths and their families, who had experienced or witnessed war trauma and torture. She developed a refugee youth leadership program, which culminated in a trip for the clients to the state capitol to receive certificates of completion and meet a state legislator. She advocated for family members with schools and local government officials in regard to the 2001 U.S. Patriot Act. She also attended meetings of the local Jobs with the Justice Immigrant Rights work group and a Stop Torture Now group. She and several youth leaders made a presentation at a social work event, and she produced a binder and video of the youth leadership program as her stipend products.

Student C (MSW) completed a practicum in a school social work setting and with a local chapter of the National Alliance for the Mentally Ill (NAMI). She counseled two adolescents on a weekly basis, and cofacilitated a high school therapy group and a parent support group. In preparation for her advocacy work with NAMI, she learned about state-level legislative issues regarding mental health issues as they relate to children and adolescents, and shared this information with students and their parents via e-mail alerts. She attended several NAMI advocacy meetings; participated in a state lobby day; and encouraged her students, their parents, and school professionals to write to state legislators. Her stipend products consisted of formal presentations to school staff, an advocacy manual, and a newsletter article for the center.

Student D (MSW) completed an out-of-state practicum with the Iowa Division of Latino Affairs in Des Moines, Iowa, where she worked to increase civic and community participation of Latino immigrants. She developed language and culturally appropriate educational programs and created a tool to ensure qualifications of language interpreters for Latinos. She carried out public awareness campaigns through the Iowa Civil Rights Commission Festival, an annual conference, and faith-based collaboration initiatives among Iowa's Latino communities. She had a unique opportunity to cofacilitate an immersion trip of school principals and teachers to Michoacán, Mexico (the state from which many Latinos in Iowa originate) on social and economic justice issues. Her stipend products consisted of the Congregation Resource Directory to improve service delivery for the Latino population, a conference brochure, and a newsletter article for the center.

Student E (MSW) carried out an international practicum with the U.S.-based SHARE Foundation and its partner organization in El Salvador, the Christian Committee for the Displaced (CRIPDES). Based in a rural area northwest of San Salvador, she partnered with local women in working for greater political rights and equitable resources; provided training on political rights, organizing, and leadership skills; and participated in planning antiglobalization marches, rallies, and press events on the negative impacts of the Central American Free Trade Agreement (CAFTA). She also participated as translator and cofacilitator in four delegations of Americans on their visit to El Salvador. For her stipend products, she gave a presentation at an event on International Social Work, compiled her findings from interviews with farmers on the impact of CAFTA (available on the SHARE Web site), and published an article on her practicum experience in the *New Social Worker* magazine.

In sum, these students have successfully made connections between micro- and macropractice, and have integrated the goals of the center. In the process, the students learn the connection between and integration of social justice and professional practice, with the hope that these experiences and the reflection occurring in supervision with their field instructor are changing their frame of reference and igniting a life-long passion for social justice.

Evaluation Findings

A qualitative content analysis of student evaluation reports, articles, presentations, and learning outcomes from the past several years yielded interesting results; namely, the social justice practicum stipend experience (a) increased exposure to new ideas and practice approaches; (b) facilitated a deeper understanding of social justice, conceptually and practically; and (c) aided in the realization of the vital role of advocacy for social workers.

First, students were challenged by new ideas and practice skills due to the requirement to connect micro-, mezzo-, and macrolevel activities. Students have expressed frequently that the stipend encouraged them to include activities that were new to them. Student C conveyed this explicitly: "I know that I would not have had this same type of experience had it not been for the stipend, . . . because I have a tendency towards clinical aspects of social work." Similarly, another student noted that "the involvement as an advocate took my interest with this population to a further level."

Another key outcome expressed by students is a deeper, more grounded understanding of social justice—both conceptually and practically—that was gained from the practicum stipend experience. For instance, a quote from Student D illustrates what occurs when students are immersed in practicum with explicit social justice goals, activities, and learning outcomes: "Social justice is really about right relationships. Right relationships are both a central ingredient to making change occur, and they are also the result of social justice being done." Another student eloquently expressed the major lesson from his practicum: "What I learned we must do as social workers striving for social justice . . . is enable [undocumented immigrants'] voices to be heard and assist them in using their power and building upon it, so that they can be agents in shaping their own future, not merely passive recipients of outside help." Students also gained perspective on the slow and long-term nature of social justice–oriented practice, which was often learned from the wisdom of field instructors and firsthand exposure: "It is idealistic to think that change will happen overnight . . . *poco a poco* . . . little by little, small changes bring about great accomplishments."

Lastly, another significant outcome among the student recipients is the realization of the vital role of social workers in advocacy and systemic change efforts. No matter what the specific client population, students recognized the importance of advocacy: "I've learned the basics of how to be an effective lobbyist. I've been able to witness the great need for social work influence in policy formation. With a broader understanding of social work at all levels, I am convinced of the need for stronger social work advocacy at the micro-, mezzo-, and macrolevels.

In addition, the experience affected students' future career goals and priorities as articulated by one student: "I can foresee the role that advocacy will play in my career, and I understand the direct impact that advocacy work has on our society and our clients." Another stated that, as a result of her experience, "We must point out the inequities in the systems that deliver care to the growing population with Alzheimer's disease and dementia . . . [and] I can see myself using advocacy in my everyday practice as a social worker."

The funding appears to have influenced students to incorporate activities that otherwise might not have been attempted or were attempted to a greater degree. In addition to this ongoing qualitative assessment, the center anticipates gaining greater insight from a recently implemented postpracticum survey to further evaluate the learning outcomes of the practicum stipends.

Practical Strategies for Implementation

Several factors could be imperative for successfully implementing this or similar models for strengthening social justice in field education. Collaboration and support from the office of field education and faculty practicum liaisons are essential to the success of the model. The field faculty and staff provide support by encouraging students to brainstorm and apply ideas about meeting the goals of the center, assist in editing drafts of the application, writing a contract, and monitoring the implementation of the activities and required paperwork. Field instructor involvement and buy-in are essential, as they must assist in brainstorming potential tasks prior to the practicum, supervise the activities, and engage in reflection within supervision, which includes discussion about social justice. Similarly, strong relationships with agency practicum sites can be important and can lead to agencies encouraging students to apply for the stipends.

Faculty support through social justice infusion in course content, as assignments, and encouragement to apply can all bolster the field-based social justice learning. Outreach to students can be accomplished through e-mail, flyers, Web sites, classroom announcements, printed admission materials, and workshops. Funding sources for stipends can be both internal (endowment, work-study funds, existing scholarships) and external (grants, contracts), and can be viewed as both program recruitment and retention tools. A version of this program could also be created without stipends, but rather by increasing the emphasis on social justice in professional practice in field education. Lastly, creating some means for evaluating student learning outcomes should be considered.

Incorporating Social Justice into Field Education

In general terms, relevant practice-learning assignments must connect to the social justice work of the students. Greater use of assignments tied to field seminars would strengthen social justice content and practice in field education. Students must also participate in supervisory, educational discussions about their learning activities and social justice with field instructors. In these reflective discussions, the link between social justice and field education must be made evident through discussion of conceptual frameworks of practice and social justice (Bogo, 2006). To implement this idea, field instructors could discuss the values and theories that support their work or the work of the student. Field instructors could also invite students to do the same, drawing upon the concepts students are learning in class. Field instructors and students may need to wrestle with their concepts of social justice, power, privilege, oppression, and other relevant concepts relative to their concept of social work practice, and have a relationship whereby they can feel comfortable struggling together with these questions (Bogo, 2006).

Field instructors may need additional educational sessions to understand or refresh their knowledge of social justice and ways in which to incorporate social justice into professional practice. For example, a dialogue using a structured set of questions could be utilized within supervision sessions to facilitate reflection on social justice, including the following:

1. How do you define social justice?
2. How can a social worker pursue social justice?
3. How do you see social justice pursued in this area of social work practice?
4. Can (or in what ways can) microlevel social work contribute to social justice?
5. What are the major competing views of social justice?
6. Discuss a microcase relative to social justice work and your definition.
7. How can social workers work to empower others (clients, staff, and the community) to work for social justice? In this setting?
8. What parts of the social structure contribute to oppression of our clients?
9. What parts of the system that, if changed, would move society closer to social justice?
10. In what ways can the (outcome of an assigned project) contribute to social justice?
11. Is it possible that social work practice contributes to social injustices? If so, in what ways?

The questions may serve to integrate students' classroom learning about social justice with the reality of social work practice as experienced in their field placement setting. These questions can also be utilized during field supervision to deepen students' understanding of social justice and reflect the importance of this core value to the profession.

Conclusion

As noted previously, the social work literature is sparse on the potential for field education to offer transformative learning opportunities for social justice education. While many schools offer stipends or scholarships for field placements, after extensive Internet searches, literature searches, and networking at conferences focused on social justice, the authors have been unable to locate any that tie stipends/scholarships to a systematic examination of social justice activities during the field experience. This model offers the potential to strengthen the focus on social justice within professional practice, and through the process, strengthen the profession's commitment to social justice as an orienting professional goal. A goal of transformation will include a model for reflection that can incorporate reflective discourse into field-education supervision. The model examined involves a proposal process with additional criteria, goals, and products beyond the traditional learning agreement. Others may find it useful to modify or adapt the model to fit specific resources and constraints. The authors share this model with the aim of strengthening field education and advancing social justice in social work education generally.

References

Abramovitz, M., & Bardill, D. R. (1993). Should all social work students be educated for social change? *Journal of Social Work Education, 29*(1), 6–18.

Barker, R. L. (2003) *Social work dictionary.* Washington, DC: NASW Press.

Bogo, M. (2006, February 8). *Partnerships for social justice and change: Opportunities and challenges for field instruction.* Presentation at the Council on Social Work Education annual program meeting, Chicago.

Conrad, A. P. (1988). The role of field instructors in the transmission of social justice values. *Journal of Teaching in Social Work, 2*(2), 63–82.

Council on Social Work Education. (2003). *Handbook of accreditation standards and procedures* (5th ed.). Alexandria, VA: Author.

Cranton, P. (1997). *Transformative learning in action: Insights from practice* (pp. 69–77). San Francisco: Jossey-Bass.

Cranton, P. (2006). *Understanding and promoting transformative learning.* San Francisco: Jossey-Bass.

Figueira-McDonough, J. (1993). Policy-practice: The neglected side of social work intervention. *Social Work, 38*(2), 179–188.

Finn, J. L., & Jacobson, M.. (2003). Just practice: Steps toward a new social work paradigm. *Journal of Social Work Education, 39*(1), 57–78.

Gamble, D. N., Shaffer, G. L., & Weil, M. O. (1994). Assessing the integrity of community organization and administration content in field practice. *Journal of Community Practice, 1*(3), 73–92.

Gambrill, E. D., & Patterson, H. (2001). Evaluating the quality of social work education: Options galore. *Journal of Social Work Education, 37*(3), 418–429.

Gil, D. G. (1998). Confronting injustice and oppression: Concepts and strategies for social workers. New York: Columbia University Press.

Gutierrez, L. (2006, February 8). *Empowerment for social justice in the 21st century.* Carl A. Scott Memorial Lecture presented at the Council on Social Work Education annual program meeting, Chicago.

Hardina, D. (2006, February 8). *People have the power: Supervising students in social justice internships.* Presentation at the Council on Social Work Education annual program meeting, Chicago.

Hawkins, L., Fook, J., & Ryan, M. (2001). Social workers' use of language of social justice. *British Journal of Social Work, 31*, 1–13.

Holody, R. (2002). Social justice and social work. *Journal of Social Work Education, 38*(1), 198–203.

Ladbrook, D. A. (1987). Roles for professional associations in international social development. *Social Development Issues, 10*(3), 70–80.

Longres, J. F., & Scanlon, E. (2001). Social justice and the research curriculum. *Journal of Social Work Education, 37*(3), 447

Mezirow, J. (1997). Transformative learning: Theory to practice. In P. Cranton (Ed.), *Transformative learning in action: Insights from practice* (pp. 69–77). San Francisco: Jossey-Bass.

Mezirow, J. (2000). *Learning as transformation: Critical perspectives on a theory in progress.* San Francisco: Jossey-Bass.

O'Connor, D. L., & O'Neill, B. J. (2004). Toward social justice: Teaching qualitative research. *Journal of Teaching in Social Work, 24*(3/4), 19–33.

Parker, L. (2003). A social justice model for clinical practice. *Journal of Women & Social Work, 18*(3), 272–288.

Patterson, F. M. (2004). Motivating students to work with elders: A strengths, social construction, human rights and social justice approach. *Journal of Teaching in Social Work, 24*(3/4), 165–181.

Pearson, D. M. (2003). *Perspectives on equity and justice in social work.* Alexandria, VA: Council on Social Work Education.

Pelton, L. H. (2001). Social justice and social work. *Journal of Social Work Education, 37*(3), 433–439.

Pilling-Cormick, J. (1997). Transformative and self-directed learning in practice. In P. Cranton (Ed.), *Transformative learning in action: Insights from practice* (pp. 69–77). San Francisco: Jossey-Bass.

Rabow. J., Stein, J. M., & Conley, T. D. (1999). Teaching social justice and encountering society. *Youth and Society, 30*(4), 483–514.

Reisch, M. (2002). Defining social justice in a socially unjust world. *Families in Society, 83*(4), 343–354.

Rocca, C. J., & McCarter, A. K. (2003–2004). Strengthening economic justice content in social work education. *Aretê, 27*(2), 1–16.

Rogge, M. E. (1993). Social work, disenfranchised communities, and the natural environment: Field education opportunities. *Journal of Social Work Education, 29*(1), 111–120.

Sachs, J., & Newdom, F. (1999). *Clinical work and social action: An integrative approach.* New York: Haworth Press.

Scanlon, E., & Longres, J. F. (2001). Social work and social justice: A reply to Leroy Pelton. *Journal of Social Work Education, 37*(3), 441.

Swenson, C. R. (1998). Clinical social work's contribution to a social justice perspective. *Social Work, 43*(6), 527–537.

Van Soest, D. (1992). Peace and social justice as an integral part of the social work curriculum: A North American perspective. *Australian Social Work, 45*(1), 29–38.

Van Soest, D. (1994). Social work education for multicultural practice and social justice advocacy. *Journal of Multicultural Social Work, 3*(1), 17–28.

Wakefield, J. C. (1998). Psychotherapy, distributive justice, and social work revisited. *Smith College Studies in Social Work, 69*(1), 25–59.

CHAPTER TWELVE

Family Network Partnership: A Model for Social Justice Education

Michael Forster

Tim Rehner

Abstract

In this chapter, practicum experiences and coursework that infuse social justice material are used as a context in which transformative learning takes place. A practicum experience within a social work program–sponsored agency, the Family Network Partnership (FNP), is described. Students are immersed in a community context characterized by material deprivation and social marginalization, a virtual social justice learning laboratory for social work students. Qualitative evidence suggests that the FNP model effectively facilitates a transformative learning experience for field placement students through a "pedagogy of engagement" process.

The University of Southern Mississippi School of Social Work offers a combined BSW/MSW program with a total enrollment of approximately 250 students. Nearly 90% of the school's students are Mississippi residents, with most from the southern half of the state. The MSW concentration is advanced generalist (McMahon, 1994), as it has been since the program's inception in 1974, in large measure due to the still relatively undeveloped social service infrastructure of the region (an infrastructure damaged severely by Hurricane Katrina in 2005).

All BSW and MSW students take a required foundation course in social and economic justice, and all master's level students take, in addition, a required community development course with a strong social justice planning and activism dimension. Other courses in the curriculum address social justice concerns with varying emphasis. Learning outcomes of the curricula target the development of "social work citizens," that is, social workers whose professional identities encompass change agency in the interest of social justice, whatever the particular arena of practice.

The following discussion focuses on the experience of those students who complete field education placements at the Family Network Partnership (FNP), a community-based youth and family service agency operated by the USM School of Social Work on the east side of Hattiesburg, Mississippi. In an FNP placement, described more fully below, students are immersed in a community context characterized by high rates of poverty, crime, family disruption, poor housing stock, minimal public services such as transportation, and a general paucity of the resources that contribute to a satisfying quality of life. In its material deprivation and social marginalization, the community may be considered a virtual social justice learning laboratory for social work students.

Academic social work has an obligation to educate students in matters of social and economic justice. This obligation is both traditional to the profession (see, e.g., Ehrenreich, 1985; Specht & Courtney, 1994) and acutely profound in the present period. Surely neither the United States nor the world has *ever* been free of injustice on a grand scale (Adams et al., 2000; Zinn, 2005). Yet the current state of affairs concerning justice is, arguably, deteriorating, with the American scene characterized by a rapidly growing class divide, declining real wages, and a political system unabashedly dominated by moneyed interests (Kivel, 2004), and the world gripped by new and strengthening globalizing forces of economic upheaval (Polack, 2004; Prigoff, 2000). The need for social work services is erupting worldwide, rendering "global social work," which is attuned to myriad needs and social justice concerns, an important emerging perspective (Sowers & Rowe, 2007). Further complicating requirements for conceptual understanding, discernment, and critical thinking is the new environment—fairly novel to American students, at least—of global terrorism, whose practitioners commonly couch their lethal actions in the legitimizing language of justice (Forster & Belton, 2002).

Effective social justice education (like education to the profession of social work practice generally) requires two complementary academic components. Certainly, conceptual knowledge in the form of well-designed coursework is, in the first place, essential. But coursework alone is insufficient. Direct experience, in the form of supervised field

education in an appropriate setting, is also indispensable to the transformation of mere students into social workers committed to efforts in
the cause of greater social justice (Goldstein, 2001).

By transformation, the authors mean the emergence and stabilization of a professional identity as "social work citizen," a professional
whose work, and view toward any future work, bears an inherent and
irreducible reference to social and economic justice concerns. Within
the social work literature, similar concepts appear to inform the work of
Drover (2000), which situates "social citizenship" in the global context,
Dudziak (2002), emphasizing the integration of personal and political
in the identity of "citizen social worker," and Fisher and Karger (1997),
who urge social workers to become change agents within the "public
world." From a somewhat broader educational perspective, Freire's
(1973) notion of praxis—action informed by consciousness of oppression and injustice, and dialogue about justice aimed at change—can
provide a conceptual touchstone for the engaged work of the social
work citizen.

The FNP model (fully in place, yet still under development) promotes
this desirable transformation. Within definite constraints imposed by
its unique characteristics, the model is at least partially replicable by
other schools in other settings. In the remainder of this chapter, we
outline the principal characteristics of the FNP model; its social justice
and educational conceptual moorings; the social justice influence on
instruction generally and the FNP field experience specifically; the
impact of the FNP program itself; and the nature of the transformational experience of FNP field students. We close with a summary of
lessons learned and requirements for model replication.

Understanding Social Justice

The FNP model embraces no refined theory of justice or social justice,
as in, for example, either the grand fashion of Rawls (2005) or the
"structural" social work perspective of Lundy (2004). The model does,
however, situate itself within the broad framework of the profession's
general understanding of social justice and its specific ethical imperative to respond to injustice. As van Wormer (2004) points out, the "usual
meaning" of social justice within the social work literature concerns
"the social rights of citizens of the social welfare state to have their
needs met" (p. 11). While concepts of "rights" and "needs"—along with
others, such as "fairness," "equity," and even "equality" (Flynn, 1995),
commonly associated with justice—leave ample room for disagreement
on specifics, social work's posture toward the social order as inherently
critical and activist is evident. Unfairness, inequality, discrimination,

and oppression are all too real; a major charge of the profession is to grind down the foundations of injustice in favor of a more socially just order. The National Association of Social Workers' *Code of Ethics* (2008) is explicit on the point that social workers are obligated to "challenge social injustice" (second of six ethical principles). Likewise, the accreditation standards of the Council on Social Work Education (2003) mandate that the social work curricula incorporate social and economic justice content, including content related to strategies to "engage in practice that advance social and economic justice" (Section 2.1.5), lending credence to Shank's contention (2007) of the essential compatibility of social work education and the Catholic Church's "preferential option for the poor" and oppressed.

The FNP model faithfully reflects the profession's commitment to social justice in the form of a principle-driven orientation to community-based practice with particular pertinence to the program's South Mississippi context. Following are four essential orienting principles, developed by the authors in dialogue with social work faculty, FNP staff, and students, advanced by the model.

RESOURCES

Progress toward social justice requires the infusion of new resources into resource-deprived communities. Service/activism that does not result in a net gain in resources—goods, funds, programs, jobs, opportunities, capacities, and competencies—for oppressed or marginalized communities and their residents cannot claim, in our view, to make a real and potentially lasting contribution to social justice, because they leave unaffected the unjust system of exchange and distribution (see Gil, 1998, p. 14). On this logic, it follows that a public university with a genuine service mission is obliged to commit and sustain a flow of resources to local resource-deprived communities. Though hardly a condition unique to the local area, state, or region, the authors consider resource deprivation especially pertinent to the communities directly served by FNP. Poverty among nearly exclusively African American residents of these communities is historically long-standing and prevalent.

RIGHTS

Community education toward a universal awareness of residents' rights—from the UN *Declaration of Human Rights* to the U.S. Bill of Rights to specific voting and other political, employment, property, and consumer rights—is essential to advancing social justice on behalf of disadvantaged populations. Context-specific legal grounding is fundamental to any meaningful empowerment of those victimized by social injustice (see Wronka, 2006.) Given the history of aggressive suppression of rights in Mississippi (Cobb, 1994), the authors believe that the right to education remains a salient concern to African American communities. (The local region, Forrest County, is named for Nathan Bedford Forrest, confederate general and a founder of the Ku Klux Klan.) In addition to the better-known rights, Medoff and Sklar's (1994) notion of "community rights," including a right to "celebrate vibrant cultural diversity" (p. 202), has appeal to the model.

RECONCILIATION

Historical divisions and conflicts among sectors of the larger community, and notably racial divisions, must be explicitly acknowledged and addressed before any efforts to "put the past behind us and move forward"—a popular local nostrum and rallying cry of status quo defenders (Davies, 2001)—can be successful. Recent renewed U.S. interest in prosecution of "cold" civil rights cases, and the attention to formal slavery "apologies" in Georgia, Virginia, and elsewhere (though not Mississippi at this point), confirm the central importance of reconciliation demonstrated in other historically divided contexts, such as South Africa and various Latin American nations (Gibson, 2004). In important respects, race remains an Achilles' heel of the state, including the local area, reflected in sharply segregated schools, churches, and neighborhoods. History still hangs heavy over daily life, calling for, we contend, forthright address.

RESPONSIBILITY

Genuine empowerment of marginalized people requires engaged activism at multiple levels, including visible and vocal citizen/political activism. The telling insight of American welfare criticism is that a provided subsistence can indeed engender a type of learned irresponsibility and inefficacy on the part of recipients. The myopia of this same criticism is that personal responsibility should be limited to economic, essentially private, self-support. On the contrary, a sense of responsibility (and consequent actions) for self, community, and the larger sociopolitical/economic order is first and foremost a function of citizenship and readiness for action in the public world (see Boggs, 2000; Dudziak, 2002). Here again, given the state's deep and lingering history of disempowering blacks and, more generally, the poor, emphasis on taking responsibility for the destiny of self and community is considered keenly pertinent to the lives of the community residents served by FNP.

Toward Field-Based Educational Theory

Field education of any type presumes that the application of knowledge is essential to skill development. It is difficult to imagine education toward a professional practice credential (the sine qua non of which is employment of knowledge in the form of practical skill) lacking a rigorous field component (see Sweitzer & King, 2004). Transformation of a mere academic student into a practicing professional is, therefore, presumed to rely on an effective process of field-based learning (Royse, Dhooper, & Rompf, 1996).

Presumption is not tantamount to theory, however, and the FNP model remains uncertain as to the dynamics occurring within the "black box" of transformational learning. Under exploration is an adaptation of David Kolb's early (1984) four-stage framework of experiential learning, which tracked the movement of learning from "concrete experience," through "reflection" and "abstract conceptualization" to "testing." Without delving into the details of difference, Kolb's formulation has been modified by the authors to become a "pedagogy of engagement" process involving three central movements:

1. Transformational learning is initiated by the direct and immediate confrontation of injustice. This phase, in which students are immersed in circumstances of material and social deprivation (for some to the point of feeling overwhelmed and perhaps reacting with a kind of disbelief) is at present tentatively conceptualized as a stage of *revelation and dissonance.*

2. Learning continues with the processing of revelatory experience under supervision and field instruction well versed in the conceptual grounding provided students by the formal curriculum. Students are encouraged (indeed, they are required by formal expectations of a field seminar course) to critically reflect upon their experience—individually, as well as in the company of fellow learners—in light of coursework learning, with emphasis upon systemic interconnections of phenomena and the unseen causal/structural circumstances that lie hidden behind, as it were, phenomenal experience. This phase is tentatively conceptualized as a stage of *integration and linkage.*

3. Learning comes to its transformational culmination in a state of new perspective stabilization, the personal dimension of which is self-awareness, identity growth, and a readiness to act purposely in novel ways. A signature statement of this phase might be, "Based on my experience and my thinking about my experience, by myself and with others, I see the world in a new way. I am different, and as a result I am prepared to act differently." This

phase is tentatively conceptualized as a stage of *consciousness and commitment*. The student who arrives at this point stands on the cusp of "social work citizenship," a dynamic state of continuous engagement is a process of progressive change, informed by a critical appreciation of the forms of mechanisms of injustice (see Drover, 2000).

This model of field-based learning is intimately related to the classroom-based curriculum. The next section focuses on the curriculum supports for social justice field education.

The Social Justice Impact on Teaching Curriculum Supports for Social Justice Education

Under the impetus of continuous curriculum assessment, the social work faculty determined to strengthen the academic preparation of students for social justice work and the development of "social worker citizenship" identities.

COURSES

Two courses, one foundational and one advanced, were reworked to serve as curriculum anchors of social justice education. At the foundational level, the social work faculty reinvented the second Human Behavior in the Social Environment course to focus exclusively on social justice concerns. The course examines the dimensions, causes, and dynamics of social injustice, extends awareness of the plight of oppressed groups, and enhances student skills in policy analysis and the creation of realistic social change proposals. The focus is on the United States, but some attention is given to structural global issues. Texts include Anderson and Middleton (2004), Adams et al. (2000), and van Wormer (2004).

At the advanced level, the Community Planning and Social Development course was significantly revised to emphasize social change in disadvantaged communities. In addition to textual study and analysis, students are required to play meaningful roles in team-oriented community-based "projects of engagement," among which are prominently featured research and activism projects related to the FNP. The principal text for the course is Homan (2007).

FNP FIELD EXPERIENCE

The school's community agency, the Family Network Partnership, serves as the field education site inspiring the model under discussion.

The FNP initiated operations in 1996 upon the request of the Hattiesburg Police Department and the Forrest County Youth Court as a
response to rising delinquency rates. The FNP was designed by the
authors (then junior faculty members and today director and associate
director of the school) to parallel the efforts of Hattiesburg's community
policing unit, the Neighborhood Enhancement Team (NET), in impoverished, high-crime, heavily African American communities. Resources
at first were limited to social work interns, under direct supervision of
the authors, operating in borrowed facility space. Student workers
focused on identifying high-risk youths and intervening with life-space
counseling (a flexible form of immediate problem-solving intervention
created by American youth work pioneers Fritz Redl and David Wineman; see Redl & Wineman, 1952), recreational activities, academic support (tutoring), and liaisons with teachers and in-home counseling to
parents when possible. In time and with grant funding, paid staff members were hired, more elaborate and formal programs developed, program and office space was secured, and the network of community
partners was significantly expanded.

Today, FNP employs nine full-time and twenty-three part-time workers and operates programs at three community sites for an average
youth population of sixty low-income African American children and
youths on any given day. It continues to provide practicum experiences
to a substantial number of students in social work and other disciplines,
and is a major volunteer opportunity for university students (and a
growing number of faculty members).

Though FNP remains very much a work in progress, its goals, theoretical bearings, and programs have crystallized as follows.

GOALS

The FNP's goals have evolved from a decade of experience, informed
by youth development (see Brendtro, Brokenleg, & van Bockern, 2001),
family support (see Kagan & Weissbourd, 1994), and university/civic
engagement perspectives (Maurrasse, 2001; Soska & Butterfield, 2005).
These perspectives complement traditional social work commitments
to systems improvements, advancing knowledge, and social justice.
Briefly stated, FNP goals are as follows:

Promote youth development. The FNP aims to provide support for
the healthy growth and development of all young people. An essentially
positive, strengths-based empowerment-through-competency approach
applies universally. At-risk youths are provided a wide variety of program opportunities to discover talents and interests, which are in turn
supported and cultivated. Applicable to all, the competency approach

has been found especially pertinent to work with troubled youngsters (Durrant, 1993; Strayhorn, 1988).

Strengthen families. The behavior, health, and mental health of children and youths cannot be understood outside the contexts of family and community. A healthier, more competent family system in particular will nearly always improve outcomes for young people (Kagan & Weissbourd, 1994).

Enrich community. Too often ignored, the strengths and deficits of communities are pivotal in the lives of young people. Generally speaking, the richer the asset base of a community—wellness-promoting opportunities of all sorts—the better children and youth will fare (see Ellis & Sowers, 2001). The FNP strives to develop indigenous resources as well as to "import" new resources.

Engage the university. Universities can offer exceptional assets to communities, to the extent that faculty and students, if not entire programs, can be mobilized (Soska & Butterfield, 2005). A major emphasis of FNP is building and strengthening a bridge between the resource-rich University of Southern Mississippi and resource-deprived communities in eastern Hattiesburg.

Improve service systems. Public systems of all types—police, housing, health and mental health, child and family welfare—frequently fail poor and minority communities, often with the best of intentions, worsening instead of improving the plights of residents (Hochman, 1997). The FNP aims to improve the effective response of service systems to the needs of its participants.

Advance the social work knowledge base. As an academic program within the university system, FNP strives continuously both to apply what is already known to promote health and well-being in individuals, families, and communities, and to increase the total store of such knowledge.

Advance social justice. A commitment to work toward greater social and economic justice on behalf of marginalized minority members is, of course, inherent in the tradition of social work, a prominent feature of the profession's ethical code and a key program objective of the School of Social Work.

THEORETICAL ANCHORS

Underlying all the goals of FNP are two primary theoretical commitments.

Risks and protective factors. First is a version of the "risk and protective factors" approach to delinquency currently favored by federally funded programs (Hawkins, Catalano, & Brewer, 1995). When possible,

FNP buffers the impact of damaging risk factors in the "external" environment; historically, the agency has targeted risks in the areas of family management, antisocial behavior, commitment to education, availability of drugs, and economic deprivation. A greater emphasis, however, has fallen on the cultivation of a "prosocial culture" replete with protective factors, notably relationships with caring adults and supportive peers, values and norms favoring education, work and responsibility for self and community, and transmission of a broad range of satisfying skills.

Indeed, skill, or competency development, is embraced as a kind of "master" personal protective factor for program participants. Competency across a broad range—academic competency; personal (e.g., anger management) and interpersonal (e.g., group problem solving) competencies; civic competency, including competency in understanding and negotiating political and service systems—is taught, experienced, practiced, and reinforced on the evidence-based premise that competency is concomitant with good choice making and general physical and mental health and well-being (Combrinck-Graham, 1990; Strayhorn, 1988). Competency is at the core of real, meaningful empowerment, and programs are designed, implemented, and evaluated for effectiveness in terms of their competency payoff for FNP participants.

The engaged university. The second theoretical commitment of FNP is to a thoroughly "engaged" form of academic social work, a form that in fact incorporates efforts to connect the entire university with the problems, concerns, and aspirations of disadvantaged local communities in the interests of broad-based community development and social and economic justice. This commitment relates to a long-running debate within the profession concerning the principal purpose of social work and the thrust of its helping mission (Reisch & Andrews, 2002; Specht & Courtney, 1994) and comes down pointedly on the side that argues for a structural perspective and an essential and sustained community focus.

Two specific practical implications follow from the orientation toward sustained engagement: First, that social work should be literally community located, with programs operating not at some remote locale, but squarely within the daily life space of participants. Second is the implication that academic social work programs should provide not only direct service to "clients," but should further provide a platform or entry point to the community—constrained by due regard for and protection of community residents—for university faculty, students, and programs of diverse disciplines. This latter implication in particular is the basis for the neighborhood university concept reflected in FNP programs. (A fuller exposition of theoretical influences on FNP appears in Forster & Rehner, 1999, 2003).

PROGRAMS

The FNP programs fall under two headings: Case Management/Family Support and the Neighborhood University. The FNP field students are assigned work in both programs.

Case Management/Family Support. This program offers direct counseling and case management services to select youths, families, and groups—those at highest risk for negative health, mental health, or behavioral outcomes, usually with involvement in the justice system and in danger of further penetration of the system. Standard social work case management methodology—assessment, planning, intervention, and evaluation—is applied to the target system of individual, family, or group. Field practicum students work side by side with seasoned staff. Until fairly recently, resource constraints limited case management services to an average of ten to twelve youths and families at any one time and counseling services to youths incarcerated in the Forrest County detention center. With an injection of new grant funding, however, the number of case management service recipients has more than doubled and is still growing.

Neighborhood University. This program refers to a broad and elastic range of after-school, weekend, and summer activity clusters, organized as "centers," as well as the occasional special event (e.g., seasonal festivals, concerts/art exhibits, holiday gatherings). Programs are scheduled at times demonstrated to pose the greatest risk for delinquent behaviors, notably in the after-school hours (Carnegie Council on Adolescent Development, 1991). At present, FNP has six activity centers in operation:

- Art Center: plastic, dramatic, and movement arts;
- Academic Enrichment Center: tutoring and remedial intervention;
- Recreation and Leisure Center: noncompetitive games and cultural enrichment;
- Aspire Center: vocational skills and entrepreneurship;
- Health and Wellness Center: community gardening, healthy lifestyle education; and
- Civic Engagement Center: community service and issue (e.g., voting rights) activism.

Neighborhood University center activities, along with community-building celebrations and special events, directly enrich resource-deprived communities with otherwise unavailable assets and serve as means by which youth and families develop and refine health-promoting competencies. In the delivery of the various center activities, as in the provision of case management services, field practicum students work alongside experienced professional staff.

RESULTS

For over ten years, FNP has worked with hundreds of low-income youth and families residing in East Hattiesburg's African American communities, specifically the Dabbs Street (which encompasses the Robinson Place housing project) and East Jerusalem neighborhoods. An estimated ten thousand documented hours of programs of all types have been provided to an average of fifty participants at any given time. Data gathered by the agency and periodically updated demonstrate that these communities are characterized by high rates of poverty, crime, exposure to violence, drugs, and a multitude of other risk factors. Protective agencies, with the exception of a handful of agencies such as FNP, are in short supply (Rehner & Forster, 1999). Referrals to FNP come from the Forrest County Youth Court, the Hattiesburg Housing Authority, the Hattiesburg Public Schools, and other agencies. In addition, many participants are self-referred, due to the favorable reputation of the agency in the community.

Perhaps the FNP's most telling measures of achievement are an extraordinarily low rate of recidivism for court-involved youths who regularly participate in FNP programs (less than 10%) and a significant, if difficult to measure, impact on overall delinquency rates on Hattiesburg's entire East Side. (Data on delinquency and recidivism rates are drawn from a database specifically designed for use in Mississippi youth courts—a distinctive outcome of an intrauniversity collaboration between Social Work and Computer Science and university/community partnership—see Rehner & Forster, 2006).

When surveyed by FNP caseworkers, moreover, parents, teachers, mental health professionals, and local community leaders consistently report improved behavior (including self-control, peer relations, and responsiveness to adult authority) in youths who participate in FNP programs. In addition, FNP participants produce highly visible works of art (including several large public pieces currently on display in the city), complete community-service projects, improve school performance and, based on public school data, graduate from secondary school at rates higher than the community average. A growing (if yet small) number of FNP graduates have gone on to pursue higher education. As a means to improving observable outcomes in at-risk youths, it would appear that providing a prosocial culture of empowerment-through-competency clearly works (Tolan & Guerra, 1998).

Throughout the course of its work, FNP has developed long-standing partner relationships with a wide range of public and private actors, including the Forrest County Youth Court, the Hattiesburg Police Department, the Hattiesburg Housing Authority, and the Hattiesburg Public Schools, as well as community health, mental health and child and family service providers, faith-based organizations, and neighborhood associations. The agency is firmly established and well received by residents of the community. Through its Neighborhood University, moreover, FNP provides a platform for extensive university-based service-learning. Students and faculty from a wide range of programs regularly volunteer at FNP.

The Student Experience

A good deal of evidence—some anecdotal and unsystematically collected, some the result of relatively consistent exit interviews with students and virtually all of it qualitative—suggests that the FNP model effectively facilitates a transformative learning experience for field placement students. The staged pedagogy of engagement process outlined above was constructed largely from the observations of FNP field instructors working with scores of practicum students over a period of years. Students placed at FNP are plunged into an asset-deficient community context and called upon to exercise a rich and challenging blend of applied skills—managing individual cases, facilitating support groups for incarcerated delinquents, conducting home visits, implementing center-based activity programs, and interfacing regularly with a variety of external system actors (e.g., schools, courts, mental health providers).

Seventy-five students to date have completed field practica at FNP. Worth noting is that the characteristics of this substantial number approximates those of the general student population of the school. Roughly half are BSW students and half MSW students; of the MSW students, about half completed foundation practica and half advanced practica. The gender/racial profile fairly closely parallels the school's overall profile as well—85% female, a 60%-40% black-white ratio among BSW students and a 60%-40% white-black ratio among MSW students. While all students indicate preferences for at least the type(s) of field placements desired and undergo preplacement interviews with the program's field coordinator and usually the prospective field instructor, students placed at FNP are not prescreened or preselected in any way; in short, they are typical students.

The process of student evaluation is readily replicable. The authors, with assistance from the FNP field instructor, have, to date, followed a four-step phenomenological method akin to that of Georgi, as described by Moustakas (1994). Generally stated, steps include (1) review of documents/transcripts; (2) identification of common concepts/themes; (3) interpretation of meaning; and (4) narrative summary of "essence."

Specifically applied to the FNP student field experience, the steps play out as follows: First, near the semester's conclusion of the field placement, weekly reflective logs are reviewed. Following the review, a sixty-minute (on average) exit interview is conducted with each student individually. Four questions form the skeleton of the interview: (1) What were your first impressions and thoughts when you began the placement? (2) Over the course of the semester, what two or three experiences do you consider most significant? How did they affect you? (3) What connections have you made or can you make between your field experience and your coursework, especially HBSE II (and, if applicable, the advanced community course)? (4) As a result of this experience, what ideas have you formed about your roles and responsibilities as a social worker? Notes of student responses to each question are compiled by the interviewers and read by the field instructor as well as the interviewers, forming a broad perspective on the student experience.

Methodological steps two, three, and four—moving from broad impressions to specific ideas and interpretations, to essential conclusions—are accomplished by the authors and field instructor, whose direct observations of students over the semester is especially valuable in making interpretations and correcting errant conclusions. The following generalizations are, then, a distillation of qualitative conclusions drawn over the most recent five-year period.

The first experience of FNP students at either level, regardless of gender or race, is likely to be momentary disorientation, sometimes tinged with fear, followed by shock and distress over the direct confrontation with program participants' poverty, food insecurity, substandard housing, lack of transportation and access to services, and such, as well as the reality of near-total de facto racial segregation. "I've never been in a neighborhood like this, where grown men spend their days on porches and street corners." "I couldn't believe it when mom told me that ten people sometimes sleep in that tiny two-bedroom house." "The boy's missed five days of school with an abscessed tooth, but there's no way to get to a dentist." "I spent all day in the community and never saw another white person." "It's hard to believe; it shouldn't be this way in America; this isn't right." This is the stage of *revelation and dissonance.*

The learning stage of *integration and linkage* emerges from the processing of experience in one-on-one supervision sessions, group discussions in case staffings and team meetings, personal reflections as recorded in logs and field seminar assignments, and directed seminar discussion on the theme of social and economic justice. Course material, previously merely academic in character, is brought to bear on phenomena personally experienced in the quotidian life space of program participants. Insight into causes and factors contributing to injustices are joined with the recognition of possibilities for meaningful change. Despair ("There is just so much *need*; how do we make a permanent dent?") and budding hopefulness ("Last night's neighborhood association meeting was great; people had a lot of ideas") can frequently change places in the emotional headlamps of students in this stage.

For the student completing the journey, a substantive existential payoff comes with the crystallization of an enriched perspective on social injustice and a broadened, deepened self-awareness. Students see themselves as progressive change agents working in a community context in which clients are partners in a process. Crystallization here is not intended to imply a static state, however. The self as change agent, as social work citizen, is, on the contrary, inherently dynamic, incorporating at least the seed of insight that continued growth from this point on is not merely possible, but likely necessary. *Consciousness and commitment* represents the stage of transformation.

Thematic analysis of placement-termination interview data collected by the authors, along with the content of the field instructor's weekly supervisory discussions with students, reveals material that fits fairly well the pedagogy of engagement pattern. Students hit repeatedly on the following themes: newfound insight into the extent and multidimensionality of poverty and its interconnected causes; recognition and rejection of stereotypes regarding poor African Americans; appreciation of personal strengths and limitations/biases as a social work practitioner; frustration over the sheer difficulty of crafting meaningful solutions to long-standing problems; interest in further social justice–related study; and commitment to pursuing postgraduation community practice and social justice work. A recent review of a limited sample of weekly reflective logs found additional evidence that our theorizing is on the right track, but the current approach to logging does not encourage the students' attention to social justice issues, and much evidence must be inferred.

The impact of an FNP placement on the formation/transformation of professional identity has not been, to be sure, equal among students. A very rough generalization is that about one-third felt a strong impact ("whatever work I do must have a strong social justice dimension"), another one-third experienced a more moderate impact ("social justice is an important part of the profession, but I can be satisfied without focusing on justice issues"), and one-third considered the placement experience "so-so," and might just as well have pursued their learning objectives elsewhere.

Lessons Learned

The principal lesson learned is that the model indeed provides an effective platform for student learning transformation. Equally important, however, is the lesson that the model's potency may be significantly enhanced by a number of program adjustments/developments. These include:

1. Greater use of the "4-R" framework of social and economic justice throughout the BSW and MSW generalist and advanced generalist curricula. Discussions of justice concerns under headings of Resources, Rights, Reconciliation, and Responsibility may take place in any and all courses, with broad applicability to the Mississippi context. Greater use of the framework would add coherence to social justice studies and underscore their value to the program as a whole.

2. Development of additional social justice elective courses. A significant proportion of the student body wants more social and economic justice instruction available to them. Course proposals under review by the faculty include Political Economics for Social Workers, Research for Organizing and Advocacy, and Social Entrepreneurship: Managing for Progressive Change.

3. Modification of field education planning and evaluation instruments, as well as seminar content and logging procedures, to encourage explicit attention to social justice issues and allow for direct and systematic assessment of the pedagogy of engagement concept.

4. Systematic assessment of the social work citizen learning outcome. The faculty is at present piloting a portfolio form of assessment that promises to provide useful data on the program's success in forming a professional identity that incorporates commitment to social justice practice.

Replication Potential

To replicate the FNP model precisely would require the existence of a fairly unique set of circumstances, notably a community agency operating directly under the auspices of a school of social work and committed to addressing social justice concerns. An approximate replication is certainly possible, however, under somewhat less stringent circumstances. Four principal components are required:

1. Coursework that prepares students conceptually for entry into social justice work: in the University of Southern Mississippi curriculum, the foundation social justice course usually precedes, but at worst must run concurrently with, field placement at the FNP agency.
2. Close affiliation with a community-based agency doing justice work: Educational program and placement agency (or agencies) must enjoy excellent communication. Field instructors should thoroughly grasp justice-oriented learning outcomes; the field education program should closely monitor learning contracts and student progress evaluations to ensure the depth and quality of the placement experience.
3. Excellent field instruction and supervision: Capable site supervision is indispensable to the pedagogy of engagement. The transformational movement of students through the stages of *revelation/ dissonance* and *integration/linkage* to *consciousness/commitment* is more likely to occur and to remain with students if facilitated and reinforced by a competent and aware supervisor.
4. Faculty and administrative attention to the curriculum implications of field experience and to continuous assessment: feedback from students and field instructors should inform curriculum development, including the content of existing coursework, development of new courses, the conduct of field seminars, preparation/ training of field instructors, and other possible curriculum modifications. The program's systematic assessment efforts should encompass tracking, in a clear and explicit manner, the student transformational learning experience.

Conclusion

Preparing students to honor their ethical obligation to work for social justice is a challenge for social work education. The field experience, already vital to the educational enterprise generally, can be especially pertinent to the formation of a social work identity that incorporates long-term commitment—what the authors conceptualize here as "social work citizenship." Field placement at FNP—a school of social work–affiliated youth and family services agency operating in impoverished Hattiesburg, Mississippi, communities—appears effective in facilitating such identity formation. The FNP model, grounded in observation and assessment of BSW and MSW students over a five-year span, suggests three phases of movement toward social work citizenship: *revelation and dissonance, integration and linkage, consciousness and commitment.* The authors believe that with appropriate adaptation, other schools of social work in other settings can replicate the model.

References

Adams, M., Blumenfeld, W., Castaneda, R., Hackman, H., Peters, M., & Zuniga, X. (2000). *Readings for diversity and social justice.* London: Routledge.

Anderson, S., & Middleton, V. (2004). *Explorations in privilege, oppression and diversity.* Belmont, CA: Wadsworth.

Boggs, C. (2000). *The end of politics.* New York: Guilford Press.

Brendtro, L. K., Brokenleg, M., & van Bockern, S. (2001) *Reclaiming youth at risk: Our hope for the future.* Bloomington, IN: National Educational Service.

Carnegie Council on Adolescent Development. (1991). *A matter of time: Risk and opportunity in the nonschool hours.* New York: Carnegie Corporation of New York.

Cobb, J. (1994). *The most southern place on Earth: The Mississippi Delta and the roots of regional identity.* New York: Oxford University Press.

Combrinck-Graham, L. (1990). *Giant steps: Therapeutic innovations in child mental health.* New York: Basic Books.

Council on Social Work Education. (2003). *Handbook of accreditation standards and procedures.* Alexandria, VA: Author.

Davies, D. (2001). *The press and race: Mississippi journalists confront the movement.* Jackson: University Press of Mississippi.

Drover, G. (2000). Redefining social citizenship in a global era. *Canadian Social Work, 2*(1), 29–49.

Dudziak, S. (2002). Educating for justice: Challenges and openings at the beginning of a new century. *Critical Social Work, 3*(1). Retrieved February 13, 2007, from http://www.criticalsocialwork.com/units/socialwork/critical

Durrant, M. (1993). *Residential treatment: A cooperative, competency-based approach to therapy and program design.* New York: Norton.

Ehrenreich, J. (1985). *The altruistic imagination: A history of social work and social policy in the United States.* Ithaca, NY: Cornell University Press.

Ellis, R. A., & Sowers, K. M. (2001). *Juvenile justice practice: A cross-disciplinary approach to intervention.* Stanford, CT: Brookes/Cole.

Fisher, R., & Karger, H. (1997). *Social work and community in a private world.* Boston: Allyn & Bacon.

Flynn, J. P. (1995). Social justice in social agencies. In R. L. Edwards (Ed.), *Encyclopedia of Social Work* (19th ed., pp. 2173–2179). Washington DC: NASW Press.

Forster, M., & Belton, W. (2002). *Some implications of "9/11" for social work education.* Proceedings of the 31st annual Alabama-Mississippi Social Work Education Conference, October 18–19, 2001. Hattiesburg: University of Southern Mississippi School of Social Work.

Forster, M., & Rehner, T. (1999). Delinquency prevention in poor and at-risk African-American youth: A social work practice innovation. *Social Thought, 19*(2), 37–52.

Forster, M., & Rehner, T. (2003). Delinquency prevention as empowerment practice: A community-based social work approach. *Journal of Race, Gender & Class, 10*(2), 109–120.

Freire, P. (1973). *Education for critical consciousness.* New York: Seabury Press.

Gibson, J. L. (2004). Does truth lead to reconciliation? Testing the causal assumptions of the South African truth and reconciliation process. *American Journal of Political Science, 48*(2), 201–217.

Gil, D. (1998). *Confronting injustice and oppression: Concepts and strategies for social workers.* New York: Columbia University Press.

Goldstein, H. (2001). *Experiential learning: A foundation for social work education and practice.* Alexandria, VA: Council on Social Work Education.

Hawkins, J., Catalano, R., & Brewer, D. (1995). Preventing serious, violent, and chronic juvenile offending. In J. C. Howell, B. Krisberg, J. Hawkins, & J. Wilson (Eds.), *Serious, violent, and chronic juvenile offenders: A sourcebook,* (pp. 47–60). Thousand Oaks, CA: Sage.

Hochman, S. (1997). School-community collaboratives: The missing links. In M. Reisch & E. Gambrill (Eds.), *Social Work in the 21st century* (pp. 260–270). Thousand Oaks, CA: Pine Forge Press.

Homan, M. (2007). *Promoting community change: Making it happen in the real world.* Stamford, CT: Brooks/Cole.

Kagan, S. L., & Weissbourd, B. (1994). *Putting families first: America's family support movement and the challenge of change.* San Francisco: Jossey-Bass.

Kivel, P. (2004). *You call this a democracy? Who benefits, who pays and who really decides?* New York: Apex Press.

Kolb, D. (1984). *Experiential learning: Experience as the source of learning and development.* Upper Saddle River, NJ: Prentice-Hall.

Lundy, C. (2004). *Social work and social justice: A structural approach to practice.* Orchard Park, NY: Broadview Press.

Maurrasse, D. (2001). *Beyond the campus: How colleges and universities form partnerships with their communities.* Philadelphia: Routledge Falmer.

McMahon, M. O. (1994). *Advanced generalist practice.* Upper Saddle River, NJ: Prentice-Hall.

Medoff, P., & Sklar, H. (1994). *Streets of hope: The fall and rise of an urban neighborhood.* Boston: South End Press.

Moustakas, C. E. (1994). *Phenomenological research methods.* Thousand Oaks, CA: Sage.

National Association of Social Workers. (2008). *Code of ethics.* Retrieved July 28, 2008, from http://www.socialworkers.org/pubs/code/code.asp

Polack, R. J. (2004). Social justice in the global economy: New challenges for social work in the 21st century. *Social Work, 49*(2), 281–290.

Prigoff, A. (2000). *Economics for social workers: Social outcomes of economic globalization with strategies for community action.* Stanford, CT: Brooks/Cole.

Rawls, J. (2005). *A theory of justice.* Cambridge, MA: Belknap Press.

Redl, F., & Wineman, D. (1952). *Controls from within: Techniques for the treatment of the aggressive child.* New York: Free Press.

Rehner, T., & Forster, M. (1999). *Risk and resource assessment.* Unpublished manuscript. Hattiesburg, MS: City of Hattiesburg.

Rehner, T., & Forster, M. (2006). *Software development through university and community collaboration: SWORD 2.0.* Proceedings of the 34th annual Alabama-Mississippi Social Work Education Conference, October 20–21, 2005. Hattiesburg: University of Southern Mississippi.

Reisch, M., & Andrews, J. (2002). *The road not taken: A history of radical social work in the United States.* New York: Brunner-Routledge.

Royse, D., Dhooper, S. S., & Rompf, E. L. (1996). *Field instruction: A guide for social work students.* Boston: Longman.

Shank, B. (2007). *A call to justice: Social work in Catholic higher education.* Proceedings of the 2007 conference of the North American Association of-Christians in Social Work, March 8–11. Retrieved July 20, 2007, from http:// www.nacsw.org/Publications/Proceedings2007

Soska, T., & Butterfield, A. K. J. (Eds.). (2005). *University-community partnerships: Universities in civic engagement.* Binghamton, NY: Haworth Social Work Practice Press.

Sowers, K. M., & Rowe, W. S. (2007). *Social work practice and social justice: From local to global perspectives.* Stanford, CT: Thompson Brooks/Cole.

Specht, H., & Courtney, M. (1994). *Unfaithful angels: How social work has abandoned its mission.* New York: Free Press.

Strayhorn, J. (1988). *The competent child.* New York: Guilford.

Sweitzer, H., & King, M. (2004). *The successful internship: Transformation and empowerment in experiential learning.* Stanford, CT: Brooks/Cole.

Tolan, P. H., & Guerra, N. (1998). *What works in reducing adolescent violence? An empirical review of the field.* Boulder: Center for the Study and Prevention of Violence, Institute of Behavioral Science, University of Colorado.

Van Wormer, K. (2004). *Confronting oppression, restoring justice: From policy analysis to social action.* Alexandria, VA: Council on Social Work Education.

Wronka, J. (2006). *Human rights and social justice.* Thousand Oaks, CA: Sage.

Zinn, H. (2005). *A people's history of the United States.* New York: Harper Perennial.

Appendix: Suggestions for Utilizing a Model for Social Justice Education

The model requires four essential steps:

1. Review and strengthen the curriculum to provide a conceptual foundation for student social justice work:
   - At USM, a social justice "anchor" course is provided at each of the foundation and advanced levels of study. This coursework prepares students conceptually for social justice activity. The foundation social justice course must at least run concurrently with, if not precede, field placement at FNP.
   - Recommended is attention in *all* courses to the four justice-oriented principles of resources, rights, reconciliation, and

      responsibility as they apply to the local context. Frequent
      attention to the principles is reinforcing to student learning
      and enhances social justice curriculum coherence.

2. Provide community-based, justice-oriented field practicum
    opportunities:
    - USM operates its own agency. Alternatively, an educational
      program should cultivate strong affiliations with agencies that
      can provide appropriate student experiences. Field instruc-
      tors should be able to craft meaningful justice-oriented
      experiences in line with learning outcomes, with progress
      toward outcomes carefully monitored by the field education
      program.
    - Practicum learning plans, it follows, should explicitly incorpo-
      rate social justice activities and learning outcome achieve-
      ment benchmarks.

3. Carefully train, supervise, and support community/agency field
    instructors. Capable site supervision is indispensable to the peda-
    gogy of engagement; that is, the transformational movement of
    students through the stages of *revelation/dissonance* and *integra-
    tion/linkage* to *consciousness/commitment:*
    - At minimum, the field instructor must be versed in the trans-
      formational learning model.
    - Ideally, field instructors should share in the instruction of
      social justice courses, strengthening the connection of class-
      room and fieldwork agency.

4. Establish assessment mechanisms to track the progress of stu-
    dents toward formation of a social work citizen identity:
    - Incorporate field education learning plans, reflective logs, and
      seminar assignments into the assessment process.
    - Conduct concluding reviews of student learning designed to
      capture rich qualitative data. The USM has used an adaptable
      four-phase phenomenological method that relies on existing
      student documentation, relatively brief exit interviews, and
      field instructor observations.

CHAPTER THIRTEEN

Cambiamos Juntos (Changing Together): Student Voices on Transformation Through a Social Work Semester in Mexico

Barbara A. Lehmann

Nancy A. Rodenborg

W. Randall Herman

Sandra C. Robin

Abstract

This chapter describes an international education program in Mexico that goes beyond transacting social work knowledge and skills. Instead, as shared by students through program evaluations, study there led to major life transformation. In this chapter we explore the intersection between social justice and transformative education in an international context.

To transform implies "a major change in form, nature or function," whereas to transact is merely "an exchange or transfer of goods, services, or funds" (Merriam Webster, 2006). This chapter describes an international education program in Mexico that goes beyond transacting social work knowledge and skills. Instead, as shared by students through program evaluations, study there led to major life transformation. In this chapter, the authors explore the intersection between social justice and transformative education in an international context.

A primary goal of this chapter is to provide information for social work educators who want to start a consortium and develop an international program. After briefly describing the Social Work in a Latin American Context (SWLAC) program and its educational theory framework and social justice focus, the authors present student voices illustrating personal transformation. These voices have been gathered and completed by and with the students from course evaluations and interviews. The authors offer lessons learned and continued challenges, and conclude with a discussion of challenges and guidance in initiating such a program.

Social Work in a Latin American Context is a program that was developed and is guided by a consortium of public and private social work programs in the upper Midwest of the United States. The mission of this consortium is to develop cross-culturally competent, ethical social work professionals with a global perspective by providing a semester of transformative, experiential learning focused on social and economic justice. The mission reflects and is congruent with the learning goals related by Ramanathan and Kondrat (1994) for studying abroad: (a) enhancing cross-cultural practice, (b) learning about practice using an alternative cultural lens, and (c) creating a practice orientation promoting skills for social development. The consortium provides students from constituent schools the opportunity to study social work for a semester in Cuernavaca, Mexico. In early 1999, the consortium developed out of a prior program that had been disbanded in response to increases in migration from Mexico to the upper Midwest. It became apparent that social workers needed to become knowledgeable about Mexico and its culture to better serve this population. This group worked together for four years to develop a semester-long program for social work juniors.

Participants enroll in accredited social work and general education courses, which are integrated into their home school's curricula that permit a study-abroad semester, typically with no delay in graduation. The program strives to provide "educational opportunities in order to foster critical analysis of local and global conditions so that personal, organizational, and systemic change takes place leading to a more just and sustainable world" (Center for Global Education, 2006b, p. 2). Coursework includes comparative social policy, comparative social work methods with groups and families, migration causes and challenges, and the Mexican cultural context. Students enhance Spanish-language and cultural competence skills through classes and in rural and urban homestays. Social work internships in Mexican social-service agencies are also offered. Finally, students participate in a two-week exchange with social work students from the Autonomous National University of Mexico in Mexico City, interacting with Mexican colleagues and learning about social work education in Mexico.

Educational Theory Framework

The educational theories that serve as the foundation for the Mexico semester program are those used by the Center for Global Education

(CGE) at Augsburg College, in Minneapolis, Minnesota, the home base of the program. The educational philosophy of CGE contains the following key elements: critical evaluation of local and global conditions; learning experiences that foster personal, organizational, and systemic change; and a focus on empowering students through rigorous academic, intercultural, experiential, transformative, and holistic learning opportunities (Augsburg College, 2006).

Lutterman-Aguilar and Gingrich (2002), CGE faculty members, state the following in a summary of the CGE educational approach:

> In the literature regarding its own educational philosophy, the faculty and staff of CGE have modified Dewey's, Kolb's and Freire's cycles of experiential education. In the CGE model of international experiential education, learners begin with their own experiences prior to studying abroad. They are then encouraged to reflect and analyze those prior experiences before they add new information regarding problem-based content in context of the host country. As students learn new information, they also engage in new experiences of entering into dialogue with diverse members of the marginal community. They then engage in fresh reflection and analysis of this new experience, now that new perspectives and experiences may have changed their earlier perceptions and hypotheses. At this point, they engage in action or reflection upon appropriate types of action, which must then be evaluated and celebrated as learning continues in new directions. (p. 19)

The CGE "cycle of transformation," which has been adapted from Paulo Freire's circle of praxis (the hermeneutic circle; Freire, 1970), embodies a model of experiential education that values and incorporates a foundation of challenging social injustice.

This educational focus on transformation is grounded in the principles of *process*—learning how to learn; *community*—learning in the context of community; *content*—curriculum content made real through experiences; *critical analysis*—solidifying the learning from experiences through reflection and analysis; and *action*—learners becoming active in social transformation (Augsburg College, 2006).

Lindsey (2005) found that social work students who travel and study internationally become more receptive to alternative ways of thinking, an "opening of the mind" (p. 236), which enhances their values development. This exposure to alternative frames of reference provides students with a psychological arena that allows the space to evaluate their personal value stances as well as those of the social work profession.

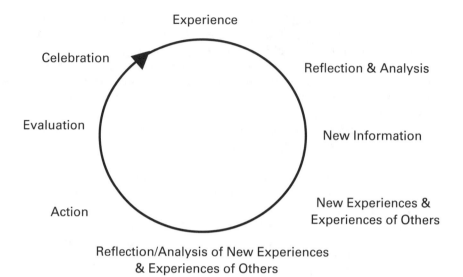

Experience

Celebration

Reflection & Analysis

Evaluation

New Information

Action

New Experiences &
Experiences of Others

Reflection/Analysis of New Experiences
& Experiences of Others

FIGURE 13.1   *Freire's Circle of Praxis*

The SWLAC program incorporates considerable opportunities for reflection on social work ethics, and values, further challenging the students to grapple with the values of the profession and their personal commitments to social justice highlighted in their experiences.

Students in the Mexico semester program live together as a community in two adjacent houses in Cuernavaca, as well as in adjoining neighborhoods during their family homestays. Students and faculty learn together through readings, lectures, discussions, and dialogue with each other and community members, as well as through experiential activities. The social work education semester embraces the CGE educational philosophy that focuses on academic, intercultural, transformative, and holistic learning activities and is designed with the intent of creating cross-culturally competent, ethical social work professionals.

Social Justice Definitions and Programmatic Underpinnings

The Mexico semester program defines social justice similar to that definition articulated by Finn and Jacobson (2003) under the rubric of "social justice social work." Following this model, social workers place justice at the heart of every social work intervention, situating their practice within the global arena. One core assumption is that social workers direct all interventions, whether at the individual, family, group, community, or policy practice level, toward increased social justice for vulnerable populations. Finn and Jacobson (2003) outline five interrelated concepts that compose the framework for social justice social work: meaning, context, power, history, and possibility. As described below, the Mexico program follows this model.

The first concept in the social justice social work model is *meaning*, which is defined as "the purpose or significance of something" and how people "make sense of the world" (Finn & Jacobson, 2003, p. 23). It is important to understand not only the ways in which clients make sense of their experience, but also the ways in which social workers interpret meaning. In the Mexico program, all coursework, internship, and service-learning experiences provide students opportunities to grapple with meaning. For example, students experience differences between their own values and assumptions and those of the Mexican people they encounter. "What did he mean?" or "She didn't understand my meaning!" are common learning moments as students gradually become aware of different understandings that are rooted in culture and experience. Learning to understand one's own meanings as well as those of their Mexican colleagues and clients is fundamental to student learning during the semester.

The second, third, and fourth concepts in the social justice framework are *context, power,* and *history* (Finn & Jacobsen, 2003), and are taught together in the Mexico program through required coursework, service-learning, field visits, and internships. Students learn that certain groups have historically had and still do have power over others. For example, the first course is mandatory for all students and addresses both historical and contemporary sources of injustice in Mexican social history. Students learn about the ways in which the conquest of Mexico during the sixteenth through the early nineteenth centuries affected marginalized populations and the ways in which pre-Colombian Mexican history served to unite indigenous groups and continues to influence contemporary Mexican culture. Students analyze the contemporary service context through discussion of current political policies such as the North American Free Trade Agreement (NAFTA) or U.S. immigration policy, learning to ask critical questions of justice and equity. Many students also take a course on comparative Mexican and U.S. social policy, in which they examine critical differences of values and ideology between the two countries and how these affect social policy.

The last concept in the social justice social work framework is *possibility* (Finn & Jacobson, 2003). Students in the Mexico semester consider possibility in at least two ways. First, most students learn their own possibility for individual foundational change; they are transformed by their experience. As described in the next section, students document profound and transformational change in themselves and the assumptions they make about their own lives and the lives of others. Many students see possibilities for themselves that they were unaware of prior to the course. Some seek to continue their involvement with international social work, a possibility that was not present prior to their Mexico semester. Second, students consider possibilities for the U.S. clients they come home to serve that are different from those recognized before. For example, as their voices describe below, some students comment on the ways in which the program changed their work with immigrants and refugees. Students describe being better able to help clients mediate their environment because they are more aware of the culture of Mexico. They are better able to form relationships with Latin American clients that were not possible prior to cross-cultural study.

TRANSFORMATIONS IN SOCIAL JUSTICE: STUDENT VOICES

The following section is a description and analysis of student comments regarding personal transformations during their semester in Mexico. These data were gathered using formal midsemester interviews in which students were asked to reflect upon each of the SWLAC program objectives, "to develop cross-culturally competent, ethical social work professionals with a global perspective by providing a semester of transformative, experiential learning focused on social and economic justice" (Center for Global Education, 2006a, p. 2). Questions were developed to assess each point of the program objectives, and students were asked to consider and discuss their assessment of their development in of these areas. During the interviews, the researchers made extensive notes, including substantial direct quotes.

The analysis involved extensive reviews of the field notes, with initial themes assigned codes based on the Lincoln and Guba (1985) comparative method of data collection. The data were then reviewed and color-coded with computer highlights to reflect thematic similarities. The color-coded data were analyzed by question and copied and cut from the narrative context and pasted into separate matrices allowing organization and analysis. This process was replicated and combined as new data were obtained. The goal of this process was to attempt to discern as accurately as possible the variety of student responses to each question and develop an accurate representation of the reality of the students' reflections on their experiences. Using Finn and Jacobson's (2003) social justice social work model as an analytic lens, the coded data were reviewed and sorted for indications of transformations in the development of meaning, understanding of power and history, and students' sense of increased possibilities.

CREATING MEANING

Being able to make sense of oneself and one's environment is the bedrock of making meaningful relationships and the enhanced understanding of context. As self-knowledge increases, one develops the opportunity to empathize with another's experience and understand more deeply the meaning of actions and attitudes. Increased empathy opens opportunities for the recognition of others' position and facilitates reparative possibilities toward the goal of social justice. The analysis of student responses indicated growth in meaning making as they reflected on gains in self-knowledge, increased cultural competencies, and the ways in which the SWLAC program's experiential pedagogy had fostered these changes.

Students related an increase in their level of self-understanding, particularly with regard to their personal stereotypes and the overt materialism they experience in the United States. One related, "My perception of what is necessary has changed, and I feel privileged." As can be expected, college-age students specifically focused on personal transformations during their time in Mexico. They reflected on experiences they found transforming as well as generalized growth during the entire program. As one student succinctly stated, "All intense experiences transform you." Another student said,

> This program was one of the best things I have ever done. I came not knowing anyone. I was able to learn my own competence. This experience reaffirmed my beliefs in myself. I feel I can handle almost anything. I am less fearful. More independent.

Still another reflected, "I am more eager to try new things. Before I would not go out of my bubble if I did not have to." One student attributed her growth to her stay with a Mexican family, "I am a shy person. I have to open up and being with others opens me up more. I needed to do a bit of self-analysis about who I am and why I am here."

Students considered how their increases in self-knowledge enhanced their ability to make meaning for themselves. Lindsey's (2005) analysis of her students' reflections found that the study-abroad experience initiated a reevaluation of one's culture, values, and norms. Our students acknowledged that they needed to learn about their own culture in order to appreciate the differences in Mexico. "[I] learned that for cultural sensitivity, it is important to know my own culture as well as that of others." And "I had never been asked to think about my own culture before." This increasing comprehension of their own position was evidenced in another student's reflection:

> Who am I—where do I come from—how does that relate to what I can do for others . . . white, upper class, suburban . . . that is not who I want to work with—but people with problems—look at what I need to do to understand . . . more than empathy.

Yet another spoke of being

> challenged (by) what we know by seeing cultural differences, (we) see what is thought of as normal and natural as different . . . I learned a lot about myself I have never realized . . . how much of who I am is culture . . . allowed me to be who I am and see myself as different.

Reflecting on their personal experiences in small villages created self-reflective moments:

> [When] people in Tlama [an isolated rural community] open to have you come into their house . . . what little they had was so valued . . . a simple life because they have to . . . would I ever invite someone of such a different class into my house . . . feels real shitty to see roles reversed.

Or more painfully:

> At my internship [I] was confronted by a woman who hated Americans. [She told me I had] no right to be in her house, my people were killing her people. I had to sit and eat with them knowing I was not welcome. It was painful and awful, my privilege shoved in my face . . . but I went back and started to explain why I was there.

Students' increase in self-knowledge included learning about their own culture, a vital step toward cultural competence (Sue, 2006). For example, one student wrote, "I've become aware of my own culture and other cultures. I see culture more strongly. I can see more differences." The experience of confronting one's own culture helped students discover their personal constructions of reality. It provided room for understanding and recognizing culturally informed meanings and enhanced recognition of embedded cultural realities; it encouraged the development of cultural competency.

The SWLAC participants were prompted to consider other areas for their developing cultural competencies. Students explored indirect versus direct communication styles, body language, differences in physical touch, and the context of communication. Conceptualizing the differences between high- and low-context cultures were important touchstones for understanding. High-context culture refers to forms "of communication in which most of the information to be conveyed is contained in the physical context or is internalized within the people who are communicating (Samovar & Porter, 1991, p. 315). Conversely, a low-context culture communicates primarily through explicit, direct communication (Samovar & Porter, 1991, p. 316). As one student reflected, "People here are more open to touch. For example, physical kissing and touch . . . and handshakes. People want to know your story, not just facts about your life, and you are going to hear their whole story."

Another important learning was about alternative perceptions of time. Students came to understand that some of their basic assumptions about being on time no longer made sense. Students also noticed an increase in their understanding of *being* rather than *doing*, and differences in the meaning of family according to culture. They were surprised by the small focus on consumerism as compared with the culture of the United States.

Yet with increased understanding, students became aware that cultural competency is a process. Another commented, "I feel I understand it better, but I am not truly competent. This is a good recognition." One student was particularly eloquent:

> [The] word "competence" implies that you know all, that you have the skills to do all, but cross-cultural competency is a journey, a continuous process for social work, you can become less and less incompetent but total competency is unattainable. As a professional we should know this, it is okay not to know all, we can't know all. The emphasis should be on the process and the steps to the journey without an end. You have to realize that the client is the expert not you— never you.

Students made meaning through their experiences in Mexico and reflected on ways to make sense of these experiences. They gained awareness of the similarities and differences of interpreted experiences. They were able to develop an understanding of the embedded nature of culture and of perception.

HISTORY, CONTEXT, AND POWER

Students were asked to reflect on the ways in which their understanding of a global perspective had changed since starting the semester. The themes of their responses centered on an appreciation of their limited understanding of the larger world they brought with them to the semester experience. They were also stuck with the power of the United States when looking from another vantage point, at the same time appreciating the economic interconnectedness of the two countries. Students related increased critical evaluation and analysis of politics and policies.

The painful confrontation of the victor's version of American history, particularly the relationship with Mexico, was enlightening to many students who "learned history is a big part of it . . . didn't know so much even about U.S. history—new ideas—have started to understand connections to life and history—so big—the conquest is still here—am still learning."

And:

> We learned that land belonged to Mexico and we had been given bad misinformation. [Our] schooling in [the] USA from [a] Euro-centric perspective [included] nothing about Latin America, only general things—now we have [the] other side of history . . . doesn't make [the] USA look perfect.

Through appreciating more of the Mexican context, students were able to comprehend more about the history of the relationship between Mexico and the United States. With this appreciation of context, students began to evaluate the challenges of migration and the immigration policies of the United States.

Through the synthesis of the curriculum's academic context, combined with experiences of hearing first-person narratives, to "hear from people who have experienced what we are taught—lived it—their lives not second- or third-hand information," students developed the ability to empathically imagine themselves in the position of a Mexican national.

Another important aspect of learning was about emigration to the United States. Students were able to see emigration through the personal narratives of those who had crossed into the United States as well as those left behind:

> I didn't know anything about immigration before coming to Mexico, either Mexican or in the United States of America— none of the process—never thought about the families left

behind and how roles have to be taken—not about change in dynamics for the family.

It was painful for many of the students to visit with U.S. embassy representatives after several months in Mexico. In contrast with their experiences of Mexican graciousness, students were shocked at "how disrespectful they are. [The] embassy showed only its own values. Having two- to three-minute immigration interviews does not match with Mexican culture. It is insensitive and shows how unaware the USA is in general in comparison to the world." Having recognized the power of their own government and its apparent cultural incompetence in dealing with difference provided fertile soil for challenging issues of power and oppression through multiple lenses.

Students began to see power dynamics both in the social context and within themselves. For example, students were able to better understand the nature of racism through reflection on its manifestations in an alien culture. One student from a small midwestern town mused with some naïveté that she "learned about racism here. It still exists here. How light skinned is beauty, and favoritism [*sic*]. Skin color still has a great impact." Another student reflected, "I think about what an emphasis there is on skin color here. I am a racial minority here and how ingrained skin color is here and it is eye-opening. I am more aware of the privilege of whiteness." Another student was shocked to recognize her own privilege of whiteness with her experience of going to bars and clubs where darker-skinned persons were standing in line while "I just walk in." Students were challenged to reflect on the meaning of their white privilege. "I learned a lot about white privilege; before, yes knew I was white and American, but now I see, even here I still have power. Here I have privilege in a country not even my own." Another stated, "Talks about racism were impactful [*sic*] and it got through to me that I am racist. I was never able to see this before, always thought it was someone else. Now I see how my culture is racist."

Students were also able to begin to critically evaluate the impacts of globalization and the power of larger nations and multinational institutions on the lives of persons in the second and third world. For example, one student responded that she could "see how things are interrelated, a million times over, everyday [things], what to buy, where to hang out . . . I now think with global effects in mind and consider macroeconomics."

Another was aware that

> getting out of the country and being challenged really made me see the effects, I was able to realize so much more. I also questioned what else don't [*sic*]. I know about, what else

could I ask about. There are many different ideas out in this world and so many I have never considered, so many I would never know to ask about.

Finally, one student recognized that "there is more, more cultural pieces but I don't have global insight to recognize what they are. It is challenging me to start talking more about global justice."

ACTION

Finn and Jacobson's (2003) model suggests that once a person has created alternative meanings and analyzed these through the lens of social history and context and power dynamics, then the possibilities for social justice actions occur. Many of the participants concluded that the program had empowered them to act based on their experiences. As one of the students put it, she has the "facts and knowledge and can now personally work with that." Another reflected on knowing now "what needs to change" and hopes she can, upon her return, "continue to see injustice and then know what to do."

One student describes this change as being "intentional about making change . . . and finds it is more pressing now to take action." She reports she is "now linking knowledge to action and am more fired up." Another student describes how she is "now able to further the cause and push on with what I have to do." She wants to do "something to educate the U.S. society" because she feels that "no one knows."

Another student mused that she was

> pushed to be more politically active—interested in [the] past but now more so because the program is empowering. It showed me there are no limits and I saw I can do anything, even little things, individual actions like saying that's not okay, showing one person can make a difference. You can take this experience and apply it, use your mind, use yourself.

In summary, as viewed through the lens of the social justice social work model, student understandings and commitment to issues of social justice appeared to have advanced during their experiences in the SWLAC program.

Collaborations That Supported Transformation

Learning through dialogue between self and others is integral to the CGE philosophy and to the mission of the consortium. Dialogue occurred continuously throughout the program but was formalized through four essential collaborations that mirrored and supported student transformation and contributed to the evolution of the program: the consortium model itself, the *grupo asesor*, the UNAM exchange, and the small town of Ixtlilco el Grande.

THE CONSORTIUM COLLABORATION

The consortium was influenced from the beginning by the relationship that CGE had with its faculty in Mexico. Prior to actual program delivery, a faculty trip composed of members from the fledgling consortium spent a week in Cuernavaca experiencing a curriculum similar to the program students would experience. This opportunity to observe and reflect on the CGE pedagogy had a profound impact on the semester program's evolution. It provided an early model of critical dialogue among the consortium members that established a collaborative process, which has flourished over the past five years. The decisions made about the Mexican semester curriculum were based on hearing from many voices from diverse settings. The consortium parallels this process in its own deliberations, and most changes made in the program have emerged from extensive dialogue among students, staff, professional advisory groups, and community programs.

GRUPO ASESOR

In the first year of the program, the combined faculty (U.S. professor and Mexican faculty and staff) realized the need for a more direct link with Mexican social workers. The visiting U.S. professor had the task of educating the Mexican staff about U.S. social work, but there was an absence of Mexican social work input for the U.S. professor, the students, and the curriculum. Consultation and supervision were necessary for field internships and service-learning opportunities, as well as for general advice. To meet this need over the first three years, a group of Mexican social workers was formed to advise and assist the program. The *convivio*, which translates as "council," assisted in locating appropriate internships, provided critique of the curriculum, and participated in the final student presentations and evaluations. At times, the *convivio* expected greater academic and professional development from our students than the abilities of the students allowed, so that many meetings were necessary to find common ground for evaluation of curriculum, assignments, and internships.

After three years, the *convivio* was formalized into the *grupo asesor* (advisory group), which has become an integral part of the program. *Grupo asesor* members expanded their input into the curriculum, and some have provided formal supervision to students in community agency settings. The need for a dedicated Spanish class to teach professional social work language/phrases was introduced as part of the Spanish-language requirement. The visiting social work professor was a crucial link to the *grupo asesor*, the Mexican staff, and to the consortium in reviewing issues of concern and addressing changes in the program.

Work with the *grupo asesor* has been an exciting and worthwhile challenge. In particular, the group has become crucial to the focus on social justice within the Mexican context. *Grupo asesor* members are helping bridge the immense gap between the U.S. students' prior social justice knowledge and that routinely required of Mexican social workers. The U.S. students have all been of traditional undergraduate age and typically arrive with limited social work experience. Their experience of the poverty and economic injustices in Mexico has been visceral and at times almost paralyzing. For the most part, the students have not brought an economic lens from which they can understand the global implications of the historical and current role of the United States in developing nations. They often lack a deep understanding of poverty in the United States, so that comparing and contrasting has been an ongoing learning process. Both the *convivio* and the *grupo asesor* have assisted with the challenge of teaching our students, adding understanding and meaning through their support, critique, and detailed attention to the curriculum.

THE MEXICAN SCHOOL OF SOCIAL WORK EXCHANGE

The *grupo asesor* contributed to an eventual decision to offer an exchange between SWLAC students and Mexican social work students at the Mexican School of Social Work (at UNAM). The social work program at UNAM is very large (two thousand students), and the university itself has over two hundred thousand students. This alone was a major culture shock for the SWLAC students in the program. A second culture shock occurred in the second year when the U.S. students visited UNAM and listened to the Mexican students' presentations about their macrolevel community research and service plans. The maturity and commitment of the Mexican students combined with their economic and political analyses intimidated the SWLAC students. This led to more in-depth discussions with the UNAM faculty and ultimately led to a legal partnership between the two programs. Currently, the collaboration with UNAM includes exchange visits between U.S. and Mexican students, during which students spend a week visiting and learning in each others' programs. This relationship continues to inspire the

SWLAC program and is helping to develop a far greater understanding of social justice social work.

COLLABORATION WITH *IXTLILCO EL GRANDE*

From the program's inception, visits to villages or other communities were an integral part of the curriculum, but each visit or homestay created new concerns, especially relative to curriculum integration. The Mexico faculty and the visiting professors from the United States spent long hours planning, implementing, and evaluating the various trips. During the previous two years a fortuitous collaboration with one village had developed, allowing the program to center all rural learning in one community. Ixtlilco el Grande is a rural community that has strong ties to Minnesota, with over 80% of the residents claiming one or more family members who have immigrated to work there. This link has become vital to the long-term goal of the program to relate the reality in Mexico to the reality of Mexicans now living in the United States.

The students begin their program in Ixtlilco el Grande and find the shock of rural poverty and isolation a counterpoint to the warm and hopeful welcome from the residents. At the end of the semester, they return for another homestay with a much more in-depth understanding of the situation. Students have case examples of community struggles in the face of massive migration and immigration as well as evidence of the strengths perspective in individual and family survival. The consequences of global politics are evident in the daily lives of the citizens of Ixtlilco el Grande and in the students who are returning to Minnesota and making contact with the family members who have immigrated to the North, who are much more aware of the complete story. The movement from an overwhelmed and deeply moved young person to an informed, critical-thinking, and compassionate social worker is evident in the feedback from the student and faculty evaluations as they comment on the role of the *convivio, grupo asesor,* UNAM exchange, and the community homestays in Ixtlilco el Grande.

Lessons Learned and Ongoing Challenges

During the five years of the program, the consortium learned several important lessons. These include, not surprisingly, the importance of effective communication, respect, intensive planning, flexibility, and open-mindedness when providing cross-institutional and cross-cultural programming. Each member institution had its own social work curriculum process, course timing, and goals for student learning, which needed to be negotiated for the program to become codified and supported by all institutions. This institutionalization required intensive work by the consortium, and considerable advocacy of the program to individual departments, as well as ongoing regular attention.

While in Mexico, there were other lessons and challenges, frequently ones requiring flexibility. Developing each social work semester required intensive group planning and a sharing of curricular emphasis throughout the program. All teaching staff met before the semester began to develop weekly metathemes in order to provide experiential options and pedagogical focus. Syllabi were altered and adjusted to meet the learning needs of the other courses or institutional needs. Cultural contexts of planning and scheduling were different from the typical university experience in the United States. Planned activities could be postponed, rescheduled, or changed on short notice. Students would receive a weekly schedule of planned activities, but there were frequently last-minute changes that were quite frustrating for students and faculty who could not rely on a set schedule for making plans as they did in their home universities. Faculty needed to develop and foster student flexibility and a cultural appreciation for being in the moment (not always an easy task). Everyone needed to develop an appreciation and appetite for the challenges inherent in the dynamic and spontaneous nature of the program. With time, most participants realized that this dynamic is one of its greatest strengths.

An important lesson and continuing challenge has been the difficulty of matching traditional social work standards in the United States with transformative cross-cultural education in a global setting. One challenge mentioned earlier was the difficulty in matching U.S. students' prior knowledge about global social and economic justice to the depth of knowledge they were required to master in order to succeed in Mexico. The UNAM social work program and Mexican social work students' competence in this area helped raise expectations. Faculty continue to stretch student learning as they and students realize the limitations of the social work curricula as presented in the United States in the areas of global social and economic justice social work.

Another example of the difficulty in bridging the homegrown and global social work expectations has centered on the decision to offer fully accredited social work practice, policy, and internship courses. The consortium has been careful to make sure all courses are essentially equivalent to those offered in the students' home schools, which can be a difficult process. For example, social work education at UNAM begins with a macrofocus linked to community-based action research. Mexican students are taught interesting macrolevel methods such as community mapping. In contrast, far more social work intervention in the United States is offered at the microlevel. The SWLAC program covers both.

The context of social work and service delivery in Mexico is also different from that in the United States. Both countries share many commonalities in the historical roots of the profession as well as in the current educational and practice standards. However, during dialogue and discussion, numerous differences have been discovered as well. Sometimes in our attempt to offer curricula that meets U.S. standards, not enough time was allowed to reflect on the Mexican social work context. As one student voiced, "Why go to Mexico to study social work if it is taught the same way as in the United States of America?" In resolving this issue, faculty have had to straddle a careful balance between CSWE accreditation standards and the professional education standards and the deeper goal of offering transformative social justice education that is authentic to the Mexican culture. The program has improved in this area through collaboration with Mexican social workers and through the cumulative experience in Mexico, and ongoing improvement is anticipated over time toward the goal of an experience that provokes profound transformation.

Conclusion

In summary, five conclusions are offered that are gleaned from SWLAC students' evaluative comments:

1. Cultural competency is directly related to student understanding of social and economic justice on a local, national, and international level.
2. Social work education is and must be transformative on both a personal and professional level. The combination of intensity and reflection inspires transformation.
3. Seeing and hearing are indeed believing. There is no substitute for experience as a learning vehicle.
4. Social work ethics are culturally defined. We must be clear about what that means for working in the United States with persons from marginalized groups or with persons from other countries or working as a social worker outside of the United States.
5. Knowledge of history and knowledge of self and others are the keystones to cross-cultural competence.

References

Augsburg College. (2006). *Program manual: Social work in a Latin American context.* Minneapolis: Center for Global Education.

Center for Global Education. (2006a). *Annual report.* Minneapolis: Augsburg College Press.

Center for Global Education. (2006b). *Program brochure.* Minneapolis: Augsburg College Press.

Finn, J. L., & Jacobson, M. (2003). *Just practice.* Peosta, IA: Eddie Bowers.

Freire, P. (1970). *Pedagogy of the oppressed.* New York: Seabury Press.

Lincoln, Y. S., & Guba, E. G. (1985). *Naturalistic inquiry.* Beverly Hills, CA: Sage.

Lindsey, E. (2005). Study abroad and values development in social work students. *Journal of Social Work Education, 41*(2), 229–249.

Lutterman-Aguilar, A., & Gingrich, O. (2002, Winter). Experiential pedagogy for study abroad: Educating for global citizenship. *Frontiers: Interdisciplinary Journal for Study Abroad,* 41–82.

Merriam Webster Online. (2006). Retrieved August 27, 2006, from http://www.m-w.com/

Ramanathan, C., & Kondrat, M. (1994). Conceptualizing and implementing a social work overseas study program in developing nations: Politics, realities, and strategies. *Social Development Issues, 16*(2), 69–85.

Samovar, L., & Porter, R. (1991). *Communication between cultures.* Belmont, CA: Wadsworth.

Sue, D. W. (2006). *Multi-cultural social work practice.* Hoboken, NJ: Wiley.

CHAPTER FOURTEEN

Transformation in Action: Service-learning to Promote Social Justice, Empowerment, and Advocacy

Carol A. Plummer

Priscilla Allen

Catherine M. Lemieux

Abstract

This chapter demonstrates ways in which social work curricular material on diversity, values and ethics, populations at risk, and social and economic justice were leveraged into social justice–oriented service-learning projects to promote student learning, reflection, and transformation in community contexts. The chapter describes the Teen Court and Neighborhood Advocacy projects, two service-learning projects that illustrate social justice issues in social work education. Described are the conception of the university/community partnerships and the academic course in which each project was nested, along with respective student learning and community change goals. Project evaluation results, transformative experiences, and suggestions for strengthening justice-oriented service-learning conclude this chapter.

Service-learning is a pedagogical approach that integrates community service with academic study to promote student reflection, critical thinking, and creative problem solving. Service-learning projects that target social justice issues increase student learning about social inequalities and the experiences of specific populations at risk, as well as ways in which to remedy these social problems through advocacy and other macropractice and applied-research activities.

This chapter discusses the leveraging of social work curricular material on social and economic justice into academic learning projects to promote student learning, reflection, and transformation in community, agency, and social contexts. To that end, service-learning is defined, and theoretical moorings shared by social justice–oriented service-learning and social work education are described. The bulk of this chapter describes ways in which service-learning was used in two different projects: the Teen Court and Neighborhood Advocacy projects. Each of the project summaries describes the way in which university/ community partnerships were conceived and the academic course in which each project was nested, as well as identifies specific learning and community change goals. Descriptions also include project evaluation results and a summary of lessons learned. This chapter provides an integrative analysis that explicates that project transactions and interactions among players evolved into learning transformations. Recommendations for the field and suggestions for strengthening justice-oriented service-learning practice and scholarship conclude this article.

Service-learning in Social Work: Definitions and Conceptual Framework

Academic service-learning is a pedagogical approach that integrates community service with academic study to promote student reflection, critical thinking, and creative problem solving. The most comprehensive definition of service-learning is offered by Bringle and Hatcher (1996): "We view service-learning as a credit-bearing educational experience in which students participate in an organized service activity that meets identified community needs and reflects on the service activity in such a way as to gain further understanding of the course content, a broader appreciation of the discipline and an enhanced sense of service responsibility" (p. 222). Community service emphasizes students' contributions to the community and the development of students' civic responsibilities. Service-learning deliberately employs pedagogical strategies that use community service as an academic learning resource. Examples of such strategies include establishing student learning goals and developing learning interventions that promote critical thinking about the service experience, such as discussions, presentations, written assignments, and journal exercises (Howard, 1993).

SERVICE-LEARNING AND SOCIAL WORK EDUCATION: EMPOWERMENT IN ACTION

Lemieux and Allen's (2007) review of service-learning in social work describes the congruence of values undergirding service-learning practice and social work education. Social work curricula are rooted in the parlance of client empowerment, which espouses principles such as capacity building, social support, strengths perspective, self-help, and antioppressive practice. Social work is well suited to curriculum-based service-learning, which is made clear in the preamble to the professional *Code of Ethics* promulgated by the National Association of Social Workers (2008), which emphasizes human well-being, empowerment, service, social justice, and social change.

Social work educators recognize the benefits of community-based learning for students. Educators who have used and tested service-learning projects (Knee, 2002; Lowe & Reisch, 1998; Rocha, 2000) believe that social work education, which historically has been characterized as field-oriented and community-based learning, offers a prototype for service-learning.

SOCIAL JUSTICE–ORIENTED SERVICE-LEARNING

Service-learning projects described in the social work literature share a common focus in that they provide students with opportunities to learn from experience in partnership with community-based providers, community residents, or both (Lemieux & Allen, 2007). Social justice–oriented service-learning projects can be distinguished from other types of service-learning experiences because they are aimed at righting societal wrongs while educating students about a specific injustice. Social justice–oriented service-learning specifically focuses on the need for social change and involves students and citizens in the change effort (Boyle-Baise & Langford, 2004). Mobley (2007) describes service-learning exercises as creating measurable differences in students' empathy related to vulnerable citizens and an enhanced competence related to social justice.

Examples of social justice–oriented service-learning projects in social work have focused on building macropractice skills in policy practice (Powell & Causby, 1994; Rocha, 2000; Rocha & Johnson, 1997). Examples of macroskills include exposure and application to social reform, often including advocacy and sometimes legislative action. Indeed, the Neighborhood Advocacy project described here takes a macro-approach. Social work students were involved in enhancing conditions in the community in tandem with an existing revitalization program related to Old South Baton Rouge. Until the completion of the service-learning activity, the oral histories were not available to community citizens. Social action was used to engage the citizens in taking leadership roles and advocacy in determining the location suitable for the maintenance of the records. Social justice service-learning education can also be accomplished using microskill development, as will be demonstrated in our description of the Teen Court project, where one-on-one contact with troubled youths created an impetus for a shift in social work student perceptions and interaction with youth. In addition, a new approach to dealing with youth offenders was made available to the community.

THEORETICAL FRAMEWORKS

Social justice–oriented service-learning is consistent with approaches in social work education that target the classroom environment and course structures to promote antioppressive learning. The classroom becomes a vehicle through which social work educators can model and teach empowerment-oriented practice, which is consistent with principles underlying adult learning theory and student-centered instruction.

Adult-learning theory. Knowles (1972) first advocated using andragogical approaches for teaching social work over thirty years ago. Andragogy, which refers to the art and science of teaching adults, is based on a particular set of assumptions about learners and teachers. Andragogy sees adult learners as mature and self-directed people who come into learning experiences to solve problems. Life experience is a valuable learning resource, and it is the demands of social roles that stimulate an adult's readiness to learn. According to Knowles (1972), the teacher is a facilitator of knowledge and is ultimately responsible for creating a comfortable and respectful learning environment. Andragogical approaches, therefore, respond to students' needs and expectations and use student-centered activities to empower them and to engage them in the learning process.

Student-directed instruction. Student-centered instruction uses pragmatic approaches to teaching that encourage self-awareness, personal responsibility for learning, and ongoing evaluation (Ephross, 1989). Student-directed instructional approaches rely on learning tools that are commonly used in service-learning classes (regardless of the curricular focus). Examples in the social work literature include case-based problem solving, journaling, and project groups (Congress, 1993; Coulshed, 1993; Davis, 1993). Learning contracts have been incorporated in a variety of ways in social work education to provide structure and guidance to student-directed learning experiences and to facilitate mutual goal setting. Huff and Johnson (1998), Knowles (1986), and Lemieux (2001) similarly used learning contracts to clarify issues and expectations around course requirements and assessment.

Social Justice–oriented Service-learning Projects in Social Work

This section describes projects that are illustrative of social justice–oriented service projects in social work by two faculty members of

Louisiana State University's (LSU) School of Social Work. The LSU School of Social Work was established in 1937, largely influenced by New Deal legislation encouraging states to meet social reform needs. The School of Social Work is one of only three accredited MSW programs within the state of Louisiana. With an annual enrollment of approximately two hundred students, the school produces the majority of the state's MSW-level social workers. Service-learning is well institutionalized at LSU, as evidenced by the Center for Community Engagement, Learning and Leadership (CCELL), which annually provides LSU faculty with service-learning incentive grants and fellowship awards, as well as offers state-of-the art training and mentorship. The Neighborhood Advocacy project described in this article was supported with a CCELL faculty incentive grants.

Teen Court Project: Overview and Description

Coauthor C. Plummer developed a service-learning project with thirty students in an advanced-year child-welfare elective course. Using a restorative justice framework, students learned about the detrimental individual and community consequences of traditional labeling and punishment of first-time youth offenders. The partner for this project was a juvenile court prosecutor's office. Students worked in task groups to identify psychoeducational theory and research-based concepts for interventions geared toward developing prosocial skills, personal awareness, and positive relationships toward engendering a sense of community responsibility in youth offenders. Students then designed, implemented, and evaluated the curriculum, learning activities, and psychoeducational intervention. Results were used for formative evaluation of the teen court project by the teen "judges," adult mentors, and the juvenile court prosecutors.

EVOLUTION OF THE PROJECT: SEEDS OF CHANGE

Teen Court is a diversion program. In brief, first-time offenders are provided with an opportunity to go before a jury of their peers—other youths—for sentencing and consequences for their offense. Youths who complete the requirements do not have a permanent record for their misdeed. Teen Court aims to be more curative than punitive; thus, it embraces principles of restorative justice, which helps to "restore" errant individuals to their rightful place in a community after they have committed a wrong. This righting of the wrong brings them fully back into group membership *after* they have demonstrated positive change, which is prompted by loving confrontation and by a demand for accountability (Wilkinson, 1997). Restorative-justice theory posits that people change, not so much by punitive ostracism, but by corrective action, which builds on strengths and prompts recognition that the wrong a youth committed is not the totality of his or her identity. Restorative justice is also pragmatic: society will never be able to incarcerate, over the long term, the majority of those who make mistakes. These individuals ultimately will return to their families and communities, so it is critical to facilitate a successful reentry, one that provides them with positive outlets in which to contribute (Nugent, Umbreit, Wiinamaki, & Paddock, 1999).

Teen Court was established at the national and local levels to address numerous problematic issues in juvenile court. The issues addressed by Teen Court include the following:

- A backlog of cases overwhelms judges and creates a gap between commission of a crime and any consequences, impeding justice for both those with serious infractions and those with petty crimes.
- There is great inequity based on race and class in juvenile court outcomes, so a Teen Court jury of peers may mete out justice in a fairer manner.
- Because first-offense pranks and mistakes are not separated from repetitive and more severe infractions, some youths are inappropriately labeled delinquent without first attempting interventions. There needs to be separation of cases based on seriousness of the offense.
- Labeling of youths prematurely as delinquent may encourage identification with the label, and thus promote future behaviors in line with the label.

A juvenile court record, once established, can affect job options and others' perception of the youth, as well as unnecessarily construct barriers to youths achieving individual, family, and academic goals. Further, the consequences can be costly to schools and to the larger community.

Linkages for the Teen Court service-learning project were initiated when a prosecutor visited the class to facilitate a mock trial experience for social work students and asked the professor to become involved. Because this relationship was already established, the groundwork was laid for an endeavor with ongoing mutual benefits. The community Teen Court organizers, including this particular prosecutor, had identified a need and were putting in place some structures, but Teen Court staff lacked adequate services. Subsequent to several planning meetings, the key community partners and the instructor defined the project based on interlocking needs for teaching tools and services for Teen Court youths.

The issues affecting juvenile court raise questions about particular issues of social justice and equality, and therefore, they can create "teachable moments" about society's reactions to and beliefs about the origins of criminality and ways in which to respond to youth crime. The Teen Court is a community-based, multidisciplinary innovation that aims to simultaneously address the above-mentioned issues by enabling a paradigm shift regarding the youths and by creating possibilities for change.

LEARNING ACTIVITIES

As mentioned, students enrolled in an elective course in child welfare undertook the Teen Court project. Students are oriented to the range of services and challenges in work with children and families who come into contact with the child welfare and juvenile justice systems. Multi-problem families and approaches to prevention, intervention, and treatment of family difficulties that result in risks for children and youth are the focus in this course. The Teen Court project specifically targeted the following course-learning objectives:

- Have awareness of the broad spectrum of social service networks that constitute child-welfare social work practice in the state and nation.
- Have the ability to critically evaluate multiproblem family situations and make accurate assessment of client problems with special sensitivity to diversity issues that influence client vulnerability and risk.
- Identify contextual elements that influence problem situations and problem resolution, including effects of individual and family developmental processes, community values, gender, race, age, and ethnicity.
- Distinguish pertinent ethical, legal, and value components of professional communication, including confidentiality and appropriate teamwork with other professionals/agencies on behalf of the client/client group.

The service-learning project required students to design, implement, and evaluate a psychoeducational group for youths "sentenced" by Teen Court. Two student task groups worked to research and design appropriate interventions for those youth whose jury of peers sentenced to a psychoeducational program. Two other student task groups implemented the six-week group intervention, which was designed to assist youths in making positive decisions, handling peer pressure, managing feelings, and setting life goals.

Under faculty supervision, the two additional social work student teams did miniassessments with the youth, which included use of a family evaluation scale provided by Teen Court staff. Use of this scale was a requirement of the grant that funded the Teen Court, yet no staff were available to assist with survey data collection. Student involvement helped the agency and also taught data-collection skills to students. The evaluation task groups also designed ways to evaluate the formative and summative outcomes of the program. Each task group separately determined how success would be defined and then developed the appropriate evaluation tools (e.g., pre- and posttests, satisfaction surveys) and processes (e.g., youth and parent self-report, focus groups). One task group used self-report data to identify the elements that youths liked and their learning from the group. These data provided information about the exercises and approaches that youth perceived as most useful so that these features could be retained in future Teen Court psychoeducation groups. The other evaluation team focused on parents' expectations and attitudes, as well as their perceptions of the program's impact upon completion. This latter focus recognized the importance of parental support and input, as well as provided an additional viewpoint to offset social desirability responses in the youths. In addition to the more formal evaluation strategies undertaken by the evaluation teams, ongoing formative evaluation processes occurred in every class session, during which student task groups reported on their activities. Weekly reports kept each team aware of the ways in which their work fit within the whole project, and gave each team the chance to learn and benefit from actions that met with varying levels of success.

The entire learning process was fed by activities experienced in the Teen Court group activities. For example, in both writing assignments and class discussions, students were asked to address the reasons why youths violate the law. This led to exploration of poverty, family dynamics, abuse, and discrimination, with many examples in the Teen Court psychoeducational groups. Beyond theory, students also grappled with program-development issues, using text to cite common challenges, and real-life experiences with time constraints, youth satisfaction, and community-partner willingness to apply those constructs. These learning goals culminated in group presentations twice during the course, with a requirement of literature bolstering the applied components. For the final student presentation, our community service-learning partners attended a celebration of our joint venture and successes, learned of the entirety of the student projects, and even requested copies of the student PowerPoint overviews.

PROJECT OUTCOMES

Youths sentenced to Teen Court needed interventions that could help provide them with new insights, positive role models, and skills in behavior management. The School of Social Work (SSW) provided two groups for a total of eight hours' contact time with each group of youths. Further, it provided empirically supported programming based on research of theoretically sophisticated approaches. Without the groups provided by the SSW graduate students, errant youths would have had restitution to pay, community service to provide, and perhaps would have had to write a letter of apology. This group learning opportunity was highly regarded by the attorneys, judges, and youths themselves. As a result, Teen Court staff requested that the program be continued, and it has been retained as a service-learning option in the second child-welfare course. Community partners and the professor hope to continue the mutually beneficial social justice effort in the foreseeable future.

EVALUATION

In addition to the evaluation of the psychoeducational groups, standard midterm and final examinations were given to the graduate students, incorporating the full range of course materials, including the service-learning project. Papers were of reduced length due to the substantial work done outside of class in the group projects. Students were given individual grades on their portion of the group in-class presentations. However, determining levels of participation from all parties can be challenging when the instructor is not present and involvement/engagement is key. To ensure fairness, students were asked to write a paragraph on the involvement of each person in their work group (development, implementation, or evaluation), detailing who was responsible for each task undertaken. They then assigned a letter grade to each person, including their self-evaluation. This approach enabled the instructor to use student-assessment data to supplement the observations of student performance provided by the community partners when assigning grades.

TRANSFORMATION

Students involved in the Teen Court process were transformed by the intersection of their contact with youths, exposure to perceptions of community partners, processing of feelings, and the professional literature. No longer an abstraction, graduate students had learned firsthand about the complexity of the questions and the shades of gray in many of the answers. They felt both amazed by the struggles they encountered and empowered by their ability to face and overcome them. In many ways, their transformation paralleled those of the youths from Teen Court whom they taught.

Theory behind social justice–oriented service-learning is congruent with all social work education, whereby students continually integrate coursework and field experience. Service-learning augments the classroom–field experience link by offering shorter-term learning opportunities, which are more directly connected to the current class in which the student is enrolled. Further, because all the classmates share the project, the diverse perspectives of the students, instructor, and community partners enrich the integration of readings and service, which is not always the case in field internships. For example, the Teen Court project required students spend a portion of each class reviewing events that occurred in the psychoeducational group and ways in which to improve them, planning for the next group, and obtaining class feedback. This level of integration was not only possible, but highly relevant to all. Ideally, teaching, practice, and social justice work should be inextricably linked in social work education. However, a theoretical understanding of suffering, inequity in service provision, and lack of resources can never equal the learning acquired through human contact, the messiness of working with community agencies, or the empowerment of seeing lives change.

LESSONS LEARNED

As a new program, Teen Court had many community players who held diverse opinions. Agency time lines were often shifted, and policies emerged that, over time, required the instructor and students to cooperatively work with multiple community groups. When partnering with a new program, our experience showed that it is essential to remain flexible at all times and to have well-defined roles for all of the key players, with one identified "point" person for the partner agency. Having a number of options for students enabled them to participate in the task groups that not only were of particular interest to them, but also were the most practical and feasible. This is especially important in graduate work, where parents with young children or rigid job schedules may prohibit some activities outside of class. Student input is critical to the learning process; thus, the manner in which course content is covered may need to be shifted in order to accommodate students' needs and experiences in the field. Task groups afforded students with opportunities to learn about cooperation, accountability to community agencies, and the importance of accommodating multiple perspectives and ideas. A ceremony or celebration whereby community partners and students can reflect on and fully appreciate their accomplishments provided for a rewarding and positive closure.

Neighborhood Advocacy Project:
Overview and Description

Coauthor L. Allen included a service-learning project in two sections of a required policy course with fifty-four advanced-year students. The goal of this service-learning project was to resolve an ongoing university/community dispute around the ownership and housing of a collection of 210 oral-history tapes. The partner agency was a neighborhood organization adjacent to the university composed primarily of African American residents and business leaders who participated in the original oral-history project (with another university department) that created the collection. Students worked in task groups to abstract, organize, and return the oral-history tape collection to the community in which the neighborhood organization resided. Students' networking, relationship building, and policy-advocacy activities culminated in a memorandum of understanding, authored by the university chancellor, which empowered the neighborhood organization to determine the repository placement of the collection.

EVOLUTION OF THE PROJECT: SEEDS OF CHANGE

The seeds of this project were planted many years prior. A rich collection of 210 oral histories of residents and leaders of the Old South Baton Rouge (OSBR) community had been carefully collected and preserved by a faculty member in the College of Education. The content of the tapes described a culturally rich and proud community. The tapes included discussions about thriving businesses and active churches; about McKinley High School, the first black high school in Louisiana; and about the first bus boycott in the nation, which actually preceded the Montgomery bus boycott. The importance of these tapes to the community is immense. For example, Dr. Martin Luther King Jr. had sought advice from OSBR residents about ways in which to implement boycotts and other forms of activism. The problem was that the tapes were not accessible to the people to whom they belonged. This had been a source of strife and ill feelings for some time, exacerbating the unsettled and sometimes tense relationship that existed between OSBR community members and the university.

The OSBR residents who requested resolution from the university made the need for reparation evident. LSU's director of the Center for Community Engagement, Learning and Leadership approached the instructor to see whether a mutually beneficial partnership could be forged among social work students and OSBR community leaders and residents.

LEARNING ACTIVITIES

The MSW students who were enrolled in the advanced required course, Community and Agency Contexts for Direct Practice, undertook the Neighborhood Advocacy project. The course focuses on the relevance of organizations and contextual forces to clients' lives and to the conduct of practice in agency and community settings. Emphasis is placed on theoretical and knowledge perspectives that provide a basis for changing political, economic, social, and organizational policies, practices, and conditions. Students learn skills for planning, implementing, and evaluating contextual change that directly benefits clients. The Neighborhood Advocacy project specifically targeted the following course-learning objectives:

- To integrate values and ethics of the profession into change efforts designed to more responsively serve clients' interests using a context-based, culturally competent approach.
- To possess knowledge of and skill in applying empowerment strategies designed to confront social injustice, institutionalized racism, sexism, agism, and oppression.
- To develop understanding of and to transfer knowledge about risk factors and predictors for vulnerable populations as a method for assessment, planning intervention, and evaluating outcomes of change efforts intended to achieve social and economic justice outcomes for clients.

The service-learning project required students to organize a community steering committee, collect information, and select relevant artifacts that highlighted themes from existing materials. Opportunities for reflection were infused throughout the course. Students maintained journals that chronicled their interactions with the community and identified instructive elements about these interactions. Reflection was monitored throughout the duration of the course. The instructor used a Web-based learning platform (BlackBoard) to show students linkages between the project goals and course objectives. In addition to other course assignments, students abstracted and organized 210 tapes and worked with the community to determine the final housing of the oral-history materials. Students presented the results of their project to the OSBR Community Revitalization Committee. Students were required to facilitate a partnership with the Carver Library and LSU Housing and

Urban Development (HUD) steering committee members (and to develop further avenues of participation, such as the Concerned Citizens and the African American Museum) to satisfy a Housing and Urban Development requirement to institute earlier collected oral histories to a public place accessible to the residents in order to reengage participation and linkage between LSU and residents within the OSBR community.

PROJECT OUTCOMES

At the end of the semester, the 210 tapes were abstracted and organized. Students learned ways to determine the final housing of the oral-history materials and maneuvered through the complex system of networking and community building. Further, approximately six months after the class commenced, an official transfer ceremony was held to house the tapes in the brand new Carver Library, complete with a state-of-the-art listening station. Multiple stakeholders attended to recognize the long-awaited passage. Several of the original architects of the project were present to mark the ceremony, and a handful of students returned to OSBR to witness their role in history making.

EVALUATION

Student-learning outcomes were assessed via students' performance on course assignments, which included journals, reflection papers, and midterm and final examinations. A graded reflection paper was required of each student, which composed a proportion of the overall project grade. Students' overall grades were composed of the group project score, individual exam scores, and scores for class participation. The accessibility and visibility of the oral histories and the openness of the dialogue between LSU and the OSBR community were community-oriented outcomes of interest. Community members, students, and the instructor evaluated project goals. Members of the HUD steering committee, which oversees broader OSBR revitalization efforts, provided feedback about the extent to which the class was successful in meeting the community-level goals of the project.

The community-action project's goals were also part of the evaluation of success. These included implementing an action plan, increasing public awareness in reaching a vulnerable group, educating the public about the implications of policy/practice, and, most important, initiating change of a specified community. The plan involved all class members and encouraged engagement of the OSBR community in social action. Through the linkage between the Carver Library and the LSU HUD steering committee, students learned from the community rather than prescribing suggestions for participation and change. A critical learning objective was for students to report their key learnings from the community. All of these goals were also reached by the service-learning project.

Students participated in a peer-evaluation process to assess the extent to which project goals and objectives were met. The instructor assessed the extent to which students were able to engage the OSBR community by soliciting feedback from OSBR community members. The action plan was carefully followed and executed. Students not only learned from the community; they received input from several invested stakeholders while increasing the visibility of the valuable oral-history materials. The students reflected that they learned unforgettable lessons about a community that they knew little or (more typically) nothing about, except negative attributes. Information shared by students who were intimately familiar with the "Bottoms" community was received as beneficial and life changing in terms of gaining exposure to leaders in the Civil Rights Movement, discovering the history of McKinley School, and the role of churches and the greater community.

TRANSFORMATION

The discord between the community and the university that was addressed by this service-learning project was at one time viewed as an intractable problem. In fact, a number of university administrators were skeptical about whether the students would be able to navigate their way through the historically rocky terrain that characterized previous university-OSBR community interactions and actually come to a resolution about where the tapes would be housed. Transformation occurred as students were able to maneuver their way through the land mines of conflict, to work through university politics, and to table issues that could create strife, such as egoism and polarity. The permanent display of the oral histories, with the students' efforts in the background of the celebration, worked perfectly, because the community was the central focus of the students' learning efforts, as it should be in service-learning.

LESSONS LEARNED

Similar to the lessons learned in Teen Court, the importance of flexibility was underscored in the Neighborhood Advocacy project. Flexibility in covering course content was critical in order to address students' emergent needs while working in the field. Further, cooperation, clear expectations, and well-defined roles all proved essential to the success of the project. The task-group experience taught students about the importance of accommodating multiple perspectives and ideas. A ceremony celebrated the final repository of the oral-history tapes, a fitting opportunity for community partners and students to acknowledge their accomplishments.

Integration and Analysis of Project Key Features

TRANSFORMATIVE ELEMENTS

Both the Teen Court and Neighborhood Advocacy projects required social work students to advocate with and on behalf of traditionally marginalized communities, albeit in distinctly different ways. As each project unfolded, students were confronted with learning situations fraught with ambiguity and unpredictability. This is unlike the orderliness and structure that is typical of traditional classroom learning. The Teen Court and Neighborhood Advocacy projects required students to work together as a collective to accomplish certain community-level outcomes. And therein lies the transformative elements of social justice–oriented service-learning: project success invariably rests upon student interdependence, investment, ownership, and mutual reliance. These latter characteristics are the hallmarks of all vital and strong communities. Transformation occurs when students consciously cocreate learning communities while working toward the goal of empowering client communities.

COLLABORATION AND INTERACTION: FACULTY, STUDENTS, COMMUNITY PARTNERS

Service-learning is a pedagogical approach that is most effective when students are afforded ready access to information and guidance and when faculty members and community partners communicate frequently to sustain a collaborative focus. This means that community partners must strike a delicate balance between meeting community needs and satisfying student learning needs. As with all newly formed groups, the beginning stages of a student service-learning task group may be characterized by identity crises, role confusion, and power struggles. Students therefore benefit from structure, clear expectations, and ongoing communication.

The OSBR Oral History Project illuminated the linkage between the classroom and the community. Students had to table their own agenda of swiftly finishing a project in neat, objective goals, and embrace the reality of connecting with stakeholders and meet the community where they were. Although buy-in may not have been 100% at the onset, there was a transition from resistance to participation, particularly after students were exposed to the shared experiences, frustrations, and joys of connecting with multiple community stakeholders. Collaboration occurred through deliberation among students. They organized tasks and contacts and met with members of key organizations who were invested in receiving the oral histories, such as the McKinley High Association, local legislators, and members of the local senior center. Relationships were developed, which is the key in productive service-learning.

Similarly, the Teen Court/child welfare project required flexibility both from students and community partners. For example, groups were not held during school breaks. Teen Court sentencing influenced the numbers of youth referred for psychoeducational groups, sometimes greatly altering student experiences. Give-and-take was evident as the relationship with our community partner grew. Appreciative Teen Court staff provided ongoing mock trial experiences and field trips for our students to the detention center or court, creating even more learning opportunities. The faculty member wrote a letter of support for their ongoing funding of Teen Court, and students even wrote a small (successful) grant for funding of necessary supplies and materials during class time, indicative of the mutual benefits that multiplied.

Service-learning to Promote Social Justice: Conclusions

The two projects described in this chapter illustrate two ways in which service-learning was used as a community-based learning tool to teach social work students about social justice, social reform, and social action. The two projects exemplify opportunities in service-learning to parallel the perspectives of social justice, social reform, and social action. As Lemieux and Allen (2007) found, these projects document the value of community partnerships in learning and, in fact, exceeded expectations because unexpected positive outcomes also resulted.

Mobley's (2007) findings that empathy increases in students and enhanced competencies develop as a result of social justice service-learning are reflected in comments from student participants. As one student put it, "Through the participation in the Neighborhood Advocacy project, I came to understand the wide range of social work skills needed to practice on a community and organizational level." Another added, "Prior to working with the Neighborhood Advocacy project, I had little connection with the outlying community. By working as partners to return the oral histories, I changed many opinions about this community that I once avoided." Likewise, students from the Teen Court project noted specific value from their experience. One graduate student stated:

> We didn't take student/teacher roles. We all learned together.
> I gained a lot of patience because I worked with different

children from different cultural backgrounds. I learned how to relate to teens in a more down-to-earth way. The Teen Court experience helped me to develop my skills in bettering my rapport with adolescents.

Service-learning is a pedagogical tool that has the potential to transform students' perceptions and empower communities. Instructors promote learning about social justice issues when students are enabled to apply the core values of social work in the context of a collective, mutually empowering experience.

References

Boyle-Baise, M., & Langford, J. (2004). There are children here: Service learning for social justice. *Equity and Excellence in Education, 37,* 55–66.

Bringle, R. G., & Hatcher, J. A. (1996). Implementing service-learning in higher education. *Journal of Higher Education, 67,* 221–239.

Congress, E. P. (1993). Teaching ethical decision making to a diverse community of students: Bringing practice into the classroom. *Journal of Teaching in Social Work, 7*(2), 23–36.

Coulshed, V. (1993) Adult learning: Implications for teaching in social work education. *British Journal of Social Work, 23*(1), 1–13.

Davis, L. (1993). Feminism and constructivism: Teaching social work practice with women. *Journal of Teaching in Social Work, 8*(1/2), 147–163.

Ephross, P. H. (1989). Teaching group therapy within social work education. *Journal of Independent Social Work, 3*(4), 87–98.

Howard, J. (1993). Community service-learning in the curriculum. In J. Howard (Ed.), *Praxis I: A faculty casebook on community service learning* (pp. 3–12). Ann Arbor: University of Michigan, OCSL Press.

Huff, M. T., & Johnson, M. M. (1998). Empowering students in a graduate level social work course. *Journal of Social Work Education, 34*(3), 375–385.

Knee, R. T. (2002). Can service-learning enhance student understanding of social work research? *Journal of Teaching in Social Work, 22*(1/2), 213–225.

Knowles, M. S. (1972). Innovations in teaching style based upon adult learning. *Journal of Education for Social Work, 8*(2), 32–39.

Knowles, M. S. (1986). *Using learning contracts.* San Francisco: Jossey Bass.

Lemieux, C. M. (2001). Learning contracts in the classroom: Tools for empowerment and accountability. *Social Work Education, 20*(2), 263–276.

Lemieux, C. M., & Allen, P. D. (2007). Service-learning in social work: Service considerations, practice conundrums, and pedagogical practicalities. *Journal of Social Work Education, 43*(2), 1–17.

Lowe, J. I., & Reisch, M. (1998). Bringing the community into the classroom: Applying the experiences of social work education to service-learning courses in sociology. *Teaching Sociology, 26*(4), 92–98.

Mobley, C. (2007). Breaking ground: Engaging undergraduates in social change through service learning. *Teaching Sociology, 35*(2), 125–137.

National Association of Social Workers. (2008). *Code of Ethics of the National Association of Social Workers*. Washington, DC: Author.

Nugent, W. R., Umbreit, M. S., Wiinamaki, L., & Paddock, J. (1999, Summer). Participation in victim-offender mediation reduces recidivism. *VOMA Connections, 3*(1), 11.

Powell, J. Y., & Causby, V. D. (1994). From classroom to the capitol, from MSW
students to advocates: Learning by doing. *Journal of Teaching in Social
Work, 9*(11/2), 141–154.

Rocha, C. J. (2000). Evaluating experiential teaching methods in a policy practice
course: The case for service learning to increase political participation. *Journal of Social Work Education, 36*(1).

Rocha, C. J., & Johnson, A. K. (1997). Teaching family policy through a policy practice framework. *Journal of Social Work Education, 33*(3), 433–444.

Wilkinson, R. A. (1997, December 1). A shifting paradigm: Modern restorative justice principles have their roots in ancient cultures. *Corrections Today*. Alexandria, VA: American Correctional Association.

Appendix: Recommendations for Service-Learning to Promote Social Justice

Developing a successful service-learning project that promotes social
justice education is worthwhile, but it also is challenging. Projects need
to fit the course objectives, meet community needs, augment student
learning in a manner that does not duplicate learning experiences
encountered in field internships, and be accomplished in one semester.
Although service-learning is specifically tailored to a unique learning
situation, the following recommendations are consistent with best
practices gleaned from existing scholarship on social work service-
learning (Lemieux & Allen, 2007):

- Partner with a community organization or agency with which you
  have a prior relationship.
- When possible, lay significant groundwork with community partners about the scope and definition of the work, recognizing the
  limitations of time imposed by a semester.
- In order to promote student investment and ownership, empower
  students to make decisions about time frames, options for tasks,
  content of program and planning.
- Maintain ongoing contact with your community partner to quickly
  solve any difficulties, anticipate changes or problems, and maintain the relationship.
- Spend time each class session to reflect upon the links between
  course materials and service-learning experiences.

- Be prepared to teach students task group approaches to help them work through conflicts that may arise due to different expectations, frustrations related to the community interface, or anxiety produced from the service-learning task.

Additional recommendations can be gleaned from the experience of facilitating these social justice–oriented service-learning projects:

- Prepare students for the possibility of group conflict. Identify potential sources and teach them ways to resolve conflict and remain goal oriented. Encourage students to approach the instructor for mediation, if necessary.
- During periods of student reflection, explicate the real-life implications of the service-learning experiences that students may not themselves have extricated from various learning opportunities.
- Be creative and fair in grading, especially if the instructor is unable to directly observe the full range of students' service-learning activities. For example, evaluate students' individual reflection papers, class presentations, and other project products and materials. In order to fully appreciate students' individual contributions to group learning, require student task groups to maintain group activity logs and to engage in structured peer assessment.
- While fulfilling community roles as a field supervisor or member of a nonprofit board of directors, keep alert to unsolved community problems that may be amenable to social justice–oriented service-learning.

The Teen Court and Neighborhood Advocacy projects described in this chapter are examples of service-learning projects in social work that addressed social change and social justice issues. The creation of student learning communities paralleled the community changes brought about by service-learning activities. These projects illustrate how social justice, empowerment, and advocacy are catalysts for transformation.

CHAPTER FIFTEEN

Organizing on Campus for Civil Liberties and Social Justice

Donna Hardina
Ruth Obel-Jorgensen

Abstract

In this chapter, the authors describe a recent opportunity that was used to teach and engage social work students in direct-action organizing. The authors use this case example to describe the process of experiential learning similar to Freire's (1970) model of popular education. Academic freedom and its importance for student learning are defined, and recent developments related to police surveillance and academic freedom at universities and colleges are described. In addition, the authors discuss the risks involved in direct-action organizing, the application of specific tactical methods, and the outcomes produced.

According to David Gil (1998), social justice is achieved when all people have equal "social, civil, and political rights and responsibilities" (p. 13). In order to expand the rights of oppressed groups or establish equality in the distribution of resources, individuals and groups typically form coalitions and social movements to acquire political power and engage in lobbying, social protest, and mass mobilization for changes in laws and social policies (Mondros & Wilson, 1994). Consequently, the achievement of social justice requires the use of a variety of strategies and tactics by social workers, their constituents, and the organizations with whom they collaborate. In some instances, it is necessary to use direct-action-related tactics in organizing campaigns (Brager, Specht, & Torczyner, 1987). Shaw (2001) defines direct action as "events that immediately confront a specific individual or organization with a set of specific demands" (p. 212).

Recent trends in social movement organizing indicate a shift from collaborative tactics to direct action and civil disobedience as a response to government and corporate initiatives to reduce political rights, limit economic opportunities for people in poverty, and harm the environment (Conway, 2003; McAdam & Tarrow, 2000). Mondros (2005) argues that the use of confrontation methods can be ethically justified in situations in which members of marginalized or historically oppressed groups are fighting for recognition of their rights or to obtain power. Consequently, social work graduates may face situations in which they must make decisions about their level of involvement in protest activities and whether to involve others in confrontation (Shaw, 2001). Some of the skills necessary to effectively engage in social justice organizing include the ability to develop collaborative partnerships with constituents, analyze the power held by the various groups involved, examine the ethical and safety concerns associated with the use of various tactics, and carry out actions that involve confrontation with powerful decision makers (Homan, 2004; Reisch & Lowe, 2000; Rivera & Erlich, 1998).

In this chapter, the authors describe a recent opportunity that was used to teach and engage social work students in direct-action organizing. This effort was in response to an incident in which six undercover officers attended a presentation by an animal rights activist. The event was sponsored by a student antiwar and social justice organization. Social work students and faculty affiliated with the Campus Peace and Civil Liberties Coalition led a successful hunger strike in response to this threat to academic freedom and civil liberties. The hunger strike resulted in the issuance of a university policy that restricted the ability of campus police to conduct surveillance operations on campus.

The authors use this case example to describe the process of experiential learning similar to Freire's (1970) model of popular education in which students and teachers engage in a participatory process that broaden their understanding of social issues, enhance their leadership skills, and achieve social justice goals. Academic freedom and its importance for student learning are defined, and recent developments related to police surveillance and academic freedom at universities and colleges are described. This case study of the campaign to oppose police surveillance at a university also provides an opportunity to identify strategies and tactics that can be used on other campuses to preserve civil liberties. In addition, the authors discuss the risks involved in direct-action organizing, the application of specific tactical methods, and the outcomes produced.

Experiential Learning and the Social Justice Curriculum

Experiential learning has been an important component of social justice–related curriculum in many schools of social work. This tradition has drawn upon Paulo Freire's (1970) model of popular education, which emphasizes the development of student self-knowledge or the critical capacity to understand social, political, and economic forces that have contributed to the oppression of marginalized groups. An important component of this approach is that the learner should engage with others in dialogue about social problems and participate in social action to address these injustices (Gutierrez & Alvarez, 2000). According to Wint and Sewpaul (2000), "learning occurs at both concrete and abstract levels, arising from introspection (reflection) and experience (external experimentation)" (p. 62). Another key component of this approach, as applied to community organization practice, is that responsibility for problem identification, solutions, and action originates among those individuals who are affected by the problem rather than being directed by teachers, organizers, or other professionals (Carroll & Minkler, 2000).

Although community-organization courses in schools of social work often teach organizing techniques using experiential methods, the focus is almost always on collaborative projects or lobbying state legislatures rather than activities such as demonstrations, boycotts, and other forms of direct action. Numerous case studies have described the successful use of experiential techniques to teach social work students about organizing communities (Danis, 2006; Gutierrez & Alvarez, 2000; Rogge & Rocha, 2004; Salcido, Ornelas, & Lee, 2002). Only a few of these case studies actually describe the use of social action or confrontational methods to challenge university administrators or elected officials (Moore, 2004; Moore & Dietz, 1999). Consequently, there is little available social work literature that describes educational outcomes or the risks inherent in using confrontation tactics in the context of a student-organizing campaign.

Defining Civil Liberties and Academic Freedom

The term "civil liberties" can be defined in terms of constitutional protections identified in the first ten amendments of the U.S. Constitution (the Bill of Rights). These rights include freedom of speech, freedom of assembly, and freedom of the press, as well as freedom of religion and protection from unreasonable search and seizure (Encyclopedia Britannica Online, 2006). Many of these freedoms have historically been eroded or suspended during periods of war. For example, during the 1960s, antiwar activists opposed to the Vietnam War were placed under surveillance by local authorities and the Federal Bureau of Investigation (Schlosberg, 2006).

The term "academic freedom" is often applied to the exercise of free speech on university campuses. The U.S. Supreme Court has recognized academic freedom as a basic right protected by the First Amendment (AAUP, 2001). The American Association of University Professors issued its first statement of principles on academic freedom in 1940. In this document, it stated that "the common good depends upon the free speech for truth and its free expression" (AAUP, 2001, p. 1). Among the principles identified were the right of faculty to engage in free expression on their subject matter and the freedom of faculty to conduct research and publish their results. Most universities and associations that represent college faculty have adopted these principles.

Although academic freedom is often framed in relation to a faculty member's right to discuss controversial materials in the classroom, it also has important implications for students. According to Free Exchange on Campus (n.d.), a group formed in Pennsylvania to preserve the free speech rights of students, academic freedom is essential because

> faculty must feel able to bring up new and sometimes controversial topics and ideas in order to challenge students to learn, analyze debate, and think for themselves. Students need an education that challenges them to become critical thinkers, to become people who come up with new ideas and analyses. (p. 2)

The AAUP (2007) defines student academic freedom as the "freedom to learn," and maintains that "students should be free to take reasoned exception to the data or views offered in any course of study" (p. 4). Although legal opinions vary about whether students have a constitutional right to academic freedom, the courts have generally ruled that universities should function as a "marketplace of ideas." Consequently, students do have the right to bring speakers with diverse views to campus or to form student groups around controversial issues (AAUP, 2007; Pavela, 2005). In 2006, in response to some universities rejecting student requests to bring controversial speakers to campus, the AAUP issued a policy statement, Academic Freedom and Outside Speakers, which restates a principle adopted by the organization in 1967:

> The freedom to hear is an essential condition of a university
> community and an inseparable part of academic freedom . . .
> [and] . . . the right to examine issues and seek the truth is
> prejudiced to the extent that the university is open to some
> but not to others whom members of the university also judge
> desirable to hear. (p. 1)

Academic Freedom Post-9/11

For many university faculty members and students, the post-9/11 era
has posed a number of threats to academic freedom. In some instances,
the right to speak freely in the classroom or to invite controversial
speakers to campus has been limited by conservative groups determined to "protect" students from controversial ideas or "unbalanced"
presentations of varying viewpoints (Friedman, 2005). For example,
filmmaker Michael Moore was barred from several campuses just prior
to the 2004 presidential election after university administrators were
pressured by conservative media pundits and university donors (Gravois, 2004). Student groups have also been ordered to cancel presentations or refrain from protesting in instances in which the substance of
the speech or protest conflicted with the prevailing doctrine at universities operated by religious groups, when ethnic or religious groups complained about the viewpoint of the speaker (most often in reference to
political conflicts in the Middle East), or when the presence of a controversial speaker was thought (often without evidence) to promote or
provoke violence by the speaker's supporters or opponents (American
Civil Liberties Union [ACLU], 2006a; Bartlett, 2006; McCarthy, 2002;
Sherman, 2005).

At some universities, conservative students have complained about
statements made by liberal or radical faculty. Recently, conservative
commentator David Horowitz (2006) published a controversial book,
The Professors: The 101 Most Dangerous Academics in America. Based on
limited concrete evidence and using some deliberate misstatements or
misrepresentations, Horowitz has listed faculty members that he felt
articulated progressive political opinions in their teaching or published
work, attempting to indoctrinate students with extremist left-wing propaganda (Jacobson, 2006). Horowitz also has campaigned to have state
governments adopt an academic bill of rights to "protect" students
from liberal bias in the classroom (Lipka, 2006). Although over a dozen
state legislatures have considered this legislation, most have declined
to adopt it after protest by student and faculty groups (Center for Campus Free Speech, 2006).

Universities have worked with local law enforcement to monitor events and rallies on campus in addition to rescinding invitations to speak on campus and challenging the right of faculty and students to articulate controversial viewpoints. In some instances, federally funded, county-level antiterrorism task forces, which include a variety of local law enforcement agencies, FBI representatives, and campus police, have conducted surveillance activities (Arnone, 2003). Some of the universities involved in surveillance have cited concerns about violence or terrorism in monitoring these events. Changes in the Patriot Act have made it easier for law enforcement to send undercover officers to public events, meetings of civic organizations, and houses of worship (Friedman, 2005). Antiwar, civil rights, and environmental activists have often been targets of surveillance. Information obtained from the Pentagon and the Federal Bureau of Investigation by the American Civil Liberties Union, in response to public records requests, has verified that groups such as Greenpeace, People for the Ethical Treatment of Animals (PETA), and the ACLU have been placed under surveillance (Lichtblau, 2005; Schlosberg, 2006).

In this chapter, we describe a series of incidents involving efforts to bar speakers from campus or place campus groups under police surveillance. These incidents occurred over a two-year period at California State University, Fresno (Fresno State). Social work students were members of groups placed under surveillance and were instrumental in coordinating a series of actions to generate public awareness of these threats to academic freedom and to pressure the university to adopt policies to restrict surveillance of on-campus groups.

Outside Speakers and Police Surveillance in Fresno, 2000–2004

A number of instances of police surveillance and efforts to stop events involving outside speakers occurred in Fresno beginning in 2000. In 2000, Students Against Sweatshops (SAS), a group made up of Fresno State students and faculty, were arrested protesting against sweatshop labor in front of the local Gap clothing store. City police told group members that they would not be permitted to protest inside the shopping mall because they were considered to be violent. Those people arrested (including the coordinator of the peace and conflict studies program at Fresno State) sued the city for false arrest. During the trial, testimony revealed that city police received information about the group from an undercover agent planted in SAS by the campus police at Fresno State. Subsequently, the plaintiffs won a large financial judgment from the city (Rhodes, 2005).

In 2003, the president of an off-campus group, Peace Fresno, found an article in a local newspaper about a deputy sheriff who had recently died in a motorcycle accident. She recognized the picture of the officer as a previous active member of Peace Fresno. The sheriff's office eventually confirmed the deputy sheriff's membership in the county antiterrorist task force as well as his presence at Peace Fresno meetings, but argued that such surveillance is legal (Marcum, 2006; Rhodes, 2005). This incident was documented in Michael Moore's film *Fahrenheit 911*.

A third event involved overt rather than covert surveillance. A number of conservative groups, including the Free Republic and the Center for Consumer Freedom, conservative faculty members, local farmers, and businesspeople attempted to put pressure on university administrators to stop a conference on revolutionary environmentalism (RE) at Fresno State in February 2003 (Center for Consumer Freedom, 2003). Invitations to speak were sent by the political science department to a variety of radical environmental activists, including several with criminal records for activities such as firebombing animal research labs and releasing animals from a mink farm. These activists included members of Earth First and a former staff member for PETA. The university responded to the political pressure by permitting the conference to proceed with heavy security. Law enforcement officials believed such measures to be necessary to prevent the panelists and conference participants from engaging in direct action against local SUV dealerships or ranchers. Local police and the groups opposed to the event characterized the radical environmentalists who spoke at the conference as "domestic terrorists" (Fogg, 2003).

Although the conference went on as scheduled, the controversy continued. A federal grand jury subpoenaed tapes of the conference (Steinberg, 2003). After consulting attorneys, the university turned over the tape of a presentation by an animal rights activist. University administrators, concerned about the opposition to the RE conference, adopted a new policy for outside speakers that required approval for events from a minimum of six university officials, including the campus police chief. Implementation of this policy made it difficult for on-campus organizations, especially student groups, to bring outside speakers to campus. The Campus Coalition for Peace and Civil Liberties (Campus Peace) was just one of the groups that subsequently experienced problems in complying with this new policy.

Starving for Civil Liberties

On November 10, 2004, the Campus Peace and Civil Liberties Coalition at California State University, Fresno, sponsored a presentation by Gary

Yourofsky, an animal rights advocate who was one of the speakers at the RE conference. On the day of the event, the Campus Police demanded that the room location be changed and raised concerns about security. The event took place without incident. A week later, the president of Campus Peace, who was also an MSW student, was asked to come to the campus police station to respond to police chief's concerns about another guest speaker, Ilan Pappe, a prominent Israeli historian and advocate for Palestinian rights. She was told that in the future, all speakers would be screened for security reasons and that the approval of the police chief would be required for all events.

During two meetings with university officials, the Campus Peace president and the faculty adviser (a faculty member in the department of social work education) were told that undercover officers were present at the Yourofsky presentation. A number of explanations were offered: security concerns, intelligence gathering, and that the presence of uniformed officers would "inflame the crowd" of vegans who attended the event.

During spring 2005, Campus Peace and the American Civil Liberties Union filed a public records request with Fresno State and raised concerns with the university administration about the impact of this surveillance on student privacy and freedom of speech. The university refused to respond to the public records request. Although at least two university officials had previously acknowledged the surveillance, senior administrators asserted that plainclothes officers were not present at the event.

In response to the university's refusal to honor the public record request, members of Campus Peace developed a well-thought-out and planned strategy to pressure administrators to publicly acknowledge the surveillance and provide information about the reasons for the incident. The strategy took into account a short time frame (the conclusion of the school year) and required the rapid escalation of tactics in order to achieve a successful outcome. Tactics used by the student activists included a letter-writing and call-in campaign, workshops on academic freedom, demonstrations, street theater performances, press conferences, and coalition building with progressive groups in the community, including those organizations previously targeted for surveillance such as Peace Fresno and Students Against Sweatshops. The faculty union provided a number of resources for the organizing efforts. Also included in the coalition were representatives of a local anarchist group.

Under pressure from local media, university administrators eventually informed Campus Peace that six undercover officers (three university police officers and three members of the county sheriff's department) attended the event for "security purposes." The university did not acknowledge that the circumstances pertaining to the surveillance represented a clear violation of privacy protections in the California constitution. In 1971, the California Supreme Court in *White v. Davis* ruled that surveillance in classrooms or during student events were strictly prohibited except in cases in which there was reasonable suspicion of criminal activity (Schlosberg, 2006).

Frustrated by the university's reluctance to provide information about the event, over a dozen members of Campus Peace staged a forty-eight-hour hunger strike outside the university administration building. The hunger strikers included a number of MSW students. Within a few hours of the start of the hunger strike, senior administrators who previously had refused to meet with members of Campus Peace quickly set up a meeting with the faculty adviser and student president to discuss the issue. Students were permitted to continue the hunger strike for the entire forty-eight-hour period. Immediately after the hunger strike concluded, the university president issued a letter assuring Campus Peace that university police would not be permitted to conduct surveillance at university events unless required by law and approved by university administration (Steinberg, 2005). The president also pledged to set up a task force to review police procedures. The task force, which included the Campus Peace adviser, concluded its work in December 2005. A variety of policies to protect the privacy of students, faculty, and university staff were recommended. In February 2007, these recommendations (with minor revisions that strengthened civil liberties protections) were approved by the faculty senate and forwarded to the university president for approval.

Dilemmas and Challenges in Organizing for Civil Liberties: Lessons for MSW Students and Community Organizers

This organizing effort posed a number of challenges for the students and faculty involved and provides a good case study for examining the use of direct-action organizing methods on college campuses. Contest- or confrontation-oriented tactics pose a number of dilemmas for participants. The challenges involved in this organizing effort include using escalating tactics, risk taking, obtaining public support and media coverage, partnering with diverse groups, and negotiating with powerful decision makers.

ESCALATING TACTICS

In many organizing situations in which negotiations fail or decision makers simply refuse to meet with representatives of the action group, constituents escalate their use of tactics, moving rapidly from cooperation, to campaign, to direct confrontation (Mondros, 2005). The negotiation and collaborative tactics used at the beginning stages of the process involved a handful of people and were largely unsuccessful. Although Campus Peace initially confirmed police presence at the Yourofsky event, they were told by senior administrators to "back off" and were, in one instance, given false information about university policies and practices on the use of undercover officers at university events. In addition, the university president and the provost simply refused a request to meet. The lack of success in finding out exact details of events required the escalation of tactics, including sponsoring a panel discussion, a number of press conferences, street theater, a letter-writing and call-in campaign, a protest outside the campus police station, and finally, the hunger strike.

One reason for this escalation was due to the time line. Campus Peace started the public information campaign and the partnership with the ACLU in late March. All action needed to be completed prior to the end of the academic year in mid-May. Another rationale for using confrontation was that public support was needed to achieve an outcome. Actions such as the media campaign and the on-campus protests helped generate public support and illustrate the seriousness of the issue. However, as noted by Mondros (2005), the use of some types of confrontation (such as civil disobedience) may drive away potential members or increase difficulties with authorities. The use of these tactics also increases the risk of harm to participants and targets and requires full disclosure to members of the group taking action (Hardina, 2002).

RISK TAKING

Both students and faculty members face a number of risks when organizing on campus. Students can be subject to disciplinary action or arrest. Faculty members may risk tenure, promotion, or other types of explicit or implicit sanctions or censure (Rogge & Rocha, 2004). In this instance, harassment or surveillance by local police agencies and the FBI were additional risks associated with the process. In addition, the hunger strike posed significant risks to participants including health risks associated with the two-day fast as well as the possibility of arrest. Campus Peace prepared for these risks by conducting extensive discussions about potential risks and benefits associated with each of the planned actions. The various organizing partners also participated in many of these discussions; in some instances partners provided substantial support including information, letters of support to university officials, and media contacts. All participants agreed that the potential harm from failing to take action outweighed the risks.

MEDIA COVERAGE IN A SMALL MEDIA MARKET

Although Campus Peace received assistance from a volunteer media consultant, the group encountered a number of problems in disseminating information to the press and the general public. In many instances, press releases or interviews conducted by the media did not result in the type of coverage expected. Press coverage was sporadic and primarily involved a number of local television and radio stations and independent media sources that provided coverage on the Internet. Although the Associated Press (a national news service) covered the events, little state or national coverage was obtained despite the obvious link to Peace Fresno and *Fahrenheit 911*. While a local newspaper reporter initially provided comprehensive coverage (including a statement confirming the surveillance from a university official), the university's press office issued a denial and the paper limited its subsequent coverage. This was particularly problematic because there is only one major newspaper serving Fresno. This experience suggests that media campaigns in small markets must be creative, developing networks with both local and national media outlets, and relying extensively on independent media sources.

PARTNERSHIPS WITH OTHERS: THE DIVERSITY OF TACTICS DILEMMA

Many antiglobalization and environmental activists have embraced the concept of "diversity of tactics," or tolerance of methods that include the destruction of property and direct confrontation with authorities (Conway, 2003). What may prove especially challenging for organizers in choosing ethical tactics are situations in which collaborative partners use less than nonviolent methods or fail to adequately inform collaborators about potential risks. One of Campus Peace's major challenges was a partnership with the anarchist group. While the group assisted us with the media campaign and recruited participants for the hunger strike, some of their tactics put the entire coalition of groups at risk. The anarchist group had been responsible for asking Campus Peace to sponsor Yourofsky's presentation on campus and had failed to disclose to the students that the event would probably generate police scrutiny. Another difficulty encountered was that during the final phase of our campaign, the same group pasted stickers on each of the university's surveillance cameras in clear violation of university policy. Campus Peace asked the group to remove the stickers. Campus Peace also found it necessary to control activities planned for an on-campus antiwar rally; one of the members of the anarchist group suggested having people "smash" television sets during the event. While our efforts to maintain peace and group solidarity would seem to violate principles of self-determination and diversity of tactics, the students believed that actions were needed to minimize risk to all members.

NEGOTIATING WITH CHANGE TARGETS

The organizer as well as members of the constituency group may be called upon to negotiate with a number of different entities: government decision makers, the police, media representatives, opponents, and members of allied groups (Salcido et al., 2002). Throughout the campaign, negotiations occurred with various university officials, including the chief of police, the provost, and the president. The level of preparation for the negotiation meetings and the results obtained varied.

Despite requests by Campus Peace to meet with the university president, initial negotiation meetings were held with the dean of student affairs and the chief of police. Attempts by Campus Peace members and their faculty advisor to obtain answers and resolve their concerns during these meetings were ignored. However, the information gained proved to be valuable in the decision to escalate tactics, in validating initial concerns, and by providing further context to the situation.

These meetings provided organizers an opportunity to assess their power to move the identified target. Negotiations can be intimidating and unpredictable. It is crucial to prepare and debrief after every meeting with a change target (Bobo, Kendall, & Max, 2001). In preparation for the negotiation meetings, the students and faculty adviser discussed their goals for the meetings, methods for achieving them, and which role each individual would fulfill. Detailed notes were also taken and documented in written statements following each meeting with administrators. In addition, organizers debriefed after the meetings to determine the next course of action.

During the initial meetings it was clear that the university administrators were not going to reconcile the situation or even acknowledge their responsibility without additional pressure. It was also clear that senior administration did not see Campus Peace as a priority since group members would not directly meet with representatives. Upon the escalation of tactics, the university president released multiple statements that confirmed that the surveillance took place but asserted that the purpose was to ensure the safety of participants. This nonresponse was discussed with Campus Peace members and allied organizations. A decision was made to start the hunger strike outside the university administration building. A few hours after the strike started, the provost called a meeting with Campus Peace representatives on behalf of the university president.

The unexpected nature of this request made it difficult for us to prepare for this meeting. While our documentation of the initial incident and subsequent meetings with midlevel administrators was extensive, we were not able to gather that information before the meeting. Our ACLU attorney accompanied us to the meeting site but was not permitted to join us in the meeting with the provost. Consequently, the group had to improvise a logical argument and verbally present evidence in response to the provost's request for information. Clarification of the goals for resolution of this issue was requested. While no direct outcome was achieved during the meeting, the provost permitted Campus Peace to remain camped outside the administration building for the entire forty-eight-hour period. After the conclusion of the hunger strike, the university president issued a statement acknowledging the surveillance and ordering the campus police to clear any future surveillance activities with his office, activities that essentially resolved the immediate issue for Campus Peace.

Given such unexpected occurrences, it is important to discuss potential issues that may arise when opportunities present themselves. However, organizers cannot always plan for negotiations with targets that may occur at unexpected times. A student from Campus Peace was casually confronted by a member of the administration during a university social event. As the conversation proceeded, the administrator told the student not to continue talking to the media about the surveillance issue. Organizers should be prepared to utilize such unexpected confrontations with change targets to further the campaign. However, safety is most important and student organizers should always remove themselves from a compromising situation with a change target.

Discussion: Learning Outcomes

Organizing against surveillance provided a unique learning experience for all who participated in the effort: students, faculty, and our allies. The campaign undertaken by the Campus Peace and Civil Liberties Coalition and allied groups was a success in that the groups were able to persuade university decision makers to improve civil liberties protections for students and faculty using direct-action organizing techniques. The ability to conduct thorough assessments of the situation at hand and the power held by various groups, establish good relationships with media, generate public support, develop partnerships with off-campus groups such as the ACLU, and take risks (such as the possibility of arrest) were critical to success.

For students, there were a number of tangible outcomes. They learned how to plan a media and a direct-action campaign and how to carry it out when faced with new information and situational changes. Students from several campus organizations, including Campus Peace, Students Against Sweatshops, and El Movimiento Estudiantil Chicano/a de Aztlán, were involved in many aspects of the campaign. Members of the student senate were instrumental in informing the university president that no uniformed officers were present at the Yourofsky event and lobbying for a resolution of the surveillance issue. These students learned to work collaboratively with a variety of student organizations and off-campus groups. They learned to negotiate with coalition members to choose strategies and tactics and with powerful decision makers such as the campus police and university administrators.

Students also learned how to engage in confrontation in a nonviolent manner and to take responsibility for their actions. The fourteen students who participated during the entire forty-eight-hour hunger strike not only abstained from eating, but risked arrest as well as the possibility of ongoing harassment or surveillance by authorities. Although no formal evaluation of the organizing campaign was completed, interviews conducted by members of the local media suggest that in addition to the successful outcome, the organizing effort also provided a rich learning opportunity for student participants. Students learned about the history of academic freedom and the importance of preserving this important civil liberty. For example, one student who attended a protest paraphrased Benjamin Franklin with this rationale for his participation, "If you trade liberty for security, you end up with tyranny" (Ndole, 2005, p. 1). Another participant in the events leading up to the hunger strike made the following statement in a letter to the campus paper, *The Collegian:*

> I would much rather have a police officer at our events than no police officer to keep order. But I am also not doing anything wrong. There is no reason to spy on us. Campus Peace has proclaimed on a weekly basis that law enforcement is welcomed to our meetings . . . just not undercover law enforcement. (Spencer, 2005, p. 3)

A number of students also were interviewed for a video produced by a local documentary filmmaker, George Ballis. In the video *We Starve for Free Speech* (Ballis & Ballis, 2005), students emphasized the importance of engaging in civil disobedience in defense of liberty. For example, one student member of Students Against Sweatshops stated:

> The reason why I'm starving myself for forty-eight hours is because I'm tired of the abuse. It's an extreme. I've never

done this before and it just represents how tired and how violated I feel I am of my civil rights, of just thinking of speaking out, and of freedom of speech.

A member of Campus Peace agreed with this rationale: "I'm here, but I don't think why I wouldn't be here. It's just kind of common sense to me. We need to defend our rights." An MSW student felt that participation in the hunger strike was important because "I think that people should live their life for what they believe, and I believe really deeply in civil liberties and student academic freedom, so I didn't see any other way." Another Campus Peace member examined the long-term policy implications associated with surveillance:

> You know, the whole point of infiltration and cops—how do they have this money, where is this money coming from? You know, right now we have huge education budget cuts going on continually but yet we have money the university can spend to watch people in meetings and who knows where else really, and when you start thinking about that paranoia, there could be cops, cameras, microphones anywhere, everywhere.

Interviewed for a documentary produced by the American Civil Liberties Union, the president of Campus Peace, Ruth Obel-Jorgensen (one of the authors of this chapter), made a statement about the importance of taking risks and accepting the consequences of one's actions when working for social justice:

> You Google my name and you come up with all this involved in peace protest, challenging authority, believing that there's being undercover surveillance going on. I can't imagine that I would ever get a job at Fresno State, that's for sure, much less I don't know that I'd ever get a job in the CSU [California State University] system. Who knows what impact that would have on me because I was trying to bring things, that of course in the end came out to be true, to the forefront? (ACLU, 2006b)

In addition to learning about the importance of fighting for civil liberties, students also learned ways to interact, on a positive basis, with media representatives. Many of the student protestors were interviewed by print, radio, and television reporters and learned to frame issues in a manner that interested the media as well as the general public. One of the more important learning opportunities for students was discovering that the media does not always report issues and events in a manner consistent with the goals of organizers or activists. Handling the disappointment of inappropriate or inaccurate reporting and changing approaches or finding alternative news outlets was one of the many challenges faced by participants in this event.

The students also learned that it is possible to successfully challenge powerful interests and fight political oppression. Another very tangible outcome of the hunger strike is that at least four of the student participants (two social work students and two political science students) have found postgraduation employment in social-action-related positions in health prevention, union organizing, environmental activism, and direct-action organizing.

While other campus organizations may be able to apply similar methods, the amount of power held by decision makers or members of the various constituency groups, the amount of media coverage, and the willingness of participants to apply a wide variety of strategies may limit the effectiveness of the model. Student groups wishing to replicate these methods will need to recognize situational demands and be ready to adjust their tactics accordingly.

Conclusion

Frameworks for tactical decision making found in the community organization literature (Brager et al., 1987; Mondros, 2005) indicate that direct-action organizing for social justice is appropriate in situations in which there are short time frames, when decision makers refused to meet with groups seeking redress, and when members of oppressed groups are fighting for their rights. The organizing campaign used to respond to police surveillance of the Campus Peace and Civil Liberties Coalition took place within the context of all three of these conditions. However, the use of direct-action methods also requires that they be used responsibly, that members weigh the risks and benefits of their action, that extensive consultation take place with constituents, and that tactical methods are used to bring opponents to the negotiating table rather than to simply escalate conflict among opposing groups.

This case study indicates that social work students can successfully apply direct-action tactics to achieve social justice. Social workers should receive education in a wide range of strategies and tactics, ranging from collaboration to social protest. The use of any of these methods is dependent on situational demands, time, resources, and the preferences of constituents or the direct beneficiaries of the organizing effort (Hardina, 2002). To limit curriculum content to collaboration or consensus-oriented initiatives severely restricts the type and range of tactical skills available to program graduates. While few practicum settings provide opportunities for direct-action organizing, faculty and students should seek out opportunities to engage in social change-related activities involving social protest. Our mandate as social workers, as identified in the NASW *Code of Ethics* (National Association of Social Workers, 2008), requires that we be able to act as advocates and take action to oppose oppression. Explicit threats to traditional constitutional protections such as freedom of speech or freedom from unreasonable search and seizure require that social workers engage in action to uphold our civil liberties and the rights of those individuals and groups served.

References

American Association of University Professors. (2001). *Two statements from policy documents and reports.* Washington, DC: Author.

American Association of University Professors. (2006). *Academic freedom and outside speakers.* Retrieved March 27, 2007, from http://www.aaup.org/AAUP/About/committees/committee + repts/CommA/outside-spkrs.htm

American Association of University Professors. (2007). *Academic freedom of students and professors and political discrimination.* Retrieved July 16, 2007, from http://www.aaup.org/AAUP/protectrifhts/legal/topics/PolDivDiscrim.htm

American Civil Liberties Union. (2006a). *ACLU files free speech suit against Rhode Island College for censoring reproductive rights display.* Retrieved July 23, 2006, from http://www.aclu.org/20061204.html

American Civil Liberties Union. (2006b). *Tracked in America.* Retrieved September 2, 2007, from http://www.trackedinamerica.org/timeline/after_911/jorgensen/

Arnone, M. (2003, April 11). Watchful eyes: The FBI steps up its work on campuses, spurring fear and anger among many academics. *Chronicle of Higher Education.* Retrieved January 19, 2006, from http://chronicle.com/weekly/V49/i3la01401.htm

Ballis, G., & Ballis M. (Prods.). (2005). *We starve for free speech: CSUF Campus Peace* [Video/Docu-poem]. Available from SunMT Productions, Box 314, Prather, CA, 93651, or http://www.sunmt.org

Bartlett, T. (2006, October 27). Boston College to veto students' speakers. *Chronicle of Higher Education.* Retrieved July 20, 2007, from http://chronicle.com/weekly/v53/i10/10a04004.htm

Bobo, K., Kendall, J., & Max, S. (2001). *Organizing for social change.* Santa Ana, CA: Seven Locks Press.

Brager, G., Specht, H., & Torczyner, J. (1987). *Community organizing.* New York: Columbia University Press.

Carroll, J., & Minkler, M. (2000). Freire's message for social workers: Looking back, looking ahead. *Journal of Community Practice, 8*(1), 21–36

Center for Campus Free Speech. (2006, March 23). *Students speak out against academic bill of restrictions.* Retrieved July 23, 2007, from http://www.campuss-peech.org/news/recent-news/students-speak-out-against-academic-bill

Center for Consumer Freedom. (2003, February 12). *Fresno braces for powder keg.* Retrieved May 28, 2006, from http://www.consumerfreedom.com/news_detail.cfm/headline/1783

Conway, J. (2003). Civil resistance and the "diversity of tactics" in the anti-globalization movement: Problems of violence, silence, and solidarity in activist politics. *Osgood Hall Law Journal, 41,* 505–529.

Danis, R. (2006). In search of a safe campus communities: A campus response to violence against women. *Journal of Community Practice, 14*(3), 29–46.

Encyclopedia Britannica Online. (2006). *Constitution of the United States of America: Civil liberties and the Bill of Rights.* Retrieved February 19, 2007, from http://searcheb.comhmlpoxy.lib.csufresno.edu/ebarticle-219002

Fogg, P. (2003, February 14). Fresno State criticized for invitations to radical environmentalists. *Chronicle of Higher Education.* Retrieved May 28, 2006, from http://chronicle.com/weekly/v49/i23a01201.htm

Free Exchange on Campus. (n.d.). *Campus voices: Students and faculty speak out on the free exchange of ideas in Pennsylvania colleges and universities.* Retrieved July 23, 2007, from http://www.exchangeoncampus.org

Freire, P. (1970). *Pedagogy of the oppressed.* New York: Continuum Books.

Friedman, J. (2005, September). Spying on the protesters. *The Nation.* Retrieved January 19, 2006, from http://www.thenationa.com/doc/20050919/friedman

Gil, D. (1998). *Confronting injustice and oppression.* New York: Columbia University Press.

Gravois, J. (2004, October 1). Students and college clash over invitation to the filmmaker Michael Moore. *Chronicle of Higher Education.* Retrieved April 6, 2005, from http://chronicle.com/prm/weeily/v51/i06/06a03601.htm

Gutierrez L., & Alvarez, A. (2000). Educating students for multicultural community practice. *Journal of Community Practice, 7*(1), 39–56.

Hardina, D. (2002). *Analytical skills for community organization practice.* New York: Columbia University Press.

Homan, M. (2004). *Promoting community change: Making it happen in the real world.* Belmont, CA: Brooks/Cole.

Horowitz, D. (2006). *The professors: The 101 most dangerous academics of all time.* Washington, DC: Regnery.

Jacobson, J. (2006, February 17). Dangerous minds. *Chronicle of Higher Education.* Retrieved on July 20, 2007, from http://chronicle.com/weekly/v52/i24/24a00601.htm

Lichtblau, E. (2005, July, 18). Protest groups cite FBI files as proof of meddling. *Fresno Bee,* p. A3.

Lipka, S. (2006, June 19). *"Academic bill of rights" criticized.* Retrieved July 20, 2007, from http://chronicle.com/weekly/v52/i40/40a01202.htm

Marcum, D. (2006, February 10). Agency may have violated civil rights. *Fresno Bee,* pp. A1, A15.

McAdam, D., & Tarrow, S. (2000). Nonviolence as contentious interaction. *Political Science & Politics, 33*, 149–154.

McCarthy, J. (2002, April 10). Florida State's radical students: The Berkeley of the South rises again. *Counterpunch.* Retrieved July 23, 2007, from http://www.counterpunch.org/mccarthy0410.html

Mondros, J. (2005). Political, social, and legislative action. In M. Weil (Ed.), *The handbook of community practice* (pp. 276–286). Thousand Oaks, CA: Sage.

Mondros, J., & Wilson, S. (1994). *Organizing for power and empowerment.* New York: Columbia University Press.

Moore, L. (2004). Opening doors to disability: A class project. *Journal of Community Practice, 12*(1/2), 89–105.

Moore, L., & Dietz, T. (1999). Four months to systems change. Teaching baccalaureate students to affect policy. *Journal of Community Practice, 6*(1), 33–44.

National Association of Social Workers. (2008). *Code of ethics.* Washington, DC: Author.

Ndole, M. (2005, April 22). Group protests near police station. *Collegian,* 1, 8.

Pavela G, (2005, May 27). Academic freedom for students has ancient roots. *Chronicle of Higher Education.* Retrieved July 20, 2007, from http://chronicle.com/weeklyv51i38/38b00801.htm

Reisch, M., & Lowe, J. I., (2000). "Of means and ends" revisited: Teaching ethical community organizing in an unethical society. *Journal of Community Practice, 7*(1), 38.

Rhodes, M. (2005, May 1). Local law enforcement violates the state constitution, continues to infiltrate Fresno peace groups. *Community Alliance, 1*(6), 10.

Rivera, F., & Erlich, J. (1998). *Community organizing in a diverse society.* Boston: Allyn & Bacon.

Rogge, M., & Rocha, C. (2004). University-community partnership centers: An important link for social work education. *Journal of Community Practice, 12*(3), 103–121.

Salcido, R., Ornelas, V., & Lee, N. (2002). Cross cultural field assignments in an undergraduate community practice course: Integrating multimedia documentation. *Journal of Community Practice, 10*(4), 49–65.

Schlosberg, M. (2006). *The state of surveillance: Government monitoring of political activity in northern and central California.* San Francisco: American Civil Liberties Union of Northern California.

Shaw, R. (2001). *The activist's handbook: A primer.* Berkeley: University of California Press.

Sherman, S. (2005, April 4). The Mideast comes to Columbia. *The Nation, 280*(13), 18, 20–24.

Spencer, A. (2005, May 4). Protesting isn't whining [Letter to the editor]. *Collegian,* p. 3.

Steinberg, J. (2003, May 10). Jury gets Fresno State eco tape. *Fresno Bee,* pp. B1, B6.

Steinberg, J. (2005, May 17). Fresno State clarifies policies on surveillance. *Fresno Bee,* pp. A1, A8.

Wint, E., & Sewpaul, V. (2000). Product and process dialectic: Developing an indigenous approach to community development training. *Journal of Community Practice, 7*(1), 57–70.

Appendix: How to Organize on Campus for Civil Liberties and Social Justice

1. Conduct a thorough analysis of the issue and the options for resolution.
2. Examine the amount of power held by members of the constituent group, opponents, and decision makers.
3. Identify resources including key individuals and allied groups that are needed to increase the power of the group or coalition that is conducting the action.
4. Engage in dialogue with constituents and allied groups to identify the best strategies and tactics and to examine the risks and benefits of the various options.
5. Reconcile opposing viewpoints among group members. Establish parameters for acceptable and unacceptable behavior among members of partner groups.
6. Establish relationships with the media. Provide information to local reporters and package your method in a manner that will resonate with the general public. Be ready to use alternative strategies such as independent media and the Internet to get the word out.
7. Take action. Use low-impact tactics first such as letter-writing campaigns and press conferences. Gradually escalate tactics in response to situational demands. Remember that all tactics, including direct action or civil disobedience, are to be used to bring decision makers to the bargaining table rather than to alienate them or the public that you are trying to influence.
8. Thoroughly consult with group members and allied organizations about changes in tactics. Try to anticipate and prepare for potential risks or unintended consequences of each action. Make sure that all members of the group engaging in the action are fully informed about potential consequence and have a chance to consent or withdraw from participation.
9. Negotiate for a resolution with decision makers. Be open to dialogue and compromise. Have a specific goal in mind prior to meeting with the decision makers. Document all interactions with decision makers immediately.
10. Be prepared to take advantage of any unexpected occurrences and opportunities and adjust your tactics accordingly!

Measurement of Transformative Education

CHAPTER SIXTEEN

Approaches to Measuring Transformative Education Experiences

R. Jan Wilson

Abstract

The Council on Social Work Education (CSWE) (2008) requires social work education programs to utilize measurable competencies that demonstrate student learning outcomes, including in the area of social justice. At the same time, there is growing interest in exploring social justice education as a transformational experience that extends into practice. This chapter addresses the measurement of transformative experiences related to social justice by providing (1) a review of current conditions that present challenges for evaluation research in social work education and practice; (2) a review of recent literature demonstrating educational evaluation of social justice teaching and practice; (3) a review of the influence of research epistemology on social work evaluation research and their implications for social work education; and (4) recommendations for improving evaluation of social justice education efforts, including the measurement of transformative learning.

Social justice, a central core value in social work values and ethics (NASW, 2008), is a good example of an educational objective that is often accepted as being understood (Gambrill, 1997), but has very little evidence to support educational outcomes. The social work literature offers prescriptions for teaching social justice and some evidence of course outcomes (Adams, Bell, & Griffin, 1997; Finn & Jacobson, 2003; Gutiérrez, Zuñiga, & Lum, 2004; Van Soest & Garcia, 2003); however, there is less attention to whether graduating social workers have actually acquired the knowledge, skills, and values reflected in institutional goals, mission statements, or in the professional standards. More importantly, few to no studies demonstrate whether students are practicing professional social work that adheres to those standards (Gambrill, 1997).

Schools of social work have been mandated by the Council on Social Work Education (CSWE) to have systems in place for evaluating their academic programs with measurable competencies that correspond to the CSWE *Education and Policy Accreditation Standards* (2008a). The CSWE introduced standards for evaluating the effectiveness of social work programs in the 1980s, updated the requirement in 1994 (Potts, Meyer-Adams, & Rosales, 2007), and strengthened it in 2005 and 2008 (CSWE, 2008b) by prescribing that each social work program have an assessment plan, procedures for evaluating program competencies, and demonstrate use-of-outcome data to improve program quality. The CSWE's mandate may prove difficult to carry out as social work programs try to allocate from among scarce resources to develop and maintain a continuous assessment program, and search for well-developed, accessible methods and tools for evaluating social work educational outcomes (CSWE, 2008; Holden, Anastas, & Meenaghan, 2005; Potts et al., 2007). The instruments that are currently being used (i.e., alumni surveys and student course evaluations) primarily rely on self-reported attitudes and opinions and have not produced useful outcome data. Recommendations have been made to move away from tools that measure student satisfaction to validated instruments that assess student learning outcomes through evidence of changes in knowledge, attitudes, and behavior (Garcia & Floyd, 2002; Pike, 1998; Wolfer & Johnson, 2003).

At the same time, there have been debates about whether all aspects of social work practice can be objectively measured, given the abstract nature of theories and concepts and the uncertainty that characterizes social work practice (Gomory, 2001; Thyer, 2001). Nathan Glazer's (1974) *Schools of the Minor Professions* named social work as one of the professions that is characterized by "ambiguous ends, shifting contexts of practice, and no fixed content of professional knowledge," (Schön, 1991, p. 45). Since then, social work has been conscious of the need to develop an empirical knowledge base that can stand up to scientific scrutiny (Gambrill, 2003b; Rosen, 1996, 2003; Rosen & Proctor, 2003; Rosen, Proctor, & Staudt, 1999). Thyer (2001) categorized social work as an "applied field," rather than an "academic discipline," and therefore, less in need of theory building and more in need of establishing legitimate forms of intervention. These concerns have also been expressed about social work education, yet there has been little progress on improving methods of evaluating educational practices (Gambrill, 1997; Ruckdeschel, Ernshaw, & Firrek, 1994).

Given CSWE's focus on educational program outcomes measures and the interest in exploring social justice education as a transformational experience that extends into practice, this chapter will provide an overview of transformative learning and social justice followed by the following sections: (1) a review of current conditions that present challenges for evaluation research in social work education and practice; (2) a review of recent literature demonstrating educational evaluation of social justice teaching and practice; (3) a review of the influence of research epistemology on social work evaluation research and the implications for social work education; and (4) recommendations for improving evaluation of social justice education efforts, including the measurement of transformative learning.

Transformative Learning in Educational Evaluation

In higher education, there has been a movement over the past decade to shift the focus of evaluation research from the educators to the learners and to align evaluation policy with institutional goals for learning (Knapper, 2001). The Council on Social Work Education's (CSWE) requirement that social work programs to develop measurable competencies that are in alignment with the *Education and Policy Accreditation Standards* (2008) follows this trend. While the process of alignment is time consuming, it can lead to an integrated, ongoing system of evaluation (Knapper, 2001).

Alverno College, a four-year liberal arts college for women in Milwaukee, Wisconsin, developed such an alignment. The college formed an alliance with several other liberal arts colleges that over a twenty-year period developed a model evaluation system for studying student learning outcomes directly linked to an educational program (Mentkowski & Associates, 2000). The well-planned evaluation collected data on multiple levels of learning and points in time throughout the students' undergraduate years and after they graduated. While a variety of data collection methods were used, qualitative methods best captured the voices of the students. The research found students responding to learning that precipitated critical thinking and self-reflection, citing that "learners go through distinct, transformative learning processes or cycles to connect reasoning and performance, and self-reflection and performance" (Mentkowski & Associates, 2000, p. 224). Reasoning and performance are connected through "metacognitive strategies" to result in competence (Mentkowski & Associates, 2000, p. 192). Self-reflection and performance are connected through critical thinking about different approaches and views that result in the making of new and expanded meanings. These findings reference the work of Schön (1991), who made the connection between transformative self-reflection and performance in the workplace, and to Brookfield (1991) and Mezirow (1991), who documented the power of self-reflection to transform the learning experience. Mentkowski and Associates (2000) concluded that "learning that lasts" (p. 227) is integrative and experiential, balanced by the student's continual integration of knowledge, reflection, and practice toward development of competency. In social work education, with its emphasis on practice/theory integration, experiential learning is provided through field education practica and other on-site or in-class course work.

Social Justice as an Educational Competency

Social justice is the predominant feature in the Preamble to the National Association of Social Workers' (NASW) *Code of Ethics* (2008). The *Social Work Dictionary* defines social justice as an "ideal condition in which all members of a society have the same basic rights, protection, opportunities, obligations, and social benefits" (Barker, 1999, p. 451.). From this very broad definition, the social work literature on social justice has spread in many directions (Finn & Jacobson, 2003; Gill, 1998; Mullaly, 2002; Pelton, 2001; Reisch, 2002; Scanlon & Longres, 2001; Swensen, 1998; Wakefield, 1998), posing more questions than answers, without a formal unifying educational framework (Snyder, Peeler, & May, 2008). This multiplicity of perspectives presents educational evaluators with difficulties in concept definition (Cowger, 2003; Gambrill, 1997; Longres & Scanlon, 2001; Scanlon & Longres, 2001). Snyder, Peeler, and May (2008) have identified a central debate as being whether social work should take a political, structural change stance in conceptualizing social justice work. This is the position taken by critical theorists, who recognize oppression and antioppressive social work practice as their central premise, considering all social work practice as political, and aiming for social change and transformation of attitudes, beliefs, and perspectives (Adams, Dominelli, & Payne, 2005; DePoy, Hartman, & Haslett, 1999).

Evaluation Research and Outcomes for Social Justice Education

In the social work literature, some promising areas of education evaluation research that fit Mertens's (2009) transformative evaluation research paradigm (to be discussed below) and illustrate the transformative learning described by Mentkowski and Associates (2000) are (1) intergroup dialogue, (2) multicultural competencies, (3) self-efficacy, (4) empowerment of social work students, (5) the longitudinal study, and (6) education in policy practice. In each case, the researchers have struggled to conduct evaluations of complex, nonobjective realities in ways that allow for a respectable degree of empiricism while incorporating social justice concerns.

INTERGROUP DIALOGUE

Intergroup dialogue (IGD) is a method of education evaluation that holds promise for measuring transformative learning. Intergroup dialogue can be defined as "a public process designed to involve individuals and groups in an exploration of societal issues such as politics, racism, religion, and culture that are often flashpoints for polarization and social conflict" (Dressel, Rogge, & Garlington, 2006, p. 303) that "involve[es] face-to-face, focused, facilitated, and confidential discussions occurring over time between two or more groups of people defined by their different social identities" (Shoem, Hurtado, Sevig, Chesler, & Sumida, 2001, p. 6). The IGD movement is focused on conflict around diversity and oppression issues and is associated with critical theory to transform perspectives and initiate social change that lessens oppressive conditions (Uehara, Sohng, Nagada, Erera, & Yamashiro, 2004).

The University of Washington and the University of Michigan have utilized IGDs. Through the University of Washington's Intergroup Dialogue, Education and Action (IDEA) Center, IGDs are integrated into the social work curriculum as a way of teaching cultural diversity and oppression. Researchers at the IDEA Center have used pre- and posttest surveys and hierarchical regression analysis of the data to assess the effects of the program (Nagada, Kim, & Truelove, 2004). The University of Michigan's Program on Intergroup Relations is in the process of a longitudinal evaluation study of four thousand college students who participated in IGDs at nine public universities. Researchers used multiple regression analysis to assess longitudinal data, some of which is derived from participant/control group comparison (Gurin, Dey, Hurtado, & Gurin, 2002; Gurin & Nagada, 2006; Hurtado, 2005).

Dressel et al. (2006) reviewed evaluation research designs for outcomes on IGDs. While early research results indicated that IDGs met intended goals, evaluation methods tended to be anecdotal and informal. More formal methods, such as mail-in surveys and focus groups were introduced, using both quantitative and qualitative questions. In all situations, the validity of studies was limited by self-selection.

Groups were evaluated using quantitative surveys, qualitative interviews, and longitudinal studies. Researchers also observed interpersonal processes at the individual, intragroup, and intergroup level. Dressel et al. (2006) called for all IGD researchers to discuss limitations of studies, make recommendations for improvement, and use methods that strengthen the "rigor" of the study (e.g., pre- and post measures of knowledge, attitude and behavior change, control groups, and longitudinal studies that would allow for higher order statistical analysis). Other recommendations were (1) mixed use of quantitative/qualitative methods; (2) strengthening qualitative methods with interrater training, systematic observation, and content analysis; (3) applying qualitative methods to assess the process within IGDs; and (4) engaging stakeholders in participatory research, development of goals, and evaluation design.

Measuring Multicultural Practice Competencies

In an effort to measure multicultural practice competencies, Krentzman and Townsend (2008) searched databases for tools from a variety of disciplines, and selected scales that had a pre- and posttest format, were easy to score, and accessible. From these, four scales were selected that demonstrated (1) construct validity, which is the extent to which the scale was based on a clear definition or theoretical model of cultural competence and demonstrated validity with diverse groups of respondents; (2) reliability, demonstrated by coefficient alphas for the total scale at or above .80 and test/retest correlations of at least .70; (3) a socially just perspective on cultural competence that recognized poverty, racism, prejudice, discrimination, and oppression as sociopolitical realities, and corresponded with NASW's *Code of Ethics* (2008) and *Standards for Culturally Competent Practice* (2001), and CSWE's *Education Policy and Accreditation Standards* (2008); (4) a broad definition of diversity with scales covering multiple areas of difference; (5) clearly written scale items; (6) a consistent response format; (7) scale items that attempted to reduce the incidence of socially desirable responses; and (8) scale items that were compatible with social work. Krentzman and Townsend's (2008, p. 20) four recommended scales for evaluating social work students' cultural competence are

1. Ethnic-Competence-Skill Model in Psychological Interventions with Minority Ethnic Children and Youth (1992), Ho (1992);
2. Miville-Guzman Universality-Diversity Scale (1992), Miville, M. L. described in Fuertes, Miville, Mohr, Sedlacek, & Gretchen (2000);

3. Multicultural Counseling Inventory (1994), Sodowsky, G. R. described in Sodowsky, Taffe, Gutkin, & Wise (1994); and
4. Multicultural Counseling Knowledge and Awareness Scale (1991), Ponterotto, J. G. described in Ponterotto & Potre (2003).

Millstein (1997) reported on a qualitative effort, based on Tatum's (1992) model, to measure the development of students' multicultural competencies in a course. As an assignment, students audiotaped their responses to an interview schedule that focused on their perceptions and experiences with difference, prejudice, discrimination, and oppression. At the end of the course, they listened to the tape and evaluated their personal changes in belief systems, attitudes, and behavior based on what they said on the tape. These essays were assessed using grounded theory method to determine the changes students experienced.

SELF-EFFICACY AS A MEASURE OF COMPETENCE

Self-efficacy is emerging as an important characteristic in measuring social work competencies, including social justice practice (Holden, Anastas, & Meenaghan, 2003, 2005). Scales that measure self-efficacy as an indicator of social work students' confidence in their professional practice skills have been developed and refined over the past decade, such as the Foundation Practice Self-Efficacy Scale (Holden et al., 2003, 2005); the Research Self-Efficacy Scale (Holden, Barker, Meenaghan, & Rosenberg, 1999); the Hospital Social Work Self-Efficacy Scale (Holden, Cuzzi, Ruttner, Chernack, & Rosenberg, 1997); and the Social Work Self-Efficacy Scale (Holden, Meenaghan, Anastas, & Metrey, 2002).

Perceived self-efficacy has been defined as "judgments of how well one can execute courses of action required to deal with prospective situations" (Bandura, 1982, p. 1). Based on evidence of the use of the construct of self-efficacy as an educational outcome in social work, and in recognition of the need for effective outcome measures, the Foundation Practice Self-Efficacy Scale was developed to provide a means of assessing outcomes of students' progress in meeting the Council on Social Work Education's Educational and Policy Accreditation Standards (EPAS) for foundation-year study (Holden et al., 2003). Foundation-year students rated their confidence level on being able to perform a number of learning objectives related to the EPAS. While the results of the studies were promising, the authors identified several threats to internal and external validity: (1) small, nonrandom convenience sample of social work students; (2) use of self-report measures, at a single point in time, in one location, with a single group of investigators; and (3) a simple pre- and posttest design. Although the scale was seen to provide a "viable addition" to student-focused outcomes measures (Holden et al., 2005, p. 568), there is a need to replicate the study.

MEASURING EMPOWERMENT AS A COMPETENCY

Van Voorhis and Hostetter (2006) studied the changes that social work graduate students made over the course of the program in perceiving their own empowerment as social workers and commitment to client empowerment through social justice advocacy. Four scales were used in a pre- and posttest format: Social Worker Empowerment Scale (Frans, 1993); Social Justice Advocacy Scale (Van Soest, 1996); Counselor Locus of Control Scale (Koeske & Kirk, 1995); and Belief in a Just World Scale (Rubin & Peplau, 1975). The data indicated an increase in the students' levels of empowerment and commitment. The researchers cited the following limitations of the study: small sample size; a convenience sample from one program; attrition between pre- and posttests; responses based on self-report; possibility of response shift bias; lack of a comprehensive instrument to measure all variables; and the inability to explain how the program affected changes in student perceptions and commitment.

LONGITUDINAL RESEARCH

In an effort to investigate the ties between curriculum and practice, including the process of practice wisdom, Fook, Ryan, and Hawkins (2000) followed social work students in Australia through two years of social work studies and three years of practice immediately following graduation. Three comparison groups were studied, each for one year during the same time period. All the studies collected qualitative data through responses to case vignettes and descriptions of critical incidents. The data were analyzed using content analysis to compare data with practice models, and inductive reasoning to develop themes of practice as perceived by the subjects. At the conclusion of the study, the researchers were able to identify patterns and stages of professional development in acquiring knowledge, skills, and values. While this study was not focused on social justice, its purpose was the same as that of the longitudinal IGD studies and those conducted by Mentkowski & Associates (2000): to follow students from coursework to graduation and into practice, using comparison groups who had not been exposed to the same curriculum, to establish whether specific learning had carried over from the curriculum to practice.

EVALUATION OF SOCIAL POLICY COURSES

Rocha (2002) attempted to evaluate whether teaching policy practice through experiential learning increased students' efficacy and actions as policy practitioners. In an attempt to increase the strength of the evaluation, Rocha (2002) sent surveys to graduates of the class and to a comparison group of students who had not had the experiential learning component in their policy course. Results indicated that both groups valued political skills, but the group members that had the experiential learning component in their course were more likely to see themselves as able to carry out policy practice and to be in policy-related activities after graduation. Limitations in this study were the need to replicate the study, the lack of pretest information, and the absence of baseline data at the point of entry into the social work program. Rocha's work offers guidelines to other educators for including experiential learning in policy courses and for evaluating whether students' understanding of social justice practice has been affected by the course content.

Evaluation Research, Social Justice, and Transformation

A definition of evaluation research in education is "the process of making judgments about the merit, value, or worth of educational programs" (Gall, Borg, & Gall, 1996, p. 680). The evaluator's clients use data for program decisions and planning, policy analysis, and advocacy for legislation and program funding. Evaluation research differs from basic research in that it has a specific purpose and is usually site-specific, not intending to examine relationships between variables or to generalize findings beyond the evaluated program (Gall et al., 1996).

The American Evaluation Association's (AEA) *Guiding Principles for Evaluators* (2004) includes the following five ethical elements: systematic inquiry, competence, integrity/honesty, respect for people, and responsibilities for general and public welfare. These principles guard against the primary objection to evaluation research: that it may become "accountability-driven," shifting "from providing services to attaining priority outcomes," overlooking the variability by which individuals respond to programs (Patton, 2002, p. 151), and losing the importance of "meaningful changes in the lives of real people" (p. 152). The AEA's *Guiding Principles* (2004) emphasize attention to the motives of the research and the rights of all stakeholders to participate in, and benefit from, the process. The evaluator's credibility depends on presenting a fair representation of the data, but with special consideration for those who will be affected by the results (House & Howe, 1998).

Evaluation research seeks to find the value for all stakeholders (Mertens, 2009; Ruckdeschel et al., 1994). Mertens (2009) sees researchers and evaluators working together with stakeholders for "personal and social transformation" in an emancipatory paradigm, influenced by critical theory, which includes "individuals who have been pushed to the societal margins throughout history and who are finding a means to bring their voices into the world of research . . . with scholars who work as their partners to support the increase of social justice and human rights" (pp. 2–3). Mertens (2009) renamed this paradigm "transformative" to highlight "the agency of the people involved in the research" (p. 2) and "to ground research and evaluation in assumptions that prioritize the furtherance of social justice and human rights . . . that will lead to a greater realization of social change" (p. 3).

Stakeholder involvement relates closely to social justice as a concept, as well as critical theory, which is highly conscious of power differentials. In the mid-1970s, Earnest House (1991) was the first to discuss his main concern for the inclusion of vulnerable and marginalized groups in the research evaluation process. House (1991, 2003) warned social scientists that the results of evaluations had the potential power to affect change in social service programs and the distribution of services. He questioned whose interests were being advanced through evaluation and introduced the "stakeholder approach" to counter a "pluralist-elitist" model (1991, p. 239), which did not represent the interests of all parties affected by the decisions based on evaluation outcomes. Later, Fetterman's (2003) "empowerment evaluation" (p. 18) was aimed at involving staff and clients in every aspect of the evaluation process to promote self-determination. In addition, Fetterman proposed the concept of "process use" (p. 49), added to involve participants in generating findings and recommendations, which was found to result in stronger ownership and use of evaluation on an everyday basis.

Dominelli (2005) cites power differentials in the research process and endorses stakeholder involvement, but like Mertens (2009), she advocates for social work research to be change oriented, and to work in collaboration with the service users as full partners. Service users' ability to contribute "remains undeveloped," and there is a long way to go before they are "integrated as equal and active subjects in research." (Dominelli, 2005, p. 235). In social work education evaluation research, little thought has been given to the fact that stakeholders include students and practitioners. Evaluation research that examines learning outcomes in social work programs and courses should consider students and practitioners as partners and decision makers in the research process.

Social service agencies and organizations have developed systems of evaluation to meet the demands of managed care and government and to justify their funding by demonstrating efficiency in reaching service and outcomes goals (Moxley & Manela, 2001). Economic conditions may force the neglect of the caring aspect of human services in favor of rational and utilitarian outcomes, influenced by those with the power to control resources and impose values that conflict with social work values and ethics. Social workers become caught up in systems that serve to "prioritize utilitarian results over compassion" (Moxley & Manela, 2001, p. 571) and may become purveyors of oppressive conditions when service choices are limited (for example, low-wage jobs instead of education and training). Evaluation researchers in this situation might have difficulties instituting Mertens's (2009) transformative, change-oriented, social justice–based paradigm. Witkin (1996) has criticized empirical practice for emphasizing goals that evaluate effectiveness without regard for the worth of the goal itself, "measurability vs. substance" (p. 71). He suggests a litmus test to assess whether a particular practice model supports social work values and ethics, promotes social justice, or serves people who are poor and marginalized.

According to the NASW *Code of Ethics* (2008) and CSWE's *Education Policy and Accreditation Standards* (2008), the purpose of evaluation research is strictly to improve the professional knowledge base, practice methods, and service delivery. Ironically, except for protections of human subjects, neither imposes a social justice paradigm. The CSWE (2008) research policy presumes that students are educated to be professional social workers capable of taking an active role in the research process of knowledge appraisal, application, and construction. There is widespread agreement that this is more of an ideal than a reality (McNeill, 2006; Rosen, Proctor, Morrow-Howell, & Staudt, 1995; Rubin & Parrish, 2007; Walker, Briggs, Koroloff, & Friesen, 2007). Social work programs must improve educational opportunities for students and practitioners that provide the knowledge and skills they need to accomplish the research accreditation standards (Drake, Hovmand, Jonson-Reid, & Zayas, 2007; Franklin & Hopson, 2007; Gambrill, 1997, 2003a, 2003b; Rubin & Parrish, 2007; Walker et al., 2007).

Influence of Research Epistemology on Social Work Evaluation Research

The debates on the epistemology of evaluation research reveal different beliefs on what constitutes knowledge and ways in which to best build a professional knowledge base, such as the importance of theory, the degree to which reality may be empirically measured, the worth and meaning of social work practitioners' use of practice wisdom as a viable professional knowledge base, and the proposed role of the social work practitioner in the development and application of research knowledge (Gomory, 2001; Thyer, 2001). The nature and importance of theory is the basis from which evaluation research diverges in two primary directions: logical positivism and postmodernism.

These two perspectives differ in beliefs about the objectivity and measurability of human behavior and the natural world. The logical positivist perspective assumes that human behavior and phenomena can be objectively measured and champions rigorous scientific methodology to test practice interventions. Positivists are concerned with building an empirically validated body of knowledge (Thyer, 2001). A postmodern perspective assumes that knowledge is relative (relativism) to those who perceive it, and therefore cannot be objectified. Postmodernists take the position that all learning comes from observation and experience. There can be no theory-free observations or facts because hypothesizing and theory building are bound up in the process of observation. Theories are considered to be always in a temporal state and are "just hypothetical and tentative human guesses about what is," (Gomory, 2001, p. 32). Qualitative research methods fit best under this framework (Gomory, 2001) and come closest to Mertens's (2009) transformative paradigm of including the voices of stakeholders.

While some still maintain extremist positions on both sides, today most evaluation researchers have come to respect both the positivist and postmodern perspectives. A growing number of social work researchers have been calling for the use of qualitative and quantitative methods as complementary to one another, allowing for a fuller understanding of evaluation outcomes (Crisp, 2004; Gambrill, 1995; Harrison, 1994; Klein & Bloom, 1995; Loneck, 1994; McNeill, 2006; Petr & Walter, 2005; Stern, 1994; Witkin & Harrison, 2001). McNeill (2006) notes the development of a postpositivist stance that accepts postmodern arguments about the "limitations of objectivity" and "reflects a more relativist version of positivism" (p. 149).

PRACTICE WISDOM

Practice wisdom is another way that practitioners are seen to build a system of knowledge about theory and practice based on the continual feedback on their actions from clients and peers. Practice wisdom, like transformative learning, is experiential, reflective, and inclusive of the social work knowledge base as it cycles repeatedly through levels of insight and understanding that result in action. Klein and Bloom (1995) defined practice wisdom as "a personal and value-driven system of knowledge that emerges out of the transaction between the phenomenological experience of the client situation and the use of scientific information (p. 799). Use of practice wisdom remains a controversial area of social work evaluation research, discounted by those who consider it to be unsubstantiated, personal, and idiosyncratic in nature (Gambrill, 1999; Munro, 2002; Rosen, 2003; Rosen & Proctor, 2003;

Thyer, 2001) and endorsed by others (Fook, 1996; Gomory, 2001; Klein & Bloom, 1995).

Practice wisdom, as described by Klein and Bloom (1995), involves the same self-reflection and critical-thinking cycles that Mentkowski and Associates (2000) link to new and expanded meanings and to competencies. Fook (1996) maintained that positivist research could not account for the entire context of practice or take in the perspectives of all "players." She believed that a reflective approach could help practitioners identify the rationale behind practice actions and theoretical assumptions. Such insight could help students link practice wisdom more directly to competencies.

Recommendations and Conclusion

Educational researchers of social justice learning efforts have struggled to conduct evaluations of complex, nonobjective realities in ways that allow for a respectable degree of empiricism while incorporating social justice concerns. There are a few suggestions to take from the review of current research about social justice learning efforts: (1) both quantitative and qualitative methods are needed to present a full picture of student learning; (2) the most challenging task in evaluating a student's transformative learning in social justice education is to extend evaluation into the graduate's practice environment to determine whether and how learning is being applied to practice; (3) a comprehensive plan for evaluation of social justice education would ensure that important points of data collection, such as preprogram and precourse, are not overlooked, and that all naturally occurring data sources are considered; and (4) refinement of the aforementioned scales and development of other instruments should be continued. Self-efficacy was mentioned as an outcome in every mode of evaluation research reported in the previous section and may hold a key to evaluating a number of social work competencies. Mertens's (2009) framework for a transformative evaluation based on social justice and human rights applies to all evaluation research in the social sciences and fits well with social work values and ethics.

Following the work of House (1991, 2003), Fetterman (2003), Dominelli (2005), and Mertens (2009), researchers studying social justice education efforts should use research designs that incorporate stakeholders in the research design process. Students in social work programs might learn to recognize, understand, and use practice wisdom in the same purposeful way as they are being trained to use evidenced-based practice. If social work education programs are to truly implement CSWE's EPAS (2008) and students are educated to be professional social workers capable of taking an active role in the research process of knowledge appraisal, application, and construction, in evaluation research of social work education and practice interventions, the application of social justice values is imperative.

References

Adams, M., Bell, L. A., & Griffin, P. (1997). *Teaching for diversity and social justice: A sourcebook*. New York: Routledge.

Adams, R., Dominelli, L., & Payne, M. (2005). *Social work futures: Crossing boundaries, transforming practice*. New York: Palgrave MacMillan.

American Evaluation Association. (2004). *Guiding principles for evaluators*. Fairhaven, MA: Author.

Bandura, A. (1982). Self-efficacy mechanism in human agency. *American Psychologist, 37*(2), 122–147.

Barker, R. L. (1999). *The social work dictionary* (4th ed.). Washington, DC: NASW Press.

Brookfield, S. D. (1991). The development of critical reflection in adulthood: Foundations of a theory of adult learning. *New Education, 13*(1), 39–48

Council on Social Work Education. (2008a). *Educational policy and accreditation standards*. Alexandria, VA: Author.

Council on Social Work Education. (2008b). *Some suggestions on educational program assessment and continuous improvement*. Alexandria, VA: Author. Retrieved December 11, 2009, from http://www.cswe.org/Accreditation.aspx

Cowger, C. D. (2003). The values of the research university should be maximized to strengthen social work education. *Journal of Social Work Education, 39*(1), 43–48.

Crisp, B. R. (2004). Evidence-based practice and the borders of data in the global information era. *Journal of Social Work Education, 40*(1), 73–86.

DePoy, E., Hartman, A., & Haslett, D. (1999). Critical action research: A model of social work knowing. *Social Work, 44*(6), 560–569.

Dominelli, L. (2005). Social work research: Contested knowledge for practice. In R. Adams, L. Dominelli, & M. Payne (Eds.), *Social work futures: Crossing boundaries, transforming practice* (2nd ed., pp. 223–236). New York: Palgrave Macmillan.

Drake, B., Hovmand, P., Jonson-Reid, M., & Zayas, L. H. (2007). Adopting and teaching evidence-based practice in master's-level social work programs. *Journal of Social Work in Education, 43*(3), 431–446.

Dressel, A., Rogge, M. E., & Garlington, S. B. (2006). Using intergroup dialogue to promote social justice and change. *Social Work, 51*(4), 303–315.

Fetterman, D. (2003). Fetterman-House: A process use distinction and a theory. In C. A. Christie (Ed.), *New directions for evaluation: The practice-theory relationship in evaluation* (pp. 47–52). American Evaluation Association (no. 97). San Francisco: Jossey-Bass Education Series, Wiley Periodicals.

Finn, J. L., & Jacobson, M. J. (2003). *Just practice: A social justice approach to social work*. Peosta, IA: Eddie Bowers.

Fook, J. (1996). *The reflective researcher: Social workers' theories of practice research.* Sydney, Australia: Allen & Unwin.

Fook, J., Ryan, M., & Hawkins, H. (2000). *Professional expertise: Practice, theory and education for working in uncertainty.* London: Whiting & Birch.

Franklin, C., & Hopson, L. M. (2007). Facilitating the use of evidence-based practice in community organizations. *Journal of Social Work Education, 43*(3), 377–404.

Frans, D. J. (1993). A scale for measuring social worker empowerment. *Research on Social Work Practice, 3,* 312–328.

Gall, M. D., Borg, W. R., & Gall, J. P. (1996). *Educational research: An introduction* (6th ed.). White Plains, NY: Longman.

Gambrill, E. (1995). Less marketing and more scholarship. *Social Work Research, 19*(1), 38–47.

Gambrill, E. (1997). Social work education: Current concerns and possible futures. In M. Reisch & E. Gambrill (Eds.), *Social work in the 21st century: Theories, knowledge, and values and the social work profession* (pp. 317–327). Thousand Oaks, CA: Pine Forge Press.

Gambrill, E. (1999). Evidence-based practice: An alternative to authority-based practice. *Families in Society: The Journal of Contemporary Human Services, 80*(4), 341–350.

Gambrill, E. (2003a). Ethics, science, and the helping professions: A conversation with Robyn Dawes. *Journal of Social Work Education, 39*(1), 27–48.

Gambrill, E. (2003b). Evidence-based practice: Sea change or the emperor's new clothes? *Journal of Social Work Education, 43*(3), 3–23.

Garcia, J. A., & Floyd, C. E. (2002). Addressing evaluative standards related to program assessment: How do we respond? *Journal of Social Work Education, 38*(3), 369–382.

Gill, D. (1998). *Confronting injustice and oppression: Concepts and strategies for social workers.* New York: Columbia University Press.

Glazer, N. (1974). School of the minor professions. *Minerva, 12*(3), 346–364.

Gomory, T. (2001). A fallibilistic response to Thyer's theory of theory-free empirical research in social work practice. *Journal of Social Work Education, 37*(1), 26–50.

Gurin, P., Dey, E. L., Hurtado, S., & Gurin, G. (2002). Diversity and higher education: Theory and impact on educational outcomes. *Harvard Educational Review, 72*(3), 330–366.

Gurin, P., & Nagada, B. A. (2006). Getting to the *what, how,* and *why* of diversity on campus. *Educational Researcher, 35*(1), 20–24.

Gutiérrez, L., Zuñiga, M., & Lum, D. (2004). *Education for multicultural social work practice: Critical viewpoints and future directions.* Alexandria, VA: Council on Social Work Education.

Harrison, W. D. (1994). The inevitability of integrated methods. In E. Sherman & J. Reid (Eds.), *Qualitative research in social work* (pp. 409–422). New York: Columbia University Press.

Holden, G., Anastas, J., & Meenaghan, T. (2003). Determining attainment of the EPAS foundation objectives: Evidence for the use of self-efficacy as an outcome. *Journal of Social Work Education, 39*(3), 425–440.

Holden, G., Anastas, J., & Meenaghan, T. (2005). EPAS objectives and foundation practice self-efficacy: A replication. *Journal of Social Work Education, 41*(3), 559–570.

Holden, G., Barker, K., Meenaghan, T., & Rosenberg, G. (1999). Research self-efficacy: A new possibility for educational outcomes assessment. *Journal of Social Work Education, 35*, 463–476.

Holden, G., Cuzzi, L. C., Ruttner, S., Chernack, P., & Rosenberg, G. (1997). The hospital social work self-efficacy scale: A replication. *Research on Social Work Practice, 7*, 490–499.

Holden, G., Meenaghan, T., Anastas, J., & Metrey, G. (2002). Outcomes of social work education: The case for social work self-efficacy. *Journal of Social Work Education, 38*(1), 115–133.

House, E. (1991). Evaluation and social justice: Where are we? In M. W. McLaughlin & D. C. Phillips (Eds.), *Evaluation and education: At quarter century, part II, Nineteenth yearbook of the National Society for the Study of Education* (pp. 233–247). Chicago: University of Chicago Press.

House, E. R. (2003). Stakeholder bias. In C. A. Christie (Ed.), *New directions for evaluation: The practice-theory relationship to evaluation* (no. 97, pp. 53–56). New Jersey: American Evaluation Association, Jossey-Bass Education Series, Wiley Periodicals.

House, E. R., & Howe, K. R. (1998). The issue of advocacy in evaluations. *American Journal of Evaluation, 19*(2), 233–237.

Hurtado, S. (2005). The next generation of diversity and intergroup relations research. *Journal of Social Issues, 61*(3), 595–610.

Klein, W. C., & Bloom, M. (1995). Practice wisdom. *Social Work, 40*(6), 799–807.

Knapper, C. (2001). Broadening our approach to teaching evaluation. In C. Knapper & P. Cranton (Eds.), *New directions for teaching and learning: Fresh approaches to the evaluation of teaching* (no. 88). New York: Jossey-Bass Education Series, Wiley.

Koeske, G. G., & Kirk, S. A. (1995). Direct and buffering effects of internal locus of control among mental health professionals. *Journal of Social Service Research, 20*(3/4), 1–28.

Krentzman, A., & Townsend, A. (2008). Review of multidisciplinary measures of cultural competence for use in social work. *Journal of Social Work Education, 44*(2), 7–31.

Loneck, B. (1994). Commentary: Practitioner-researcher perspective on the integration of qualitative and quantitative research methods. In E. Sherman & W. J. Reid (Eds.), *Qualitative research in social work* (pp. 435–444). New York: Columbia University Press.

Longres, J. F., & Scanlon, E. (2001). Social justice and the research curriculum. *Journal of Social Work Education, 37*(3), 447–463.

McNeill, T. (2006). Evidence-based practice in an age of relativism: Toward a model for practice. *Social Work, 51*(2), 147–156.

Mentkowski, M., & Associates. (2000). *Learning that lasts: Integrating learning, development, and performance in college and beyond.* San Francisco: Jossey-Bass.

Mertens, D. M. (2009). *Transformative research and evaluation.* New York: Guilford Press.

Mezirow, J. (1991). *Transformative dimensions of adult learning.* San Francisco: Jossey-Bass.

Millstein, K. H. (1997). The taping project: A method for self-evaluation and "informed consciousness" in race courses. *Journal of Social Work Education, 33*(3), 491–506.

Moxley, D. P., & Manela, R. W. (2001). Expanding the conceptual basis of outcomes and their use in the human services. *Families in Society: The Journal of Contemporary Human Services, 82*(6), 570–577.

Mullaly, B. (2002). *Challenging oppression: A critical social work approach.* New York: Oxford University Press.

Munro, E. (2002). The role of theory in social work research: A further contribution to the debate. *Journal of Social Work Education, 38*(3), 461–481.

Nagada, B. A., Kim, C., & Truelove, Y. (2004). Learning about difference, learning with others, learning to transgress. *Journal of Social Issues, 60*(1), 195–214.

National Association of Social Workers. (2001). *Standards for culturally competence practice.* Washington DC: Author.

National Association of Social Workers. (2008). *Code of ethics.* Washington, DC: Author.

Patton, M. Q. (2002). *Qualitative research and evaluation methods.* Thousand Oaks, CA: Sage.

Pelton, L. H. (2001). Social justice and social work. *Journal of Social Work Education, 37*(3), 433–439.

Petr, C. G., & Walter, U. M. (2005). Best practices inquiry: A multidimensional, value-critical framework. *Journal of Social Work Education, 41*(2), 251–267.

Pike, C. (1998). A validation study of an instrument designed to measure teaching effectiveness. *Journal of Social Work Education, 34,* 261–271.

Potts, M. K., Meyer-Adams, N., & Rosales, A. M. (2007, October). *Education outcomes assessment: From conceptualization to use of results.* Paper presented at CSWE 53rd annual Program Meeting, San Francisco.

Reisch, M. (2002). Defining social justice in a socially unjust world. *Families in Society: The Journal of Contemporary Human Services, 83*(4), 343–351.

Rocha, C. J. (2002). Evaluating experiential teaching methods in a policy practice course: The case for service learning to increase political participation. *Journal of Social Work Education, 36*(1), 53–439.

Rosen, A. (1996). The scientific practitioner revisited: Some obstacles and prerequisites for fuller implementation in practice. *Social Work Research, 20*(2), 105–111.

Rosen, A. (2003). Evidence-based social work practice: Challenges and promise. *Social Work Research, 27*(4), 197–208.

Rosen, A., & Proctor, E. K. (2003). Developing practice guidelines for social work intervention: Issues, methods, and research agenda. New York: Columbia University Press.

Rosen, A., Proctor, E., Morrow-Howell, N., & Staudt, M. (1995). Rationales for practice decisions: Variations in knowledge use by decision task and social work service. *Research on Social Work Practice, 5,* 501–523.

Rosen, A., Proctor, E. K., & Staudt, M. (1999). Social work research and the quest for effective practice. *Social Work Research, 23,* 4–14.

Rubin, A., & Parrish, D. (2007). Challenges to the future of evidence-based practice in social work education. *Journal of Social Work in Education, 43*(3), 405–428.

Rubin, Z., & Peplau, L. A. (1975). Who believes in a just world? *Journal of Social Issues, 31*(3), 65–89.

Ruckdeschel, R., Earnshaw, P., & Firrek, A. (1994). The qualitative case study and evaluation: Issues, methods, and examples. In E. Sherman & W. J. Reid (Eds.), *Qualitative research in social work* (pp. 251–264). New York: Columbia University Press.

Scanlon, E., & Longres, J. F. (2001). Social work and social justice: A reply to Leroy Pelton. *Journal of Social Work Education, 37*(3), 441–444.

Schön, D. (1991). *The reflective practitioner: How professionals think in action.* Aldershot, UK: Ashgate.

Schoem, D., Hurtado, S., Sevig, T., Chesler, M., & Sumida, S. H. (2001). Intergroup dialogue: Democracy at work in theory and practice. In D. Schoem & S. Hurtado (Eds.), *Intergroup dialogue: Deliberative democracy in school, college, community, and workplace* (pp. 1–21). Ann Arbor: University of Michigan Press.

Snyder, C., Peeler, J., & May, J. D. (2008). Combining human diversity and social justice education: A conceptual framework. *Journal of Social Work Education, 44*(1), 145–161.

Stern, S. B. (1994). Commentary: Wanted! Social work practice evaluation and research—all methods considered. In E. Sherman & W. J. Reid (Eds.), *Qualitative research in social work* (pp. 285–290). New York: Columbia University Press.

Swensen, C. R. (1998). Clinical social work's contribution to a social justice perspective. *Social Work, 43*(6), 527–537.

Tatum, B. D. (1992). Talking about race, learning about racism: The application of racial identity development theory in the classroom. *Harvard Educational Review, 62*(1), 1–24.

Thyer, B. A. (2001). What is the role of theory in research on social work practice? *Journal of Social Work Education, 37*(1), 9–25.

Uehara, E. S., Sohng, S. S. L., Nagada, B. A., Erera, P., & Yamashiro, G. (2004). Multiculturalism, social justice, and social inquiry issues for social work research education. In L. Gutiérrez, M. E. Zuñiga, & D. Lum (Eds.), *Education for multicultural social work practice: Critical viewpoints and future directions.* Alexandria, VA: Council on Social Work Education.

Van Soest, D. (1996). Impact of social work education on student attitudes and behavior concerning oppression. *Journal of Social Work Education, 32*(2), 191–202.

Van Soest, D., & Garcia, B. (2003). *Diversity education for social justice: Mastering teaching skills.* Alexandria, VA: Council on Social Work Education.

Van Voorhis, R. M., & Hostetter, C. (2006). The impact of MSW education on social worker empowerment and commitment to client empowerment through social justice advocacy. *Journal of Social Work Education, 42*(1), 105–121.

Walker, J. S., Briggs, H. E., Koroloff, N., & Friesen, B. J. (2007). Implementing and sustaining evidence-based practice in social work. *Journal of Social Work Education, 43*(3), 361–375.

Wakefield, J. C. (1998). Psychotherapy, distributive justice and social work revisited. *Smith College Studies in Social Work, 69*(1), 25–57.

Witkin, S. L. (1996). If empirical practice is the answer, then what is the question? *Social Work Research, 20*(2), 69–75.

Witkin, S. L., & Harrison, W. D. (2001). Whose evidence and for what purpose? *Social Work, 46*(4), 293–296.

Wolfer, T. A., & Johnson, M. M. (2003). Re-evaluating student evaluation of teaching: The teaching evaluation form. *Journal of Social Work Education, 39*(1), 111–121.

About the Authors

Priscilla Allen, PhD, MSW, is associate professor in the LSU School of Social Work and associate director of the LSU Life Course and Aging Center. She served as an appointed member on the LSU Service-Learning Advisory Council from 2006 to 2008. Dr. Allen is a gerontologist and advocate for citizens in the nursing home setting.

Julie Birkenmaier, PhD, is associate professor and director of field education at Saint Louis University School of Social Work. Her publication topics include social justice, field education, and financial credit and low-income families.

Ashley Cruce, MA, MSW, is currently assistant director of field education at Hunter College School of Social Work in New York City. Previously, she served as director of the Doerr Center for Social Justice Education and Research in the School of Social Work at Saint Louis University for five years. Her teaching, scholarly interests, and publications have focused on social justice education, international social work, field education, community/university partnerships, and community development in the United States and East Africa.

Linda Ferrise, MSW, is clinical associate professor and BSW program director in the Division of Social Work at West Virginia University.

Dolly Ford, MSW, LGSW MPA, is a clinical therapist in the Department of Behavioral Medicine and Psychiatry, University Health Associates, and adjunct faculty in the Division of Social Work at West Virginia University.

Michael Forster and **Tim Rehner** are professors of social work at the University of Southern Mississippi. They cofounded Family Network

Partnership in 1996 in response to community requests to help address a rising local juvenile delinquency problem; the agency has operated continuously since. In 2007, the university recognized their achievements in the form of the Innovation Partnership Award, a specialized research award. From 2000 to 2008, Forster and Rehner served as director and associate director, respectively, of the School of Social Work. In mid-2008, Forster began service as interim dean of the university's College of Health, as Rehner assumed responsibilities as interim director of the School of Social Work.

Donna Hardina, PhD, is professor in the Department of Social Work Education at California State University, Fresno. Her social work practice experience includes coordinating a statewide antihunger organization and employment as a community organizer in the Hyde Park neighborhood of Chicago. She is the author of *Analytical Skills for Community Organization Practice* and *An Empowering Approach to Managing Social Service Organizations.*

W. Randall Herman, MSW, LICSW, M.Phil, EdD, is professor emeritus at the College of St. Catherine and the University of St. Thomas School of Social Work. He has taught in both the BSW and MSW programs and was the BSW program director before retiring. He has taught in Mexico, Nicaragua, Guatemala, Australia, and New Zealand. His research interests are varied and include work on retirement and purpose in the second phase of life, international education/experiential learning, and end-of-life planning. He is currently a consultant and clinical supervisor.

David R. Hodge, PhD, is assistant professor, School of Social Work, Arizona State University, and senior nonresident fellow, Program for Research on Religion and Urban Civil Society, University of Pennsylvania.

Philip Young P. Hong, PhD, is assistant professor, School of Social Work, Loyola University Chicago. His main academic interest is in poverty and workforce development. In particular, his research program focuses on structural poverty in the United States and international/ comparative social welfare. He is currently partnering with local workforce development initiatives to develop bottom-up strategies for empowering low-income individuals and families in their quest to achieve self-sufficiency.

Barbara A. Lehmann, PhD, LICSW, has thirty years of social work practice and teaching experience. She is the chair of the executive committee for the Social Work in a Latin American Context consortium program and taught for two years in residence in the program. Her research interests include social work education and stigmatization of visual differences.

Catherine M. Lemieux, PhD, ACSW, LCSW, serves as the Margaret Champagne Womack Associate Professor in Addictive Disorders at the LSU School of Social Work, where she has taught graduate-level research and practice courses and electives in the areas of addiction and domestic violence since 1995. For over eighteen years Dr. Lemieux served as a clinician and supervisor in a variety of outpatient and institutional settings, with individuals and families affected by substance abuse. She has fulfilled a number of leadership roles at the LSU School of Social Work, serving as interim dean from May 2002 through August 2003 and as MSW program director from August 2006 through May 2009.

Ruth Obel-Jorgensen, MSW, is an alumna of California State University, Fresno, where she obtained a master's in social work, emphasizing in community organizing and advocacy, and an American Humanics certificate in nonprofit management and leadership. Ruth has organized statewide grassroots campaigns to increase access to higher education and mobilize youth voters with the University of California Student Association. She has overseen the collaboration of state and regional Gay-Straight Alliance (GSA) Networks across the country with the GSA Network. She currently coordinates professional development and advocacy projects for afterschool professionals throughout California with the California School-Age Consortium.

A former director of New York's Food & Hunger Hotline and Artists to End Hunger, **Stephen Pimpare** is associate professor of political science at Yeshiva College and the Wurzweiler School of Social Work. He is the author of *The New Victorians: Poverty, Politics and Propaganda in Two Gilded Ages* (2004) and *A People's History of Poverty in America* (2008).

Carol A. Plummer, PhD, LCSW, is the child welfare instructor and Title IV-E project director at the LSU School of Social Work. As assistant professor, she spent most of her social work career as a child abuse prevention specialist, therapist, and consultant. Her areas of specialization include interpersonal violence, disaster, and trauma.

The professional career of **Rene Pogue**, PhD, spans more than twenty years. Her experience includes practice in the fields of geriatric, forensic, community, and mental health social work and twelve years as a social work educator. Her research interests focus on interpersonal violence, the criminal justice system, higher education processes and outcomes, and social justice issues.

Michael Reisch, PhD, is the Daniel Thursz Distinguished Professor of Social Justice at the University of Maryland, where he teaches graduate courses on the history and philosophy of social welfare, community organization theory and practice, the nonprofit sector, and contemporary social policy. He is the author or editor of over twenty books and monographs and nearly one hundred articles and book chapters, which have been translated into French, German, Italian, Japanese, Korean, Spanish, and Bulgarian. He has lectured widely in Europe, Australia, and Latin America and has held leadership positions in national and state advocacy, professional, and social change organizations.

Sandra C. Robin, MSW, PhD, LISW, is professor of Social Work at St. Cloud State University. Her research interests include public, child, and family services as well as social work education.

Nancy A. Rodenborg, PhD, MSW, has over twenty years of experience in social work practice, teaching, and research on diversity and inequality in both national and international contexts. She teaches diversity courses to MSW and BSW students and has served on Augsburg's diversity committees and on community advisory boards for several years. Her current research explores intergroup dialogue as a method of reducing prejudice and increasing understanding among diverse groups.

Julie Schroeder, PhD, is an associate professor in the Jackson State University School of Social Work, teaching across the curriculum focusing on research methods, policy, and social justice issues.

Carla J. Sofka, PhD, MSW, is associate professor of social work at Siena College in Loudonville, New York. Her research interests include the ways in which museums and memorials serve as healing spaces, public responses to tragedy, and the use of technology in social work education and grief counseling/death education.

Diana Strock-Lynskey, MSW, is professor of social work at Siena College in Loudonville, New York. Some of her major research interests include death, grief, loss, and trauma, restorative justice, cemetery restoration work, peace building, community development, and disability and social work practice.

Cecilia Thomas, MSW, PhD, has been at the University of North Texas, Denton, Texas, since 2001. She teaches solely in an undergraduate social work program, teaching primarily the first practice course, a diversity and integrative seminar for seniors. She is a licensed social worker and has over twenty years of social work practice experience including mental health, health services, and child welfare. Her scholarship interest has included social work education and practice with vulnerable populations.

Following twenty-five years in professional social work practice, **R. Jan Wilson**, PhD, joined the School of Social Work faculty in 1996 as a member of an innovative field education team and a specialist in family practice and school social work. She received her doctorate in higher education in 2006, focusing on issues of educational equity and multicultural competence in higher education.

Index

338   Index